The scene of "The Knapsack" is laid in Sweden, to produce variety; and to show that the rich and poor, the young and old, in all countries, are mutually serviceable to each other; and to portray some of those virtues which are peculiarly amiable in the character of a soldier.

"Angelina" is a female Forester. The nonsense of sentimentality is here aimed at with the shafts of ridicule, instead of being combated by serious argument. With the romantic eccentricities of Angelina are contrasted faults of a more common and despicable sort. Miss Burrage is the picture of a young lady who meanly natters persons of rank; and who, after she has smuggled herself into good company, is ashamed to acknowledge her former friends, to whom she was bound by the strongest ties of gratitude.

"Mademoiselle Panache" is a sketch of the necessary consequences of imprudently trusting the happiness of a daughter to the care of those who can teach nothing but accomplishments.

"The Prussian Vase" is a lesson against imprudence, and on exercise of judgment, and an eulogium upon our inestimable trial by jury. This tale is designed principally for young gentlemen who are intended for the bar.

"The Good Governess" is a lesson to teach the art of giving lessons.

In "The Good Aunt," the advantages which a judicious early education confers upon those who are intended for public seminaries are pointed out. It is a common error to suppose that, let a boy be what he may, when sent to Eton, Westminster, Harrow, or any great school, he will be moulded into proper form by the fortuitous pressure of numbers; that emulation will necessarily excite, example lead, and opposition polish him. But these are vain hopes: the solid advantages which may be attained in these large nurseries of youth must be, in a great measure, secured by previous domestic instruction.

These Tales have been written to illustrate the opinions delivered in "Practical Education." As their truth has appeared to me to be confirmed by increasing experience, I sat down with pleasure to write this preface for my daughter. It is hoped that the following stories will afford agreeable relaxation from severer studies, and that they will be thought—what they profess to be—Moral Tales.

R.L. EDGEWORTH

FORESTER

Forester was the son of an English gentleman, who had paid some attention to his education, but who had some singularities of opinion, which probably influenced him in his conduct toward his children.

Young Forester was frank, brave, and generous, but he had been taught to dislike politeness so much, that the common forms of society appeared to him either odious or ridiculous; his sincerity was seldom restrained by any attention to the feelings of others. His love of independence was carried to such an extreme, that he was inclined to prefer the life of Robinson Crusoe in his desert island, to that of any individual in cultivated society. His attention had been early fixed upon the follies and vices of the higher classes of people; and his contempt for selfish indolence was so strongly associated with the name of gentleman, that he was disposed to choose his friends and companions from amongst his inferiors: the inequality between the rich and the poor shocked him; his temper was enthusiastic as well as benevolent; and he ardently wished to be a man, and to be at liberty to act for himself, that he might reform society, or at least his own neighbourhood. When he was about nineteen years old, his father died, and young Forester was sent to Edinburgh, to Dr. Campbell, the gentleman whom his father had appointed his guardian. In the choice of his mode of travelling his disposition appeared. The stage-coach and a carrier set out nearly at the same time from Penrith. Forester, proud of bringing his principles immediately into action, put himself under the protection of the carrier, and congratulated himself upon his freedom from prejudice. He arrived at Edinburgh in all the glory of independence, and he desired the carrier to set him down at Dr. Campbell's door.

"The doctor is not at home," said the footman, who opened the door.

"He is at home," exclaimed Forester with indignation; "I see him at the window."

"My master is just going to dinner, and can't see any body now," said the footman; "but if you will call again at six o'clock, maybe he may see you, my good lad."

"My name is Forester—let me in," said Forester, pushing-forwards.

"Forester!—Mr. Forester!" said the footman; "the young gentleman that was expected in the coach to-day?" Without deigning to give the footman any explanation, Forester took his own portmanteau from the carrier; and Dr. Campbell came down-stairs just when the footman was officiously struggling with the young gentleman for his burden. Dr. Campbell received his pupil very kindly; but Forester would not be prevailed upon to rub his shoes sufficiently upon the mat at the bottom of the stairs, or to change his disordered dress before he made his appearance in the drawing-room. He entered with dirty shoes, a threadbare coat, and hair that looked as if it never had been combed; and he was much surprised by the effect which his singular appearance produced upon the risible muscles of some of the company.

"I have done nothing to be ashamed of," said he to himself; but, notwithstanding all his efforts to be and to appear at ease, he was constrained and abashed. A young laird, Mr. Archibald Mackenzie, seemed to enjoy his confusion with malignant, half-suppressed merriment, in which Dr. Campbell's son was too good-natured, and too well-bred, to participate. Henry Campbell was three or four years older than Forester, and though he looked like a gentleman, Forester could not help being pleased with the manner in which he drew him into conversation. The secret magic of politeness relieved him insensibly from the torment of false shame.

"It is a pity this lad was bred up a gentleman," said Forester to himself, "for he seems to have some sense and goodness."

Dinner was announced, and Forester was provoked at being interrupted in an argument concerning carts and coaches, which he had begun with Henry Campbell. Not that Forester was averse to eating, for he was at this instant ravenously hungry: but eating in company he always found equally repugnant to his habits and his principles. A table covered with a clean table-cloth; dishes in nice order; plates, knives, and forks, laid at regular distances, appeared to our young Diogenes absurd superfluities, and he was ready to exclaim, "How many things I do not want!" Sitting down to dinner, eating, drinking, and behaving like other people, appeared to him difficult and disagreeable ceremonies. He did not perceive that custom had rendered all these things perfectly easy to every one else in company; and as soon as he had devoured his food his own way, he moralized in silence upon the good sense of Sancho Panza,

Tales & Novels by Maria Edgeworth

Volume I (of II)

Maria Edgeworth was born at Black Bourton, Oxfordshire on January 1st 1768. Her early years were with her mother's family in England. Sadly, her mother died when Maria was five.

Maria was educated at Mrs Lattafière's school in Derby in 1775. There she studied dancing, French and other subjects. Maria transferred to Mrs Devis's school in Upper Wimpole Street, London. Her father began to focus more attention on Maria in 1781 when she nearly lost her sight to an eye infection.

She returned home to Ireland at 14 and took charge of her younger siblings. She herself was home-tutored by her father in Irish economics and politics, science, literature and law. Despite her youth literature was in her blood. Maria also became her father's assistant in managing the family's large Edgeworthstown estate.

Maria first published 1795 with 'Letters for Literary Ladies'. That same year 'An Essay on the Noble Science of Self-Justification', written for a female audience, advised women on how to obtain better rights in general and specifically from their husbands.

'Practical Education' (1798) is a progressive work on education. Maria's ambition was to create an independent thinker who understands the consequences of his or her actions.

Her first novel, 'Castle Rackrent' was published anonymously in 1800 without her father's knowledge. It was an immediate success and firmly established Maria's appeal to the public.

Her father married four times and the last of these to Frances, a year younger and a confidante of Maria, who pushed them to travel more widely: London, Britain and Europe were all now visited.

The second series of 'Tales of Fashionable Life' (1812) did so well that she was now the most commercially successful novelist of her age.

She particularly worked hard to improve the living standards of the poor in Edgeworthstown and to provide schools for the local children of all and any denomination.

After a visit to see her relations Maria had severe chest pains and died suddenly of a heart attack in Edgeworthstown on 22nd May 1849. She was 81.

Index of Contents

PREFACE

It has been somewhere said by Johnson, that merely to invent a story is no small effort of the human understanding. How much more difficult is it to construct stories suited to the early years of youth, and, at the same time, conformable to the complicate relations of modern society—fictions, that shall display examples of virtue, without initiating the young reader into the ways of vice—narratives, written in a style level to his capacity, without tedious detail, or vulgar idiom! The author, sensible of these difficulties, solicits indulgence for such errors as have escaped her vigilance.

In a former work the author has endeavoured to add something to the increasing stock of innocent amusement and early instruction, which the laudable exertions of some excellent modern writers provide for the rising generation; and, in the present, an attempt is made to provide for young people, of a more advanced age, a few Tales, that shall neither dissipate the attention, nor inflame the imagination.

In a work upon education, which the public has been pleased to notice, we have endeavoured to show that, under proper management, amusement and instruction may accompany each other through many paths of literature; whilst, at the same time, we have disclaimed and reprehended all attempts to teach in play. Steady, untired attention is what alone produces excellence. Sir Isaac Newton, with as much truth as modesty, attributed to this faculty those discoveries in science, which brought the heavens within the grasp of man, and weighed the earth in a balance. To inure the mind to athletic vigour is one of the chief objects of good education; and we have found, as far as our limited experience has extended, that short and active exertions, interspersed with frequent agreeable relaxation, form the mind to strength and endurance, better than long-continued feeble study.

Hippocrates, in describing the robust temperament, tells us that the athletae prepare themselves for the gymnasium by strong exertion, which they continued till they felt fatigue; they then reposed till they felt returning strength and aptitude for labour: and thus, by alternate exercise and indulgence, their limbs acquire the firmest tone of health and vigour. We have found, that those who have tasted with the keenest relish the beauties of Berquin, Day, or Barbauld, pursue a demonstration of Euclid, or a logical deduction, with as much eagerness, and with more rational curiosity, than is usually shown by students who are nourished with the hardest fare, and chained to unceasing labour.

"Forester" is the picture of an eccentric character—a young man who scorns the common forms and dependencies of civilized society; and who, full of visionary schemes of benevolence and happiness, might, by improper management, or unlucky circumstances, have become a fanatic and a criminal.

who preferred eating an egg behind the door to feasting in public; and he recollected his favourite traveller Le Vaillant's(1) enthusiastic account of his charming Hottentot dinners, and of the disgust that he afterwards felt, on the comparison of European etiquette and African simplicity.

(Footnote 1: Le Vaillant's Travels in Africa, vol. i. p. 114.)

"Thank God, the ceremony of dinner is over," said Forester to Henry Campbell, as soon as they rose from table.

All these things, which seemed mere matter of course in society, appeared to Forester strange ceremonies. In the evening there were cards for those who liked cards, and there was conversation for those who liked conversation. Forester liked neither; he preferred playing with a cat; and he sat all night apart from the company in a corner of a sofa. He took it for granted that the conversation could not be worth his attention, because he heard Lady Catherine Mackenzie's voice amongst others; he had conceived a dislike, or rather a contempt for this lady, because she showed much of the pride of birth and rank in her manners. Henry Campbell did not think it necessary to punish himself for her ladyship's faults, by withdrawing from entertaining conversation; he knew that his father had the art of managing the frivolous subjects started in general company, so as to make them lead to amusement and instruction; and this Forester would probably have discovered this evening, had he not followed his own thoughts, instead of listening to the observations of others. Lady Catherine, it is true, began with a silly history of her hereditary antipathy for pickled cucumbers; and she was rather tiresome in tracing the genealogy of this antipathy through several generations of her ancestry; but Dr. Campbell said "that he had heard, from an ingenious gentleman of her ladyship's family, that her ladyship's grandfather, and several of his friends, nearly lost their lives by pickled cucumbers;" and thence the doctor took occasion to relate several curious circumstances concerning the effects of different poisons.

Dr. Campbell, who plainly saw both the defects and the excellent qualities of his young ward, hoped that, by playful raillery, and by well-timed reasoning, he might mix a sufficient portion of good sense with Forester's enthusiasm, might induce him gradually to sympathize in the pleasures of cultivated society, and might convince him that virtue is not confined to any particular class of men; that education, in the enlarged sense of the word, creates the difference between individuals more than riches or poverty. He foresaw that Forester would form a friendship with his son, and that this attachment would cure him of his prejudices against gentlemen, and would prevent him from indulging his taste for vulgar company. Henry Campbell had more useful energy, though less apparent enthusiasm, than his new companion: he was always employed; he was really independent, because he had learned how to support himself either by the labours of his head or of his hands; but his independence did not render him unsociable; he was always ready to sympathize with the pleasures of his friends, and therefore he was beloved: following his father's example, he did all the good in his power to those who were in distress; but he did not imagine that he could reform every abuse in society, or that he could instantly new-model the universe. Forester became, in a few days, fond of conversing, or rather of holding long arguments, with Henry; but his dislike to the young laird, Archibald Mackenzie, hourly increased. Archibald and his mother, Lady Catherine Mackenzie, were relations to Mrs. Campbell, and they were now upon a visit at her house. Lady Catherine, a shrewd woman, fond of precedence, and fully sensible of the importance that wealth can bestow, had sedulously inculcated into the mind of her son all the maxims of worldly wisdom which she had collected in her intercourse with society; she had inspired him with family pride, but at the same time had taught him to pay obsequious court to his superiors in rank or fortune: the art of rising in the world, she knew, did not entirely depend upon virtue or ability; she was consequently more solicitous about her son's manners than his morals, and was more anxious that he should form high connexions, than that he should apply to the severe studies of a profession. Archibald was nearly what might be expected from his education, alternately supple to his superiors, and insolent to his inferiors: to insinuate himself into the favour of young men of rank and fortune, he affected to admire extravagance; but his secret maxims of parsimony operated even in the midst of dissipation. Meanness and pride usually go together. It is not to be supposed that young Forester had such quick penetration, that he could discover the whole of the artful Archibald's character in the course of a few days' acquaintance; but he disliked him for good reasons, because he was a laird, because he had laughed at his first entrée, and because he was learning to dance.

THE SKELETON

About a week after our hero's arrival at Dr. Campbell's, the doctor was exhibiting some chemical experiments, with which Henry hoped that his young friend would be entertained; but Forester had scarcely been five minutes in the laboratory, before Mackenzie, who was lounging about the room, sneeringly took notice of a large hole in his shoe. "It is easily mended," said the independent youth; and he immediately left the laboratory, and went to a cobbler's, who lived in a narrow lane, at the back of Dr. Campbell's house. Forester had, from his bed-chamber window, seen this cobbler at work early every morning; he admired his industry, and longed to be acquainted with him. The good-humoured familiarity of Forester's manner pleased the cobbler, who was likewise diverted by the eagerness of the young gentleman to mend his own shoe. After spending some hours at the cobbler's stall, the shoe was actually mended, and Forester thought that his morning's work was worthy of admiration. In a court (or, as such places are called in Edinburgh, a close) near the cobbler's, he saw some boys playing at ball: he joined them; and, whilst they were playing, a dancing-master with his hair powdered, and who seemed afraid of spattering his clean stockings, passed through the court, and interrupted the ball players for a few seconds. The boys, as soon as the man was out of hearing, declared that he passed through their court regularly twice a day, and that he always kicked their marbles out of the ring. Without staying to weigh this evidence scrupulously, Forester received it with avidity, and believed all that had been asserted was true, because the accused was a dancing-master; from his education he had conceived an antipathy to dancing-masters, especially to such as wore silk stockings, and had their heads well powdered. Easily fired at the idea of any injustice, and eager to redress the grievances of the poor, Forester immediately concerted with these boys a scheme to deliver them from what he called the insolence of the dancing-master, and promised that he would compel him to go round by another street.

In his zeal for the liberty of his new companions, our hero did not consider that he was infringing upon the liberties of a man who had never done him any injury, and over whom he had no right to exercise any control.

Upon his return to Dr. Campbell's, Forester heard the sound of a violin; and he found that his enemy, M. Pasgrave, the dancing-master, was attending Archibald Mackenzie: he learnt, that he was engaged to give another lesson the next evening; and the plans of the confederates in the ball-alley were arranged accordingly. In Dr. Campbell's room Forester remembered to have seen a skeleton in a glass case; he seized upon it, carried it down to his companions, and placed it in a niche in the wall, on the landing-place of a flight of stone stairs down which the dancing-master was obliged to go. A butcher's son (one of Forester's new companions) he instructed to stand at a certain hour behind the skeleton, with two rushlights, which he was to hold up to the eye-holes in the skull.

The dancing-master's steps were heard approaching at the expected hour; and the boys stood in ambush to enjoy the diversion of the sight. It was a dark night; the fiery eyes of the skeleton glared suddenly upon the dancing-master, who was so terrified at the spectacle, and in such haste to escape, that his foot slipped, and he fell down the stone steps: his ankle was sprained by the fall, and he was brought to Dr. Campbell's. Forester was shocked at this tragical end of his intended comedy. The poor man was laid upon a bed, and he writhed with pain. Forester, with vehement expressions of concern, explained to Dr. Campbell the cause of this accident, and he was much touched by the dancing-master's good nature, who, between every twinge of pain, assured him that he should soon be well, and endeavoured to avert Dr. Campbell's displeasure. Forester sat beside the bed, reproaching himself bitterly; and he was yet more sensible of his folly, when he heard, that the boys, whose part he had hastily taken, had frequently amused themselves with playing mischievous tricks upon this inoffensive man, who declared, that he had never purposely kicked their marbles out of the ring, but had always implored them to make way for him with all the civility in his power.

Forester resolved, that before he ever again attempted to do justice, he would, at least, hear both sides of the question.

THE ALARM

Forester would willingly have sat up all night with M. Pasgrave, to foment his ankle from time to time, and, if possible, to assuage the pain: but the man would not suffer him to sit up, and about twelve o'clock he retired to rest. He had scarcely fallen asleep, when his door opened, and Archibald Mackenzie roused him, by demanding, in a peremptory tone, how he could sleep when the whole family were frightened out of their wits by his pranks?

"Is the dancing-master worse? What's the matter?" exclaimed Forester in great terror.

Archibald replied, that he was not talking or thinking about the dancing-master, and desired Forester to make haste and dress himself, and that he would then soon hear what was the matter.

Forester dressed himself as fast as he could, and followed Archibald through a long passage, which led to a back staircase. "Do you hear the noise?" said Archibald.

"Not I," said Forester.

"Well, you'll hear it plain enough presently," said Archibald: "follow me down-stairs."

He followed, and was surprised, when he got into the hall, to find all the family assembled. Lady Catherine had been awakened by a noise, which she at first imagined to be the screaming of an infant. Her bedchamber was on the ground floor, and adjoining to Dr. Campbell's laboratory, from which the noise seemed to proceed. She awakened her son Archibald and Mrs. Campbell; and, when she recovered her senses a little, she listened to Dr. Campbell, who assured her, that what her ladyship thought was the screaming of an infant was the noise of a cat: the screams of this cat were terrible; and, when the light approached the door of the laboratory, the animal flew at the door with so much fury, that nobody could venture to open it. Every body looked at Forester, as if they suspected that he had confined the cat, or that he was in some way or other the cause of the disturbance. The cat, which, from his having constantly fed and played with it, had grown extremely fond of him, used to follow him often from room to room; and he now recollected, that it followed him the preceding evening into the laboratory, when he went to replace the skeleton. He had not observed whether it came out of the room again, nor could he now conceive the cause of its yelling in this horrible manner. The animal seemed to be mad with pain. Dr. Campbell asked his son whether all the presses were locked. Henry said he was sure they were all locked. It was his business to lock them every evening; and he was so exact, that nobody doubted his accuracy.

Archibald Mackenzie, who all this time knew, or at least suspected the truth, held himself in cunning silence. The preceding evening he, for want of something to do, had strolled into the laboratory, and, with the pure curiosity of idleness, peeped into the presses, and took the stoppers out of several of the bottles. Dr. Campbell happened to come in, and carelessly asked him if he had been looking in the presses; to which question Archibald, though with scarcely any motive for telling a falsehood, immediately replied in the negative. As the doctor turned his head, Archibald put aside a bottle, which he had just before taken out of the press; and, fearing that the noise of replacing the glass stopper would betray him, he slipped it into his waistcoat pocket. How much useless cunning! All this transaction was now fully present to Archibald's memory: and he was well convinced that Henry had not seen the bottle when he afterwards went to lock the presses; that the cat had thrown it down; and that this was the cause of all the yelling that disturbed the house. Archibald, however, kept his lips fast closed; he had told one falsehood; he dreaded to have it discovered; and he hoped the blame of the whole affair would rest upon Forester. At length the animal flew with diminished fury at the door; its screams became feebler and feebler, till, at last, they totally ceased. There was silence: Dr. Campbell opened the door: the cat was seen stretched upon the ground, apparently lifeless. As Forester looked nearer at the poor animal, he saw a twitching motion in one of its hind legs; Dr. Campbell said, that it was the convulsion of death. Forester was just going to lift up his cat, when his friend Henry stopped his hand, telling him, that he would burn himself, if he touched it. The hair and flesh of the cat on one side were burnt away, quite to the bone. Henry pointed to the broken bottle, which, he said, had contained vitriolic acid.

Henry in vain attempted to discover by whom the bottle of vitriolic acid had been taken out of its place. Suspicion naturally fell upon Forester, who, by his own account, was the last person in the room before the presses had been locked for the night. Forester, in warm terms, asserted, that he knew nothing of the matter. Dr. Campbell coolly observed, that Forester ought not to be surprised at being suspected upon this occasion; because every body had the greatest reason to suspect the person, whom they had detected in one practical joke, of planning another.

"Joke!" said Forester, looking down upon his lifeless favourite; "do you think me capable of such cruelty? Do you doubt my truth?" exclaimed Forester, haughtily. "You are unjust. Turn me out of your house this instant. I do not desire your protection, if I have forfeited your esteem."

"Go to bed for to-night in my house," said Dr. Campbell; "moderate your enthusiasm, and reflect coolly upon what has passed."

Dr. Campbell, as Forester indignantly withdrew, said, with a benevolent smile, as he looked after him, "He wants nothing but a little common sense. Henry, you must give him a little of yours."

In the morning, Forester first went to inquire how the dancing-master had slept, and then knocked impatiently at Dr. Campbell's door.

"My father is not awake," said Henry; but Forester marched directly up to the side of the bed, and, drawing back the curtain with no gentle hand, cried, with a loud voice, "Dr. Campbell, I am come to beg your pardon. I was angry when I said you were unjust."

"And I was asleep when you begged my pardon," said Dr. Campbell, rubbing his eyes.

"The dancing-master's ankle is a great deal better; and I have buried the poor cat," pursued Forester: "and I hope now, doctor, you'll at least tell me, that you do not really suspect me of any hand in her death."

"Pray let me go to sleep," said Dr. Campbell, "and time your explanations a little better."

THE GERANIUM

The dancing-master gradually recovered from his sprain; and Forester spent all his pocket-money in buying a new violin for him, as his had been broken in his fall; his watch had likewise been broken against the stone steps. Though Forester looked upon a watch as a useless bauble, yet he determined to get this mended; and his friend Henry went with him for this purpose to a watchmaker's.

Whilst Henry Campbell and Forester were consulting with the watchmaker upon the internal state of the bruised watch, Archibald Mackenzie, who followed them for a lounge, was looking over some new watches, and ardently wished for the finest that he saw. As he was playing with this fine watch, the watchmaker begged that he would take care not to break it.

Archibald, in the insolent tone in which he was used to speak to a tradesman, replied, that if he did break it, he hoped he was able to pay for it. The watchmaker civilly answered, "he had no doubt of that, but that the watch was not his property; it was Sir Philip Gosling's, who would call for it, he expected, in a quarter of an hour."

At the name of Sir Philip Gosling, Archibald quickly changed his tone: he had a great ambition to be of Sir Philip's acquaintance, for Sir Philip was a young man who was to have a large fortune when he should come of age, and who, in the meantime, spent as much of it as possible, with great spirit and little judgment. He had been sent to Edinburgh for his education; and he spent his time in training horses, laying bets, parading in the public walks, and ridiculing, or, in his own phrase, quizzing every sensible young man, who applied to literature or science. Sir Philip, whenever he frequented any of the professor's classes, took care to make it evident to every body present, that he did not come there to learn, and that he looked down with contempt upon all who were obliged to study; he was the first always to make any disturbance in the classes, or, in his elegant language, to make a row.

This was the youth of whose acquaintance Archibald Mackenzie was ambitious. He stayed in the shop, in hopes that Sir Philip would arrive: he was not disappointed; Sir Philip came, and, with address which Lady Catherine would perhaps have admired, Archibald entered into conversation with the young baronet, if conversation that might be called, which consisted of a species of fashionable dialect, devoid of sense, and destitute of any pretence to wit. To Forester this dialect was absolutely unintelligible: after he had listened to it with sober contempt for a few minutes, he pulled Henry away, saying, "Come, don't let us waste our time here; let us go to the brewery that you promised to show me."

Henry did not immediately yield to the rough pull of his indignant friend, for at this instant the door of a little back parlour behind the watchmaker's shop opened slowly, and a girl of about seven years old appeared, carrying, with difficulty, a flower-pot, in which there was a fine large geranium in full flower. Henry, who saw that the child was scarcely able to carry it, took it out of her hands, and asked her, "Where she would like to have it put?"

"Here, for to-day!" said the little girl, sorrowfully; "but to-morrow it goes away for ever."

The little girl was sorry to part with this geranium, because "she had watched it all the winter," and said, "that she was very fond of it; but that she was willing to part with it, though it was just come into flower, because the apothecary had told her, that it was the cause of her grandmother's having been taken ill. Her grandmother lodged," she said, "in that little room, and the room was very close, and she was taken ill in the night—so ill, that she could hardly speak or stir; and when the apothecary came, he said," continued the little girl, "it was no wonder any body was ill, who slept in such a little close room, with such a great geranium in it, to poison the air. So my geranium must go!" concluded she with a sigh: "but, as it is for grandmother, I shall never think of it again."

Henry Campbell and Forester were both struck with the modest simplicity of this child's countenance and manner, and they were pleased with the unaffected generosity with which she gave up her favourite geranium. Forester noted this down in his mind as a fresh instance in favour of his exclusive good opinion of the poor. This little girl looked poor, though she was decently dressed; she was so thin, that her little cheek-bones could plainly be seen; her face had not the round, rosy beauty of cheerful health: she was pale and sallow, and she looked in patient misery. Moved with compassion, Forester regretted that he had no money to give where it might have been so well bestowed. He was always extravagant in his generosity; he would often give five guineas where five shillings would have been enough, and by these means he reduced himself to the necessity sometimes of refusing assistance to deserving objects. On his journey from his father's house to Edinburgh, he lavished, in undistinguishing charity, a considerable sum of money; and all that he had remaining of this money he spent in purchasing the new violin for M. Pasgrave. Dr. Campbell absolutely refused to advance his ward any money till his next quarterly allowance should become due. Henry, who always perceived quickly what passed in the minds of others, guessed at Forester's thoughts by his countenance, and forebore to produce his own money, though he had it just ready in his hand: he knew that he could call again at the watchmaker's, and give what he pleased, without ostentation.

Upon questioning the little girl further, concerning her grandmother's illness, Henry discovered, that the old woman had sat up late at night knitting, and that, feeling herself extremely cold, she got a pan of charcoal into her room; that, soon afterwards, she felt uncommonly drowsy; and when her little grand-daughter spoke to her, and asked her why she did not come to bed, she made no answer: a few minutes after this, she dropped from her chair. The child was extremely frightened, and though she felt it very difficult to rouse herself, she said, she got up as fast as she could, opened the door, and called to the watchmaker's wife, who luckily had been at work late, and was now raking the kitchen fire. With her assistance the old woman was brought into the air, and presently returned to her senses: the pan of charcoal had been taken away before the apothecary came in the morning; as he was in a great hurry when he called, he made but few inquiries, and consequently condemned the geranium without sufficient evidence. As he left the house, he carelessly said, "My wife would like that geranium, I think." And the poor old woman, who had but a very small fee to offer, was eager to give any thing that seemed to please the doctor.

Forester, when he heard this story, burst into a contemptuous exclamation against the meanness of this and of all other apothecaries. Henry informed the little girl, that the charcoal had been the cause of her grandmother's illness, and advised them never, upon any account, to keep a pan of charcoal again in her bedchamber; he told her, that many people had been killed by this practice. "Then," cried the little girl, joyfully, "if it was the charcoal, and not the geranium, that made grandmother ill, I may keep my beautiful geranium:" and she ran immediately to gather some of the flowers, which she offered to Henry and to Forester. Forester, who was still absorbed in the contemplation of the apothecary's meanness, took the flowers, without perceiving that he took them, and pulled them to pieces as he went on thinking. Henry, when the little girl held the geraniums up to him, observed, that the back of her hand was bruised and black; he asked her how she had hurt herself, and she replied innocently, "that she had not hurt herself, but that her schoolmistress was a very strict woman." Forester, roused from his reverie, desired to hear what the little girl meant by a strict woman, and she explained herself more fully: she said, that, as a favour, her grandmother had obtained leave from some great lady to send her to a charity school: that she went there every day to learn to read and work, but that the mistress of the charity school used her scholars very severely, and often kept them for hours, after they had done their own tasks, to spin for her; and that she beat them if they did not spin as much as she expected. The little girl's grandmother then said, that she knew all this, but that she did not dare to complain, because the schoolmistress was under the patronage of some of "the grandest ladies in Edinburgh," and that, as she could not afford to pay for her little lass's schooling, she was forced to have her taught as well as she could for nothing.

Forester, fired with indignation at this history of injustice, resolved, at all events, to stand forth immediately in the child's defence; but, without staying to consider how the wrong could be redressed, he thought only of the quickest, or, as he said, the most manly means of doing the business: he declared, that if the little girl would show him the way to the school, he would go that instant and speak to the woman in the midst of all her scholars. Henry in vain represented that this would not be a prudent mode of proceeding.

Forester disdained prudence, and, trusting securely to the power of his own eloquence, he set out with the child, who seemed rather afraid to come to open war with her tyrant. Henry was obliged to return home to his father, who had usually business for him to do about this time. The little girl had stayed at home on account of her grandmother's illness, but all the other scholars were hard at work, spinning in a close room, when Forester arrived.

He marched directly into the schoolroom. The wheels stopped at once on his appearance, and the schoolmistress, a raw-boned, intrepid-looking woman eyed him with amazement: he broke silence in the following words:—

"Vile woman, your injustice is come to light! How can you dare to tyrannize over these poor children? Is it because they are poor? Take my advice, children, resist this tyrant, put by your wheels, and spin for her no more."

The children did not move, and the schoolmistress poured out a torrent of abuse in broad Scotch, which, to the English ear of Forester, was unintelligible. At length she made him comprehend her principal questions—Who he was? and by whose authority he interfered between her and her scholars? "By nobody's authority," was Forester's answer; "I want no authority to speak in the cause of injured innocence." No sooner had the woman heard these words, than she called to her husband, who was writing in an adjoining room: without further ceremony, they both seized upon our hero, and turned him out of the house.

The woman revenged herself without mercy upon the little girl whom Forester had attempted to defend, and dismissed her, with advice never more to complain of being obliged to spin for her mistress.

Mortified by the ill success of his enterprise, Forester returned home, attributing the failure of his eloquence chiefly to his ignorance of the Scotch dialect.

THE CANARY BIRD

At his return, Forester heard, that all Dr. Campbell's family were going that evening to visit a gentleman who had an excellent cabinet of minerals. He had some desire to see the fossils; but when he came to the gentleman's house, he soon found himself disturbed at the praises bestowed by some ladies in company upon a little canary bird, which belonged to the mistress of the house. He began to kick his feet together, to hang first one arm and then the other over the back of his chair, with the obvious expression of impatience and contempt in his countenance. Henry Campbell, in the meantime, said, without any embarrassment, just what he thought about the bird. Archibald Mackenzie, with artificial admiration, said a vast deal more than he thought, in hopes of effectually recommending himself to the lady of the house. The lady told him the history of three birds, which had successively inhabited the cage before the present occupier. "They all died," continued she, "in a most extraordinary manner, one after another, in a short space of time, in convulsions."

"Don't listen," whispered Forester, pulling Henry away from the crowd who surrounded the bird-cage; "how can you listen, like that polite hypocrite, to this foolish woman's history of her extraordinary favourites? Come down-stairs with me, I want to tell you my adventure with the schoolmistress; we can take a turn in the hall, and come back before the cabinet of minerals is opened, and before these women have finished the ceremony of tea. Come."

"I'll come presently," said Henry; "I really want to hear this."

Henry Campbell was not listening to the history of the lady's favourite birds like a polite hypocrite, but like a good-natured sensible person; the circumstances recalled to his memory the conversation that we formerly mentioned, which began about pickled cucumbers, and ended with Dr. Campbell's giving an account of the effects of some poisons. In consequence of this conversation, Henry's attention had been turned to the subject, and he had read several essays, which had informed him of many curious facts. He recollected, in particular, to have met with the account(2) of a bird that had been poisoned, and whose case bore a strong resemblance to the present. He begged leave to examine the cage, in order to discover whether there were any lead about it, with which the birds could have poisoned themselves. No lead was to be found: he next examined whether there were any white or green paint about it; he inquired whence the water came which the birds had drunk; and he examined the trough which held their seeds. The lady, whilst he was pursuing these inquiries, said she was sure that the birds could not have died either for want of air or exercise, for that she often left the cage open on purpose, that they might fly about the room. Henry immediately looked round the room, and at length he observed in an inkstand, which stood upon a writing table, a number of wafers, which were many of them chipped round the edges; upon sweeping out the bird-cage, he found a few very small bits of wafer mixed with the seeds and dust; he was now persuaded that the birds had eaten the wafers, and that they had been poisoned by the red lead which they contained; he was confirmed in this opinion, by being told, that the wafers had lately been missed very frequently, and it had been imagined that they had been used by the servants. Henry begged the lady would try an experiment, which might probably save the life of her new favourite; the lady, though she had never before tried an experiment, was easily prevailed upon. She promised Henry that she would lock up the wafers; and he prophesied that her bird would not, like his predecessors, come to an untimely end. Archibald Mackenzie was vexed to observe, that knowledge had in this instance succeeded better, even with a lady, than flattery. As for Forester, he would certainly have admired his friend Henry's ingenuity, if he had been attending to what had passed; but he had taken a book, and had seated himself in an arm-chair, which had been placed on purpose for an old gentleman in company, and was deep in the history of a man who had been cast away, some hundred years ago, upon a desert island.

(Footnote 2: Falconer, on the Poison of Lead and Copper.)

He condescended, however, to put down his book when the fossils were produced: and, as if he had just awakened from a dream, rubbed his eyes, stretched himself, and joined the rest of the company. The malicious Archibald, who observed that Forester had seated himself, through absence of mind, in a place which prevented some of the ladies from seeing the fossils, instantly made a parade of his own politeness, to contrast himself advantageously with the rude negligence of his companion; but Archibald's politeness was always particularly directed to the persons in company whom he thought of the most importance. "You can't see there," said Forester, suddenly rousing himself, and observing that Dr. Campbell's daughter, Miss Flora Campbell, was standing behind him; "had you not better sit down in this chair? I don't want it, because I can see over your head; sit down." Archibald smiled at Forester's simplicity, in paying his awkward compliment to the young lady, who had, according to his mode of estimating, the least pretensions to notice of any one present. Flora Campbell was neither rich nor beautiful, but she had a happy mixture in her manners of Scottish sprightliness and English reserve. She had an eager desire to improve herself, whilst a nice sense of propriety taught her never to intrude upon general notice, or to recede from conversation with airs of counterfeit humility. Forester admired her abilities, because he imagined that he was the only person who had ever discovered them; as to her manners, he never observed these, but even whilst he ridiculed politeness he was anxious to find out what she thought polite. After he had told her all that he knew concerning the fossils, as they were produced from the cabinet—and he was far from ignorant—he at length perceived that she knew full as much of natural history as he did, and he was surprised that a young lady should know so much, and should not be conceited. Flora, however, soon sunk many degrees in his opinion; for, after the cabinet of mineralogy was shut, some of the company talked of a ball, which was to be given in a few days, and Flora, with innocent gaiety, said to Forester, "Have you learnt to dance a Scotch reel since you came to Scotland?" "I!" cried Forester with contempt; "do you think it the height of human perfection to dance a Scotch reel?—then that fine young laird, Mr. Archibald Mackenzie, will suit you much better than I shall." And Forester returned to his arm-chair and his desert island.

THE KEY

It was unfortunate that Forester retired from company in such abrupt displeasure at Flora Campbell's question, for had he borne the idea of a Scotch reel more like a philosopher, he would have heard of something interesting relative to the intended ball, if any thing relative to a ball could be interesting to him. It was a charity-ball, for the benefit of the mistress of the very charity-school(3) to which the little girl with the bruised hand belonged. "Do you know," said Henry to Forester, when they returned home, "that I have great hopes we shall be able to get justice done to the poor children? I hope the tyrannical schoolmistress may yet be punished. The lady, with whom we drank tea yesterday is one of the patronesses of the charity-school."

(Footnote 3: There is no charity-school of this description in Edinburgh; this cannot, therefore, be mistaken for private satire.)

"Lady patronesses!" cried Forester; "we need not expect justice from a lady patroness, depend upon it, especially at a ball; her head will be full of feathers, or some such things. I prophesy you will not succeed better than I have."

The desponding prophecies of Forester did not deter Henry from pursuing a scheme which he had formed. The lady, who was the mistress of the canary bird, came in a few days to visit his mother, and she told him that his experiment had succeeded, that she had regularly locked up the wafers, and that her favourite bird was in perfect health. "And what fee, doctor," said she, smiling, "shall I give you for saving his life?"

"I will tell you in a few minutes," replied Henry; and in a few minutes the little girl and her geranium were sent for, and appeared. Henry told the lady all the circumstances of her story with so much feeling, and at the same time with so much propriety, that she became interested in the cause: she declared that she would do every thing in her power to prevail upon the other ladies to examine into the conduct of the schoolmistress, and to have her dismissed immediately, if it should appear that she had behaved improperly.

Forester, who was present at this declaration, was much astonished, that a lady, whom he had seen caressing a canary-bird, could speak with so much decision and good sense. Henry obtained his fee: he asked and received permission to place the geranium in the middle of the supper-table at the ball; and he begged that the lady would take an opportunity, at supper, to mention the circumstances which he had related to her; but this she declined, and politely said, that she was sure Henry would tell the story much better than she could.

"Come out and walk with me," said Forester to Henry, as soon as the lady was gone. Henry frequently left his occupations with great good-nature, to accompany our hero in his rambles, and he usually followed the subjects of conversation which Forester started. He saw, by the gravity of his countenance, that he had something of importance revolving in his mind. After he had proceeded in silence for some time along the walk, under the high rock called Arthur's Seat, he suddenly stopped, and, turning to Henry, exclaimed, "I esteem you; do not make me despise you!"

"I hope I never shall," said Henry, a little surprised by his friend's manner; "what is the matter?"

"Leave balls, and lady patronesses, and petty artifices, and supple address, to such people as Archibald Mackenzie," pursued Forester, with enthusiasm:

"Who noble ends by noble means pursues—"
"Will scorn canary birds, and cobble shoes,"

Replied Henry, laughing; "I see no meanness in my conduct: I do not know what it is you disapprove."

"I do not approve," said Forester, "of your having recourse to mean address to obtain justice."

Henry requested to know what his severe friend meant by address; but this was not easily explained. Forester, in his definition of mean address, included all that attention to the feelings of others, all those honest arts of pleasing, which make society agreeable. Henry endeavoured to convince him, that it was possible for a person to wish to please, nay, even to succeed in that wish, without being insincere. Their argument and their walk continued, till Henry, who, though very active, was not quite so robust as his friend, was completely tired, especially as he perceived that Forester's opinions remained unshaken.

"How effeminate you gentlemen are!" cried Forester: "see what it is to be brought up in the lap of luxury. Why, I am not at all tired; I could walk a dozen miles further, without being in the least fatigued!"

Henry thought it a very good thing to be able to walk a number of miles without being fatigued, but he did not consider it as the highest perfection of human nature. In his friend's present mood, nothing less could content him, and Forester went on to demonstrate to the weary Henry, that all fortitude, all courage, and all the manly virtues, were inseparably connected with pedestrian indefatigability. Henry, with good-natured presence of mind, which perhaps his friend would have called mean address, diverted our hero's rising indignation by proposing that they should both go and look at the large brewery which was in their way home, and with which Forester would, he thought, be entertained.

The brewery fortunately turned the course of Forester's thoughts, and, instead of quarrelling with his friend for being tired, he condescended to postpone all further debate. Forester had, from his childhood, a habit of twirling a key, whenever he was thinking intently: the key had been produced, and had been twirling upon its accustomed thumb during the argument upon address; and it was still in Forester's hand when they went into the brewery. As he looked and listened, the key was essential to his power of attending; at length, as he stopped to view a large brewing vat, the key unluckily slipped from his thumb, and fell to the bottom of the vat: it was so deep, that the tinkling sound of the key, as it touched the bottom, was scarcely heard. A young man who belonged to the brewery immediately descended by a ladder into the vat, to get the key, but scarcely had he reached the bottom, when he fell down senseless. Henry Campbell was speaking to one of the clerks of the brewery when this accident happened: a man came running to them with the news, "The vat has not been cleaned; it's full of bad air." "Draw him up, let down a hook and cords for him instantly, or he's a dead man," cried Henry, and he instantly ran to the place. What was his terror, when he beheld Forester descending the ladder! He called to him to stop; he assured him that the man could be saved without his hazarding his life: but Forester persisted; he had one end of a cord in his hand, which he said he could fasten in an instant round the man's body. There was a skylight nearly over the vat, so that the light fell directly upon the bottom.

Henry saw his friend reach the last step of the ladder. As Forester stooped to put the rope round the shoulders of the man, who lay insensible at the bottom of the vat, a sudden air of idiocy came over his animated countenance; his limbs seemed no longer to obey his will; his arms dropped, and he fell insensible.

The spectators, who were looking down from above, were so much terrified, that they could not decide to do any thing; some cried, "It's all over with him! Why would he go down?" Others ran to procure a hook—others called to him to take up the rope again, if he possibly could: but Forester could not hear or understand them, Henry Campbell was the only person who, in this scene of danger and confusion, had sufficient presence of mind to be of service.

Near the large vat, into which Forester had descended, there was a cistern of cold water. Henry seized a bucket, which was floating in the cistern, filled it with water, and emptied the water into the vat, dashing it against the sides, to disperse the water, and to displace the mephitic air(4), He called to the people, who surrounded him, for assistance; the water expelled the air; and, when it was safe to descend, Henry instantly went down the ladder himself, and fastened the cord round Forester, who was quite helpless.

(Footnote 4: Carbonic acid gas.)

"Draw him up!" said Henry, They drew him up. Henry fastened another cord round the body of the other man, who lay at the bottom of the vessel, and he was taken up in the same manner. Forester soon returned to his senses, when he was carried into the air; it was with more difficulty that the other man, whose animation had been longer suspended, was recovered; at length, however, by proper application, his lungs played freely, he stretched himself, looked round upon the people who were about him with an air of astonishment, and was some time before he could recollect what had happened to him. Forester, as soon as he had recovered the use of his understanding, was in extreme anxiety to know whether the poor man, who went down for his key, had been saved. His gratitude to Henry, when he heard all that had passed, was expressed in the most enthusiastic manner.

"I acted like a madman, and you like a man of sense," said Forester. "You always know how to do good: I do mischief, whenever I attempt to do good. But now, don't expect, Henry, that I should give up any of my opinions to you, because you have saved my life. I shall always argue with you just as I did before. Remember, I despise address, I don't yield a single point to you. Gratitude shall never make me a sycophant."

THE FLOWERPOT

Eager to prove that he was not a sycophant, Forester, when he returned home with his friend Henry, took every possible occasion to contradict him, with even more than his customary rigidity; nay, he went further still, to vindicate his sincerity.

Flora Campbell had never entirely recovered our hero's esteem, since she had unwittingly expressed her love for Scotch reels; but she was happily unconscious of the crime she had committed, and was wholly intent upon pleasing her father and mother, her brother Henry, and herself. She had a constant flow of good spirits, and the charming domestic talent of making every trifle a source of amusement to herself and others: she was sprightly, without being frivolous; and the uniform sweetness of her temper showed, that she was not in the least in want of flattery, or dissipation, to support her gaiety. But Forester, as the friend of her brother, thought it incumbent upon him to discover faults in her which no one else could discover, and to assist in her education, though she was only one year younger than himself. She had amused herself, the morning that Forester and her brother were at the brewery, with painting a pasteboard covering for the flower-pot which held the poor little girl's geranium. Flora had heard from her brother of his intention to place it in the middle of the supper-table, at the ball; and she flattered herself, that he would like to see it ornamented by her hands at his return. She produced it after dinner. Henry thanked her, and her father and mother were pleased to see her eagerness to oblige her brother. The cynical Forester alone refused his sympathy. He looked at the flower-pot with marked disdain. Archibald, who delighted to contrast himself with the unpolished Forester, and who remarked that Flora and her brother were both somewhat surprised at his unsociable silence, slyly said, "There's something in this flower-pot Miss Campbell, which does not suit Mr. Forester's correct taste; I wish he would allow us to profit by his criticisms."

Forester vouchsafed not a reply.

"Don't you like it, Forester?" said Henry.

"No, he does not like it," said Flora, smiling; "don't force him to say that he does."

"Force me to say I like what I don't like!" repeated Forester; "no, I defy any body to do that."

"But why," said Dr. Campbell, laughing, "why such a waste of energy and magnanimity about a trifle? If you were upon your trial for life or death, Mr. Forester, you could not look more resolutely guarded—more as if you had 'worked up each corporal agent' to the terrible feat!"

"Sir," said Forester, who bore the laugh that was raised against him with the air of a martyr, "I can bear even your ridicule in the cause of truth." The laugh continued at the solemnity with which he pronounced these words. "I think," pursued Forester, "that those who do not respect truth in trifles, will never respect it in matters of consequence."

Archibald Mackenzie laughed more loudly, and with affectation, at this speech: Henry and Dr. Campbell's laughter instantly ceased.

"Do not mistake us," said Dr. Campbell; "we did not laugh at your principles, we only laughed at your manner."

"And are not principles of rather more consequence than manners?"

"Of infinitely more consequence," said Dr. Campbell: "but why, to excellent principles, may we not add agreeable manners? Why should not truth be amiable, as well as respectable? You, who have such enlarged views for the good of the whole human race, are, I make no doubt, desirous that your fellow-creatures should love truth, as well as you love it yourself."

"Certainly, I wish they did," said Forester.

"And have your observations upon the feelings of others, and upon your own, led you to conclude, that we are most apt to like those things which always give us pain? And do you, upon this principle, wish to make truth as painful as possible, in order to increase our love for it?"

"I don't wish to make truth painful," said Forester; "but, at the same time, it is not my fault if people can't bear pain. I think people who can't bear pain, both of body and mind, cannot be good for any thing; for, in the first place, they will always," said Forester, glancing his eye at Flora and her flower-pot,—"they will always prefer flattery to truth, as all weak people do."

At this sarcastic reflection, which seemed to be aimed at the sex, Lady Catherine, Mrs. Campbell, and all the ladies present, except Flora, began to speak at once in their own vindication.

As soon as there was any prospect of peace, Dr. Campbell resumed his argument in the calmest voice imaginable.

"But, Mr. Forester, without troubling ourselves for the present with the affairs of the ladies, or of weak people, may I ask what degree of unnecessary pain you think it the duty of a strong person, a moral Samson, to bear?"

"Unnecessary pain! I do not think it is any body's duty to bear unnecessary pain."

"Nor to make others bear it?"

"Nor to make others bear it."

"Then we need argue no further. I congratulate you, Mr. Forester, upon your becoming so soon a proselyte to politeness."

"To politeness!" said Forester, starting back.

"Yes, my good sir; real politeness only teaches us to save others from unnecessary pain; and this you have just allowed to be your wish.—And now for the grand affair of Flora's flower-pot. You are not bound by politeness to tell any falsehoods; weak as she is, and a woman, I hope she can bear to hear the painful truth upon such an important occasion."

"Why," said Forester, who at last suffered his features to relax into a smile, "the truth then is, that I don't know whether the flower-pot be pretty or ugly, but I was determined not to say it was pretty."

"But why," said Henry, "did you look so heroically severe about the matter?"

"The reason I looked grave," said Forester, "was, because I was afraid your sister Flora would be spoiled by all the foolish compliments that were paid to her and her flower-pot."

"You are very considerate; and Flora, I am sure, is much obliged to you," said Dr. Campbell, smiling, "for being so clear-sighted to the dangers of female vanity. You would not then, with a safe conscience, trust the completion of her education to her mother, or to myself?"

"I am sure, sir," said Forester, who now, for the first time, seemed sensible that he had not spoken with perfect propriety, "I would not interfere impertinently for the world. You are the best judges; only I thought parents were apt to be partial. Henry has saved my life, and I am interested for every thing that belongs to him. So I hope, if I said any thing rude, you will attribute it to a good motive. I wish the flower-pot had never made its appearance, for it has made me appear very impertinent."

Flora laughed with so much good humour at this odd method of expressing his contrition, that even Forester acknowledged the influence of engaging manners and sweetness of temper. He lifted up the flower-pot, so as completely to screen his face, and, whilst he appeared to be examining it, he said, in a low voice, to Henry, "She is above the foibles of her sex."

"Oh, Mr. Forester, take care!" cried Flora.

"Of what?" said Forester, starting.

"It is too late now," said Flora.

And it was too late. Forester, in his awkward manner of lifting the flower-pot and its painted case, had put his thumbs into the mould, with which the flower-pot had been newly filled. It was quite soft and wet. Flora, when she called to him, saw the two black thumbs just ready to stamp themselves upon her work, and her warning only accelerated its fate; for, the instant she spoke, the thumbs closed upon the painted covering, and Forester was the last to perceive the mischief that he had done.

There was no possibility of effacing the stains, nor was there time to repair the damage, for the ball was to commence in a few hours, and Flora was obliged to send her disfigured work, without having had the satisfaction of hearing the ejaculation which Forester pronounced in her praise behind the flower-pot.

THE BALL

Henry seized the moment when Forester was softened by the mixed effect of Dr. Campbell's raillery and Flora's good humour, to persuade him, that it would be perfectly consistent with sound philosophy to dress himself for a ball, nay, even to dance a country-dance. The word reel, to which Forester had taken a dislike, Henry prudently forbore to mention; and Flora, observing, and artfully imitating her brother's prudence, substituted the word hays instead of reels in her conversation. When all the party were ready to go to the ball, and the carriages at the door, Forester was in Dr. Campbell's study, reading the natural history of the elephant.

"Come," said Henry, who had been searching for him all over the house, "we are waiting for you; I'm glad to see you dressed—come!"

"I wish you would leave me behind," said Forester, who seemed to have relapsed into his former unsociable humour, from having been left half an hour in his beloved solitude; nor would Henry probably have prevailed, if he had not pointed to the print of the elephant(5). "That mighty animal, you see, is so docile, that he lets himself be guided by a young boy," said Henry; "and so must you."

(Footnote 5: Cabinet of Quadrupeds.)

As he spoke he pulled Forester gently, who thought he could not show less docility than his favourite animal. When they entered the ball-room, Archibald Mackenzie asked Flora to dance, whilst Forester was considering where he should put his hat. "Are you going to dance without me? I thought I had asked you to dance with me. I intended it all the time we were coming in the coach."

Flora thanked him for his kind intentions; whilst Archibald, with a look of triumph, hurried his partner away, and the dance began. Forester saw this transaction in the most serious light, and it afforded him subject for meditation till at least half a dozen country-dances had been finished. In vain the Berwick Jockey, the Highland Laddie, and the Flowers of Edinburgh, were played; "they suited not the gloomy habit" of his soul. He fixed himself behind a pillar, proof against music, mirth, and sympathy: he looked upon the dancers with a cynical eye. At length he found an amusement that gratified his present splenetic humour; he applied both his hands to his ears, effectually to stop out the sound of the music, that he might enjoy the ridiculous spectacle of a number of people capering about, without any apparent motive. Forester's attitude caught the attention of some of the company; indeed, it was strikingly awkward. His elbows stuck out from his ears, and his head was sunk beneath his shoulders. Archibald Mackenzie was delighted beyond measure at his figure, and pointed him out to his acquaintance with all possible expedition. The laugh and the whisper circulated with rapidity. Henry, who was dancing, did not perceive what was going on till his partner said to him, "Pray, who is that strange mortal?"

"My friend," cried Henry: "will you excuse me for one instant?" And he ran up to Forester, and roused him from his singular attitude. "He is," continued Henry, as he returned to his partner, "an excellent young man, and he has superior abilities; we must not quarrel with him for trifles."

With what different eyes different people behold the same objects! Whilst Forester had been stopping his ears, Dr. Campbell, who had more of the nature of the laughing than of the weeping philosopher, had found much benevolent pleasure in contemplating the festive scene. Not that any folly or ridicule escaped his keen penetration; but he saw every thing with an indulgent eye, and, if he laughed, laughed in such a manner, that even those who were the objects of his pleasantry could scarcely have forborne to sympathize in his mirth. Folly, he thought, could be as effectually corrected by the tickling of a feather, as by the lash of the satirist. When Lady Margaret M'Gregor, and Lady Mary Macintosh, for instance, had almost forced their unhappy partners into a quarrel to support their respective claims to precedency, Dr. Campbell, who was appealed to as the relation of both the furious fair ones, decided the difference expeditiously, and much to the amusement of the company, by observing, that, as the pretensions of each of the ladies were incontrovertible, and precisely balanced, there was but one possible method of adjusting their precedency—by their age. He was convinced, he said, that the youngest lady would with pleasure yield precedency to the elder. The contest was now, which should stand the lowest, instead of which should stand the highest, in the dance: and when the proofs of seniority could not be settled, the fair ones drew lots for their places, and submitted that to chance which could not be determined by prudence.

Forester stood beside Dr. Campbell whilst all this passed, and wasted a considerable portion of virtuous indignation upon the occasion. "And look at that absurd creature!" exclaimed Forester, pointing out to Dr. Campbell a girl who was footing and pounding for fame at a prodigious rate. Dr. Campbell turned from the pounding lady to observe his own daughter Flora, and a smile of delight came over his countenance: for "parents are apt to be partial"—especially those who have such daughters as Flora. Her light figure and graceful agility attracted the attention even of many impartial spectators; but she was not intent upon admiration: she seemed to be dancing in the gaiety of her heart; and that was a species of gaiety in which every one sympathized, because it was natural, and of which every one approved, because it was innocent. There was a certain delicacy mixed with her sportive humour, which seemed to govern, without restraining, the tide of her spirits. Her father's eye was following her as she danced to a lively Scotch tune, when Forester pulled Dr. Campbell's cane, on which he was leaning, and exclaimed, "Doctor, I've just thought of an excellent plan for a tragedy!"

"A tragedy!" repeated Dr. Campbell, with unfeigned surprise; "are you sure you don't mean a comedy?"

Forester persisted that he meant a tragedy, and was proceeding to open the plot. "Don't force me to your tragedy now," said Dr. Campbell, "or it will infallibly be condemned. I cannot say that I have my buskin on! and I advise you to take yours off. Look, is that the tragic muse?"

Forester was astonished to find, that so great a man as Dr. Campbell had so little the power of abstraction; and he retired to muse upon the opening of his tragedy in a recess under the music gallery. But here he was not suffered long to remain undisturbed; for, near this spot, Sir Philip Gosling presently stationed himself; Archibald Mackenzie, who left off dancing as soon as Sir Philip entered the room, came to the half-intoxicated baronet; and they, with some other young men, worthy of their acquaintance, began so loud a contest concerning the number of bottles of claret which a man might, could, or should drink at a sitting, that even Forester's powers of abstraction failed, and his tragic muse took her flight.

"Supper! Supper! thank God!" exclaimed Sir Philip, as supper was now announced. "I'd never set my foot in a ballroom," added he, with several suitable oaths, "if it were not for the supper."

"Is that a rational being?" cried Forester to Dr. Campbell, after Sir Philip had passed them.

"Speak a little lower," said Dr. Campbell, "or he will infallibly prove his title to rationality by shooting you, or by making you shoot him, through the head."

"But, sir," said Forester, holding Dr. Campbell fast, whilst all the rest of the company were going down to supper, "how can you bear such a number of foolish, disagreeable people with patience?"

"What would you have me do?" said Dr. Campbell. "Would you have me get up and preach in the middle of a ball-room? Is it not as well, since we are here, to amuse ourselves with whatever can afford us any amusement, and to keep in good humour with all the world, especially with ourselves?—and had we not better follow the crowd to supper?"

Forester went down-stairs; but, as he crossed an antechamber, which led to the supper-room, he exclaimed, "If I were a legislator, I would prohibit balls."

"And if you were a legislator," said Dr. Campbell, pointing to a tea-kettle, which was on the fire in the antechamber, and from the spout of which a grey cloud of vapour issued—"if you were a legislator, would not you have stoppers wedged tight into the spouts of all tea-kettles in your dominions?"

"No, sir," said Forester; "they would burst."

"And do you think that folly would not burst, and do more mischief than a tea-kettle in the explosion, if you confined it so tight?"

Forester would willingly have stayed in the antechamber, to begin a critical dissection of this allusion; but Dr. Campbell carried him forwards into the supper-room. Flora had kept a seat for her father; and Henry met them at the door.

"I was just coming to see for you, sir," said he to his father. "Flora began to think you were lost."

"No," said Dr. Campbell, "I was only detained by a would-be Cato, who wanted me to quarrel with the whole world, instead of eating my supper. What would you advise me to eat, Flora?" said he, seating himself beside her.

"Some of this trifle, papa;" and as she lightly removed the flowers with which it was ornamented, her father said, "Yes, give me some trifle, Flora. Some characters are like that trifle—flowers and light froth at the top, and solid, good sweetmeat, beneath."

Forester immediately stretched out his plate for some trifle. "But I don't see any use in the flowers, sir," said he.

"Nor any beauty," said Dr. Campbell.

Forester picked the troublesome flowers out of his trifle, and ate a quantity of it sufficient for a Stoic. Towards the end of the supper, he took some notice of Henry, who had made several ineffectual efforts to amuse him by such slight strokes of wit as seemed to suit the time and place. Time and place were never taken into Forester's consideration: he was secretly displeased with his friend Henry for having danced all the evening instead of sitting still; and he looked at Henry's partner with a scrutinizing eye. "So," said he, at last, "I observe I have not been thought worthy of your conversation to-night: this is what gentlemen, polite gentlemen, who dance reels, call friendship!"

"If I had thought that you would have taken it ill I should dance reels," said Henry, laughing, "I would have made the sacrifice of a reel at the altar of friendship; but we don't come to a ball to make sacrifices to friendship, but to divert ourselves."

"If we can," said Forester, sarcastically: here he was prevented from reproaching his friend any longer, for a party of gentlemen began to sing catches, at the desire of the rest of the company.

Forester was now intent upon criticising the nonsensical words that were sung; and he was composing an essay upon the power of the ancient bards, and the effect of national music, when Flora's voice interrupted him: "Brother," said she, "I have won my wager." The wager was, that Forester would not during supper observe the geranium that was placed in the middle of the table.

As soon as the company were satisfied, both with their supper and their songs, Henry, whose mind was always present, seized the moment when there was silence to turn the attention of the company towards the object upon which his own thoughts were intent. The lady-patroness, the mistress of the canary-bird, had performed her promise: she had spoken to several of her acquaintance concerning the tyrannical schoolmistress; and now, fixing the attention of the company upon the geranium, she appealed to Henry Campbell, and begged him to explain its history. A number of eager eyes turned upon him instantly; and Forester felt, that if he had been called upon in such a manner he could not have uttered a syllable. He now felt the great advantage of being able to speak, without hesitation or embarrassment, before numbers. When Henry related the poor little girl's story, his language and manner were so unaffected and agreeable, that he interested every one who heard him in his cause. A subscription was immediately raised; every body was eager to contribute something to the child, who had been so ready, for her old grandmother's sake, to part with her favourite geranium. The lady who superintended the charity-school agreed to breakfast the next morning at Dr. Campbell's, and to go from his house to the school precisely at the hour when the schoolmistress usually set her unfortunate scholars to their extra task of spinning.

Forester was astonished at all this; he did not consider that negligence and inhumanity are widely different. The lady-patronesses had, perhaps, been rather negligent in contenting themselves with seeing the charity-children show well in procession to Church, and they had not sufficiently inquired into the conduct of the schoolmistress; but, as soon as the facts were properly stated, the ladies were eager to exert themselves, and candidly acknowledged that they had been to blame in trusting so much to the reports of the superficial visitors, who had always declared that the school was going on perfectly well.

"More people who are in the wrong," said Dr. Campbell to Forester, "would be corrected, if some people who are in the right had a little candour and patience joined to their other virtues."

As the company rose from the supper-table, several young ladies gathered round the geranium to admire Flora's pretty flower-pot. The black stains, however, struck every eye. Forester was standing by rather embarrassed. Flora, with her usual good-nature, refrained from all explanation, though the exclamations of "How was that done?"—"Who could have done that?" were frequently repeated.

"It was an accident," said Flora; and, to change the conversation, she praised the beauty of the geranium; she gathered one of the fragrant leaves, but, as she was going to put it amongst the flowers in her bosom, she observed she had dropped her moss-rose. It was a rarity at this time of year: it was a rose which Henry Camphell had raised in a conservatory of his own construction.

"Oh, my brother's beautiful rose!" exclaimed Flora.

Forester, who had been much pleased by her good-nature about the stains on the flower-pot, now, contrary to his habits, sympathized with her concern for the loss of her brother's moss-rose. He even exerted himself so far as to search under the benches and under the supper-table. He was fortunate enough to find it; and eager to restore the prize, he with more than his usual gallantry, but not with less than his customary awkwardness, crept from under the table, and, stretching half his body over a bench, pushed his arm between two young ladies into the midst of the group which surrounded Flora. As his arm extended his wrist appeared, and at the sight of that wrist all the young ladies shrank back, with unequivocal tokens of disgust. They whispered—they tittered; and many expressive looks were lost upon our hero, who still resolutely held out the hand upon which every eye was fixed. "Here's your rose! Is not this the rose?" said he, still advancing the dreaded hand to Flora, whose hesitation and blushes surprised him. Mackenzie burst into a loud laugh; and in a whisper, which all the ladies could hear, told Forester, that "Miss Campbell was afraid to take the rose out of his hands, lest she should catch from him what he had caught from the carter who had brought him to Edinburgh, or from some of his companions at the cobbler's."

Forester flung the rose he knew not where, sprung over the bench, rushed between Flora and another lady, made towards the door in a straight line, pushing every thing before him, till a passage was made for him by the astonished crowd, who stood out of his way as if he had been a mad dog.

"Forester!" cried Henry and Dr. Campbell, who were standing upon the steps before the door, speaking about the carriages, "what's the matter? where are you going? The carriage is coming to the door."

"I had rather walk—don't speak to me," said Forester; "I've been insulted: I am in a passion, but I can command myself. I did not knock him down. Pray let me pass!"

Our hero broke from Dr. Campbell and Henry with the strength of an enraged animal from his keepers; and he must have found his way home by instinct, for he ran on without considering how he went. He snatched the light from the servant who opened the door at Dr. Campbell's—hurried to his own apartment—locked, double-locked, and bolted the door—flung himself into a chair, and, taking breath, exclaimed, "Thank God! I've done no mischief. Thank God! I didn't knock him down. Thank God! he is out of my sight, and I am cool now—quite cool: let me recollect it all."

Upon the coolest recollection, Forester could not reconcile his pride to his present circumstances. "Archibald spoke the truth—why am I angry? why was I angry, I mean!" He reasoned much with himself upon the nature of true and false shame: he represented to himself that the disorder which disfigured his hands was thought shameful only because it was vulgar; that what was vulgar was not therefore immoral; that the young tittering ladies who shrunk back from him were not supreme judges of right and wrong; that he ought to despise their opinions, and he despised them with all his might for two or three hours, as he walked up and down his room with unremitting energy. At length our peripatetic philosopher threw himself upon his bed, determined that his repose should not be disturbed by such trifles: he had by this time worked himself up to such a pitch of magnanimity, that he thought he could with composure meet the disapproving eyes of millions of his fellow-creatures; but he was alone when he formed this erroneous estimate of the strength of the human mind. Wearied with passion and reason, he fell asleep, dreamed that he was continually presenting flowers, which nobody would accept; awakened at the imaginary repetition of Archibald's laugh, composed himself again to sleep, and dreamed that he was in a glover's shop, trying on gloves, and that, amongst a hundred pair which he pulled on, he could not find one that would fit him. Just as he tore the last pair in his hurry, he awakened, shook off his foolish dream, saw the sun rising between two chimneys many feet below his windows, recollected that in a short time he should be summoned to breakfast, that all the lady-patronesses were to be at this breakfast, that he could not breakfast in gloves, that Archibald would perhaps again laugh, and Flora perhaps again shrink back. He reproached himself for his weakness in foreseeing and dreading this scene: his aversion to lady-patronesses and to balls was never at a more formidable height; he sighed for liberty and independence, which he persuaded himself were not to be had in his present situation. In one of his long walks he remembered to have seen, at some miles' distance from the town of Edinburgh, a gardener and his boy, who were singing at their work. These men appeared to Forester to be yet happier than the cobbler, who formerly was the object of his admiration; and he was persuaded that he should be much happier at the gardener's cottage than he could ever be at Dr. Campbell's house.

"I am not fit," said he to himself, "to live amongst idle gentlemen and ladies; I should be happy if I were a useful member of society; a gardener is a useful member of society, and I will be a gardener, and live with gardeners."

Forester threw off the clothes which he had worn the preceding night at the fatal ball, dressed himself in his old coat, tied up a small bundle of linen, and took the road to the gardener's.

BREAKFAST

When Henry found that Forester was not in his room in the morning, he concluded that he had rambled out towards Salisbury Craigs, whither he talked the preceding day of going to botanize.

"I am surprised," said Dr. Campbell, "that the young gentleman is out so early, for I have a notion that he has not had much sleep since we parted, unless he walks in his sleep, for he has been walking over my poor head half the night."

Breakfast went on—no Forester appeared. Lady Catherine began to fear that he had broken his neck upon Salisbury Craigs, and related all the falls she had ever had, or had ever been near having, in carriages, on horseback, or otherwise. She then entered into the geography of Salisbury Craigs, and began to dispute upon the probability of his having fallen to the east or to the west.

"My dear Lady Catherine," said Dr. Campbell, "we are not sure that he has been upon Salisbury Craigs; whether he has fallen to the east or to the west, we cannot, therefore, conveniently settle."

But Lady Catherine, whose prudential imagination travelled fast, went on to inquire of Dr. Campbell, to whom the great Forester estate would go in case of any accident having happened or happening to the young gentleman before he should come of age.

Dr. Campbell was preparing to give her ladyship satisfaction upon this point, when a servant put a letter into his hands. Henry looked in great anxiety. Dr. Campbell glanced his eye over the letter, put it into his pocket, and desired the servant to show the person who brought the letter into his study.

"It's only a little boy," said Archibald; "I saw him as I passed through the hall."

"Cannot a little boy go into my study?" said Dr. Campbell, coolly.

Archibald's curiosity was strongly excited, and he slipped out of the room a few minutes afterward, resolved to speak to the boy, and to discover the purpose of his embassy. But Dr. Campbell was behind him before he was aware of his approach, and just as Archibald began to cross-examine the boy in these words, "So you came from a young man who is about my size?" Dr. Campbell put both his hands upon his shoulders, saying, "He came from a young man who does not in the least resemble you, believe me, Mr. Archibald Mackenzie."

Archibald started, turned round, and was so abashed by the civilly contemptuous look with which Dr. Campbell pronounced these words, that he retired from the study without even attempting any of his usual equivocating apologies for his intrusion. Dr. Campbell now read Forester's letter. It was as follows:—

"Dear Sir,

"Though I have quitted your house thus abruptly, I am not insensible of your kindness. For the step I have taken, I can offer no apology merely to my guardian; but you have treated me, Dr. Campbell, as your friend, and I shall lay my whole soul open to you.

"Notwithstanding your kindness,—notwithstanding the friendship of your son Henry, whose excellent qualities I know how to value,—I most ingenuously own to you that I have been far from happy in your house. I feel that I cannot be at ease in the vortex of dissipation; and the more I see of the higher ranks of society, the more I regret that I was born a gentleman. Neither my birth nor my fortune shall, however, restrain me from pursuing that line of life which, I am persuaded, leads to virtue and tranquillity. Let those who have no virtuous indignation obey the voice of fashion, and at her commands let her slaves eat the bread of idleness till it palls upon the sense! I reproach myself with having yielded, as I have done of late, my opinions to the persuasions of friendship; my mind has become enervated, and I must fly from the fatal contagion. Thank Heaven, I have yet the power to fly: I have yet sufficient force to break my chains. I am not yet reduced to the mental degeneracy of the base monarch, who hugged his fetters because they were of gold.

"I am conscious of powers that fit me for something better than to waste my existence in a ball-room; and I will not sacrifice my liberty to the absurd ceremonies of daily dissipation. I, that have been the laughing-stock of the mean and frivolous, have yet sufficient manly pride, unextinguished in my breast, to assert my claim to your esteem: to assert, that I never have committed, or shall designedly commit, any action unworthy of the friend of your son.

"I do not write to Henry, lest I should any way involve him in my misfortunes: he is formed to shine in the polite world, and his connexion with me might tarnish the lustre of his character in the eyes of the 'nice-judging fair.' I hope, however, that he will not utterly discard me from his heart, though I cannot dance a reel. I beg that he will break open the lock of the trunk that is in my room, and take out of it my Goldsmith's Animated Nature, which he seemed to like.

"In my table-drawer there are my Martyn's Letters on Botany, in which you will find a number of plants that I have dried for Flora—Miss Flora Campbell, I should say. After what passed last night, I can scarcely hope they will be accepted. I would rather have them burned than refused; therefore please to burn them, and say nothing more upon the subject. Dear sir, do not judge harshly of me; I have had a severe conflict with myself before I could resolve to leave you. But I would rather that you should judge of me with severity than that you should extend to me the same species of indulgence with which you last night viewed the half-intoxicated baronet.

"I can bear any thing but contempt.

"Yours, &c.

"P.S. I trust that you will not question the bearer; he knows where I am; I therefore put you on your guard. I mean to earn my own bread as a gardener; I have always preferred the agricultural to the commercial system."

To this letter, in which the mixture of sense and extravagance did not much surprise Dr. Campbell, he returned the following answer:—

"My dear cobbler, gardener, orator, or by whatever other name you choose to be addressed, I am too old to be surprised at any thing, otherwise I might have been rather surprised at some things in your eloquent letter. You tell me that you have the power to fly, and that you do not hug your chains, though they are of gold! Are you an alderman, or Daedalus? or are these only figures of speech? You inform me, that you cannot live in the vortex of dissipation, or eat the bread of idleness, and that you are determined to be a gardener. These things seem to have no necessary connexion with each other. Why you should reproach yourself so bitterly for having spent one evening of your life in a ball-room, which I suppose is what you allude to when you speak of a vortex of dissipation, I am at a loss to discover. And why you cannot, with so much honest pride yet unextinguished in your breast, find any occupation more worthy of your talents, and as useful to society, as that of a gardener, I own, puzzles me a little. Consider these things coolly; return to dinner, and we will compare at our leisure the advantages of the mercantile and the agricultural system. I forbear to question your messenger, as you desire; and I shall not show your letter to Henry till after we have dined. I hope by that time you will insist upon my burning it; which, at your request, I shall do with pleasure, although it contains several good sentences.

As I am not yet sure you have departed this life, I shall not enter upon my office of executor; I shall not break open the lock of your trunk (of which I hope you will some time, when your mind is less exalted, find the key), nor shall I stir in the difficult case of Flora's legacy. When next you write your will, let me, for the sake of your executor, advise you to be more precise in your directions; for what can be done if you order him to give and burn the same thing in the same sentence? As you have, amongst your other misfortunes, the misfortune to be born heir to five or six thousand a year, you should learn a little how to manage your own affairs, lest you should, amongst your poor or rich companions, meet with some who are not quite so honest as yourself.

"If, instead of returning to dine with us, you should persist in your gardening scheme, I shall have less esteem for your good sense, but I shall forbear to reproach you. I shall leave you to learn by your own experience, if it be not in my power to give you the advantages of mine gratis. But, at the same time, I shall discover where you are, and shall inform myself exactly of all your proceedings. This, as your guardian, is my duty. I should further warn you, that I shall not, whilst you choose to live in a rank below your own, supply you with your customary yearly allowance. Two hundred guineas a year would be an extravagant allowance in your present circumstances. I do not mention money with any idea of influencing your generous mind by mercenary motives; but it is necessary that you should not deceive yourself by inadequate experiments: you cannot be rich and poor at the same time. I gave you the day before yesterday five ten-pound notes for your last quarterly allowance; I suppose you have taken these with you, therefore you cannot be in any immediate distress for money. I am sorry, I own, that you are so well provided, because a man who has fifty guineas in his pocket-book cannot distinctly feel what it is to be compelled to earn his own bread.

"Do not, my dear ward, think me harsh; my friendship for you gives me courage to inflict present pain, with a view to your future advantage. You must not expect to see any thing of your friend Henry until you return to us. I shall, as his father and your guardian, request that he will trust implicitly to my prudence upon this occasion; that he will make no inquiries concerning you; and that he will abstain from all connexion with you whilst you absent yourself from your friends. You cannot live amongst the vulgar (by the vulgar I mean the ill-educated, the ignorant, those who have neither noble sentiments nor agreeable manners), and at the same time enjoy the pleasures of cultivated society. I shall wait, not without anxiety, till your choice be decided.

"Believe me to be

"Your sincere friend and guardian,

"H. CAMPBELL."

As soon as Dr. Campbell had despatched this letter, he returned to the company. The ladies, after breakfast, proceeded to the charity-school; but Henry was so anxious to learn what was become of his friend Forester, that he could scarcely enjoy the effects of his own benevolent exertions. It was with difficulty, such as he had never before experienced, that Dr. Campbell obtained from him the promise to suspend all intercourse with Forester. Henry's first impulse, when he read the letter, which his father now found it prudent to show him, was to search for his friend instantly. "I am sure," said he, "I shall be able to find him out; and if I can but see him, and speak to him, I know I could prevail upon him to return to us."

"Yes," said Dr. Campbell, "perhaps you might persuade him to return; but that is not the object: unless his understanding be convinced, what should we gain?"

"It should be convinced. I could convince him," cried Henry.

"I have, my dear son," said Dr. Campbell, smiling, "the highest opinion of your logic and eloquence; but are your reasoning powers stronger to-day than they were yesterday? Have you any new arguments to produce? I thought you had exhausted your whole store without effect."

Henry paused.

"Believe me," continued his father, lowering his voice, "I am not insensible to your friend's good, and, I will say, great qualities; I do not leave him to suffer evils, without feeling as much perhaps as you can do; but I am convinced, that the solidity of his character, and the happiness of his whole life, will depend upon the impression that is now made upon his mind by realities. He will see society as it is. He has abilities and generosity of mind which will make him a first-rate character, if his friends do not spoil him out of false kindness."

Henry, at these words, held out his hand to his father, and gave him the promise which he desired.

"But," added he, "I still have hopes from your letter—I should not be surprised to see Forester at dinner to-day."

"I should," said Dr. Campbell.

Dr. Campbell, alas! was right. Henry looked eagerly towards the door every time it opened, when they were at dinner: but he was continually disappointed. Flora, whose gaiety usually enlivened the evenings, and agreeably relieved her father and brother after their morning studies, was now silent.

Whilst Lady Catherine's volubility overpowered even the philosophy of Dr. Campbell, she wondered—she never ceased wondering—that Mr. Forester did not appear, and that the doctor and Mrs. Campbell, and Henry and Flora, were not more alarmed. She proposed sending twenty different messengers after him. She was now convinced, that he had not fallen from Salisbury Craigs, because Dr. Campbell assured her ladyship, that he had a letter from him in his pocket, and that he was safe; but she thought that there was imminent danger of his enlisting in a frolic, or, perhaps, marrying some cobbler's daughter in a pet. She turned to Archibald Mackenzie, and exclaimed, "He was at a cobbler's; it could not be merely to mend his shoes. What sort of a lassy is the cobbler's daughter? or has the cobbler a daughter?"

"She is hump-backed, luckily," said Dr. Campbell, coolly.

"That does not signify," said Lady Catherine; "I'm convinced she is at the bottom of the whole mystery; for I once heard Mr. Forester say—and I'm sure you must recollect it, Flora, my dear, for he looked at you at the time—I once heard him say, that personal beauty was no merit, and that ugly people ought to be liked—or some such thing—out of humanity. Now, out of humanity, with his odd notions, it's ten to one, Dr. Campbell, he marries this cobbler's hump-backed daughter. I'm sure, if I were his guardian, I could not rest an instant with such a thought in my head."

"Nor I," said Dr. Campbell, quietly; and in spite of her ladyship's astonishment, remonstrances, and conjectures, he maintained his resolute composure.

THE GARDENER

The gardener who had struck Forester's fancy, was a square, thick, obstinate-eyed, hard-working, ignorant, elderly man, whose soul was intent upon his petty daily gains, and whose honesty was of that "coarse-spun, vulgar sort(6)," which alone can be expected from men of uncultivated minds. Mr. M'Evoy, for that was the gardener's name, was both good-natured and selfish; his views and ideas all centered in his own family; and his affection was accumulated and reserved for two individuals, his son and his daughter. The son was not so industrious as the father; he was ambitious of seeing something of the world, and he consorted with all the young 'prentices in Edinburgh, who would condescend to forget that he was a country boy, and to remember that he expected, when his father should die, to be rich. Mr. M'Evoy's daughter was an ugly, cross-looking girl, who spent all the money that she could either earn or save upon ribands and fine gowns, with which she fancied she could supply all the defects of her person.

(Footnote 6: Mrs. Barbauld'a Essay on the Inconsistency of Human Expectations.)

This powerful motive for her economy operated incessantly upon her mind, and she squeezed all that could possibly be squeezed for her private use from the frugal household. The boy, whose place Forester thought himself so fortunate to supply, had left the gardener, because he could not bear to work and be scolded without eating or drinking.

The gardener willingly complied with our hero's first request; he gave him a spade, and he set him to work. Forester dug with all the energy of an enthusiast, and dined like a philosopher upon long kail; but long kail did not charm him so much the second day as it had done the first; and the third day it was yet less to his taste; besides, he began to notice the difference between oaten and wheaten bread. He, however, recollected that Cyrus lived, when he was a lad, upon water-cresses—the black broth of the Spartans he likewise remembered, and he would not complain. He thought, that he should soon accustom himself to his scanty, homely fare. A number of the disagreeable circumstances of poverty he had not estimated when he entered upon his new way of life; and though at Dr. Campbell's table he had often said to himself, "I could do very well without all these things," yet, till he had actually tried the experiment, he had not clear ideas upon the subject. He missed a number of little pleasures and conveniences, which he had scarcely noticed, whilst they had every day presented themselves as matters of course. The occupation of digging was laborious, but it afforded no exercise to his mind, and he felt most severely the want of Henry's agreeable conversation; he had no one to whom he could now talk of the water-cresses of Cyrus, or the black broth of the Spartans; he had no one with whom he could dispute concerning the Stoic or the Epicurean doctrines, the mercantile or the agricultural system. Many objections to the agricultural system, which had escaped him, occurred now to his mind; and his compassion for the worms, whom he was obliged to cut in pieces continually with his spade, acted every hour more forcibly upon his benevolent heart. He once attempted to explain his feelings for the worms to the gardener, who stared at him with all the insolence of ignorance, and bade him mind his work, with a tone of authority which ill suited Forester's feelings and love of independence.

"Is ignorance thus to command knowledge? Is reason thus to be silenced by boorish stupidity?" said Forester to himself, as he recollected the patience and candour with which Dr. Campbell and Henry used to converse with him. He began to think, that in cultivated society he had enjoyed more liberty of mind, more freedom of opinion, than he could taste in the company of an illiterate gardener. The gardener's son, though his name was Colin, had no Arcadian simplicity, nothing which could please the classic taste of Forester, or which could recall to his mind the Eclogues of Virgil, or the golden age; the Gentle Shepherd, or the Ayrshire Ploughman. Colin's favourite holiday's diversion was playing at goff; this game, which is played with a bat loaded with lead, and with a ball, which is harder than a cricket-ball, requires much strength and dexterity. Forester used, sometimes, to accompany the gardener's son to the Links,(7) where numbers of people, of different descriptions are frequently seen practising this diversion. Our hero was ambitious of excelling at the game of goff; and, as he was not particularly adroit, he exposed himself, in his first attempts, to the derision of the spectators, and he likewise received several severe blows. Colin laughed at him without mercy; and Forester could not help comparing the rude expressions of his new companion's untutored vanity with the unassuming manners and unaffected modesty of Henry Campbell. Forester soon took an aversion to the game of goff, and recollected Scotch reels with less contempt.

(Footnote 7: A lea or common near Edinburgh.)

One evening, after having finished his task of digging (for digging was now become a task), he was going to take a walk to Duddingstone lake, when Colin, who was at the same instant setting out for the Links, roughly insisted upon Forester's accompanying him. Our hero, who was never much disposed to yield to the taste of others, positively refused the gardener's son, with some imprudent expressions of contempt. From this moment Colin became his enemy, and, by a thousand malicious devices, contrived to show his vulgar hatred.

Forester now, to his great surprise, discovered that hatred could exist in a cottage. Female vanity, he likewise presently perceived, was not confined to the precincts of a ball-room; he found that Miss M'Evoy spent every leisure moment in the contemplation of her own coarse image in a fractured looking-glass. He once ventured to express his dislike of a many-coloured plaid in which Miss M'Evoy had arrayed herself for a dance; and the fury of her looks, and the loud-toned vulgarity of her conceit, were strongly contrasted with the recollection of Flora Campbell's gentle manners and sweetness of temper. The painted flower-pot was present to his imagination, and he turned from the lady who stood before him with an air of disgust, which he had neither the wish nor the power to conceal. The consequences of offending this high-spirited damsel our hero had not sufficiently considered: the brother and sister, who seldom agreed in any thing else, now agreed, though from different motives, in an eager desire to torment Forester. Whenever he entered the cottage, either to rest himself, or to partake of those "savoury messes, which the neat-handed Phillis dresses," he was received with sullen silence, or with taunting reproach. The old gardener, stupid as he was, Forester thought an agreeable companion, compared with his insolent son and his vixen daughter. The happiest hours of the day, to our hero, were those which he spent at his work; his affections, repressed and disappointed, became a source of misery to him.

"Is there nothing in this world to which I can attach myself?" said Forester, as he one day leaned upon his spade in a melancholy mood. "Must I spend my life in the midst of absurd altercations? Is it for this that I have a heart and an understanding? No one here comprehends one word I say—I am an object of contempt and hatred, whilst my soul is formed for the most benevolent feelings, and capable of the most extensive views. And of what service am I to my fellow-creatures? Even this stupid gardener, even a common labourer, is as useful to society as I am. Compared with Henry Campbell, what am I? Oh, Henry!—Flora!—could you see me at this instant, you would pity me."

But the fear of being an object of pity wakened Forester's pride; and though he felt that he was unhappy, he could not bear to acknowledge that he had mistaken the road to happiness. His imaginary picture of rural felicity was not, to be sure, realized; but he resolved to bear his disappointment with fortitude, to fulfil his engagements with his master, the gardener, and then to seek some other more eligible situation. In the meantime, his benevolence tried to expand itself upon the only individual in this family who treated him tolerably well: he grew fond of the old gardener, because there was nothing else near him to which he could attach himself, not even a dog or a cat. The old man, whose temper was not quite so enthusiastical as Forester's, looked upon him as an industrious simple young man, above the usual class of servants, and rather wished to keep him in his service, because he gave him less than the current wages. Forester, after his late reflections upon digging, began to think, that, by applying his understanding to the business of gardening, he might perhaps make some discoveries, which should excite his master's everlasting gratitude, and immortalize his own name. He pledged a shirt and a pair of stockings at a poor bookseller's stall, for some volumes upon gardening; and these, in spite of the ridicule of Colin and Miss M'Evoy, he studied usually at his meals. He at length met with an account of some experiments upon fruit-trees, which he thought would infallibly make the gardener's fortune.

"Did you not tell me," said Forester to the gardener, "that cherries were sometimes sold very high in Edinburgh?"

"Five a penny," said the gardener; and he wished, from the bottom of his heart, that he had a thousand cherry-trees, but he possessed only one.

He was considerably alarmed, when Forester proposed to him, as the certain means of making his fortune, to strip the bark off this cherry-tree, assuring him, that a similar experiment had been tried and had succeeded; that his cherry-tree would bear twice as many cherries, if he would only strip the bark from it. "Let me try one branch for an experiment—I will try one branch!"

But the gardener peremptorily forbade all experiments, and, shutting Forester's book, bade him leave such nonsense, and mind his business.

Provoked by this instance of tyrannical ignorance, Forester forgot his character of a servant boy, and at length called his master an obstinate fool.

No sooner were these words uttered, than the gardener emptied the remains of his watering-pot coolly in Forester's face, and, first paying him his wages, dismissed him from his service.

Miss M'Evoy, who was at work, seated at the door, made room most joyfully for Forester to pass, and observed, that she had long since prophesied he would not do for them.

Forester was now convinced, that it was impossible to reform a positive old gardener, to make him try new experiments upon cherry-trees, or to interest him for the progress of science. He deplored the perversity of human nature, and he began, when he reflected upon the characters of Miss M'Evoy and her brother, to believe, that they were beings distinct from the rest of their species; he was, at all events, glad to have parted with such odious companions. On his road to Edinburgh he had time for various reflections.

"Thirty shillings, then, with hard bodily labour, I have earned for one month's service!" said Forester to himself. "Well, I will keep to my resolution. I will live upon the money I earn, and upon that alone; I will not have recourse to my bank notes till the last extremity." He took out his pocket-book, however, and looked at them, to see that they were safe. "How wretched," thought he, "must be that being, who is obliged to purchase, in his utmost need, the assistance of his fellow-creatures with such vile trash as this! I have been unfortunate in my first experiment; but all men are not like this selfish gardener and his brutal son, incapable of disinterested friendship."

Here Forester was interrupted in his meditations by a young man, who accosted him with—"Sir, if I don't mistake, I believe I have a key of yours."

Forester looked up at the young man's face, and recollected him to be the person who had nearly lost his life in descending for his key into the brewing-vat.

"I knew you again, sir," continued the brewer's clerk, "by your twirling those scissors upon your finger, just as you were doing that day at the brewery."

Forester was not conscious, till this moment, that he had a pair of scissors in his hand: whilst the gardener was paying him his wages, to relieve his mauvaise honte, our hero took up Miss M'Evoy's scissors, which lay upon the table, and twirled them upon his fingers, as he used to do with a key. He was rather ashamed to perceive, that he had not yet cured himself of such a silly habit. "I thought the lesson I got at the brewery," said he, "would have cured me for ever of this foolish trick; but the diminutive chains of habit(8), as somebody says, are scarcely ever heavy enough to be felt, till they are too strong to be broken."

(Footnote 8: Dr. Johnson's Vision of Theodore.)

"Sir!" said the astonished clerk.

"Oh, I beg your pardon," said our hero, who now perceived by his countenance that his observation on the peculiar nature of the chains of habit was utterly unintelligible to him; "pray, sir, can you tell me what o'clock it is?"

"Half after four—I am—sir," said the clerk, producing his watch, with the air of a man who thought a watch a matter of some importance. "Hum! He can't be a gentleman; he has no watch!" argued he with himself; and he looked at Forester's rough apparel with astonishment. Forester had turned back, that he might return Miss M'Evoy her scissors. The brewer's clerk was going in the same direction to collect some money for his master. As they walked on, the young man talked to our hero with good-nature, but with a species of familiarity, which was strikingly different from the respectful manner in which he formerly addressed Forester, when he had seen him in a better coat, and in the company of a young gentleman.

"You have left Dr. Campbell's, then?" said he, looking with curiosity. Forester replied, that he had left Dr. Campbell's, because he preferred earning his own bread to living an idle life among gentlemen and ladies.

The clerk, at this speech, looked earnestly in Forester's face, and began to suspect that he was deranged in his mind.

As the gravity of our hero's looks, and the sobriety of his demeanour, did not give any strong indications of insanity, the clerk, after a few minutes' consideration, inclined to believe, that Forester concealed the truth from him; that probably he was some dependant of Dr. Campbell's family; that he had displeased his friends, and had been discarded in disgrace. He was confirmed in these suppositions by Forester's telling him, that he had just left the service of a gardener; that he did not know where to find a lodging for the night; and that he was in want of some employment, by which he might support himself independently.

The clerk, who remembered with gratitude the intrepidity with which Forester had hazarded his life to save him the morning that he was at the brewery, and who had also some compassion for a young gentleman reduced to poverty, told him that if he could write a good hand, knew any thing of accounts, and could get a character for punctuality (meaning to include honesty in this word) from any creditable people, he did not doubt that his master, who had large concerns, might find employment for him as an under-clerk. Forester's pride was not agreeably soothed by the manner of this proposal, but he was glad to hear of a situation, to use the clerk's genteel expression; and he moreover thought, that he should now have an opportunity of comparing the commercial and agricultural systems.

The clerk hinted, that he supposed Forester would choose to "make himself smart," before he called to offer himself at the brewery, and advised him to call about six, as by that time in the evening his master was generally at leisure.

A dinner at a public-house (for our hero did not know where else to dine), and the further expense of a new pair of shoes, and some other articles of dress, almost exhausted his month's wages: he was very unwilling to make any of these purchases, but the clerk assured him, that they were indispensable; and, indeed, at last, his appearance was scarcely upon a par with that of his friendly adviser.

THE BET

Before we follow Forester to the brewery, we must request the attention of our readers to the history of a bet of Mr. Archibald Mackenzie's.

We have already noticed the rise and progress of this young gentleman's acquaintance with Sir Philip Gosling. Archibald,

"Whose ev'ry frolic had some end in view,
Ne'er played the fool, but played the rascal too,"
—Anonymous

cultivated assiduously the friendship of this weak, dissipated, vain young baronet, in hopes that he might, in process of time, make some advantage of his folly. Sir Philip had an unfortunately high opinion of his own judgment; an opinion which he sometimes found it difficult to inculcate upon the minds of others, till he hit upon the compendious method of laying high wagers in support of all his assertions. Few people chose to venture a hundred guineas upon the turn of a straw. Sir Philip, in all such contests, came off victorious; and he plumed himself much upon the success of his purse. Archibald affected the greatest deference for Sir Philip's judgment; and, as he observed that the baronet piqued himself upon his skill as a jockey, he flattered him indefatigably upon this subject. He accompanied Sir Philip continually in his long visits to the livery-stables; and he made himself familiarly acquainted with the keeper of the livery-stables, and even with the hostlers. So low can interested pride descend! All this pains Archibald took, and more, for a very small object. He had set his fancy upon Sawney, one of his friend's horses; and he had no doubt, but that he should either induce Sir Philip to make him a present of this horse, or that he should jockey him out of it, by some well-timed bet.

In counting upon the baronet's generosity, Archibald was mistaken. Sir Philip had that species of good-nature which can lend, but not that which can give. He offered to lend the horse to Archibald most willingly; but the idea of giving it was far distant from his imagination. Archibald, who at length despaired of his friend's generosity, had recourse to his other scheme of the wager. After having judiciously lost a few guineas to Sir Philip in wagers, to confirm him in his extravagant opinion of his own judgment, Archibald, one evening, when the fumes of wine and vanity, operating together, had somewhat exalted the man of judgment's imagination, urged him, by artful, hesitating contradiction, to assert the most incredible things of one of his horses, to whom he had given the name of Favourite. Archibald knew, from the best authority—from the master of the livery-stables, who was an experienced jockey—that Favourite was by no means a match for Sawney; he therefore waited quietly till Sir Philip Gosling laid a very considerable wager upon the head of his "Favourite." Archibald immediately declared, he could not, in conscience—that he could not, for the honour of Scotland, give up his friend Sawney.

"Sawney!" cried Sir Philip; "I'll bet fifty guineas, that Favourite beats him hollow at a walk, trot, or gallop, whichever you please."

Archibald artfully affected to be startled at this defiance, and, seemingly desirous to draw back, pleaded his inability to measure purses with such a rich man as Sir Philip.

"Nay, my boy," replied Sir Philip, "that excuse shan't stand you in stead. You have a pretty little pony there, that Lady Catherine has just given you; if you won't lay me fifty guineas, will you risk your pony against my judgment?"

Archibald had now brought his friend exactly to the point at which he had been long aiming. Sir Philip staked his handsome horse Sawney against Archibald's sorry pony, upon this wager, that Favourite should, at the first trials, beat Sawney at a walk, a trot, and a gallop.

Warmed with wine, and confident in his own judgment, the weak baronet insisted upon having the bet immediately decided. The gentlemen ordered out their horses, and the wager was to be determined upon the sands of Leith.

Sir Philip Gosling, to his utter astonishment, found himself for once mistaken in his judgment. The treacherous Archibald coolly suffered him to exhale his passion in unavailing oaths, and at length rejoiced to hear him consoling himself with the boast, that this was the first wager upon horse-flesh that he had ever lost in his life. The master of the livery-stables stared with well-affected incredulity, when Sir Philip, upon his return from the sands of Leith, informed him, that Favourite had been beat hollow by Sawney; and Archibald, by his additional testimony, could scarcely convince him of the fact, till he put two guineas into his hand, when he recommended his new horse Sawney to his particular care. Sir Philip, who was not gifted with quick observation, did not take notice of this last convincing argument. Whilst this passed, he was talking eagerly to the hostler, who confirmed him in his opinion, which he still repeated as loud as ever, "that Favourite ought to have won." This point Archibald prudently avoided to contest; and he thus succeeded in duping and flattering his friend at once.

"Sawney for ever!" cried Archibald, as soon as Sir Philip had left the stables. "Sawney for ever!" repeated the hostler, and reminded Mackenzie, that he had promised him half a guinea. Archibald had no money in his pocket; but he assured the hostler, that he would remember him the next day. The next day, however, Archibald, who was expert in parsimonious expedients, considered that he had better delay giving the hostler his half-guinea, till it had been earned by his care of Sawney.

It is the usual error of cunning people to take it for granted, that others are fools. This hostler happened to be a match for our young laird in cunning, and, as soon as he perceived that it was Archibald's intention to cheat him of the interest of his half-guinea, he determined to revenge himself in his care of Sawney. We shall hereafter see the success of his devices.

THE SADDLE AND BRIDLE

Scarcely had Archibald Mackenzie been two days in possession of the long-wished-for object of his mean soul, when he became dissatisfied with his own saddle and bridle, which certainly did not, as Sir Philip observed, suit his new horse. The struggles in Archibald's mind, betwixt his taste for expense and his habits of saving, were often rather painful to him. He had received from Lady Catherine a ten-guinea note, when he first came to Dr. Campbell's; and he had withstood many temptations to change it. One morning (the day that he had accompanied Henry and Forester to the watchmaker's) he was so strongly charmed by the sight of a watch-chain and seals, that he actually took his bank-note out of his scrutoire at his return home, put it into his pocket, when he dressed for dinner, and resolved to call that evening at the watchmaker's to indulge his fancy, by purchasing the watch-chain, and to gratify his family pride, by getting his coat of arms splendidly engraven upon the seal. He called at the watchmaker's, in company with Sir Philip Gosling, but he could not agree with him respecting the price of the chain and seals; and Archibald consoled himself with the reflection, that his bank-note would still remain. He held the note in his hand, whilst he higgled about the price of the watch-chain.

"Oh, d—n the expense!" cried Sir Philip.

"Oh, I mind ten guineas as little as any man," said Archibald, thrusting the bank-note, in imitation of the baronet, with affected carelessness, into his waistcoat-pocket. He was engaged that night to go to the play with Sir Philip, and he was much hurried in dressing. His servant observed that his waistcoat was stained, and looked out another for him.

Now this man sometimes took the liberty of wearing his master's clothes; and, when Archibald went to the play, the servant dressed himself in the stained waistcoat, to appear at a ball, which was given that night in the neighbourhood, by some "gentleman's gentleman." The waistcoat was rather too tight for the servant: he tore it, and instead of sending it to the washerwoman's, to have the stain washed out, as his master had desired, he was now obliged to send it to the tailor's to have it mended.

Archibald's sudden wish for a new saddle and bridle for Sawney could not be gratified without changing the bank-note; and, forgetting that he had left it in the pocket of his waistcoat the night that he went to the play, he searched for it in the scrutoire, in which he was accustomed to keep his treasures. He was greatly disturbed, when the note was not to be found in the scrutoire; he searched over and over again;

not a pigeon-hole, not a drawer, remained to be examined. He tried to recollect when he had last seen it, and at length remembered, that he put it into his waistcoat-pocket, when he went to the watchmaker's; that he had taken it out to look at, whilst he was in the shop; but whether he had brought it home safely or not he could not precisely ascertain. His doubts upon this subject, however, he cautiously concealed, resolved, if possible, to make somebody or other answerable for his loss. He summoned his servant, told him that he had left a ten-guinea bank-note in his waistcoat-pocket the night that he went to the play, and that, as the waistcoat was given into his charge, he must be answerable for the note. The servant boldly protested, that he neither could nor would be at the loss of a note which he had never seen.

Archibald now softened his tone; for he saw, that he had no chance of bullying the servant. "I desired you to send it to the washerwoman's," said he.

"And so I did, sir," said the man.

This was true, but not the whole truth. He had previously sent the waistcoat to the tailor's to have the rent repaired, which it received the night he wore it at the ball. These circumstances the servant thought proper to suppress; and he was very ready to agree with his master in accusing the poor washerwoman of having stolen the note. The washerwoman was extremely industrious, and perfectly honest; she had a large family, that depended upon her labour, and upon her character, for support. She was astonished and shocked at the charge that was brought against her, and declared, that if she were able, she would rather pay the whole money at once, than suffer any suspicion to go abroad against her. Archibald rejoiced to find her in this disposition; and he assured her, that the only method to avoid disgrace, a lawsuit, and ruin, was instantly to pay, or to promise to pay, the money. It was out of her power to pay it; and she would not promise what she knew she could not perform.

Archibald redoubled his threats; the servant stood by his master. The poor woman burst into tears; but she steadily declared that she was innocent; and no promise could be extorted from her, even in the midst of her terror. Though she had horrible, perhaps not absolutely visionary, ideas of the dangers of a lawsuit, yet she had some confidence in the certainty that justice was on her side. Archibald said, that she might talk about justice as much as she pleased, but that she must prepare to submit to the law. The woman trembled at the sound of these words; but, though ignorant, she was no fool, and she had a friend in Dr. Campbell's family, to whom she resolved to apply in her distress. Henry Campbell had visited her little boy when he was ill, and had made him some small present; and, though she did not mean to encroach upon Henry's good-nature, she thought, that he had so much learning, that he certainly could, without its costing her any thing, put her in the right way to avoid the law, with which she had been threatened by Archibald Mackenzie and his servant.

Henry heard the story with indignation, such as Forester would have felt in similar circumstances; but prudence tempered his enthusiastic feelings; and prudence renders us able to assist others, whilst enthusiasm frequently defeats its own purposes, and injures those whom it wildly attempts to serve. Henry, knowing the character of Archibald, governed himself accordingly; he made no appeal to his feelings; for he saw that the person must be deficient in humanity, who could have threatened a defenceless woman with such severity; he did not speak of justice to the tyrannical laird, but spoke of law. He told Archibald, that being thoroughly convinced of the woman's innocence, he had drawn up a statement of her case, which she, in compliance with his advice, was ready to lay before an advocate, naming the first counsel in Edinburgh.

The young laird repeated, with a mixture of apprehension and suspicion, "Drawn up a case! No; you can't know how to draw up cases; you are not a lawyer—you only say this to bully me."

Henry replied, that he was no lawyer; that he could, notwithstanding, state plain facts in such a manner, he hoped, as to make a case intelligible to any sensible lawyer; that he meant to show what he had written to his father.

"You'll show it to me, first, won't you?" said Archibald, who wished to gain time for consideration.

Henry put the paper, which he had drawn up, into his hands, and waited with a determined countenance beside him, whilst he perused the case. Archibald saw that Henry had abilities and steadiness to go through with the business; the facts were so plainly and forcibly stated, that his hopes even from law began to falter. He therefore talked about humanity—said, he pitied the poor woman; could not bear to think of distressing her; but that, at the same time, he had urgent occasion for money; that, if he could even recover five guineas of it, it would be something. He added, that he had debts, which he could not, in honour, delay to discharge.

Now Henry had five guineas, which he had reserved for the purchase of some additions to his cabinet of mineralogy, and he offered to lend this money to Archibald, to pay the debts that he could not, in honour, delay to discharge, upon express condition, that he should say nothing more to the poor woman concerning the bank-note.

To this condition Archibald most willingly acceded; and as Henry, with generous alacrity, counted the five guineas into his hand, this mean, incorrigible being said to himself, "What fools these bookish young men are, after all! Though he can draw up cases so finely, I've taken him in at last; and I wish it were ten guineas instead of five!"

Fatigued with the recital of the various petty artifices of this avaricious and dissipated young laird, we shall now relieve ourselves, by turning from the history of meanness to that of enthusiasm. The faults of Forester we hope and wish to see corrected; but who can be interested for the selfish Archibald Mackenzie?

FORESTER, A CLERK

We left Forester when he was just going to offer himself as clerk to a brewer. The brewer was a prudent man; and he sent one of his porters with a letter to Dr. Campbell, to inform him that a young lad, whom he had formerly seen in company with Mr. Henry Campbell, and who, he understood, was the doctor's ward, had applied to him, and that he should be very happy to take him into his service, if his friends approved of it, and could properly recommend him. In consequence of Dr. Campbell's answer to the brewer's letter, Forester, who knew nothing of the application to his friends, obtained the vacant clerkship. He did not, however, long continue in his new situation. At first he felt happy, when he found himself relieved from the vulgar petulance of Miss M'Evoy and her brother Colin: in comparison with their rude ill-humours, the clerks who were his companions appeared patterns of civility. By hard experience, Forester was taught to know, that obliging manners in our companions add something to the happiness of our lives. "My mind to me a kingdom is," was once his common answer to all that his friend Henry could urge in favour of the pleasures of society; but he began now to suspect, that separated from social intercourse, his mind, however enlarged, would afford him but a dreary kingdom.

He flattered himself, that he could make a friend of the clerk who had found his key: this young man's name was Richardson; he was good-natured, but ignorant; and neither his education nor his abilities distinguished him from any other clerk in similar circumstances. Forester invited him to walk to Arthur's Seat, after the monotonous business of the day was over, but the clerk preferred walking on holidays in Prince's-street; and, after several ineffectual attempts to engage him in moral and metaphysical arguments, our hero discovered the depth of his companion's ignorance with astonishment. Once, when he found that two of the clerks, to whom he had been talking of Cicero and Pliny, did not know any thing of these celebrated personages, he said, with a sigh,

"But knowledge to their eyes her ample page,
Rich with the spoils of time, did ne'er unroll;
Chill penury repressed their noble rage,
And froze the genial current of their soul."

The word penury, in this stanza, the clerks at least understood, and it excited their "noble rage;" they hinted, that it ill became a person, who did not dress nearly as well as themselves, to give himself such airs, and to taunt his betters with poverty; they said that they supposed, because he was an Englishman, as they perceived by his accent, he thought he might insult Scotchmen as he pleased. It was vain for him to attempt any explanation; their pride and their prejudices combined against him: and, though their dislike to him was not so outrageous as that of the gardener, gentle Colin, yet it was quite sufficient to make him uneasy in his situation. Richardson was as steady as could reasonably be expected; but he showed so little desire to have "the ample page, rich with the spoils of time," unrolled to him, that he excited our young scholar's contempt. No friendships can be more unequal than those between ignorance and knowledge. We pass over the journal of our hero's hours, which were spent in casting up and verifying accounts; this occupation, at length he decided, must be extremely injurious to the human understanding: "All the higher faculties of my soul," said he to himself, "are absolutely useless at this work, and I am reduced to a mere machine." But there were many other circumstances in the mercantile system, which Forester had not foreseen, and which shocked him extremely. The continual attention to petty gain, the little artifices which a tradesman thinks himself justifiable in practising upon his customers, could not be endured by his ingenuous mind. One morning the brewery was in an uncommon bustle; the clerks were all in motion. Richardson told Forester that they expected a visit in a few hours from the gauger and the supervisor, and that they were preparing for their reception. When the nature of these preparations was explained to Forester; when he was made to understand that the business and duty of a brewer's clerk was to assist his master in evading certain clauses in certain acts of parliament; when he found, that to trick a gauger was thought an excellent joke, he stood in silent moral astonishment. He knew about as much of the revenue laws as the clerks did of Cicero and Pliny; but his sturdy principles of integrity could not bend to any of the arguments, founded on expediency, which were brought by his companions in their own and their master's justification. He declared that he must speak to his master upon the subject immediately. His master was as busy as he could possibly be; and, when Forester insisted upon seeing him, he desired that he would speak as quickly as he could, for that he expected the supervisor every instant. Our hero declared, that he could not, consistently with his principles, assist in evading the laws of his country. The brewer stared, and then laughed; assured him that he had as great a respect for the laws as other people; that he did nothing but what every person in his situation was obliged to do in their own defence. Forester resolutely persisted in his determination against all clandestine practices. The brewer cut the matter short, by saying, he had not time to argue; but that he did not choose to keep a clerk who was not in his interests; that he supposed the next thing would be, to betray him to his supervisor.

"I am no traitor!" exclaimed Forester; "I will not stay another instant with a master who suspects me."

The brewer suffered him to depart without reluctance; but what exasperated Forester the most was the composure of his friend Richardson during this scene, who did not even offer to shake hands with him, when he saw him going out of the house: for Richardson had a good place, and did not choose to quarrel with his master, for a person whom he now verily believed to be, as he had originally suspected, insane.

"This is the world!—this is friendship!" said Forester to himself.

His generous and enthusiastic imagination supplied him with eloquent invectives against human nature, even while he ardently desired to serve his fellow-creatures. He wandered through the streets of Edinburgh, indulging himself alternately in misanthropic reflections and benevolent projects. One instant, he resolved to study the laws, that he might reform the revenue laws; the next moment, he recollected his own passion for a desert island, and he regretted that he could not be shipwrecked in Edinburgh.

The sound of a squeaking fiddle roused Forester from his reverie; he looked up, and saw a thin, pale man fiddling to a set of dancing dogs, that he was exhibiting upon the flags, for the amusement of a crowd of men, women, and children. It was a deplorable spectacle; the dogs appeared so wretched, in the midst of the merriment of the spectators, that Forester's compassion was moved, and he exclaimed—

"Enough, enough!—They are quite tired; here are some halfpence!"

The showman took the halfpence; but several fresh spectators were yet to see the sight; and though the exhausted animals were but little inclined to perform their antic feats, their master twitched the rope, that was fastened round their necks, so violently, that they were compelled to renew their melancholy dance.

Forester darted forward, stopped the fiddler's hand, and began an expostulation, not one word of which was understood by the person to whom it was addressed. A stout lad, who was very impatient at this interruption of his diversion, began to abuse Forester, and presently from words he proceeded to blows.

Forester, though a better orator, was by no means so able a boxer as his opponent. The battle was obstinately fought on both sides; but, at length, our young Quixote received what has no name in heroic language, but in the vulgar tongue is called a black eye; and, covered with blood and bruises, he was carried by some humane passenger into a neighbouring house. It was a printer and bookseller's shop. The bookseller treated him with humanity; and, after advising him not to be so hastily engaged to be the champion of dancing dogs, inquired who he was, and whether he had any friends in Edinburgh, to whom he could send.

This printer, from having been accustomed to converse with a variety of people, was a good judge of the language of gentlemen; and, though there was nothing else in Forester's manners which could have betrayed him, he spoke in such good language, that the bookseller was certain that he had received a liberal education.

Our hero declined telling his history; but the printer was so well pleased with his conversation, that he readily agreed to give him employment; and, as soon as he recovered from his bruises, Forester was eager to learn the art of printing.

"The art of printing," said he, "has emancipated mankind, and printers ought to be considered as the most respectable benefactors of the human race."

Always warm in his admiration of every new phantom that struck his imagination, he was now persuaded that printers' devils were angels, and that he should be supremely blessed in a printer's office.

"What employment so noble!" said he, as he first took the composing-stick in his hand; "what employment so noble, as that of disseminating knowledge over the universe!"

FORESTER, A PRINTER

It was some time before our hero acquired dexterity in his new trade: his companions formed, with amazing celerity, whole sentences, while he was searching for letters, which perpetually dropped from his awkward hands: but he was ashamed of his former versatility, and he resolved to be steady to his present way of life. His situation, at this printer's, was far better suited to him than that which he had quitted, with so much disgust, at the brewer's. He rose early, and, by great industry, overcame all the difficulties which at first so much alarmed him. He soon became the most useful journeyman in the office. His diligence and good behaviour recommended him to his master's employers. Whenever any work was brought, Forester was sent for. This occasioned him to be much in the shop, where he heard the conversation of many ingenious men who frequented it; and he spent his evenings in reading. His understanding had been of late uncultivated; but the fresh seeds that were now profusely scattered upon the vigorous soil took root, and flourished.

Forester was just at that time of life when opinions are valued for being new: he heard varieties of the most contradictory assertions in morals, in science, in politics. It is a great advantage to a young man to hear opposite arguments, to hear all that can be said upon every subject.

Forester no longer obstinately adhered to the set of notions which he had acquired from his education; he heard many, whom he could not think his inferiors in abilities, debating questions which he formerly imagined scarcely admitted of philosophic doubt. His mind became more humble; but his confidence in his own powers, after having compared himself with numbers, if less arrogant, was more secure and rational: he no longer considered a man as a fool the moment he differed with him in opinion; but he was still a little inclined to estimate the abilities of authors by the party to which they belonged. This failing was increased, rather than diminished, by the company which he now kept.

Amongst the young students who frequented Mr.—'s, the bookseller, was Mr. Thomas —, who, from his habit of blurting out strange opinions in conversation, acquired the name of Tom Random. His head was confused between politics and poetry; his arguments were paradoxical, his diction florid, and his gesture something between the spouting action of a player, and the threatening action of a pugilist.

Forester was caught by the oratory of this genius from the first day he heard him speak.

Tom Random asserted, that "this great globe, and all that it inhabits," must inevitably be doomed to destruction, unless certain ideas of his own, in the government of the world, were immediately adopted by universal acclamation.

It was not approbation, it was not esteem, which Forester felt for his new friend it was for the first week blind, enthusiastic admiration—every thing that he had seen or heard before appeared to him trite and obsolete; every person who spoke temperate common sense he heard with indifference or contempt; and all who were not zealots in literature, or in politics, he considered as persons whose understandings were so narrow, or whose hearts were so depraved, as to render them "unfit to hear themselves convinced."

Those who read and converse have a double chance of correcting their errors.

Forester most fortunately, about this time, happened to meet with a book which in some degree counteracted the inflammatory effects of Random's conversation, and which had a happy tendency to sober his enthusiasm, without lessening his propensity to useful exertions: this book was the Life of Dr. Franklin.

The idea that this great man began by being a printer interested our hero in his history; and whilst he followed him, step by step, through his instructive narrative, Forester sympathized in his feelings, and observed how necessary the smaller virtues of order, economy, industry, and patience were to Franklin's great character and splendid success. He began to hope that it would be possible to do good to his fellow-creatures, without overturning all existing institutions.

About this time another fortunate coincidence happened in Forester's education. One evening his friend, Tom Random, who was printing a pamphlet, came, with a party of his companions, into Mr.—, the bookseller's shop, enraged at the decision of a prize in a literary society to which they belonged.

All the young partisans who surrounded Mr. Random loudly declared that he had been treated with the most flagrant injustice; and the author himself was too angry to affect any modesty upon the occasion.

"Would you believe it?" said he to Forester—"my essay has not been thought worthy of the prize! The medal has been given to the most wretched, tame, commonplace performance you ever saw. Every thing in this world is done by corruption, by party, by secret influence!"

At every pause the irritated author wiped his forehead, and Forester sympathized in his feelings.

In the midst of the author's exclamations, a messenger came with the manuscript of the prize essay, and with the orders of the society to have a certain number of copies printed off with all possible expedition.

Random snatched up the manuscript, and, with all the fury of criticism, began to read aloud some of the passages which he disliked.

Though it was marred in the reading, Forester could not agree with his angry friend in condemning the performance. It appeared to him excellent writing and excellent sense.

"Print it—print it then, as fast as you can—that is your business—that's what you are paid for. Every one for himself," cried Random, insolently throwing the manuscript at Forester; and, as he flung out of the shop with his companions, he added, with a contemptuous laugh, "A printer's devil setting up for a critic! He may be a capital judge of pica and brevier, perhaps—but let not the compositor go beyond his stick."

"Is this the man," said Forester, "whom I have heard so eloquent in the praise of candour and liberality? Is this the man who talks of universal toleration and freedom of opinion, and who yet cannot bear that any one should differ from him in criticising a sentence? Is this the man who would have equality amongst all his fellow-creatures, and who calls a compositor a printer's devil? Is this the man who cants about the pre-eminence of mind and the perfections of intellect, and yet now takes advantage of his rank, of his supporters, of the cry of his partisans, to bear down the voice of reason?—'Let not the compositor go beyond his composing-stick!'—And why not? Why should not he be a judge of writing?" At this reflection, Forester eagerly took up the manuscript, which had been flung at his feet. All his indignant feelings instantly changed into delightful exultation—he saw the hand—he read the name of Henry Campbell. The title of the manuscript was, "An Essay on the best Method of reforming Abuses." This was the subject proposed by the society; and Henry had written upon the question with so much moderation, and yet with such unequivocal decision had shown himself the friend of rational liberty, that all the members of the society who were not borne away by their prejudices were unanimous in their preference of this performance.

Random's declamation only inflamed the minds of his own partisans. Good judges of writing exclaimed, as they read it, "This is all very fine; but what would this man be at? His violence hurts the cause he wishes to support."

Forester read Henry Campbell's essay with all the avidity of friendship; he read it again and again—his generous soul was incapable of envy; and whilst he admired, he was convinced by the force of reason.

His master desired that he would set about the essay early in the morning; but his eagerness for his friend Henry's fame was such, that he sat up above half the night hard at work at it. He was indefatigable the next day at the business; and as all hands were employed on the essay, it was finished that evening.

Forester rubbed his hands with delight, when he had set the name of Henry Campbell in the title-page—but an instant afterwards he sighed bitterly.

"I am only a printer," said he to himself. "These just arguments, these noble ideas, will instruct and charm hundreds of my fellow-creatures: no one will ever ask, 'Who set the types?'"

His reflections were interrupted by the entrance of Tom Random and two of his partisans: he was extremely displeased to find that the printers had not been going on with his pamphlet; his personal disappointments seemed to increase the acrimony of his zeal for the public good: he declaimed upon politics—upon the necessity for the immediate publication of his sentiments, for the salvation of the state. His action was suited to his words: violent and blind to consequences, with one sudden kick, designed to express his contempt for the opposite party, this political Alnaschar unfortunately overturned the form which contained the types for the newspaper of the next day, which was just going to the press—a newspaper in which he had written splendid paragraphs.

Forester, happily for his philosophy, recollected the account which Franklin, in his history of his own life, gives of the patience with which he once bore a similar accident. The printers, with secret imprecations against oratory, or at least against those orators who think that action is every thing, set to work again to repair the mischief.

Forester, much fatigued, at length congratulated himself upon having finished his hard day's work, when a man from the shop came to inquire whether three hundred cards, which had been ordered the week before to be printed off, were finished. The man to whom the order was given had forgotten it, and he was going home: he decidedly answered, "No; the cards can't be done till to-morrow: we have left work for this night, thank God."

"The gentleman says he must have them," expostulated the messenger.

"He must not, he cannot have them. I would not print a card for his majesty at this time of night," replied the sullen workman, throwing his hat upon his head, in token of departure.

"What are these cards?" said Forester.

"Only a dancing-master's cards for his ball," said the printer's journeyman. "I'll not work beyond my time for any dancing-master that wears a head."

The messenger then said, that he was desired to ask for the manuscript card.

This card was hunted for all over the room; and, at last, Forester found it under a heap of refuse papers: his eye was caught with the name of his old friend, Monsieur Pasgrave, the dancing-master, whom he had formerly frightened by the skeleton with the fiery eyes.

"I will print the cards for him myself; I am not at all tired," cried Forester, who was determined to make some little amends for the injury which he had formerly done to the poor dancing-master. He resolved to print the cards for nothing, and he stayed up very late to finish them. His companions all left him, for they were in a great hurry to see, what in Edinburgh is a rare sight, the town illuminated.

These illuminations were upon account of some great naval victory.

Forester, steady to Monsieur Pasgrave's cards, did what no other workman would have done; he finished for him, on this night of public joy, his three hundred cards. Every now and then, as he was quietly at work, he heard the loud huzzas in the street: his waning candle sunk in the socket, as he had just packed up his work.

By the direction at the bottom of the cards, he learned where M. Pasgrave lodged, and, as he was going out to look at the illuminations, he resolved to leave them himself at the dancing-master's house.

THE ILLUMINATIONS

The illuminations were really beautiful. He went up to the Castle, whence he saw a great part of the Old Town, and all Prince's-street, lighted up in the most splendid manner. He crossed the Earth-mound into Prince's-street. Walking down Prince's-street, he saw a crowd of people gathered before the large illuminated window of a confectioner's shop. As he approached nearer, he distinctly heard the voice of Tom Random, who was haranguing the mob. The device and motto which the confectioner displayed in his window displeased this gentleman, who, beside his public-spirited abhorrence of all men of a party opposite to his own, had likewise private cause of dislike to this confectioner, who had refused him his daughter in marriage.

It was part of Random's new system of political justice to revenge his own quarrels.

The mob, who are continually, without knowing it, made the instruments of private malice, when they think they are acting in a public cause, readily joined in Tom Random's cry of "Down with the motto! Down with the motto!"

Forester, who, by his lesson from the dancing dogs, had learned a little prudence, and who had just printed Henry Campbell's Essay on the best Means of reforming Abuses, did not mix with the rabble, but joined in the entreaties of some peaceable passengers, who prayed that the poor man's windows might be spared. The windows were, notwithstanding, demolished with a terrible crash, and the crowd, then alarmed at the mischief they had done, began to disperse. The constables, who had been sent for, appeared. Tom Random was taken into custody. Forester was pursuing his way to the dancing-master's, when one of the officers of justice exclaimed, "Stop!—stop him!—he's one of 'em: he's a great friend of Mr. Random: I've seen him often parading arm in arm in High-street with him."

This, alas! was too true: the constables seized Forester, and put him, with Tom Random, and the ringleader of the riot, into a place of confinement for the night.

Poor Forester, who was punished for the faults of his former friend and present enemy, had, during this long night, leisure for much wholesome reflection upon the danger of forming imprudent intimacies. He resolved never to walk again in High-street arm in arm with such a man as Tom Random.

The constables were rather hasty in the conclusion they drew from this presumptive evidence.

Our hero, who felt the disgrace of his situation, was not a little astonished at Tom Random's consoling himself with drinking instead of philosophy. The sight of this enthusiast, when he had completely intoxicated himself, was a disgusting but useful spectacle to our indignant hero. Forester was shocked at the union of gross vice and rigid pretensions to virtue: he could scarcely believe that the reeling, stammering idiot whom he now beheld was the same being from whose lips he had heard declamations upon the omnipotence of intellect—from whose pen he had seen projects for the government of empires.

The dancing-master, who, in the midst of the illuminations, had regretted that his cards could not be printed, went early in the morning to inquire about them at the printer's.

The printer had learnt that one of his boys was taken up amongst the rioters: he was sorry to find that Forester had gotten himself into such a scrape: but he was a very cautious snug man, and he did not choose to interfere: he left him quietly to be dealt with according to law.

The dancing-master, however, was interested in finding him out, because he was informed that Forester had sat up almost all night to print his cards, and that he had them now in his pocket.

M. Pasgrave at length gained admittance to him in his confinement: the officers of justice were taking him and Random before Mr. W—, a magistrate, with whom informations had been lodged by the confectioner, who had suffered in his windows.

Pasgrave, when he beheld Forester, was surprised to such a degree, that he could scarcely finish his bow, or express his astonishment, either in French or English. "Eh, monsieur! mon Dieu! bon Dieu! I beg ten million pardons—I am come to search for a printer who has my cards in his pocket."

"Here are your cards," said Forester: "let me speak a few words to you." He took M. Pasgrave aside. "I perceive," said he, "that you have discovered who I am. Though in the service of a printer, I have still as much the feelings and principles of a gentleman as I had when you saw me in Dr. Campbell's house. I have particular reasons for being anxious to remain undiscovered by Dr. Campbell, or any of his family: you may depend upon it that my reasons are not dishonourable. I request that you will not, upon any account, betray me to that family. I am going before a magistrate, and am accused of being concerned in a riot, which I did every thing in my power to prevent."

"Ah! monsieur," interrupted the dancing-master, "but you see de grand inconvenience of concealing your rank and name. You, who are comme il faut, are confounded with the mob: permit me at least to follow you to Mr. W—, the magistrate: I have de honneur to teach les demoiselles his daughters to dance; dey are to be at my ball—dey take one half dozen tickets. I must call dere wid my cards; and I shall, if you will give me leave, accompany you now, and mention dat I know you to be un homme comme il faut, above being guilty of an unbecoming action. I flatter myself I have some interest wid de ladies of de family, and dat dey will do me de favour to speak to monsieur leur cher père sur votre compte."

Forester thanked the good-natured dancing-master, but he proudly said, that he should trust to his own innocence for his defence.

M. Pasgrave, who had seen something more of the world than our hero, and who was interested for him, because he had once made him a present of an excellent violin, and because he had sat up half the night to print the ball cards, resolved not to leave him entirely to his innocence for a defence: he followed Forester to Mr. W—'s. The magistrate was a slow, pompous man, by no means a good physiognomist, much less a good judge of character. He was proud of his authority, and glad to display the small portion of legal knowledge which he possessed. As soon as he was informed that some young men were brought before him, who had been engaged the preceding night in a riot, he put on all his magisterial terrors, and assured the confectioner, who had a private audience of him, that he should have justice, and that the person or persons concerned in breaking his window or windows should be punished with the utmost severity that the law would allow. Contrary to the humane spirit of the British law, which supposes every man to be innocent till it is proved that he is guilty, this harsh magistrate presumed that every man who was brought before him was guilty till he was proved to be innocent. Forester's appearance was not in his favour: he had been up all night; his hair was dishevelled; his linen was neither fine nor white; his shoes were thick-soled and dirty; his coat was that in which he had been at work at the printer's the preceding day; it was in several places daubed with printers' ink; and his unwashed hands bespoke his trade. Of all these circumstances the slow circumspect eye of the magistrate took cognizance one by one. Forester observed the effect which this survey produced upon his judge; and he felt that appearances were against him, and that appearances are sometimes of consequence. After having estimated his poverty by these external symptoms, the magistrate looked, for the first time, in his face, and pronounced that he had one of the worst countenances he ever beheld. This judgment once pronounced, he proceeded to justify, by wresting to the prisoner's disadvantage every circumstance that appeared. Forester's having been frequently seen in Tom Random's company was certainly against him: the confectioner perpetually repeated that they were constant companions; that they were intimate friends; that they were continually walking together every Sunday; and that they often had come arm in arm into his shop, talking politics; that he believed Forester to be of the same way of thinking with Mr. Random; and that he saw him close behind him, at the moment the stones were thrown that broke the windows. It appeared that Mr. Random was at that time active in encouraging the mob. To oppose the angry confectioner's conjectural evidence, the lad who threw the stone, and who was now produced, declared that Forester held back his arm, and said, "My good lad, don't break this man's windows: go home quietly; here's a shilling for you." The person who gave this honest testimony, in whom there was a strange mixture of the love of mischief and the spirit of generosity, was the very lad who fought with Forester, and beat him, about the dancing dogs. He whispered to Forester, "Do you remember me? I hope you don't bear malice." The magistrate, who heard this whisper, immediately construed it to the prisoner's disadvantage. "Then, sir," said he, addressing himself to our hero, "this gentleman, I understand, claims acquaintance with you; his acquaintance really does you honour, and speaks, strongly in favour of your character. If I mistake not, this is the lad whom I sent to the Tolbooth, some little time ago, for a misdemeanour; and he is not, I apprehend, a stranger to the stocks."

Forester commanded his temper as well as he was able, and observed, that whatever might be the character of the young man who had spoken in his favour, his evidence would, perhaps, be thought to deserve some credit, when the circumstances of his acquaintance with the witness were known. He then related the adventure of the dancing dogs, and remarked, that the testimony of an enemy came with double force in his favour. The language and manner in which Forester spoke surprised all who were present; but the history of the dancing dogs appeared so ludicrous and so improbable, that the magistrate decidedly pronounced it to be "a fabrication, a story invented to conceal the palpable collusion of the witnesses." Yet, though he one moment declared that he did not believe the story, he the next inferred from it, that Forester was disposed to riot and sedition, since he was ready to fight with a vagabond in the streets for the sake of a parcel of dancing dogs.

M. Pasgrave, in the meantime, had, with great good-nature, been representing Forester in the best light he possibly could to the young ladies, the magistrate's daughters. One of them sent to beg to speak to their father. M. Pasgrave judiciously dwelt upon his assurances of Forester's being a gentleman: he told Mr. W— that he had met him in one of the best families in Edinburgh; that he knew he had some private reasons for concealing that he was a gentleman: "perhaps the young gentleman was reduced to temporary distress," he said; but whatever might be these reasons, M. Pasgrave vouched for his having very respectable friends and connexions. The magistrate wished to know the family in which M. Pasgrave had met Forester; but he was, according to his promise, impenetrable on this subject. His representations had, however, the desired effect upon Mr. W—: when he returned to the examination of our hero, his opinion of his countenance somewhat varied; he despatched his other business; bailed Tom Random on high sureties; and, when Forester was the only person that remained, he turned to him with great solemnity; bade him sit down; informed him that he knew him to be a gentleman; that he was greatly concerned that a person like him, who had respectable friends and connexions, should involve himself in such a disagreeable affair; that it was a matter of grief and surprise to him, to see a young gentleman in such apparel; that he earnestly recommended to him to accommodate matters with his friends; and, above all things, to avoid the company of seditious persons. Much good advice, but in a dictatorial tone, and in cold, pompous language, he bestowed upon the prisoner, and at length dismissed him. "How different," said Forester to himself, "is this man's method of giving advice from Dr. Campbell's!"

This lesson strongly impressed, however, upon our hero's mind the belief, that external appearance, dress, manners, and the company we keep, are the usual circumstances by which the world judge of character and conduct. When he was dismissed from Mr. W—'s august presence, the first thing he did was to inquire for Pasgrave: he was giving the magistrate's daughters a lesson, and could not be interrupted; but Forester left a note for him, requesting to see him at ten o'clock the next day, at Mr. —, the bookseller's. New mortifications awaited our hero: on his return to his master's, he was very coldly received; Mr. — let him know, in unqualified terms, that he did not like to employ any one in his work who got into quarrels at night in the public streets. Forester's former favour with his master, his industry and talents, were not considered without envy by the rest of the journeymen printers; and they took advantage of his absence to misrepresent him to the bookseller: however, when Forester came to relate his own story, his master was convinced that he was not to blame; that he had worked extremely hard the preceding day; and that, far from having been concerned in a riot, he had done every thing in his power to prevent mischief. He desired to see the essay, which was printed with so much expedition: it was in the hands of the corrector of the press. The sheets were sent for, and the bookseller was in admiration at the extraordinary correctness with which it was printed; the corrector of the press scarcely had occasion to alter a word, a letter, or a stop. There was a quotation in the manuscript from Juvenal. Henry Campbell had, by mistake, omitted to name the satire and line, and the author from which it was taken, though he had left a blank in which they were to be inserted. The corrector of the press, though a literary gentleman, was at a stand. Forester immediately knew where to look for the passage in the original author: he found it, and inserted the book and line in their proper place. His master did not suffer this to pass unobserved; he hinted to him, that it was a pity a young man of his abilities and knowledge should waste his time in the mere technical drudgery of printing. "I should be glad now," continued the bookseller, "to employ you as a corrector of the press, and to advance you, according to your merits, in the world; but," glancing his eye at Forester's dress, "you must give me leave to say, that some attention to outward appearance is necessary in our business. Gentlemen call here, as you well know, continually, and I like to have the people about me make a creditable appearance. You have earned money since you have been with me—surely you can afford yourself a decent suit of clothes and a cleaner shirt. I beg your pardon for speaking so freely; but I really have a regard for you, and wish to see you get forward in life."

FORESTER, A CORRECTOR OF THE PRESS

Forester had not, since he left Dr. Campbell's, been often spoken to in a tone of friendship. The bookseller's well-meant frank remonstrance made its just impression; and he resolved to make the necessary additions to his wardrobe; nay, he even went to a hair-dresser, to have his hair cut and brought into decent order. His companions, the printers, had not been sparing in their remarks upon the meanness of his former apparel, and Forester pleased himself with anticipating the respect they would feel for him, when he should appear in better clothes. "Can such trifles," said he to himself, "make such a change in the opinion of my fellow-creatures? And why should I fight with the world for trifles? My real merit is neither increased nor diminished by the dress I may happen to wear; but I see, that unless I waste all my life in combating the prejudices of superficial observers, I should avoid all those peculiarities in my external appearance which prevent whatever good qualities I have from obtaining their just respect." He was surprised at the blindness of his companions, who could not discover his merit through the roughness of his manners and the disadvantages of his dress; but he determined to shine out upon them in the superior dress and character of a corrector of the press. He went to a tailor's, and bespoke a suit of clothes. He bought new linen; and our readers will perhaps hear with surprise, that he actually began to consider very seriously whether he should not take a few lessons in dancing. He had learned to dance formerly, and was not naturally either inactive or awkward: but his contempt for the art prevented him, for some years, from practising it; and he had nearly forgotten his wonted agility. Henry Campbell once, when Forester was declaiming against dancing, told him, that if he had learned to dance, and excelled in the art, his contempt for the trifling accomplishment would have more effect upon the minds of others, because it could not be mistaken for envy. This remark made a deep impression upon our hero, especially as he observed that his friend Henry was not in the least vain of his personal graces, and had cultivated his understanding, though he could dance a Scotch reel. Scotch reels were associated in Forester's imagination with Flora Campbell; and in balancing the arguments for and against learning to dance, the recollection of Archibald Mackenzie's triumphant look, when he led her away as his partner at the famous ball, had more influence perhaps upon Forester's mind than his pride and philosophy apprehended. He began to have some confused design of returning, at some distant period, to his friends; and he had hopes that he should appear in a more amiable light to Flora, after he had perfected himself in an accomplishment which he fancied she admired prodigiously. His esteem for that lady was rather diminished by this belief; but still a sufficient quantity remained to excite in him a strong ambition to please. The agony he felt the night he left the ball-room was such, that he could not even now recollect the circumstances without confusion and anguish of mind. His hands were now such as could appear without gloves; and he resolved to commence the education of his feet.

M. Pasgrave called upon him, in consequence of the message which he left at the magistrate's: his original design in sending for the dancing-master was to offer him some acknowledgment for his obliging conduct. "M. Pasgrave," said he, "you have behaved towards me like a man of honour; you have kept my secret; I am convinced that you will continue to keep it inviolate." As he spoke, he produced a ten-guinea bank-note, for at length he had prevailed upon himself to have recourse to his pocket-book, which, till this day, had remained unopened. Pasgrave stared at the sight of the note, and withdrew his hand at first, when it was offered; but he yielded at length, when Forester assured him that he was not in any distress, and that he could perfectly well afford to indulge his feelings of gratitude. "Nay," continued Forester, who, if he had not always practised the maxims of politeness, notwithstanding possessed that generosity of mind and good sense on which real politeness must depend—"you shall not be under any obligation to me, M. Pasgrave: I am just going to ask a favour from you. You must teach me to dance." "Wid de utmost pleasure," exclaimed the delighted dancing-master; and the hours of his attendance were soon settled. Whatever Forester attempted, he pursued with energy. M. Pasgrave, after giving him a few lessons, prophesied that he would do him infinite credit; and Forester felt a secret pride in the idea that he should surprise his friends, some time or other, with his new accomplishment.

He continued in the bookseller's service, correcting the press for him, much to his satisfaction; and the change in his personal appearance pleased his master, as it showed attention to his advice. Our hero, from time to time, exercised his talents in writing; and, as he inserted his compositions under a fictitious signature, in his master's newspaper, he had an opportunity of hearing the most unprejudiced opinions of a variety of critics, who often came to read the papers at their house. He stated, in short essays, some of those arguments concerning the advantages and disadvantages of politeness, luxury, the love of society, misanthropy, &c., which had formerly passed between him and Henry Campbell; and he listened to the remarks that were made upon each side of the question. How it happened, we know not; but after he had taken lessons for about six weeks from M. Pasgrave, he became extremely solicitous to have a solution of all his Stoical doubts, and to furnish himself with the best possible arguments in favour of civilized society. He could not bear the idea that he yielded his opinions to any thing less than strict demonstration: he drew up a list of queries, which concluded with the following question:—"What should be the distinguishing characteristics of the higher classes of people in society?" This query was answered in one of the public papers, a few days after it appeared in Mr. —'s paper, and the answer was signed H.C., a Friend to Society. Even without these initials, Forester would easily have discovered it to be Henry Campbell's writing; and several strokes seemed to be so particularly addressed to him, that he could not avoid thinking Henry had discovered the querist. The impression which arguments make upon the mind varies with time and change of situation. Those arguments in favour of subordination in society, in favour of agreeable manners, and attention to the feelings of others in the small as well as in the great concerns of life, which our hero had heard with indifference from Dr. Campbell and Henry in conversation, struck him, when he saw them in a printed essay, with all the force of conviction; and he wondered how it had happened that he never before perceived them to be conclusive.

He put the newspaper, which contained this essay, in his pocket; and, after he had finished his day's work, and had taken his evening lesson from M. Pasgrave, he went out with an intention of going to a favourite spot upon Arthur's Seat, to read the essay again at his leisure.

But he was stopped at the turn from the North Bridge, into High-street, by a scavenger's cart. The scavenger, with his broom which had just swept the High-street, was clearing away a heap of mud. Two gentlemen on horseback, who were riding like postilions, came up during this operation—Sir Philip Gosling and Archibald Mackenzie. Forester had his back towards them, and he never looked round, because he was too intent upon his own thoughts. Archibald was mounted upon Sawney, the horse which he had so fairly won from his friend Sir Philip. The half-guinea which had been promised to the hostler had not yet been paid; and the hostler, determined to revenge himself upon Archibald, invented an ingenious method of gratifying his resentment. He taught Sawney to rear and plunge whenever his legs were touched by the broom with which the stables were swept. When Sawney was perfectly well trained to this trick, the cunning hostler communicated his design, and related his cause of complaint against Archibald, to a scavenger, who was well known at the livery stables. The scavenger entered into his friend the hostler's feeling, and promised to use his broom in his cause, whenever a convenient and public opportunity should offer. The hour of retribution was now arrived: the scavenger saw his young gentleman in full glory, mounted upon Sawney; he kept his eye upon him, whilst, in company with the baronet, he came over the North Bridge: there was a stop, from the meeting of carts and carriages. The instant Archibald came within reach of the broom, the scavenger slightly touched Sawney's legs; Sawney plunged and reared, and reared and plunged. The scavenger stood grinning at the sight. Forester attempted to seize the horse's bridle; but Sawney, who seemed determined upon the point, succeeded. When Forester snatched at his bridle, he reared, then plunged; and Archibald Mackenzie was fairly lodged in the scavenger's cart. Whilst the well-dressed laird floundered in the mud, Forester gave the horse to the servant, who had now ridden up; and, satisfied that Mackenzie had received no material injury, inquired no further. He turned to assist a poor washerwoman, who was lifting a large basket of clean linen into her house, to get it out of the way of the cart. As soon as he had helped her to lift the basket into her passage, he was retiring, when he heard a voice at the back-door, which was at the other end of the passage. It was the voice of a child; and he listened, for he thought he had heard it before. "The door is locked," said the washerwoman. "I know who it is that is knocking; it is only a little girl who is coming for a cap which I have there in the basket." The door was unlocked, and Forester saw the little girl to whom the fine geranium belonged. What a number of ideas she recalled to his mind! She looked at him, and hesitated, courtesied, then turned away, as if she was afraid she was mistaken, and asked the washerwoman if she had plaited her grandmother's cap. The woman searched in her basket, and produced the cap nicely plaited. The little girl, in the meantime, considered Forester with anxious attention. "I believe," said she, timidly, "you are, or you are very like, the gentleman who was so good as to—" "Yes," interrupted Forester, "I know what you mean. I am the man who went with you to try to obtain justice from your tyrannical schoolmistress: I did not do you any good. Have you seen—have you heard any thing of—?" Such a variety of recollections pressed upon Forester's heart, that he could not pronounce the name of Henry Campbell; and he changed his question. "Is your old grandmother recovered?"

"She is quite well, thank you, sir; and she is grown young again, since you saw her: perhaps you don't know how good Mr. Henry and the young lady have been to us. We don't live now in that little, close, dark room at the watchmaker's. We are as happy, sir, as the day is long." "But what of Henry? what of—?" "Oh, sir! but if you are not very busy, or in a great hurry—it is but a little way off—if you could come and look at our new house—I don't mean our house, for it is not ours; but we take care of it, and we have two little rooms to ourselves; and Mr. Henry and Miss Flora very often come to see us. I wish you could come to see how nice our rooms are! The house is not far off, only at the back of the Meadows." "Go, show me the way—I'll follow you," said Forester, after he had satisfied himself that there was no danger of his meeting any of Dr. Campbell's family.

THE MEADOWS

Our hero accompanied the little girl with eager, benevolent curiosity. "There," said she, when they came to the Meadows, "do you see that white house, with the paling before it?" "But that cannot be your house!" "No, no, sir: Dr. Campbell and several gentlemen have the large room, and they come there twice a-week to teach something to a great many children. Grandmother can explain all that better to you, sir, than I can; but all I know is, that it is our business to keep the room aired and swept, and to take care of the glass things which you'll see; and you shall see how clean it is: it was I swept it this morning."

They had now reached the gate which was in the paling before the house. The old woman came to the door, clean, neat, and cheerful; she recollected to have seen Forester in company with Henry Campbell at the watchmaker's; and this was sufficient to make him a welcome guest. "God bless the family, and all that belongs to them, for ever and ever!" said the woman. "This way, sir." "Oh, don't look into our little rooms yet: look at the great room first, if you please, sir," said the child.

There was a large table in the middle of this long room, and several glass retorts, and other chemical vessels, were ranged upon shelves; wooden benches were placed on each side of the table. The grandmother, to whom the little girl had referred for a clear explanation, could not, however, tell Forester very exactly the use of the retorts; but she informed him that many of the manufacturers in Edinburgh sent their sons hither twice a-week; and Dr. Campbell, and Mr. Henry Campbell, and some other gentlemen, came by turns to instruct them. Forester recollected now that he once heard Henry talking to his father about a scheme for teaching the children of the manufacturers of Edinburgh some knowledge of chemistry, such as they might afterwards apply advantageously to the arts and every-day business of life.

"I have formed projects, but what good have I ever actually done to my fellow-creatures?" said Forester to himself. With melancholy steps he walked to examine every thing in the room. "Dr. Campbell sits in this arm-chair, does not he? And where does Henry sit?" The old woman placed the chairs for him as they usually were placed. Upon one of the shelves there was a slate, which, as it had been written upon, the little girl had put by very carefully; there were some calculations upon the weight of different gases, and the figures Forester knew to be Henry's: he looked at every thing that was Henry's with pleasure. "Because I used to be so rough in my manner to him," said Forester to himself, "I dare say that he thinks I have no feeling, and I suppose he has forgotten me by this time: I deserve, indeed, to be forgotten by every body! How could I leave such friends!" On the other side of the slate poor Forester saw his own name written several times over, in his friend's hand-writing, and he read two lines of his own poetry, which he remembered to have repeated to Henry the day that they walked to Arthur's Seat. Forester felt much pleasure from this little proof of his friend's affection. "Now won't you look at our nice rooms?" said the child, who had waited with some patience till he had done pondering upon the slate.

The little rooms were well arranged, and their neatness was not now as much lost upon our hero as it would have been some time before. The old woman and her grand-daughter, with all the pride of gratitude, exhibited to him several little presents of furniture which they had received from Dr. Campbell's family. "Mr. Henry gave me this! Miss Flora gave me that!" was frequently repeated. The little girl opened the door of her own room. On a clean white deal bracket, which "Mr. Henry lad put up with his own hands," stood the well-known geranium in its painted flower-pot. Forester saw nothing else in the room, and it was in vain that both the old woman and her grand-daughter talked to him at once; he heard not a word that was said to him. The flowers were all gone, and the brown calyces of the geranium flowers reminded him of the length of time which had elapsed since he had first seen them. "I am sorry there are no flowers to offer you," said the little girl, observing Forester's melancholy look; "but I thought you did not like geraniums; for I remember when I gave you a fine flower in the watchmaker's shop you pulled it to pieces, and threw it on the ground." "I should not do so now," said Forester. The black marks on the painted flower-pot had been entirely effaced: be turned away, endeavoured to conceal his emotion, and took leave of the place as soon as the grateful inhabitants would suffer him to depart. The reflection that he had wasted his time, that he had never done any good to any human being, that he had lost opportunities of making both himself and others happy, pressed upon his mind; but his Stoical pride still resisted the thought of returning to Dr. Campbell's. "It will be imagined that I yield my opinions from meanness of spirit," said he to himself. "Dr. Campbell certainly has no further regard or esteem for me; neither he nor Henry have troubled themselves about my fate: they are doing good to more deserving objects; they are intent upon literary pursuits, and have not time to bestow a thought upon me. And Flora, I suppose, is as gay as she is good. I alone am unhappy,—a wanderer,—an outcast,—a useless being."

Forester, whilst he was looking at the geranium, or soon afterwards, missed his handkerchief; the old woman and her grand-daughter searched for it all over the house, but in vain: he then thought he must have left it at the washerwoman's, where he met the little girl; he called to inquire for it, upon his return to Edinburgh. When he returned to this woman's house for his handkerchief, he found her sitting upon a low stool, in her laundry, weeping bitterly; her children stood round her. Forester inquired into the cause of her distress, and she told him that a few minutes after he left her, the young gentleman who had been thrown from his horse into the scavenger's cart was brought into her house, whilst his servant went home for another suit of clothes for him. "I did not at first guess that I had ever seen the young gentleman before," continued she; "but when the mud was cleared from his face I knew him to be Mr. Archibald Mackenzie. I am sure I wish I had never seen his face then or at any time. He was in a very bad humour after his tumble, and he began again to threaten me about a ten-guinea bank-note, which he and his servant declare they sent in his waistcoat pocket to be washed: I'm sure I never saw it. Mr. Henry Campbell quieted him about it for awhile; but just now he began again with me, and he says he has spoken to a lawyer, and that he will make me pay the whole note; and he swore at me as if I had been the worst creature in the world; and, God knows, I work hard for my children, and never wronged any one in my days!"

Forester, who forgot all his own melancholy reflections as soon as he could assist any one who was in distress, bade the poor woman dry her tears, and assured her that she had nothing to fear; for he would instantly go to Dr. Campbell, and get him to speak to Mackenzie. "If it is necessary," said he, "I'll pay the money myself." She clasped her hands joyfully as he spoke, and all her children joined in an exclamation of delight. "I'll go to Dr. Campbell's this instant," said our hero, whose pride now yielded to the desire of doing justice to this injured woman; he totally forgot himself, and thought only of her: "I'll go to Dr. Campbell's, and I will speak to Mr. Mackenzie immediately."

A SUMMONS

Whilst Forester was walking through the streets, with that energy which the hope of serving his fellow-creatures always excited in his generous mind, he even forgot a scheme which he had, in spite of his Stoical pride and his dread of being thought to give up his opinions from meanness, resolved in his imagination. He had formed the design of returning to his friends an altered being in his external appearance: he had ordered a fashionable suit of clothes, which were now ready. He had laid aside the dress and manners of a gentleman from the opinion that they were degrading to the character of a man: as soon as this prejudice had been conquered, he began to think he might resume them. Many were the pleasing anticipations in which he indulged himself: the looks of each of his friends, the generous approving eye of Henry, the benevolent countenance of Dr. Campbell, the arch smile of Flora, were all painted by his fancy; and he invented every circumstance that was likely to happen—every word that would probably be said by each individual. We are sure that our readers will give our enthusiastic hero credit for his forgetting these pleasing reveries—for his forgetting himself, nay, even Flora Campbell—when humanity and justice called upon him for exertion.

When he found himself in George's-square, within sight of Dr. Campbell's house, his heart beat violently, and he suddenly stopped to recollect himself. He had scarcely stood a few instants, when a hard, stout-looking man came up to him, and asked him if his name were Forester: he started, and answered, "Yes, sir, what is your business with me?" The stranger replied by producing a paper, and desiring him to read it. The paper, which was half printed, half written, began with these words:—"You are hereby required to appear before me—"

"What is all this?" exclaimed our hero. "It is a summons," replied the stranger: "I am a constable, and you will please to come with me before Mr. W—. This is not the first time you have been before him, I am told." To this last insolent taunt Forester made no reply, but in a firm tone said that he was conscious of no crime, but that he was ready to follow the constable, and to appear before Mr. W—, or any other magistrate, who wished to inquire into his conduct. Though he summoned all his fortitude, and spoke with composure, he was much astonished by this proceeding; he could not help reflecting, that an individual in society who has friends, an established character, and a home, is in a more desirable situation than an unconnected being, who has no one to answer for his conduct,—no one to rejoice in his success, or to sympathize in his misfortunes. "Ah, Dr. Campbell! happy father! in the midst of your own family, you have forgotten your imprudent ward!" said Forester to himself, while his mind revolted from seeking his friend's assistance in this discreditable situation. "You do not know how near he is to you! you do not know that he was just returning to you! you do not see that he is, at this moment, perhaps, on the brink of disgrace!"

THE BANK-NOTES

Forester was mistaken in his idea that Dr. Campbell had forgotten him; but we shall not yet explain further upon this subject; we only throw out this hint, that our readers may not totally change their good opinion of the doctor. We must now beg their attention to the continuation of the history of Archibald Mackenzie's bank-note.

Lady Catherine Mackenzie one day observed that the colours were changed in one spot on the right-hand pocket of her son's waistcoat. "My dear Archibald," said she, "what has happened to your smart waistcoat? What is that terrible spot?" "Really, ma'am, I don't know," said Archibald, with his usual soft voice and deceitful smile. Henry Campbell observed that it seemed as if the colours had been discharged by some acid. "Did you wear that waistcoat, Mr. Mackenzie," said he, "the night the large bottle of vitriolic acid was broken—the night that poor Forester's cat was killed: don't you remember?" "Oh, I did not at first recollect; I cannot possibly remember, indeed,—it is so long ago,—what waistcoat I wore on that particular night." The extreme embarrassment in Archibald's manner surprised Henry. "I really don't perceive your drift," continued Mackenzie: "what made you ask the question so earnestly?" He was relieved when Henry answered, that he only wished to know whether it was probable that it was stained with vitriolic acid; "because," said he, "I think that is the pocket in which you said you left your ten-guinea note; then, perhaps, the note may have been stained." "Perhaps so," replied Mackenzie dryly. "And if it were, you could identify the note: you have forgotten the number; but if the note has been stained with vitriolic acid, we should certainly be able to know it again: the acid would have changed the colour of the ink." Mackenzie eagerly seized this idea; and immediately, in pursuance of Henry's advice, went to several of the principal bankers in Edinburgh, and requested that if a note, stained in such a manner, should be presented to them, they would stop payment of it till Mackenzie should examine it. Some time elapsed, and nothing was heard of the note. Mackenzie gave up all hopes of recovering it; and in proportion as these hopes diminished, his old desire of making the poor washerwoman answerable for his loss increased. We have just heard this woman's account of his behaviour to her, when he came into her house to be refitted, after his tumble from Sawney into the scavenger's cart. All his promises to Henry he thought proper to disregard: promises appeared to him mere matters of convenience; and the idea of "taking in" such a young man as Henry Campbell was to him an excellent joke. He resolved to keep the five guineas quietly which Henry lent him; and, at the same time, to frighten this innocent industrious woman into paying him the value of his bank-note.

Upon Mackenzie's return to Dr. Campbell's, after his fall from Sawney, the first thing he heard was that his note was found; that it had been stopped at the bank of Scotland; and that one of the clerks of the bank, who brought it for his examination, had been some time waiting for his return from riding. When the note was produced, Henry saw that two or three of the words which had been written in ink, the name of the person to whom it was payable, and the date of the month and year, were so pale as to be scarcely visible; and that there was a round hole through one corner of the paper. This round hole puzzled Henry, but he had no doubt that the ink had been thus nearly obliterated by vitriolic acid. He poured a few drops, diluted with water, upon some printing, and the ink was quickly turned to nearly the same pale colour as that in Mackenzie's note. The note was easily traced, as it had not passed through many hands—our readers will be sorry to hear it—to M. Pasgrave, the dancing-master. Mackenzie and the clerk went directly to his house, found him at home, and without much preface, informed him of their business. The dancing-master trembled from head to foot, and, though innocent, exhibited all the signs of guilt; he had not the slightest knowledge of business, and the manner and language of the banker's clerk who accompanied Mackenzie terrified him beyond measure, because he did not comprehend one word in ten that he said about checks, entries, and day-books; and he was nearly a quarter of an hour before he could recover sufficient presence of mind to consider from whom he received the note. At length, after going over, in an unintelligible manner, all the puzzled accounts of monies received and paid which he kept in his head, he declared that he clearly recollected to have received the ten-guinea note at Mr. Macpherson's, the tailor; that he went a few weeks ago to settle his year's account with him; and that in change for a twenty-pound note, he received that which the banker's clerk now produced. To Mackenzie it was perfectly indifferent who was found guilty, so that he could recover his money. "Settle it as you will amongst you," said he, "the money must be refunded, or I must have you all before a magistrate directly." Pasgrave, in great perturbation, set out for Mr. Macpherson's, showed him the note, and reminded him of the day when he paid his account. "If you received the note from us, sir," said the master-tailor, very calmly, "it must be entered in our books, for we keep regular accounts." The tailor's foreman, who knew much more of the affair than his master, appealed, with assumed security, to the entry in the books. By this entry it appeared that M. Pasgrave settled his account the 17th of October; that he paid the balance by a twenty-pound note, and that he received in change a ten-guinea note on Sir William Forbes's bank. "You see, sir," said the tailor, "this cannot possibly be Mr. Mackenzie's; for his note is on the bank of Scotland. Our entry is as full as possible; and I am ready to produce my books, and to abide by them, in any court of justice in the world." M. Pasgrave was totally at a loss; he could only repeat, that he remembered to have received Mackenzie's note from one of the tailor's men, who brought it to him from an inner room. The foreman boldly asserted, that he brought the change exactly as his master gave it to him, and that he knew nothing more of the matter. But, in fact, he knew a great deal more: he had found the note in the pocket of Mackenzie's waistcoat, which his servant had left to be mended, after he had torn it furtively, as has been already related. When his master called him into the inner room, to give him the change for Pasgrave, he observed that there was a ten-guinea note wrapped up with some halfpence; and he thought that it would be a prudent thing to substitute Mackenzie's note, which he had by him, in the place of this. He accordingly gave Pasgrave Mackenzie's note, and thrust the note which he had received from his master into a corner of his trunk, where he usually kept little windfalls, that came to him by the negligence of customers—toothpick-cases, loose silver, odd gloves, &c., all which he knew how to dispose of. But this bank-note was a higher prize than usual, and he was afraid to pass it till all inquiry had blown over. He knew his master's regularity; and he thought that if the note was stopped afterwards at any of the banks, it could never be traced further than to M. Pasgrave. He was rejoiced to see that this poor man was in such trepidation of mind that he could not, in the least, use his understanding; and he saw, with much satisfaction, that his master, who was a positive man, and proud of the accuracy of his books, was growing red in the face in their defence. Mackenzie, in the meantime, who had switched his boots with great impatience during their debate, interfered at last with, "Come, gentlemen, we can't stand here all day to hear you give one another the lie. One of you, it's plain, must shell out your corianders; but, as you can't settle which, we must put you to your oath, I see." "Mr. W—'s is not far off, and I am ready to go before him with my books this instant," said the fiery master-tailor. "My books were never called in question since I was in trade till this instant; and nobody but a French dancing-master, who understands no more of debtor and creditor than my goose, would stand out against such an entry as this." To Mr. W—'s the tailor, his foreman, the dancing-master, the banker's clerk, and Mackenzie, repaired. Pasgrave turned paler than ever dancer turned before; and gave himself, his character, and his wife and children, all up for lost, when he heard that he was to be put upon his oath. He drew back when Mr. W— held the book to him, and demanded whether he would swear to the person from whom he received the note. He said he could not swear; but to the best of his belief—en conscience—en honneur—foi d'honnête homme—he was convinced he received it from Mr. Macpherson's foreman. The foreman, who, from one step in villany, found himself hurried on to another and another, now scrupled not to declare that he was ready to take his oath that he delivered the note and change, just as his master gave it to him, to M. Pasgrave. The magistrate turned to the paler, conscientious, incapacitated dancing-master, and in a severe tone said—"Appearances are strangely against you, M. Pasgrave. Here's a young gentleman has lost a bank-note—it is stopped at the bank of Scotland—it is traced home to you—you say you got it from Mr. Macpherson or his foreman—his books are produced—the entry in them is clearly against you; for it states that the note given to you in change was one of Sir William Forbes's bank; and this which I hold now in my hand is of the Bank of Scotland. Please now to tell how this note of the Bank of Scotland, which has been proved to be the property of Mr. Mackenzie, came into your possession? From whom did you receive it? or how did you come by it? I am not surprised that you decline taking an oath upon this occasion." "Ah, monsieur, ayez pitié de moi!" cried the innocent, but terrified man, throwing himself upon one knee, in an attitude, which, on the stage, would have produced a sublime effect—"Ah, monsieur, ayez pitié de moi! I have no more dan de child no sense in affairs." Mackenzie interrupted him with a brutal laugh. The more humane banker's clerk was moved by the simplicity of this avowed ignorance of business. He went up to the distracted dancer, and said, "It is not to be expected that every body should understand business as we do, sir: if you are innocent, only give yourself time to recollect; and though it's unfortunate that you never keep any regular accounts, maybe we shall be able to make out this affair of the entry. If Mr. W— will give me leave to take this pen and ink, and if you will try to recollect all the persons from whom you have received money lately—" "Ah, mon Dieu! dat is impossible." Then he began to name the quarterly and half-yearly payments that he had received from his various pupils. "Did any of them lately give you a ten-guinea note?" "Ah, oui, je me rappelle—un jeune monsieur—un certain monsieur, qui ne veut pas que—qui est là incognito—who I would not betray for the world; for he has behave wid de most parfaite générosité to me." "But did he give you a ten-guinea bank-note? that is all we want to know," said the magistrate. "Mais—oui—yes." "About what time?" said the clerk. It was about the beginning of October: and this was so near the time when he settled accounts with Mr. Macpherson, the tailor, that he even himself began to believe it possible that he had mistaken one note for the other. "When the young gentleman gave you the note," said the banker's clerk, "surely you must have looked at it—you must have observed these remarkable stains?" Pasgrave replied, that he did look at it, he supposed; that he saw it was a ten-guinea note; it might be stained, it might not be stained; he could not pretend to be certain about it. He repeated his assurances that he was ignorant of business, and of every thing in this world but dancing. "Pour la danse, je m'y connois—pour les affaires, je n'en sais rien, moi." He, with his usual simplicity, added, that if Mr. W— would give him leave, he would go to the young gentleman, his friend, and learn from him exactly the number of the note which he had given him; that he was sure he could recollect his own note immediately. Mackenzie, who thought that this was merely pretence, in order to escape, told him that he could not be suffered to go out upon his parole. "But," said Mr. W—, "tell us the name of this young gentleman who has so much generosity, and who lives incognito. I don't like gentlemen who live incognito. I think I had a young man here before me, about two months ago, charged with breaking a confectioner's windows in a riot, the night of the great illuminations—Hey? don't I remember some such thing? And you, M. Pasgrave, if I mistake not, interested yourself mightily about this young man, and told me and my daughters, sir, that he was a young gentleman incognito. I begin to see through this affair. Perhaps this is the same young gentleman from whom you received the note. And pray what value did you give for it?" Pasgrave, whose fear of betraying Forester now increased his confusion, stammered, and first said the note was a present, but afterwards added, "I have been giving de young person lessons in dancing for des six week."

"Well, then, we must summon this young person," said Mr. W—. "Tell us his name, if you please," said Mackenzie; "I have some suspicion that I know your gentleman incognito." "You need not trouble him," said the magistrate; "I know the name already, and I know where the bird is to be found: his name, if he has not changed it since he was last in this room, is Forester." "Forester!" exclaimed Mackenzie; "I thought so! I always thought how he would turn out. I wonder what his friends, the Campbells, will have to say for him now!"

Mr. W—'s pen stopped. "His friends, the Campbells—humph! So the Campbells are his friends, are they?" repeated he. "They were his friends," answered Mackenzie; "but Mr. Forester thought proper, nobody knows why, to run away from them, some months ago; the only reason I could ever learn was that he did not like to live amongst gentlemen: and he has been living ever since incognito, amongst blackguards, and we see the fruits of it." Mackenzie eagerly handed the summons, as soon as it was signed, to a constable; and Mr. W— directed the constable to Mr. —'s, the bookseller, adding, "Booksellers and printers are dangerous persons." The constable, who had seen Forester the night that he was confined with Tom Random, knew his face and person; and we have told our readers that he met Forester in George's-square, going to Dr. Campbell's, to vindicate the innocence of the poor washerwoman.

The tailor's foreman was not a little alarmed when the summons was sent for our hero; he dreaded that the voice of truth should be heard, and he skulked behind the rest of the company. What astonishment did Forester feel when he entered the room, and saw the group that surrounded the justice's table!—Archibald Mackenzie, with an insulting sneer on his lips—Pasgrave, with eyes fixed upon him in despair—Mr. Macpherson, the tailor, pointing to an entry in his book—his foreman shrinking from notice—the banker's clerk, with benevolent scepticism in his countenance—and the justice, with a portentous scowl upon his brow.

"Come forward, Mr. Forester," said the magistrate, as our hero made a sudden pause of astonishment; "come forward, sir!" Forester advanced with calm intrepidity. "You are better dressed than when I had the honour of seeing you here some time ago, sir. Are you a printer still, or a gentleman? Your dress certainly bespeaks a change in your condition." "I am sure I should hardly know Mr. Forester again, he has grown such a beau—comparatively speaking, I mean," said Mackenzie. "But certainly, M. Pasgrave, you must have made some mistake; I don't know how to believe my senses! Is this the young gentleman to whom you alluded? do you know him—?" "Give me leave, Mr. Mackenzie," interrupted the justice: "I shall examine this young incognito myself. I think I know how to come at the truth. Will you do me the favour, sir, to inform me whether you recollect any thing of a ten-guinea bank-note which you gave or paid, some time in last October, to this gentleman?" pointing to M. Pasgrave. "I do," replied Forester, in a distinct, unembarrassed voice, "perfectly well remember giving M. Pasgrave a ten-guinea bank-note." "Ah, monsieur, je ne suis pas un ingrat. Ne pensez pas que—" "Oh, M. Pasgrave," interrupted Mackenzie, "this is no time for compliments and fine speeches: for God's sake, let us get to the bottom of this affair without further ceremony!" "Sir," said the banker's clerk, "all we want to know is the number of your note, and the firm of the house. Was your note one of Sir William Forbes's, or of the Bank of Scotland?" Forester was silent. "I do not recollect," said he, after some pause. "You don't recollect, sir," said the justice, "is something like an evasive answer. You must have a vast number of bank-notes then, we must presume, if you cannot recollect to what bank your ten-guinea note belonged." Forester did not understand this logic; but he simply repeated his assertion. "Pray, sir," said the tailor, who could no longer restrain his impatience—"Pray, sir," said the magistrate, in a solemn manner, "be silent. I shall find out the truth. So, Mr. Forester, you cannot possibly recollect the house of your note? You will tell us next, I dare say, that you cannot possibly recollect how you came by it." "Sir," said Forester, "if it is necessary, I can readily tell you how I came by it." "It is very necessary, sir, for your own credit." "I received it from Dr. Campbell." "Dr. Campbell!" repeated the magistrate, changing his tone. "And I have some idea that the doctor gave me a list of the numbers of that and four other notes, with which I fortunately have not parted." "Some idea means nothing in a court of justice, sir; if you have any such paper, you can do us the favour to produce it." Now this list was locked up in the trunk, of which the key was dropped into the brewing-vat. Richardson, the clerk, had returned the key to him; but, such is the force of habit, he had not cured himself of the foolish trick of twirling it upon his thumb; and about two months ago he dropped it in one of his walks to Arthur's Seat. He long searched for it amongst the rocky fragments, but at last gave it up—he little imagined of how much consequence it might be to him. Dr. Campbell had once refused to break open the lock, and he felt very unwilling to apply to him in his present circumstances. However, he wrote a few lines to Henry Campbell; but, as soon as he had written them, his pride again revolted from the thoughts of supplicating the assistance of his friend in such a disgraceful situation. "If you don't choose to write," said the officious malevolence of Archibald, "I can, however, speak; I'll desire Dr. Campbell to open your trunk, and search for the paper." He left the room before Forester could make any further opposition.

"I have answered, I hope, both distinctly and respectfully, all the questions that you have asked me," said Forester, turning to Mr. W—. "I hope you will no longer keep me in the dark. Of what am I suspected?" "I will tell you, sir," replied the deliberate, unfeeling magistrate; "you are suspected of having, I will not say stolen, but you are more than suspected of having come unfairly by a certain ten-guinea bank-note, which the young gentleman who has just left the room lost a few months ago." Forester, as this speech was slowly pronounced, sat down, folded his arms, and appeared totally insensible—quite unconscious that he was in the presence of a magistrate, or that any human being was observing him. "Ah, mon cher monsieur, pardonnez!" cried Pasgrave, bursting into tears. "N'en parlons plus," added he, turning to the magistrate. "Je payerai tout ce qu'il faut. I will pay de ten guineas. I will satisfy every body. I cannot never forgive myself if I bring him into any disgrace." "Disgrace!" exclaimed Forester, starting up, and repeating the word in a tone which made every person in the room, not excepting the phlegmatic magistrate, start and look up to him, with a sudden feeling of inferiority. His ardent eye spoke the language of his soul. No words could express his emotion. The master-tailor dropped his day-book. "Constable—call a constable!" cried the justice. "Sir, you forget in whose presence you are—you think, I suppose, that your friends, the Campbells, will bear you out. Sir, I would have you to know that all the Campbells in Scotland can't bail you for a felony. Sir, philosophers should know these things. If you cannot clear yourself to my entire satisfaction, Mr. Forester, I shall commit you—in one word—to gaol: yes—look as you please, sir—to gaol. And if the doctor and his son, and all his family, come up to bail you, I shall, meo periculo, refuse their bail. The law, sir, is no respecter of persons. So none of your rhodomontades, young gentleman, in my presence; but step into this closet, if you please; and, I advise you, bring your mind into a becoming temperament, whilst I go to dinner. Gentlemen," continued he to Macpherson and Pasgrave, "you'll be so good to wait here in this apartment. Constable, look to your prisoner," pointing to the door of the closet. "John, let me know when Dr. Campbell arrives; and tell them to send up dinner directly," said the justice to his butler.

Whilst he dines, we must leave the tailor complaining that he was wasting precious time; the foreman in the panic of guilt; and the good-natured dancing-master half distracted betwixt his fears and his ignorance. He looked from time to time through the key-hole of the closet in which Forester was confined, and exclaimed, "Grand Dieu! comme il a l'air noble à cet instant! Ah! lui coupable! he go to gaol! it is impossible!"

"We shall see how that will be presently," said the foreman, who had hitherto preserved absolute silence. "I abide by my books," said the master-tailor; "and I wish Dr. Campbell would make haste. I have lost a day!"

In spite of the tailor's imperial exclamation, he was obliged to wait some time longer. When Mackenzie arrived at Dr. Campbell's, Henry was not at home: he was gone to the house at the back of the meadows, to prepare some chemical experiments for the next day's lecture. Mackenzie, however, found Dr. Campbell at home in his study; and, in a soft hypocritical voice, lamented that he was obliged to communicate some disagreeable circumstances relating to young Mr. Forester. "You do not, I presume, know where that unfortunate, misguided youth is at present—at this moment, I mean." "I do not know where he is at this moment," said Dr. Campbell, calmly; "but I know where he has been for some time—at Mr. —'s, the bookseller. I have had my eye upon him ever since he left this house. I have traced him from place to place. Though I have said little about him, Mr. Mackenzie, I have a great regard for my unfortunate ward." "I am sorry for it, sir," said Mackenzie: "I fear I must wound your feelings the more deeply." "What is the matter? pray speak at once," cried Dr. Campbell, who now forgot all his usual calmness. "Where is Forester?" "He is at this moment before Mr. W—, the magistrate, sir, charged with—but, I own, I cannot believe him guilty—" "Charged with what? For God's sake, speak plainly, Mr. Mackenzie!" "Then, in one word, sir, my lost bank-note is traced home to Mr. Forester. M. Pasgrave says he received it from him." "Surely, sir," said Dr. Campbell, with indignation, "you would not insinuate that Forester has stolen your bank-note?" "I insinuate nothing, doctor," said Archibald; "but, I fear, the thing is too plainly proved. My bank-note has certain stains, by which it has been identified. All that I know is, that Mr. W— says he can take no bail; and that he must commit Mr. Forester to gaol, unless he can clear himself. He says, that a few days before he left your house, you paid him his quarterly allowance of fifty guineas, in five ten-guinea bank-notes." "He says true—I did so," said Dr. Campbell eagerly. "And he says that you gave them to him wrapped in a piece of paper, on which the numbers of the notes were written." "I remember it distinctly: I desired him to take care of that paper." "He is not famous for taking care, you know, sir, of any thing. He says, he believes he threw it into his trunk; but he has lost the key of the trunk, I understand." "No matter; we can break it open this instant, and search for the paper," cried Dr. Campbell, who was now extremely alarmed for his ward. Mackenzie stood by without offering any assistance, whilst Dr. Campbell broke open the trunk, and searched it with the greatest anxiety. It was in terrible disorder. The coat and waistcoat which Forester wore at the ball were crammed in at the top; and underneath appeared unfolded linen, books, boots, maps, shoes, cravats, fossils, and heaps of little rumpled bits of paper, in which the fossils had once been contained. Dr. Campbell opened every one of these. The paper he wanted was not amongst them. He took every thing out of the box, shook and searched all the pockets of the coat, in which Forester used, before his reformation, to keep hoards of strange papers. No list of bank-notes appeared. At length, Dr. Campbell espied the white corner of a paper-mark in a volume of Goldsmith's Animated Nature, He pulled out this mark, and to his great joy, he found it to be the very paper he wanted. "So it's found, is it?" said Mackenzie, disappointed; whilst Dr. Campbell seized his hat, left every thing upon the floor, and was very near locking the door of the room upon Mackenzie. "Don't lock me in here, doctor—I am going back with you to Mr. W—'s" said Arcibald. "Won't you stay? dinner's going up—Mr. W— was going this dinner when I came away." Without listening to him, Dr. Campbell just let him out, locked the door, and hurried away to his poor ward.

"I have let things go to far," said he to himself. "As long as Forester's credit was not in danger, as long as he was unknown, it was very well; but now his character is at stake; he may pay too dear for his experience."

"Dr. Campbell," said the pompous magistrate, who hated philosophers, rising from table as Dr. Campbell entered, "do not speak to me of bailing this ward of yours—it is impossible, sir; I know my duty." "I am not come to offer bail for my ward," said Dr. Campbell, "but to prove his innocence." "We must hope the best," said Mr. W—; and, having forced the doctor to pledge him in a bumper of port, "Now I am ready to proceed again to the examination of all parties concerned."

Dr. Campbell was now shown into the room where Mr. Macpherson, his foreman and Pasgrave, were waiting. "Ah, monsieur, Dieu merci, vous voila!" exclaimed Pasgrave. "You may go," said Mr. W— to the constable: "but wait below stairs." He unlocked the closet-door. Forester, at the sight of Dr. Campbell, covered his face with his hands; but, an instant afterwards, advanced with intrepidity. "You cannot, I am sure, believe me to be guilty of any meanness, Dr. Campbell," said he. "Imprudent I have been, and I suffer for my folly." "Guilty!" cried Dr. Campbell; "no: I could almost as soon suspect my own son of such an action. But my belief is nothing to the purpose. We must prove your innocence." "Ah, oui, monsieur—and mine too; for I am innocent, I can assure you," cried M. Pasgrave.

"The whole business, sir," said the banker's clerk, who had, by this time, returned to hear the termination of the affair—"the whole thing can be settled in two minutes, by a gentleman like you, who understands business. Mr. Forester cannot recollect the number or the firm of a ten-guinea bank-note which he gave to M. Pasgrave. M. Pasgrave cannot recollect either; and he is in doubt whether he received this stained note, which Mr. Mackenzie lost, from Mr. Forester or from Mr. Macpherson, the tailor." "There can be no doubt about me," said Macpherson. "Dr. Campbell, will you be so good to look at the entry? I acknowledge, I gave M. Pasgrave a ten-guinea note; but here's the number of it, 177, of Forbes's bank. Mr. Mackenzie's note, you see, is of the bank of Scotland; and the stains upon it are so remarkable, that, if I had ever seen it before, I should certainly remember it. I'll take my oath I never saw it before." "Sir," said Forester eagerly to Dr. Campbell, "you gave me five ten-guinea notes: here are four of them in this pocket-book; the fifth I gave to M. Pasgrave. Can you tell me the number of that note?" "I can," said Dr. Campbell, producing the paper which he found in Goldsmith's Animated Nature. "I had the precaution to write down the numbers of all your notes myself: here they are." Forester opened his pocket-book: his four remaining notes were compared, and perfectly agreed with the numbers in the list. The fifth, the number of the note which he gave to Pasgrave, was 1260, of the New Bank. "One of your ten-guinea notes," said Dr. Campbell to Pasgrave, "you paid into the bank of Scotland; and this gentleman," pointing to the banker's clerk, "stopped it this morning. Now you have had another ten-guinea note; what became of that?" Pasgrave, who understood Dr. Campbell's plain method of questioning him, answered immediately, "I did give the other to my hair-dresser, not long ago, who lives in — street." Dr. Campbell instantly went himself to the hair-dresser, found that he had the note still in his possession, brought him to Mr. W—'s, and, when the note was examined, it was found to be 1260 of the New Bank, which exactly corresponded with the entry in the list of notes which Dr. Campbell had produced.

"Then all is right," said Dr. Campbell. "Ah, oui!—Ah, non!" exclaimed Pasgrave. "What will become of me?" "Compose yourself, my good sir," said Dr. Campbell. "You had but two ten-guinea notes, you are sure of that?" "But two—but two: I will swear but two." "You are now certain which of these two notes you had from my ward. The other, you say, you received from —" "From dis gentleman, I will swear," cried Pasgrave, pulling the tailor's foreman forwards. "I can swear now I am in no embarras: I am sure I did get de oder note from dis gentleman." The master-tailor was astonished to see all the pallid marks of guilt in his foreman's countenance. "Did you change the note that I gave you in the inner room?" said Mr. Macpherson. The foreman, as soon as he could command his voice, denied the charge; and persisted in it that he gave the note and change, which his master wrapped up, exactly as it was, to the dancing-master. Dr. Campbell proposed that the tailor's shop, and the foreman's room, should be searched. Mr. W— sent proper people to Mr. Macpherson's; and whilst they are searching his house, we may inquire what has become of Henry Campbell.

THE CATASTROPHE

Henry Campbell, the last time we heard of him, was at the house at the back of the meadows. When he went into the large room to his chemical experiments, the little girl, who was proud of having arranged it neatly, ran on before him, and showed him the places where all his things were put. "The writing and the figures are not rubbed off your slate—there it is, sir," said she, pointing to a high shelf. "But whose handkerchief is this?" said Henry, taking up a handkerchief which was under the slate. "Gracious! that must be the good gentleman's handkerchief; he missed it just as he was going out of the house. He thought he had left it at the washerwoman's, where I met him; and he's gone back to look for it there. I'll run with it to the washerwoman's,—maybe she knows where to find him." "But you have not told me who he is. Whom do you mean by the good gentleman?" "The good gentleman, sir, that I saw with you at the watchmaker's, the day that you helped me to carry the great geranium out of my grandmother's room." "Do you mean that Forester has been here?" exclaimed Henry. "I never heard his name, sir; but I mean that the gentleman has been here, whom I call the good gentleman, because it was he who went with me to my cross schoolmistress, to try to persuade her to use me well. She beat me, to be sure, after he was gone, for what he had said; but I'm not the less obliged to him, because he did every thing as he thought for the best. And so I'll run with his handkerchief to the woman's, who will give it safe to him."

Henry recollected his promise to his father. It required all his power over himself to forbear questioning the child, and endeavouring to find out something more of his friend. He determined to mention the circumstance to his father, and to Flora, as soon as he returned home. He was always impatient to tell any thing to his sister that interested himself or his friends; for Flora's gaiety was not of that unfeeling sort which seeks merely for amusement, and which, unmixed with sympathy for others, may divert in a companion, but disgusts in a friend.

Whilst Henry was reflecting upon the manner in which he might most expeditiously arrange his chemical experiments and return home, the little girl came running back, with a face of great distress. As soon as she had breath to speak, she told Henry that when she went to the washerwoman's with the handkerchief, she was told a sad piece of news; that Mr. Forester had been taken up, and carried before Mr. W—, the magistrate. "We don't know what he has done: I'm sure I don't think he can have done any thing wrong." Henry no sooner heard these words than he left all his retorts, rushed out of the house, hurried home to his father, and learned from Flora, with great surprise, that his father had already been sent for, and was gone to Mr. W—'s. She did not know the circumstances that Mackenzie related to Dr. Campbell, but she told him that her father seemed much alarmed; that she met him crossing the hall, and that he could not stop to speak to her. Henry proceeded directly to Mr. W—'s, and he arrived there just as the people returned from the search of the tailor's house. His opinion of Forester's innocence was so strong, that when he entered the room, he instantly walked up to him, and embraced him, with a species of frank confidence in his manner which, to Forester, was more expressive than any thing that he could have said. The whole affair was quickly explained to him; and the people who had been sent to Mr. Macpherson's now came up-stairs to Mr. W—, and produced a ten-guinea bank-note, which was found in the foreman's box. Upon examination, this note was discovered to be the very note which Mr. Macpherson sent with the change to Pasgrave. It was No. 177, of Sir William Forbes's bank, as mentioned in the circumstantial entry in the day-book. The joy of the poor dancing-master at this complete proof of his innocence was rapturous and voluble. Secure of the sympathy of Forester, Henry, and Dr. Campbell, he looked at them by turns, whilst he congratulated himself upon this "éclaircissement," and assured the banker's clerk that he would in future keep accounts. We are impatient to get rid of the guilty foreman: he stood a horrible image of despair. He was committed to gaol; and was carried away by the constables, without being pitied by any person present. Every body, however, was shocked. Mackenzie broke silence first, by exclaiming, "Well, now, I presume, Mr. W—, I may take possession of my bank-note again." He took up all the notes which lay upon the table to search amongst them for his own. "Mine, you know, is stained," said Archibald. "But it is very singular," said Henry Campbell, who was looking over his shoulder, "that here are two stained notes. That which was found in the foreman's box is stained in one corner, exactly as yours was stained, Mr. Mackenzie." Macpherson, the tailor, now stooped to examine it. "Is this No. 177, the note that I sent in change, by my foreman, to M. Pasgrave? I'll take my oath it was not stained in that manner when I took it out of my desk. It was a new and quite clean note: it must have been stained since." "And it must have been stained with vitriolic acid," continued Henry. "Ay, there's cunning for you," cried Archibald. "The foreman, I suppose, stained it, that it might not be known again." "Have you any vitriolic acid in your house?" pursued Henry, addressing himself to the master-tailor. "Not I, indeed, sir; we have nothing to do with such things. They'd be very dangerous to us." "Pray," said Henry, "will you give me leave, Mr. W—, to ask the person who searched the foreman's box a few questions?" "Certainly sir," said Mr. W—; "though, I protest, I cannot see what you are driving at." Henry inquired what was found in the box with the bank-note. The man who searched it enumerated a variety of things. "None of these," said Henry, "could have stained the note: are you sure that there was nothing else?" "Nothing in the world; nothing but an old glass stopper, I believe." "I wish I could see that stopper," said Henry. "This note was rolled round it," said the man: "but I threw it into the box again. I'll go and fetch it, sir, if you have any curiosity to see it." "Curiosity to see an old stopper? No!" cried Archibald Mackenzie, with a forced laugh; "what good would that do us? We have been kept here long enough. I move that we go home to our dinners." But Dr. Campbell, who saw that Henry had some particular reason for wishing to see this glass stopper, seconded his son. The man went for it; and when he brought it into the room, Henry Campbell looked at it very carefully, and then decidedly said, fixing his eyes upon Archibald Mackenzie, who in vain struggled to keep his countenance from changing. "This glass stopper, Mr. Mackenzie, is the stopper of my father's vitriolic acid bottle, that was broken the night the cat was killed. This stopper has stained both the bank-notes. And it must have been in the pocket of your waistcoat." "My pocket!" interrupted Archibald: "how should it come into my pocket? It never was in my pocket, sir." Henry pointed to the stain on his waistcoat. He wore the very waistcoat in question. "Sir," said Archibald, "I don't know what you mean by pointing at my waistcoat. It is stained, it is true, and very likely by vitriolic acid; but, as I have been so often in the doctor's laboratory, when your chemical experiments have been going on, is it not very natural to suppose that a drop of one of the acids might have fallen on my clothes? I have seen your waistcoats stained, I am sure. Really, Mr. Campbell, you are unfriendly, uncharitable; your partiality for Mr. Forester should not blind you, surely. I know you want to exculpate him from having any hand in the death of that cat: but that should not, my dear sir, make you forget what is due to justice. You should not, permit me to say, endeavour to criminate an innocent person." "This is all very fine," said Henry; "and you may prove your innocence to me at once, Mr. Mackenzie, if you think proper, by showing that the waistcoat was really, as you assert, stained by a drop of vitriolic acid falling upon the outside of it. Will you show us the inside of the pocket?" Mackenzie, who was now in too much confusion to know distinctly what Henry meant to prove, turned the pocket inside out, and repeated, "That stopper was never in my pocket, I'll swear." "Don't swear to that, for God's sake," said Henry. "Consider what you are saying. You see that there is a hole burnt in this pocket. Now if a drop of acid had fallen, as you said, upon the outside of the waistcoat, it must have been more burnt on the outside than on the inside." "I don't know—I can't pretend to be positive," said Archibald; "but what signifies all this rout about the stopper?" "It signifies a great deal to me," said Dr. Campbell, turning away from Mackenzie with contempt, and addressing himself to his ward, who met his approving eye with proud delight—"it signifies a great deal to me. Forgive me, Mr. Forester, for having doubted your word for a moment." Forester held his guardian's hand, without being able for some instants to reply. "You are coming home with us, Forester?" said Henry. "No," said Dr. Campbell, smiling; "you must not ask him to come home with us to-night. We have a little dance at our house to-night. Lady Catherine Mackenzie wished to take leave of her Edinburgh friends. She goes from us to-morrow. We must not expect to see Forester at a ball; but to-morrow morning—" "I see," said Forester, smiling, "you have no faith in my reformation. Well, I have affairs to settle with my master, the printer. I must go home, and take leave of him. He has been a good master to me; and I must go and finish my task of correcting. Adieu." He abruptly left Dr. Campbell and Henry, and went to the bookseller's, to inform him of all that had passed, and to thank him for his kindness. "You will be at a loss to-morrow for a corrector of the press," said he. "I am determined you shall not suffer for my vagaries. Send home the proof-sheets of the work in hand to me, at Dr. Campbell's, and I will return them to you punctually corrected. Employ me till you have provided yourself with another, I will not say a better hand. I do not imagine," continued Forester, "that I can pay you for your kindness to me by presents; indeed, I know you are in such circumstances that you disdain money. But I hope you will accept of a small mark of my regard—a complete font of new types."

Whilst Forester's generous heart expanded with joy at the thoughts of returning once more to his friends, we are sorry to leave him, to finish the history of Archibald Mackenzie. He sneaked home after Dr. Campbell and Henry, whose silent contempt he well understood. Dr. Campbell related all that had passed to Lady Catherine. Her ladyship showed herself more apprehensive that her son's meanness should be made known to the world, than indignation or sorrow for his conduct. Archibald, whilst he was dressing for the ball, began to revolve in his mind certain words which his mother had said to him about his having received the lie direct from Henry Campbell—his not having the spirit of a gentleman. "She certainly meant," said he to himself, "that I ought to fight him. It's the only way I can come off, as he spoke so plainly before Mr. W—, and all those people: the banker's clerk too was by; and, as my mother says, it will be talked of. I'll get Sir Philip Gosling to go with my message. I think I've heard Dr. Campbell say, he disapproved of duels. Perhaps Henry won't fight. Has Sir Philip Gosling sent to say, whether he would be with us at the ball to-night?" said Archibald to the servant who was dressing his hair. "No, sir," replied the servant: "Sir Philip's man has not been here: but Major O'Shannon has been here twice since you were away, to see you. He said he had some message to deliver from Sir Philip to you." "To me! message to me!" repeated Archibald, turning pale. Archibald knew Major O'Shannon, who had of late insinuated himself into Sir Philip Gosling's favour, had a particular dislike to him, and had successfully bullied him upon one or two occasions. Archibald had that civil cowardice, which made him excessively afraid of the opinion of the world; and Major O'Shannon, a gamester, who was jealous of his influence over the rich dupe, Sir Philip, determined to entangle him in a quarrel. The major knocked at the door a third time before Archibald was dressed; and when he was told that he was dressing, and could not see any one, he sent up the following note:—

"SIR,
"The last time I met you at the livery-stables, in company with my friend, Sir Philip Gosling, I had the honour of telling you my mind, in terms sufficiently explicit, concerning a transaction, which cannot have escaped your memory. My friend, Sir Philip, declares you never hinted that the pony was spavined. I don't pretend to be so good a jockey as you, but you'll excuse my again saying, I can't consider your conduct as that of a gentleman. Sir Philip is of my mind; and if you resent my interference, I am ready to give you the satisfaction of a gentleman. If not, you will do well to leave Edinburgh along with your mother to-morrow morning; for Edinburgh is no place for cowards, as long as one has the honour of living in it, who calls himself (by courtesy)

"Your humble servant,

"CORNELIUS O'SHANNON.
"P.S. Sir Philip is at your service, after your settling with me."

Archibald, oppressed with the sense of his own meanness, and somewhat alarmed at the idea of fighting three duels, to retrieve his credit, thought it best to submit, without struggle, in the first instance, to that public disgrace which he had merited. He wrote a shabby apology to Major O'Shannon and Sir Philip, concluding with saying, that rather than lose a friend he so much valued as Sir Philip Gosling, he was willing to forget all that had passed, and even to take back the pony, and to return Sawney, if the matter could, by this means, be adjusted to his satisfaction. He then went to his mother, and talked to her, in a high style, of his desperate intentions with respect to Henry Campbell. "Either he or I must fall, before we quit the ground," said the artful Archibald—well knowing that Lady Catherine's maternal tenderness would be awakened by these ideas. Other ideas were also awakened in the prudent mother's mind. Dr. Campbell was nearly related to a general officer, from whom she looked for promotion for her son. She repented, upon reflection, of what she had hastily said concerning the lie direct, and the spirit of a gentleman; and she softened down her pride, and talked of her dislike to breaking up old family friendships. Thence she digressed into hints of the advantages that might accrue from cultivating Dr. Campbell's good opinion; admitted that Henry was strangely prejudiced in favour of his rough friend Forester; but observed that Mr. Forester, after all, though singular, was a young man of merit, and at the head of a very considerable estate. "Archibald," said she, "we must make allowances, and conciliate matters—unless you make this young gentleman your friend, you can never hope to be on an eligible footing with his guardian. His guardian, you see, is glad to get him back again, and, I dare say, has his reasons. I never saw him, and I know him well, in such spirits in my life as he was when he came back to us to announce the probability of his ward's return to-morrow morning. The doctor, I dare say, has good reasons for what he does; and I understand his ward is reconciled to the idea of living in the world, and enjoying his fine fortune like other people. So I hope you and he, and of course you and the doctor, and Henry Campbell, will be very good friends. I shall leave you at Edinburgh for a few months, till we get our commission; and I shall beg the doctor to introduce you to his friend and relation, General D—. If he can do nothing for you, you may look towards the Church. I trust to your prudence, not to think of Flora Campbell, though I leave you in the house with her; for you can't afford, Archibald, to marry a girl with so small a fortune; and, you may be sure, her friends have other views for her. Pray let me hear no more of duels and quarrels. And let us go down into the ball-room; for Miss Campbell has been dressed and down-stairs this half hour; and I would not have you inattentive—that might displease as much as the other extreme. In short, I may safely leave you to your own discretion." Lady Catherine, after this prudent exhortation, entered the ball-room, where all the company soon after assembled. Seated in gay ranges, the well-dressed belles were eager for the dancing to commence. Lady Catherine stood by Dr. Campbell; and as soon as the ball began, when the music played, and she saw every one absorbed in themselves, or in their partners, she addressed herself to the doctor on the subject which was next her heart, or rather next her imagination. "The general is to be with you shortly, I understand," said she. Dr. Campbell coldly answered in the affirmative. "To be candid with you, doctor, if you'll sit down, I want to have a little chat with you about my Archibald. He is not every thing I could wish, and I see you are displeased with him about this foolish business that has just happened. For my own part, I think him to blame; but we must pardon, we must make allowances for the errors of youth; and I need not, to a man of your humanity, observe what a cruel thing it is to prejudice the world against a young man, by telling little anecdotes to his disadvantage. Relations must surely uphold one another;

and I am convinced you will speak of Archibald with candour and friendship." "With candour and with truth," replied Dr. Campbell. "I cannot pretend to feel friendship merely on the score of relationship."

The proud blood mounted into Lady Catherine's face, and she replied, "Some consideration of one's own relations, I think, is not unbecoming. Archibald, I should have thought, had as strong a claim upon Dr. Campbell's friendship as the son of an utter stranger to the family. Old Mr. Forester had a monstrous fortune, 'tis true; but his wife, who was no grand affair, I believe—a merchant's daughter, I'm told— brought him the greatest part of it; and yet, without any natural connexion between the families, or any thing very desirable, setting fortune out of the question, you accept the guardianship of this young man, and prefer him, I plainly see, to my Archibald. I candidly ask you the question, and answer me candidly."

"As you have explicitly asked the question, I will answer your ladyship candidly. I do prefer my ward to your son. I have avoided drawing comparisons between your son and Forester; and I now wish to avoid speaking of Mr. Archibald Mackenzie, because I have little hope of being of service to him."

"Nay," said Lady Catherine, softening her tone, "you know you have it in your power to be of the greatest service to him."

"I have done all I could," said Dr. Campbell, with a sigh; "but habits of—"

"Oh, but I'm not talking of habits," interrupted Lady Catherine. "I'll make him alter his habits. We shall soon turn him into what you like: he's very quick; and you must not expect every young man to be just cut out upon the pattern of our dear Henry. I don't want to trouble you to alter his habits, or to teach him chemistry, or any of those things. But you can, you know, without all that, do him an essential service."

"How?" said Dr. Campbell.

"Why how? I don't know you this evening, you are so dry. Ken you not what I mean? Speak three words for him to your friend, the general."

"Your ladyship must excuse me," said Dr. Campbell.

Lady Catherine was stunned by this distinct refusal. She urged Dr. Campbell to explain the cause of his dislike to her son.

"There is a poor washerwoman now below stairs," replied Dr. Campbell, "who can explain to you more than I wish to explain; and a story about a horse of Sir Philip Gosling was told to me the other day, by one of the baronet's friends, which I should be glad Mr. Archibald Mackenzie could contradict effectually."

"Archibald, come here," said Lady Catherine: "before the next dance begins, I must speak to you. What is this about a horse of Sir Philip Gosling?"

"Ma'am!" said Archibald, with great astonishment. At this instant one of Dr. Campbell's servants came into the room, and gave two notes to Archibald, which, he said, two gentlemen had just left, and desired him to deliver to Mr. Mackenzie whilst he was in the ball-room, if possible.

"What is it?—What are they, child?" cried Lady Catherine. "I will see them." Her ladyship snatched the notes, read, and when she saw that her son, in the grossest terms, was called a coward, for refusing the challenges of two such fashionable men as Sir Philip Gosling and Major O'Shannon, all her hopes of him were at an end. "Our family is disgraced for ever!" she exclaimed; and then, perceiving that she had uttered this unguarded sentence loud enough for several of the company to hear, she endeavoured to laugh, and fell into violent hysterics. She was carried out of the ball-room. A whisper now ran round the room of—"What's the matter with Lady Catherine Mackenzie?" It was at an unfortunate moment that she was carried out, for all the dancers had just seated themselves, after a brisk country dance; and the eyes of all the young and old were upon her ladyship as she made her exit. A young man, a friend of Major O'Shannon, who was present, whispered the secret to his partner; she, of course, to her next neighbour. Archibald saw that the contents of the notes were made public; and he quitted the apartment, "to inquire how his mother did."

The buzz of scandal was general for some moments; but a new object soon engrossed the attention of the company. "Pray," said a young lady, who was looping up Flora Campbell's gown, "who is this gentleman, who is just coming into the room?" Flora looked up, and saw a well-dressed stranger entering the room, who had much the appearance of a gentleman. He certainly resembled a person she had seen before; but she could scarcely believe that her eyes did not deceive her. Therefore she hesitatingly replied to the young lady's question, "I don't know—I am not sure." But she, an instant afterwards, saw her brother Henry and her father advance so eagerly to meet the stranger, that her doubts vanished; and, as he now directed his steps towards the spot where she was standing, she corrected her first answer to her companion's question, and said, "Yes, I fancy—it certainly is—Mr. Forester." Forester, with an open countenance, slightly tinged with the blush of ingenuous shame, approached her, as if he was afraid she had not forgotten some things which he wished to be forgotten; and yet as if he was conscious that he was not wholly unworthy of her esteem. "Amongst other prejudices of which I have cured myself," said he to Dr. Campbell, "since we parted, I have cured myself of my foolish antipathy to Scotch reels."

"That I can scarcely believe," said Dr. Campbell, with an incredulous smile.

"I will convince you of it," said Forester, "if you will promise to forget all my other follies."

"All!" said Dr. Campbell. "Convince me first; and then it will be time enough to make such a desperate promise."

Flora was rather surprised when our once cynical hero begged the favour of her hand, and led her to dance a reel. M. Pasgrave would have been in ecstasy if he had seen his pupil's performance.

"And now, my dear Forester," said Dr. Campbell, as his ward returned to claim his promise of a general amnesty, "if you do not turn out a coxcomb, if you do not 'mistake reverse of wrong for right,' you will infallibly be a very great man. Give me a pupil who can cure himself of any one foible, and I have hope of him. What hope must I not have of him who has cured himself of so many!"

Frederick the Second, king of Prussia, after his conquest of Saxony, transported, it is said(1), by force, several manufacturers from Dresden to Berlin, where he was very desirous of establishing the manufacture of china. These unfortunate people, separated from their friends, their home, and their native country, were compelled to continue their labours for the profit and for the glory of their conqueror. Amongst the number of those sufferers was Sophia Mansfeld. She was young, handsome, and possessed considerable talents. Several pieces of porcelain of her design and modelling were shown to Frederick, when he visited the manufactory at Meissen, in Saxony; and their taste and workmanship appeared to him so exquisite, that he determined to transport the artist to his capital. But from the time of her arrival at Berlin, Sophia Mansfeld's genius seemed to forsake her. It was her business to sketch designs, and to paint them on the porcelain; but either she could not or would not execute these with her former elegance: the figures were awkward and spiritless, and it was in vain that the overseer of the works attempted to rouse her to exertion; she would sit for hours, with her pencil in her hand, in a sort of reverie. It was melancholy to see her. The overseer had compassion upon her; but his compassion was not so great as his dread of the king's displeasure; and he at length declared, that the next time Frederick visited the works, he must complain of her obstinate idleness.

(Footnote 1: Vide Wraxall'g Memoirs of the Court of Berlin.)

The monarch was expected in a few days; for, in the midst, of his various occupations, Frederick, who was at this time extremely intent upon the establishment of the porcelain manufactory at Berlin, found leisure frequently to inspect it in person. The king, however, was prevented from coming at the appointed hour by a review at Potzdam. His majesty had formed the singular project of embodying, and training to the science of arms, the Jews in his dominions(2). They were rather awkward in learning the manual exercise; and the Jewish review, though it afforded infinite amusement to the spectators, put Frederick so much out of humour, that, as soon as it was over, he rode to his palace of Sans Souci, and shut himself up for the remainder of the morning. The preceding evening an English traveller, who had passed some time at Paris with the Count de Lauragais, in trying experiments upon porcelain clays, and who had received much instruction on this subject from Mr. Wedgewood, of Etruria, had been presented to the king, and his majesty had invited him to be present at a trial of some new process of importance, which was to be made this morning at his manufactory. The English traveller, who was more intent upon his countryman Mr. Wedgewood's fame than upon the martial manoeuvres of the Jews, proceeded, as soon as the review was finished, to exhibit his English specimens to a party of gentlemen, who had appointed to meet him at the china-works at Berlin.

(Footnote 2: Wraxall's Memoirs of the Court of Berlin, &c.)

Of this party, was a youth of the name of Augustus Laniska, who was at this time scarcely seventeen years old. He was a Pole by birth—a Prussian by education. He had been bred up at the military school at Potzdam, and being distinguished by Frederick as a boy of high spirit and capacity, he was early inspired with enthusiastic admiration of this monarch. His admiration, however, was neither blind nor servile. He saw Frederick's faults as well as his great qualities; and he often expressed himself with more openness and warmth upon this subject than prudence could justify. He had conversed with unusual freedom about Frederick's character with our English traveller; and whilst he was zealous to display every proof of the king's greatness of mind, he was sometimes forced to acknowledge that "there are disadvantages in living under the power of a despotic sovereign."

"A despotic sovereign! You will not then call your Frederick a despot?" whispered the English traveller to the young Pole, as they entered the china-works at Berlin. "This is a promising manufactory, no doubt," continued he; "and Dresden china will probably soon be called Berlin china, by which the world in general will certainly be much benefited. But in the meantime look around you, and read your monarch's history in the eyes of those prisoners of war—for such I must call these expatriated manufacturers."

There were, indeed, many countenances in which great dejection was visible. "Look at that picture of melancholy," resumed the Englishman, pointing to the figure of Sophia Mansfeld—"observe even now, whilst the overseer is standing near her, how reluctantly she works! 'Tis the way with all slaves. Our English manufacturers (I wish you could see them) work in quite another manner—for they are free—"

"And are free men, or free women, never ill?" said Laniska; "or do you Englishmen blame your king, whenever any of his subjects turn pale?—The woman at whom you are now looking is evidently ill. I will inquire from the overseer what is the matter with her."

Laniska then turned to the overseer, and asked him in German several questions, to which he received answers that he did not translate to the English traveller; he was unwilling that any thing unfavourable to the cause of his sovereign should appear; and, returning to his companion, he changed the conversation. When all the company were occupied round the furnaces, attending to the Englishman's experiments, Laniska went back to the apartment where Sophia Mansfeld was at work. "My good girl," said he to her, "what is the matter with you? The overseer tells me, that since you came here you have done nothing that is worth looking at; yet this charming piece (pointing to a bowl of her painting, which had been brought from Saxony) is of your design, is it not?"

"Yes, sir," replied Sophia, "I painted it—to my sorrow. If the king had never seen or liked it, I should now be—" The recollection of her home, which at this instant rushed full upon her mind, overpowered her, and she paused.

"You would now be in Saxony," resumed Laniska; "but forget Saxony, and you will be happy at Berlin."

"I cannot forget Saxony, sir," answered the young woman, with modest firmness; "I cannot forget a father and mother whom I love, who are old and infirm, and who depended on me for their support. I cannot forget every thing—every body that I have ever loved: I wish I could."

"Sir," whispered a Prussian workman, who stood by—"sir, she has a lover in Saxony, to whom she was just going to be married, when she was carried off from her cottage, and brought hither."

"Cannot her lover follow her?" said Laniska.

"He is in Berlin, in concealment," replied the workman, in a whisper; "you won't betray him, I am sure."

"Not I," said Laniska; "I never betrayed any one, and I never shall—much less the unfortunate. But why is her lover in concealment?"

"Because it is the king's pleasure," replied the Prussian, "that she should no longer consider him as her lover. You know, sir, several of these Saxon women have been compelled, since their arrival at Berlin, to marry Prussians. Sophia Mansfeld has fallen to the lot of a Prussian soldier, who swears that if she delays another month to marry him, he will complain to the king of her obstinacy. Our overseer, too, threatens to complain of her idleness. She is ruined if she go on in this way: we tell her so, but she seems to have lost all sense; for she sits as she does now, like one stupified, half the day, let us say what we will to her. We pity her; but the king knows best: the king must be obeyed."

"Slave!" exclaimed Laniska, bursting into a sudden transport of indignation, "slave! you are fit to live only under a tyrant. The king knows best! the king must be obeyed! What! when his commands are contrary to reason, to justice, to humanity?" Laniska stopped short, but not before the high tone of his voice, and the boldness of the words he uttered, had astonished and dismayed all present,—all except Sophia Mansfeld: her whole countenance became suddenly illuminated; she started up, rushed forwards, threw herself at the feet of Laniska, and exclaimed, "Save me! you can save me! you have courage; and you are a powerful lord, and you can speak to the king. Save me from this detested marriage!"

The party of gentlemen who had been in the next chamber now entered the room, curious to know what had drawn thither such a crowd of workmen. On seeing them enter, Sophia, recollecting herself, rose, and returned to her work quietly; whilst Laniska, much agitated, seized hold of the Englishman's arm, and hurried out of the manufactory.

"You are right, you are right," cried he, "Frederick is a tyrant! But how can I save his victim?"

"Not by violence, my Augustus; not by violence!" replied a young man of the name of Albert, who followed Laniska, anxious to restrain the impetuosity of his friend's temper, with which he was well acquainted. "By imprudence," said he, "you will but expose yourself to danger; you will save, you will serve no one."

"Tame prudence will neither save nor serve any one, however it may prevent its possessor from exposing himself to danger," retorted Laniska, casting upon Albert a look of contemptuous reproach. "Prudence be your virtue,—courage mine."

"Are they incompatible?" said Albert, calmly.

"I know not," replied Laniska; "but this I know, that I am in no humour to reason that point, or any other, according to all those cursed forms of logic, which, I believe, you love better than any thing else."

"Not better than I love you, as I prove by allowing you to curse them as much and as often as you think proper," replied Albert, with a smile, which could not, however, force one from his angry friend.

"You are right to practise logic and rhetoric," resumed Laniska, "as much and as often as you can, since in your profession you are to make your bread by your tongue and your pen. I am a soldier, or soon to be a soldier, and have other arms and other feelings."

"I will not dispute the superiority of your arms," replied Albert; "I will only beg of you to remember, that mine will be at your service whenever you want or wish for them."

This temperate and friendly reply entirely calmed Laniska. "What would become of Augustus Laniska," said he, giving Albert his hand, "if he had not such a friend as you are? My mother may well say this, as she does ten times a-day; but now take it in your sober manner, what can we do for this poor woman? for something must be done."

After some consideration, Albert and Laniska determined to draw up a petition for Sophia, and to present it to the king, who was known to pay ready and minute attention to every application made to him in writing, even by the meanest of his subjects. The petition was presented, and an answer anxiously expected. Frederick, when at Potzdam, often honoured the Countess Laniska with a visit. She was a woman of considerable information and literature, acquirements not common amongst the Polish or Prussian ladies; and the king distinguished the countess by his approbation, in order to excite some emulation amongst his female subjects. She held a sort of conversazione at her house, which was frequented by all foreigners of distinction, and especially by some of the French literati, who were at this time at Frederick's court.

One evening—it was a few days after Sophia Mansfeld's petition had been presented—the king was at the Countess Laniska's, and the company were conversing upon some literary subject, when Frederick, who had been unusually silent, suddenly turned to the English traveller, who was one of the company, and asked him whether his countryman, Mr. Wedgewood, had not made a beautiful imitation of the Barberini, or Portland Vase?

The Englishman replied, that the imitation was so exquisite, as scarcely to be known by the best judges from the original: and he went on, with much eagerness, to give a description of the vase, that he might afterward, for the honour of his country, repeat some lines written upon the subject by an English poet(3). Frederick was himself a poet, and a judge of poetry; he listened to the lines with attention; and, as soon as the Englishman had finished speaking, he exclaimed, "I will write a description of the Prussian vase myself."

(Footnote 3: Darwin.—See his description of the Barberini vase in the Botanic Garden. We hope our readers will pardon this anachronism.)

"The Prussian Vase!" said the English traveller: "I hope I may have the honour of seeing it before I leave Berlin."

"If you prolong your stay another month, your curiosity will probably be gratified," replied Frederick. "The Prussian Vase is not yet in being; but I have this day determined to offer a reward, that I know will produce a vase worthy of Prussia. Those who have the command of motives, and know their power, have also the command of all that the arts, or what is called a genius for the arts, can produce. The human mind, and human fingers, are much the same in Italy, in England, and in Prussia. Then, why should not we have a Prussian as as well as a Wedgewood's or a Barberini Vase? We shall see. I do not understand mon métier de roi, if I cannot call forth talents where I know them to exist. There is," continued the king, fixing his eyes full upon Laniska, "there is, in my porcelain manufactory at Berlin, a woman of considerable talents, who is extremely anxious to return, along with some lovers of hers, to Saxony. Like all other prisoners of war, she must purchase her liberty from the conqueror; and if she cannot pay her ransom in gold, let her pay it by her talents. I do not give premiums to idleness or obstinacy. The king must be obeyed, whether he knows how to command or not: let all the world, who are able to judge, decide." Frederick, as soon as he had finished this speech, which he pronounced in a peremptory tone, left the room; and Laniska's friend, who perceived that the imprudent words he had uttered in Berlin had reached the king's ear, gave the young man up for lost. To their surprise, however, the king took no further notice of what had happened, but received Laniska the next day at Sans Souci with all his usual kindness. Laniska, who was of an open, generous temper, was touched by this conduct; and, throwing himself at Frederick's feet, he exclaimed:—

"My king! forgive me, if in a moment of indignation I called you a tyrant."

"My friend, you are yet a child, and I let children and fools speak of me as they please," replied Frederick. "When you are an older man, you will judge more wisely, or, at least, you will speak with more discretion within twenty miles of a tyrant's palace. Here is my answer to your Sophia Mansfeld's petition," added he, giving Laniska the paper, which Albert had drawn up; at the bottom of which was written, in the king's own hand, these words:—

"I will permit the artist who shall produce, before this day month, the most beautiful vase of Berlin china, to marry or not to marry, whomsoever he or she shall think proper, and to return to Saxony with all imaginable expedition. If the successful artist choose to remain at Berlin, I will add a reward of 500 crowns. The artist's name shall be inscribed on the vase, which shall be called the Prussian Vase." No sooner had Sophia Mansfeld read these words, than she seemed animated with new life and energy. She was likely to have many competitors; for, the moment the king's intentions were made known in the manufactory, all hands and heads were at work. Some were excited by the hope of regaining their liberty; others stimulated by the mention of 500 crowns; and some were fired with ambition to have their name inscribed on the Prussian Vase. But none had so strong a motive for exertion as Sophia. She was indefatigable. The competitors consulted the persons whom they believed to have the best taste in Berlin and Potzdam. Sophia's designs were shown, as soon as they were sketched, to the Countess Laniska, whose advice was of material use to her.

At length, the day which was to decide her fate arrived. The vases were all ranged, by the king's order, in his gallery of paintings at Sans Souci; and in the evening, when Frederick had finished the business of the day, he went thither to examine them. Laniska and some others were permitted to accompany him: no one spoke, whilst Frederick was comparing the works of the different competitors.

"Let this be the Prussian Vase," said the king. It was Sophia Mansfeld's. Laniska just stayed to show her name, which was written underneath the foot of the vase, and then he hurried away to communicate the happy news to Sophia, who was waiting, with her lover, at the house of the Countess Laniska, in Potzdam, impatient to hear her fate. She heard it with inexpressible joy; and Laniska's generous heart sympathized in her happiness. It was settled that she should the next morning be married to her lover, and return with him to her father and mother in Saxony. The happy couple were just taking leave of the young count and his mother, when they were alarmed by the sound of many voices on the great staircase. Some persons seemed to be disputing with the countess's servants for admittance. Laniska went out to inquire into the cause of the disturbance. The hall was filled with soldiers.

"Are you the young Count Laniska?" said an officer to him, the moment he appeared.

"I am the young Count Laniska," replied he, in a firm tone. "What do you want with me? and why this disturbance in my mother's house at this unseasonable hour?"

"We come here by the king's orders," replied the soldier. "Is not there in this house a woman of the name of Sophia Mansfeld?"

"Yes," replied Laniska: "what do you want with her?"

"She must come with us; and you are our prisoner, count," replied the soldier.

It was in vain to ask for further explanation. The soldiers could give none; they knew nothing, but that their orders were to convey Sophia Mansfeld immediately to Meissen in Saxony, and to lodge Count Laniska in the castle of Spandau, a state prison.

"I must know my crime before I submit to punishment," cried Laniska, in a passionate voice; but he restrained the natural violence of his temper, on seeing his mother appear, and, at her request, yielded himself up a prisoner without resistance, and without a murmur. "I depend on your innocence, my son, and on the justice of the king," said the countess; and she took leave of him without shedding a tear. The next day, even before the king arrived at Potzdam, she went to the palace, determined to wait there till she could see him, that she might hear from his own lips the cause of her son's imprisonment. She waited a considerable time—for, without alighting from horseback, Frederick proceeded to the parade, where he was occupied for some hours; at length he alighted, and the first person he saw, on entering his palace, was the Countess Laniska.

"I am willing to believe, madam," said he, "that you have no share in your son's folly and ingratitude."

"My son is, I hope, incapable of ingratitude, sir," answered the countess, with an air of placid dignity. "I am well aware that he may have been guilty of great imprudence."

"At six o'clock this evening let me see you, madam," replied the king, "at Sans Souci, in the gallery of paintings, and you shall know of what your son is accused."

At the appointed hour she was in the gallery of paintings at Sans Souci. No one was there. She waited quietly for some time, then walked up and down the gallery with extreme impatience and agitation; at last, she heard the king's voice and his step; the door opened, and Frederick appeared. It was an awful moment to the mother of Laniska. She stood in silent expectation.

"I see, madam," said the king, after fixing his penetrating eye for some moments on her countenance, "I see that you are, as I believe you to be, wholly ignorant of your son's folly." As he spoke, Frederick put his hand upon the vase made by Sophia Mansfeld, which was placed on a small stand in the middle of the gallery. The countess, absorbed by her own reflections, had not noticed it.

"You have seen this vase before," said the king; "and you have probably seen the lines which are inscribed on the foot of it."

"Yes," said the countess, "they are my son's writing."

"And they are written by his own hand," said the king.

"They are. The poor Saxon woman who draws so admirably cannot write; and my son wrote the inscription for her."

"The lines are in a high strain of panegyric," said the king; and he laid a severe emphasis on the word panegyric.

"Whatever may be my son's faults," said the countess, "your majesty cannot suspect him of being a base flatterer. Scarcely a month has elapsed since his unguarded openness exposed him to your displeasure. Your majesty's magnanimity, in pardoning his imprudent expressions, convinced him at once of his error in having used them; and, in the fit of enthusiasm with which your kindness upon that occasion inspired him, he, who is by no means a poet by profession, composed the two lines of panegyric which seem to have given your majesty offence, but which I should never have conceived could be the cause of his imprisonment."

"You plead like a mother, madam," said the king; "but you reason like a woman. Have I ever said that your son was imprisoned for having written two lines of flattery? No, madam: I know how to smile both at flattery and satire, when they are undisguised; but there is a degree of baseness which I cannot so easily pardon. Be patient, madam; I will listen to all you can say in your son's defence, when you have read this inscription. But, before you read it, understand that I was upon the point of sending this vase to Paris. I had actually given orders to the man who was packing up that case (pointing to a half-packed case of porcelain) to put up the Prussian Vase as a present for a Prussian bel esprit of your acquaintance. The man showed me the inscription at the bottom of the vase. I read the flattering lines with pleasure, and thought them—as people usually think flattering lines made on themselves—excellent. I was even fool enough immediately to consider how I could reward the author, when my friend, the packer, interrupted the course of my thoughts, by observing, with some exclamation of astonishment, that the blue colour of the vase came off in one spot, where he had been rubbing it. I looked, and saw that part of the inscription at the bottom of the vase had been covered over with blue paint. At first sight, I read the words, 'On the character of Frederick the Great;' the blue paint had concealed the next word, which is now, madam, sufficiently legible." The word to which the king pointed was—tyrant. "Those flattering lines, madam, you comprehend, were written—'On the character of Frederick, the great tyrant.'

"I shall spare you, madam, all the reflections I have made on this occasion. Tyrant as I am, I shall not punish the innocent mother for the follies of her son. I shall be at your house, along with the rest of your friends, on Tuesday evening."

The unhappy mother of Laniska withdrew from the presence of the king, without attempting any reply. Her son's conduct admitted, she thought, of no apology, if it were really true that he had written the words to which his name was signed. Of this she doubted; but her consternation was at first so great, that she had not the power to think. A general belief remained in her mind of her son's innocence; but then a number of his imprudent words and actions came across her memory; the inscription was, apparently, in his own hand-writing. The conversation which had passed in the porcelain manufactory at Berlin corroborated the idea expressed in this inscription. The countess, on her return home, related the circumstances, with as much composure as she could, to Albert, who was waiting to hear the result of her interview with the king. Albert heard her relation with astonishment; he could not believe in his friend's guilt, though he saw no means of proving his innocence. He did not, however, waste his time in idle conjectures, or more idle lamentations: he went immediately to the man who was employed to pack up the vase; and, after questioning him with great care, he went to Berlin to the porcelain manufactory, and inquired whether any persons were present when Laniska wrote the inscription for Sophia Mansfeld. After Albert had collected all the information that could be obtained, his persuasion of Laniska's innocence was confirmed.

On Tuesday Frederick had promised to come to the countess's conversazione. The company, previous to his majesty's arrival, were all assembled round the sofa, on which she was seated, and they were eagerly talking over Laniska's affair. "What a blessing it is," cried the English traveller, "to live in a country where no man can be imprisoned without knowing of what he is accused! What a blessing it is to live under a government where no man can be condemned without trial, and where his trial must be carried on in open day, in the face of his country, his peers, his equals!"—The Englishman was in the midst of a warm eulogium upon the British mode of trial by jury, when Frederick entered the room, as it was his custom, without being announced: and the company were so intently listening to our traveller, they did not perceive that the king was one of his auditors. "Would to Heaven," cried the Countess Laniska, when the Englishman paused—"would to Heaven my son could have the advantage of such a trial!"

"And would to Heaven," exclaimed Albert, "that I might plead his cause!"

"On one condition," said Frederick; and, at the sound of his voice, every one started—"on one condition, young man, your prayer shall be granted. You shall plead your friend's cause, upon condition that, if you do not convince his judges of his innocence, you shall share his punishment. His punishment will be a twelvemonth's imprisonment in the castle of Spandau; and yours the same, if you fail to establish your cause and his. Next to the folly of being imprudent ourselves, that of choosing imprudent friends is the most dangerous. Laniska shall be tried by his equals; and, since twelve is the golden, harmonic, divine number, for which justice has a blind predilection, let him have twelve judges, and call them, if you please, a jury. But I will name my counsel, and you counsel for Laniska. You know the conditions—do you accept of them?"

"Willingly, sire!" cried Albert, joyfully. "You will permit me to have access to the prisoner in the castle of Spandau?"

"That is a new condition; but I grant it. The governor shall have orders to admit you to see and converse with his prisoner for two hours; but if, after that conversation, your opinion of your friend should change, you will not blame me if I hold you to your word."

Albert declared that he desired no more: and the Countess Laniska, and all who were present, joined in praising Frederick's clemency and Albert's generosity. The imprisonment of Laniska had been much talked of, not only in public companies at Potzdam and at Berlin, but, what affected Frederick much more nearly, it had become the subject of conversation amongst the literati in his own palace at Sans Souci. An English traveller, of some reputation in the literary world, also knew the circumstances, and was interested in the fate of the young count. Frederick seems to have had a strong desire to be represented in an amiable point of view by writers who, he believed, could transmit his fame to posterity. Careless of what might be said of him, he was anxious that nothing should be printed derogatory to his reputation. Whether the desire to give to foreigners a striking proof of his magnanimity, or whether his regard for the young count, and his friendship for his mother, were his motives in granting to Laniska this trial by jury, cannot and need not be determined. Unmixed virtue is not to be expected from kings more than from common men.

After his visit to the prisoner in the castle of Spandau, Albert felt no inclination to recede from the agreement into which he had entered; but Laniska was much alarmed when he was told of what had passed. "Oh, my generous friend!" exclaimed the young count, "why did you accept of the conditions offered to you by the king? You may—I am sure you do—believe in my innocence; but you will never be able to prove it. You will soon be involved in my disgrace."

"I shall think it no disgrace," replied Albert, "to be the fellow-prisoner of an innocent friend."

"Do not you remember," said Laniska, "that, as we were returning from Berlin, after my unlucky visit to the porcelain manufactory, you promised me, that whenever I should be in want of your weapons, they should be at my service? I little thought that I should so soon be in such need of them. Farewell—I pray for their success."

On the day appointed for the trial of Laniska, crowds of people of all ranks flocked to hear the proceedings. A spacious building in Potzdam, intended for a barrack, was, upon this occasion, converted into a hall of justice; a temporary gallery was erected for the accommodation of the audience; and a platform was raised in the centre of the hall, where the judge's chair was placed: on the right hand of his chair a space was railed in for the reception of the twelve young gentlemen, who were to act as jurors; on the left another space was railed in for spectators. In the front there was a large table, on each side of which were benches for the counsel and witnesses: those for the crown on the right hand; those for the prisoner on the left. Every thing had, by the king's orders, been prepared in this manner, according to the English custom.

The Countess Laniska now entered the court, with a few friends, who had not yet forsaken her. They took their seats at the lower end of the gallery; and as every eye turned upon the mother, who waited to hear the trial of her son, an awful silence prevailed. This lasted but for a few moments; it was succeeded by a general whispering amongst the crowds, both in the hall and in the gallery. Each individual gave his opinion concerning the event of the trial: some declared that the circumstances which must appear against Laniska were so strong, that it was madness in Albert to undertake his defence; others expressed great admiration of Albert's intrepid confidence in himself and his friend. Many studied the countenance of the king, to discover what his wishes might be; and a thousand idle conjectures were formed from his most insignificant movements.

At length, the temporary judge having taken his seat, twelve young gentlemen were chosen, from the most respectable families in Potzdam, to act as jurors. The prisoner was summoned to answer to the charges brought against him, in the name of Frederick the Second, king of Prussia. Laniska appeared, guarded by two officers: he walked up to the steps of the platform with an air of dignity, which seemed expressive of conscious innocence; but his countenance betrayed involuntary marks of emotion, too strong for him to command, when, on raising his eyes, he beheld his friend Albert, who stood full in his view. Albert maintained an immovable composure of countenance. The prisoner was now asked whether he had any objections to make to any of the twelve persons who had been selected to judge his cause. He made none. They proceeded to take an oath, "that, in their decision, they would suffer no motives to influence them but a sense of truth and justice." The judge then rose, and addressing himself to the jury, said:—

"Gentlemen,

"You are here, by the king's order, to form your opinions concerning the guilt or innocence of the prisoner, commonly known by the name of Count Augustus Laniska. You will learn the nature and circumstances of the accusation against him from Mr. Warendorff, the gentleman on my right hand, who in this cause has the honour of being counsel for his majesty. You will hear from the gentleman on my left, Albert Altenburg, all that can be said in defence of the prisoner, for whom he voluntarily offers himself as counsel. After having listened to the arguments that may be adduced, and to the witnesses that shall be examined on each side, you are, gentlemen, according to the tenour of the oath which has just been administered to you, to decide, without regard to any consideration but truth and justice. Your opinion is to be delivered to me by the eldest amongst you, and it is to be expressed in one or other of these phrases—guilty or not guilty.

"When I shall have heard your decision, I am, in his majesty's name, to pronounce sentence accordingly. If the prisoner be judged by you not guilty, I am to announce to him that he is thenceforward at liberty, and that no stain affixes to his honour from the accusation that has been preferred against him, or from his late imprisonment, or from this public trial. If, on the contrary, your judgment shall be, that the prisoner is guilty, I am to remand him to the castle of Spandau, where he is to remain confined for twelve months from this day. To the same punishment I am also to condemn Albert Altenburg, if he fail to establish in your minds the innocence of the Count Laniska. It is upon this condition that he is permitted to plead the cause of his friend.

"Gentlemen, you are called upon to give impartial attention in this cause, by your duty to your king and to your country."

As soon as the judge, after making this short address to the jury, had seated himself, Mr. Warendorff, counsel for the crown, rose, and spoke in the following manner:—

"My lord, and gentlemen of the jury,

"It is with inexpressible concern that I find myself called upon to plead in this cause. To be the accuser of any man is an invidious task: to be the accuser of such a man as I once thought—as you perhaps still think—the young Count Laniska must, to a person of generous feelings, be in a high degree difficult and distressing. I do not pretend to more generosity or delicacy of sentiment than others; but I beg any of you, gentlemen, to imagine yourselves for a moment in my place, and to conceive what must be my sensations as a man, and as an advocate. I am not ignorant how popular the name of Augustus Laniska is, both in Berlin and Potzdam. I am not ignorant that the young count has been in the habit of living amongst you, gentlemen, on terms of familiarity, friendship, and confidence; nor can I doubt that the graceful, manly manner, and open deportment, for which he is so eminently distinguished, must have strongly prepossessed you in his favour. I am not ignorant that I have to plead against him before his friends, in the presence of his mother—a mother respected even in a higher degree than her son is beloved; respected for her feminine virtues—for her more than feminine endowments; who, had she no other claim upon your hearts, must, by the unfortunate situation in which she now appears, command your sympathy.

"You must all of you feel, likewise, strongly prepossessed in favour of that noble-minded youth, who has undertaken to defend the prisoner's cause, at the hazard of sharing his punishment. I respect the general character of Albert Altenburg; I admire his abilities; I applaud him, for standing forward in defence of his friend; I pity him, because he has a friend, for whom, I fear, even he will find it impossible to establish any plausible defence. But the idea that he is acting handsomely, and that he has the sympathy of numbers in his favour, will doubtless support the young advocate in his arduous task. He appears in this court in the striking character of counsel, disinterested counsel, for his friend.

"Gentlemen, I also appear in this court as counsel, disinterested counsel for a friend. Yes, gentlemen, I am permitted to call Frederick the Great my friend. He is not, as other great monarchs have been, ambitious to raise himself above the sphere of humanity; he does not desire to be addressed in the fulsome strains either of courtly or of poetical adulation: he wishes not to be worshipped as a god, but to be respected as a man(4). It is his desire to have friends that shall be faithful, or subjects that shall be obedient. Happy his obedient subjects—they are secure of his protection: happy, thrice happy, his faithful friends—they are honoured with his favour and his confidence. It was in the power of the prisoner now before you to have been in this enviable class. You all of you know that the Countess

Laniska, his mother, has for years been honoured by the friendship of her sovereign; even the conduct of her son has not been able to shake his confidence in her. A Pole by birth, Augustus Laniska was educated amongst the first of the Prussian nobility, at the military academy at Potzdam, that nursery of heroes. From such an education—from the son of such a mother—honourable sentiments and honourable conduct were to be expected. Most confidently were they expected by his king, who distinguished the young count, as you all know, even in his boyish days. The count is said to be of a temper naturally impetuous: the errors into which such a temper too publicly betrayed him were pardoned by the indulgence of his king. I am compelled to recall one recent instance of the truth of these assertions, as it is immediately connected with the present cause."

(Footnote 4: AEschylus.)

Here Mr. Warendorff related all that had passed at the porcelain manufactory at Berlin, and the king's subsequent conduct towards Count Laniska. On the magnanimity of his majesty, the eloquent counsel expatiated for a considerable time; but the applauses with which this part of his oration was received by a party in the gallery, who were seated near the king, were so loud, as almost to drown the voice of the orator, and effectually to distract the attention of those employed to take down his words. When he could again be heard distinctly, he resumed as follows:

"I am not surprised at these testimonies of admiration which burst from the warm hearts of his majesty's subjects; I am only surprised that a heart could be found in his dominions on whom such magnanimity could make no impression. I am shocked, I am grieved, when I find such a heart in the person of Count Laniska. Can it be believed that, in the course of one short month after this generous pardon, that young nobleman proved himself the basest of traitors—a traitor to the king, who was his friend and benefactor? Daring no longer openly to attack, he attempted secretly to wound the fame of his sovereign. You all of you know what a degree of liberty, even licence, Frederick the Great permits to that species of satirical wit with which the populace delight to ridicule their rulers. At this instant there are various anonymous pasquinades on the garden-gates at Sans Souci, which would have provoked the resentment—the fatal resentment—of any other monarch upon earth. It cannot be doubted that the authors of these things could easily be discovered, if the king condescended to make any inquiries concerning them: it cannot be doubted that the king has power to punish the offenders: yet they remain untouched, perhaps unknown. Our sovereign is not capable of feeling the petty emotions of vulgar spleen or resentment; but he could not be insensible to the treacherous ingratitude of one, whom he imagined to have been attached to him by every tie of kindness and of duty. That the Count Laniska should choose the instant when the king was showing him unusual favour, to make that favour an instrument of his base malice, is scarcely credible. Yet, Prussians, incredible as it sounds to us, it is true. Here are my proofs: here are my witnesses."

Mr. Warendorff, at this instant, uncovered the Prussian Vase, and then pointed to a Jew, and to the master of the porcelain manufactory, who stood beside him, ready to give their evidence. We omit that part of Mr. Warendorff's speech which contained the facts that have been already related. The Prussian Vase was handed to the jury: the verses in praise of Frederick the Great were read, and the word tyrant was seen, afterward, with the utmost surprise. In the midst of the general indignation, Mr. Warendorff called upon the Jew to come forward and give his evidence. This Jew was an old man, and there was something remarkable in his looks. His head was still; his neck was stiff; but his eyes moved with incessant celerity from side to side, and he seemed uneasy at not being able to see what was passing behind him: there was a certain firmness in his attitude, but his voice trembled when he attempted to speak. All these circumstances prepossessed Laniska's friends against the Jew the moment he appeared;

and it was justly observed, that his having the misfortune to be a Jew was sufficient to prejudice many of the populace against him, even before a word he uttered reached their ears. But impartial spectators judged that the poor man was only terrified at being called upon to speak in so large an assembly. Solomon (for that was the name of the Jew), after having taken an oath upon the Talmud that he would speak nothing but the truth, made the following answers to the questions put to him by Mr. Warendorff:—

Mr. Warendorff.—"Did you ever see this vase before?"

Solomon.—"Yes."

Mr. Warendorff.—"Where? when? Tell all you know about it to the gentlemen of the jury."

Solomon.—"The first time I saw that vase was in the gallery of paintings, at the king's palace of Sans Souci; to the best of my recollection, it was on the night of the first day of the month, about ten o'clock, or, perhaps, it might be eleven: I wish to be exact; but I cannot be certain as to the hour precisely."

Mr. Warendorff.—"The exact hour is not of any consequence: proceed. Tell us how you came to see this vase. Take your time to speak. We are in no hurry: the truth will appear sooner or later."

Solomon.—"His majesty himself put the vase into my hands, and commanded me to pack it up, with some other china, which he was going to send as a present to a gentleman at Paris. I am something of a judge of china myself, being used to selling small pieces of it up and down the town and country. So I was struck with the first sight of this beautiful vase; I looked at it very carefully, and wiped away, with my handkerchief, the dust which had settled on the white figures: here is the very handkerchief. I wiped the vase all over; but, when I came to rub the bottom, I stopped to read the verses on the character of Frederick the Great; and having read these, I rubbed the white letters quite clean: the ground on which they were written was blue. I found that some of the blue colour came off upon my handkerchief, which surprised me a good deal. Upon examining further, I perceived that the colour came off only in one spot, of about an inch long, and half an inch broad. The king was at this time standing with his back to me, looking at a new picture which had just been hung up in the gallery; but hearing me make an exclamation ('Father Abraham!' I believe it was that I said), his majesty turned round. 'What is the matter with you, Solomon? You look wondrous wise,' his majesty was pleased to say. 'Why do you call on Father Abraham at this time of day? Do you expect that he will help you to pack up that china—hey, Solomon, my friend?' I had no power to answer this question, for by this time, to my utter astonishment, I had discovered that, on the spot where I had rubbed off the blue paint, there was a word written—the word was tyrant. 'On the character of Frederick, the great tyrant!' Said I to myself— 'what can this mean?' The king snatched the vase from my hands, read what I had read, saw the paint which had been rubbed off upon my handkerchief, and without saying one word left the gallery. This is all I know about the matter."

The Jew bowed to the court, and Mr. Warendorff told him that, having closed his evidence, he might depart. But Albert rose to desire that the judge would order him to remain in court, as he purposed to examine, or, according to the English term, to cross-examine him further, at a proper time. The judge ordered the Jew to remain in court. The next witness called, on the part of the crown, was the master of the porcelain manufactory of Berlin; to whom Mr. Warendorff put the following questions:—

Q.—"Have you seen the verses which are inscribed on the foot of this vase?"

Answer.—"Yes, I have."

Q.—"Do you recollect what words are written over the verses?"

Answer.—"I do: the words are—'On the character of Frederick, the great tyrant.'"

Q.—"Do you know by whom those words and these verses were written?"

Answer.—"I believe that they were written by Count Augustus Laniska."

Q.—"How do you know? or why do you believe it?"

Answer.—"I was present when Sophia Mansfeld, the woman by whom the vase was designed, told the count that she did not know how to write, and that she would be obliged to him if he would write the inscription himself on it. The vase at this time had not been put into the furnace. It was in what we call biscuit. The Count Laniska took a proper tool, and said that he would write the inscription as she desired. I saw him writing on the bottom of the vase for some minutes. I heard him afterward call to one of the workmen, and desire that he would put the vase into the furnace: the workman accordingly carried it into the next room to the furnace, as I believe."

Q.—"Did you see the inscription on the vase after it was taken out of the furnace? and was the word 'tyrant' then on it?"

Answer.—"I did not see the vase immediately upon its being taken out of the furnace; but I saw it about an hour afterward. At that time I read the inscription: the word 'tyrant' was not then visible on the vase; the place where it now appears was blue. I carried it myself, along with some others, to the king's palace at Sans Souci. The night of the first day of this month his majesty sent for me, and showed me the word tyrant on the vase: I had never seen it there till then. It could not have been written after the china was baked: it must have been written whilst the biscuit was soft; and it must have been covered over with the blue paint after the vase was taken out of the furnace. I believe the word was written by Count Laniska, because I saw nobody else write upon the vase but him; because the word exactly resembles the handwriting of the rest of the inscription; and because I, upon a former occasion, heard the count make use of that very word in speaking of Frederick the Great."

Here the master of the porcelain manufactory finished speaking, and was going, with Mr. Warendorff's permission, to retire; but Albert signified his intention to cross-examine him also, and the judge commanded that he should remain in court. The two next witnesses who were produced and examined were the workman who carried the vase to the furnace, and the man whose business it was to put the biscuit into the furnace. Neither of these witnesses could write or read. The workman deposed, that he carried the Prussian Vase, as he was desired, to the furnace; that no one touched it on the way thither. The man whose business it was to put the biscuit into the furnace swore that he put it along with several other vases into the furnace; that he attended the fire, and that no one touched any of them till they were baked and taken out by him. Here the evidence for the prosecution closed. Mr. Warendorff observed, that he should forbear to expatiate further upon the conduct of the prisoner; that he had been ordered by his sovereign to speak of him with all possible moderation; that he earnestly hoped the defence that should be made for Count Laniska might be satisfactory; and that the mode of trial which had been granted to him by the king was a sufficient proof of the clemency of his majesty, and of his earnest desire to allow the prisoner every possible means of re-establishing his character in the eyes of the public. Albert now rose. The Count Laniska, who had appeared unmoved during Mr. Warendorff's oration, changed countenance the moment Albert rose in his defence; the Countess Laniska leaned forward over the rails of the gallery in breathless anxiety: there was no sound heard in the whole gallery, except the jingling of the chain of the king's sword, with which he was playing.

"I shall not attempt, gentlemen," said Albert, "to move your sympathy by a pathetic description of my own feelings as a man, and as an advocate. Whatever mine may be, it is my wish and my duty to repress them. I have need of that calm possession of my understanding, which will be necessary to convince yours of the innocence of my friend. To convince is my object. If it were in my power, I should, upon the present occasion, disdain to persuade. I should think it equally incompatible with my own honour and that of the Count Laniska. With these sentiments, I refrain, Prussians, from all eulogium upon the magnanimity of your king. Praises from a traitor, or from the advocate of a traitor, must be unworthy of a great monarch, or of a generous people. If the prisoner before you shall be proved to be no traitor, he will doubtless have opportunities of expressing by actions, better than I can by words, his gratitude to his sovereign, for having allowed him this public trial by his equals—men who are able to discern and to assert the truth. It cannot have escaped their observation, that no positive evidence whatever has yet been produced against the prisoner. No one has yet been heard to swear that he saw Count Laniska write the word tyrant upon this vase. The first witness, Solomon the Jew, has informed us of what our senses could not leave us room to doubt, that the word is actually engraved upon the porcelain: further, he has told us that it was covered over with blue paint, which he rubbed off with his handkerchief. All this may be true; but the wisdom of Solomon, united to that of Baron Warendorff, has failed to point out to us any certain connexion between this blue paint, this handkerchief, and the supposed guilt of the Count Laniska. The master of the porcelain manufactory came next, and I apprehended that, as being a more respectable witness than the Jew, it was reserved for him to supply this link in the chain of evidence. But this respectable witness simply swore, that he heard a woman say she could not write or read; that she asked Count Laniska to write an inscription upon a vase for her; that, in consequence of this request, the count wrote something upon the vase, he does not pretend to know what; but he believes that the word tyrant must have been one of the words then written by the count, because he saw no one else write on the vase; because the hand-writing of that word resembles the rest of the inscription; and because the count, in his hearing, had, upon a former occasion, made use of the same expression in speaking of the king. I recapitulate this evidence, to show that it is in no part positive: that it all rests upon circumstances. In order to demonstrate to you that the word in question could not have been written by any person but Laniska, two witnesses are produced—the workman who carried the vase to the furnace, and he who put it into the fire. The one has positively sworn that no person touched the vase on the way to the furnace. The other as positively swears that no one meddled with the vase after it was put into the furnace.

"It is granted that the word could not have been engraved after the biscuit was baked. The witness, however, has not sworn, or asserted, that there was no interval of time between his receiving the vase and his putting it into the fire. What became of it during this interval? How long did it last? Will the witness swear that no one touched it during this interval?

"These are questions which I shall put to him presently. I hope I have established my first assertion, that you have no positive evidence of the prisoner's guilt.

"You well know, gentlemen, that where positive evidence of any supposed fact cannot be produced, our judgments must be decided by the balance of probabilities; and it is for this reason that the study of probabilities, and the power of comparing them, has, in a late celebrated essay, been called the Science of Judges.(5) To you, judges of my friend, all the probabilities of his supposed guilt have been stated. Weigh and compare them with those which I shall produce in favour of his innocence. His education, his character, his understanding, are all in his favour. The Count Laniska must be much below the common standard of human virtue and capacity, if, without any assignable motive, he could have committed an action at once so base and so absurd as this of which he is accused. His temper is naturally or habitually open and impetuous, even to extreme imprudence. An instance of this imprudence, and of the manner in which it was pardoned by the king, has been stated to you. Is it probable that the same man should be both ingenuous and mean? Is it probable that the generosity with which he was treated made no impression upon his heart? His heart must, upon this supposition, be selfish and unfeeling. Look up, gentlemen, towards that gallery—look at that anxious mother! those eager friends! Could Laniska's fate excite such anxiety, if he were selfish and unfeeling? Impossible! But, suppose him destitute of every generous sentiment, you cannot imagine Count Laniska to be a fool. You have been lately reminded that he was early distinguished for his abilities by a monarch, whose penetration we cannot doubt. He was high in the favour of his sovereign: just entering upon life—a military life; his hopes of distinction resting entirely upon the good opinion of his general and his king: all these fair expectations he sacrifices—for what? for the pleasure—but it could be no pleasure—for the folly of writing a single word. Unless the Count Laniska be supposed to have been possessed with an insane desire of writing the word tyrant, how can we account for his writing it upon this vase? Did he wish to convey to France the idea, that Frederick the Great is a tyrant? A man of common sense could surely have found, at least, safer methods of doing so than by engraving it as his opinion upon a vase which he knew was to pass through the hands of the sovereign whom he purposed thus treacherously to insult. The extreme improbability that any man in the situation, with the character, habits, and capacity of Count Laniska, should have acted in this manner amounts, in my judgment, almost to a moral impossibility. I knew nothing more, gentlemen, of this cause, when I first offered to defend Laniska at the hazard of my liberty: it was not merely from the enthusiasm of friendship that I made this offer; it was from the sober conviction of my understanding, founded upon the accurate calculation of moral probabilities.

(Footnote 5: Voltaire—*Essai sur les Probabilités en fait de Justice.*)

"It has been my good fortune, gentlemen, in the course of the inquiries which I have since made, to obtain further confirmation of my opinion. Without attempting any of that species of oratory which may be necessary to cover falsehood, but which would encumber instead of adorning truth, I shall now, in the simplest manner in my power, lay the evidence before the court."

The first witness Albert called was the workman who carried the vase to the man at the furnace. Upon his cross-examination, he said that he did not deliver the vase into the hands of the man at the furnace, but that he put it, along with several other pieces, upon a tray, on a table, which stood near the furnace.

Albert.—"You are certain that you put it upon a tray?"

Witness.—"Quite certain."

Albert.—"What reason have you for remembering that circumstance particularly?"

Witness.—"I remember it, because I at first set this vase upon the ledge of the tray, and it was nearly falling. I was frightened at that accident, which makes me particularly remember the thing. I made room upon the tray for the vase, and left it quite safe upon the tray: I am positive of it."

Albert.—"That is all I want with you, my good friend."

The next witness called was the man whose business it was to put the vases into the furnace.

Albert.—"Did you see the witness who was last examined put this vase upon a tray when he left it under your care?"

Witness.—"I did."

Albert.—"You are certain that he put it upon the tray? What reason have you to remember that circumstance particularly?"

Witness.—"I remember it, because I heard the witness cry out, 'There, William, I had like to have thrown down this cursed vase; but, look you here, I've left it quite safe upon the tray.' Upon this, I turned and looked, and saw that vase standing upon the tray, safe, with some others."

Albert.—"Do you recollect any thing else that passed?"

Witness.—"Only that the witness told me I must put it—the vase, I mean—into the furnace directly; and I answered to that, 'All in good time; the furnace is not ready yet; it will go in along with the rest.'"

Albert.—"Then you did not put it into the furnace immediately after it was left with you?"

Witness.—"No, I did not—but that was not my fault—I could not; the furnace was not hot enough."

Albert.—"How long do you think it was, from the time it was left upon the tray, till you put it into the furnace?"

Witness.—"I don't know—I can't be positive: it might be a quarter of an hour, or twenty minutes; or it might be half an hour. I cannot be positive, sir; I cannot be positive."

Albert.—"You need not be positive. Nobody wants you to be positive. Nobody wants to entrap you, my good friend. During this quarter of an hour, or twenty minutes, or half an hour, that you speak of, did you ever lose sight of this vase?"

Witness.—"To be sure I did. I did not stand watching it all the while. Why should I? It was safe enough."

Albert.—"Do you recollect where you found the vase when you took it to put it into the furnace?"

Witness.—"Yes: it was standing as it might be here, in the middle of the table."

Albert.—"Do you recollect whether it was standing upon the tray or not?"

Witness.—"It was not upon the tray, as I recollect: no, I'm sure it was not, for I carried to the furnace first the tray and all that was on it, and then I remember, I came back for this, which was standing, as I said before, as it might be here, in the middle of the table."

Albert.—"Was any body, except yourself, at the furnace, or in the room, from the time that this vase was brought to you, till you put it into the furnace?"

Witness.—"Not as I remember. It was our dinner-time. All the men, except myself, were gone to dinner: I stayed to mind the furnace."

Albert.—"It was you, then, that took this vase off the tray, was it?"

Witness.—"No, it was not. I never took it off the tray. I told you it was not upon the tray with the others; I told you it was upon the table, as it might be here."

Albert.—"Yes, when you were going to put it into the furnace, you said that you saw it standing in the middle of the table; but you recollect that you saw the workman who brought it put it upon the tray. You told us you remembered that circumstance perfectly."

Witness.—"Yes, so I do."

Albert.—"The vase could not have got off the tray of itself. You did not take it off. How came it off, do you think?"

Witness.—"I don't know. I can't tell. Somebody, to be sure, must have taken it off. I was minding the furnace. My back was to the door. I don't recollect seeing any body come in; but many might have come in and out, without my heeding them."

Albert.—"Take your own time, my good friend. Recollect yourself; perhaps you may remember."

Witness.—"Oh, yes, now you put me upon recollecting, I do remember that Solomon the Jew came in, and asked me where Sophia Mansfeld was; and it certainly must have been he who took the vase off the tray; for now I recollect, as I looked round once from the furnace, I saw him with it in his hand; he was looking at the bottom of it, as I remember: he said, here are some fine verses, or some such thing; but I was minding the furnace. That's all I know about the matter."

Albert.—"That is enough."

The next witness who came forward was the husband of Sophia Mansfeld.—He deposed, that on the 29th of April, the day on which the Prussian Vase was finished, as stated by the former evidence, and sent to be put into the furnace, he met Sophia Mansfeld in the street: she was going home to dinner. He asked to see the vase: she said that it was, she believed, put into the furnace, and that he could not then see it; that she was sorry he had not come sooner, for that he could have written the inscription on it for her, and that would have spared her the shame of telling Count Laniska that she could not read or write. She added, that the count had written all that was wanting for her. The witness, being impatient to see the vase, went as fast as he could to the manufactory, in hopes of getting a sight of it before it was put into the furnace. He met Solomon the Jew at the door of the manufactory, who told him that he was too late, that all the vases were in the furnace; he had just seen them put in. The Jew, as the witness now recollects, though it did not strike him at the time, was eager to prevent him from going into the furnace-room. Solomon took him by the arm, and walked with him up the street, talking to him of some money which he was to remit to Meissen, to Sophia Mansfeld's father and mother.

Albert asked the witness on whose account this money was to be remitted by the Jew to Meissen.

Witness.—"The money was to be remitted on Sophia Mansfeld's account."

Albert.—"Did she borrow it from the Jew?"

Witness.—"No; the Jew owed it to her for work done by her. She had the art of painting on glass. She had painted some glasses for a large magic lantern, and several small pictures on glass. She did these things at the hours when she was not obliged to be at the manufactory. She rose very early in the morning and worked hard. She sold her work to the Jew upon condition that he would remit the price agreed upon to her father and mother, who were old, and depended on her for support."

Albert.—"Was the money punctually remitted to her father and mother by the Jew?"

Witness.—"Not a farthing of it was remitted by him, as Sophia discovered since her return to Meissen."

Albert.—"Did you ever hear this Jew say any thing about Sophia Mansfeld's returning to Saxony?"

Witness.—"Yes; I once heard the Jew say that he hoped she never would leave Berlin, because she was of great use to him. He advised me to settle in Berlin. This passed about six weeks ago. About a week before the prize was decided by the king, I met the Jew, and told him Sophia had good hopes of getting back to Saxony. He looked very much vexed, and said, 'She is not sure of that.'"

Albert.—"Did you ever hear this Jew speak of Count Laniska?"

Witness.—"Yes, about two months ago I saw him in the street when I was speaking to Solomon, and I asked the Jew who he was. He answered, 'He is the Count Laniska—a man that I hate, and on whom I will be revenged some time or other.' I asked why he hated the count. The Jew replied, 'Because the Christian dog has made the corps of Jews his laughing-stock. This day, when my son was going through his manual exercise before the king, Count Laniska was holding his sides with laughter. I'll be revenged upon him some time or other.'"

Albert.—"I have no occasion, sir, to trouble you with any farther questions."

The next witness who appeared was a druggist of Berlin. He deposed, that, on the 30th of April, Solomon the Jew came to his shop and asked for blue paints; that, after trying the colours very carefully upon the back of a letter, which he took out of his pocket, he bought a small quantity of a shade of blue, which the witness produced in court.

Albert ordered that the paint should be handed to the gentlemen of the jury, that they might compare it with the blue ground of the Prussian Vase. With this it was found, upon comparison, to match exactly.

Albert to the druggist.—"Do you know what became of the paper upon which you say the Jew tried your colours?"

Witness.—"Yes; here it is. I found it under the counter, after the Jew went away, and I kept it to return to him, as I saw there was an account on the other side of the paper, which I imagined he might want. He never happened to call at my shop afterwards, and I forgot that I had such a paper, till you, sir, called upon me about a week ago, to make inquiry on this subject. You desired me to keep the paper carefully, and not to let any one know that it was in my possession, till the day on which the trial of Count Laniska was to come on. I have complied with your request, and here is the paper."

The paper was handed to the jury; and one of the shades of blue exactly matched that of the ground of the Prussian Vase. Albert now called upon the Jew to produce, once more, the handkerchief with which he had rubbed off the paint. The chain of evidence was now complete, for the blue on the handkerchief was precisely the same as the colours on the paper and on the vase. After the jury had satisfied themselves of this resemblance, Albert begged that they would read what was written upon the paper. The first thing that struck their eyes was the word tyrant frequently repeated, as if by some one who had been practising to write different hands. One of these words was an exact resemblance of the word tyrant on the Prussian Vase; and Albert pointed out a circumstance, which had till now escaped attention, that the letter r, in this word, was made differently from all the ars in the rest of the inscription. The writing of the Count Laniska had, in every other respect, been successfully imitated.

After Albert had shown these things to the jury, he here closed the evidence in favour of the prisoner, observing, that the length of time which the trial had lasted seemed to have somewhat fatigued both the judge and jury; and, knowing that it was now their usual hour of dinner, he prudently forbore to make a long speech upon the evidence which had been laid before them in favour of his friend: he left it to their own understandings to determine the balance of probabilities between the honour of Count Laniska and the honesty of Solomon the Jew.

The judge, in a manner which would have done honour even to the English bench, summed up the evidence on both sides, and gave a distinct and impressive charge to the jury, who, without leaving the court, gave a verdict in favour of the prisoner. Loud acclamations filled the hall. In the midst of these acclamations, the word—"Silence!" was pronounced by that voice which never failed to command instantaneous obedience in Prussia. All eyes turned upon the monarch.

"This court is now dissolved," said his majesty. "My judgment confirms the verdict of the jury. Count Laniska, I took your sword from you too hastily. Accept of mine in its stead." And as he pronounced these words, Frederick ungirded his sword, and presented it to the young count. "As for you, sir," continued the king, addressing himself to Albert, "you want no sword for the defence of your friends. Your arms are superior to ours. Let me engage them in my service; and, trust me, I shall not leave them long unemployed, or unrewarded."

There was but one person present to whom this speech seemed to give no satisfaction. This person was Solomon the Jew, who stood apart, waiting in black silence to learn his own fate. He was sentenced, not to a year's imprisonment in the castle of Spandau, but to sweep the streets of Potzdam (including the court in front of Count Laniska's palace) for a twelvemonth.

After having heard this sentence, which was universally approved of, the spectators began to retire.

The king dined—it is always important to know where great men dine—Frederick the Great dined this day at the Countess Laniska's, in company with her son, his friend Albert, and the English traveller. After dinner, the king withdrew to attend parade; and it was observed that he wore the Count Laniska's sword.

"You will allow," said the countess to the English traveller, "that our king is a great man; for none but great men can bear to acknowledge that they have been mistaken."

"You will allow, madam," replied the Englishman, "that it was our English trial by jury which convinced the king of his mistake."

"And you applaud him for granting that trial," said Albert.

"To a certain degree I do," said the Englishman, from whom it was difficult to extort praise of a despotic king—"to a certain degree, I do; but you will observe, that this trial by jury, which is a matter of favour to you Prussians, is a matter of right to us Englishmen. Much as I admire your king of Prussia, I admire our English constitution more."

THE GOOD AUNT

Charles Howard was left an orphan when he was very young. His father had dissipated a large fortune, and lost his life in a duel, about some debt of honour, which had been contracted at the gaming-table. Without fortune and without friends, this poor boy would probably have lived and died in wretchedness, but for the humanity of his good aunt, Mrs. Frances Howard. This lady possessed a considerable fortune, which, in the opinion of some of her acquaintance, was her highest merit: others respected her as the branch of an ancient family: some courted her acquaintance because she was visited by the best company in town: and many were ambitious of being introduced to her, because they were sure of meeting at her house several of those distinguished literary characters who throw a radiance upon all who can contrive to get within the circle of their glories. Some few, some very few of Mrs. Howard's acquaintance, admired her for her real worth, and merited the name of friends.

She was a young and cheerful woman when she first undertook the education of her little nephew. She had the courage to resist the allurements of dissipation, or all that by her sex are usually thought allurements. She had the courage to apply herself seriously to the cultivation of her understanding: she educated herself, that she might be able to fulfil the important duty of educating a child. Hers was not the foolish fondness of a foolish aunt; she loved her nephew, and she wished to educate him, so that her affection might increase, instead of diminishing, as he grew up. By associating early pleasure with reading, little Charles soon became fond of it: he was never forced to read books which he did not understand; his aunt used, when he was very young, to read aloud to him any thing entertaining that she met with; and whenever she perceived by his eye that his attention was not fixed, she stopped. When he was able to read fluently to himself, she selected for him passages from books, which she thought would excite his curiosity to know more; and she was not in a hurry to cram him with knowledge, but rather anxious to prevent his growing appetite for literature from being early satiated. She always encouraged him to talk to her freely about what he read, and to tell her when he did not like any of the books which she gave him. She conversed with him with so much kindness and cheerfulness; she was so quick at perceiving his latent meaning; and she was so gentle and patient when she reasoned with him, that he loved to talk to her better than to any body else; nor could little Charles ever thoroughly enjoy any pleasure without her sympathy.

The conversation of the sensible, well-informed people who visited Mrs. Howard contributed to form her nephew's taste. A child may learn as much from conversation as from books—not so many historic facts, but as much instruction. Greek and Latin were the grand difficulties. Mrs. Howard did not understand Greek and Latin; nor did she, though a woman, set too high or too low a value upon the learned languages. She was convinced that a man might be a great scholar without being a man of sense; she was also persuaded that a man of sense might be a good scholar. She knew that, whatever abilities her nephew might possess, he could not be upon a footing with other men in the world, without possessing that species of knowledge which is universally expected from gentlemen, as an essential proof of their having received a liberal education; nor did she attempt to undervalue the pleasures of classic taste merely because she was not qualified to enjoy them: she was convinced, by the testimony of men of candour and judgment, that a classical taste is a source of real enjoyment, and she wished her nephew's literary pleasures to have as extensive a range as possible.

To instruct her nephew in the learned languages, she engaged a good scholar and a man of sense: his name—for a man is nothing without a name—was Russell(1). Little Charles did not at first relish Latin; he used sometimes to come from his Latin lessons with a very dull, stupified face, which gradually brightened into intelligence, after he had talked for a few minutes with his aunt. Mrs. Howard, though pleased to perceive that he was fond of her, had not the weakness to sacrifice his permanent advantage to her transient gratification. One evening Charles came running up-stairs to his aunt, who was at tea; several people happened to be present. "I have done with Mr. Russell, and my Latin, ma'am, thank goodness—now may I have the elephant and the camel, or the bear and her cubs, that you marked for me last night?"

(Footnote 1: RUSSELL.—This name is chosen for that of a good tutor, because it was the name of Mr. Edgeworth's tutor, at Oxford: Mr. Russell was also tutor to the late Mr. Day. Both by Mr. Day and Mr. Edgeworth he was respected, esteemed, and beloved, in no common degree.)

The company laughed at this speech of Charles: and a silly lady—for even Mrs. Howard could not make all her acquaintance wise—a silly lady whispered to Charles, "I've a notion, if you'd tell the truth, now, that you like the bear and her cubs a great deal better than you do Latin and Mr. Russell."

"I like the bear a great deal better than I do Latin, to be sure," said the boy; "but as for Mr. Russell—why, I think," added he, encouraged by the lady's smiles, "I think I like the bear better than Mr. Russell."

The lady laughed affectedly at this sally.

"I am sure," continued Charles, fancying that every person present was delighted with his wit, "I am sure, at any rate, I like the learned pig fifty times better than Mr. Russell!"

The judicious lady burst into a second fit of laughter. Mrs. Howard looked very grave. Charles broke from the lady's caresses, and going up to his aunt, timidly looking up in her face, said, "Am I a fool?"

"You are but a child," said Mrs. Howard; and, turning away from him, she desired the servant, who waited at tea, to let Mr. Russell know that she desired the honour of his company. Mrs. Holloway—for that was the silly lady's name—at the words, "honour of his company," resumed her gravity, but looked round to see what the rest of the company thought.

"Give me leave, Mr. Russell," said Mrs. Howard, as soon as he came into the room, "to introduce you to a gentleman, for whose works I know you have a great esteem." The gentleman was a celebrated traveller, just returned from abroad, whose conversation was as much admired as his writings.

The conversation now took a literary turn. The traveller being polite, as well as entertaining, drew out Mr. Russell's knowledge and abilities. Charles now looked up to his tutor with respect. Children have sufficient penetration to discover the opinions of others by their countenance and manner, and their sympathy is quickly influenced by the example of those around them. Mrs. Howard led the traveller to speak of what he had seen in different countries—of natural history—of the beaver, and the moose-deer, and the humming-bird, that is scarcely larger than a bumble bee; and the mocking-bird, that can imitate the notes of all other birds. Charles niched himself into a corner of the sofa upon which the gentlemen were sitting, and grew very attentive. He was rather surprised to perceive that his tutor was as much entertained with the conversation as he was himself.

"Pray, sir," said Mrs. Howard to the traveller, "is it true that the humming-bird is a passionate little animal? Is the story told by the author of the Farmer's Letters true?"

"What story?" said Charles, eagerly.

"Of a humming-bird that flew into a fury with a flower, and tore it to pieces, because it could not get the honey out of it all at once."

"Oh, ma'am," said little Charles, peeping over his tutor's shoulders, "will you show me that? Have you got the book, dear aunt?"

"It is Mr. Russell's book," said his aunt.

"Your book!" cried Charles: "what, and do you know all about animals, and those sorts of entertaining things, as well as Latin? And can you tell me, then, what I want very much to know, how they catch the humming-bird?"

"They shoot it."

"Shoot it! but what a large hole they must make in its body and beautiful feathers! I thought you said its whole body was no bigger than a bee—a humble bee."

"They make no hole in its body—they shoot it without ruffling even its feathers."

"How, how?" cried Charles, fastening upon his tutor, whom he now regarded no longer as a mere man of Latin.

"They charge the gun with water," said Mr. Russell, "and the poor little humming-bird is stunned by the discharge."

The conversation next turned upon the entertaining chapter on instinct, in Dr. Darwin's Zoonomia. Charles did not understand all that was said, for the gentlemen did not address themselves to him. He never listened to what he did not understand: but he was very quick at hearing whatever was within the limits of his comprehension. He heard of the tailor-bird, that uses its long bill as a needle, to sew the dead and the living leaf together, of which it makes its light nest, lined with feathers and gossamer: of the fish called the 'old soldier,' that looks out for the empty shell of some dead animal, and fits this armour upon himself: of the Jamaica spider, that makes himself a house under ground, with a door and hinges, which door the spider and all the members of his family take care to shut after them, whenever they go in and out.

Little Charles, as he sat eagerly attentive in his corner of the sofa, heard of the trumpet of the common gnat(2), and of its proboscis, which serves at once for an awl, a saw, and a pump.

(Footnote 2: St. Pierre, Études de la Nature.)

"Are there any more such things," exclaimed Charles, "in these books?"

"A great many," said Mr. Russell.

"I'll read them all," cried Charles, starting up—"may I? may not I, aunt?"

"Ask Mr. Russell," replied his aunt: "he who is obliged to give you the pain of learning what is tiresome, should have the pleasure of rewarding you with entertaining books. Whenever he asks me for Dr. Darwin and St. Pierre, you shall have them. We are both of one mind. We know that learning Latin is not the most amusing occupation in the world, but still it must be learned."

"Why," said Charles modestly, "you don't understand Latin, aunt, do you?"

"No," said Mrs. Howard, "but I am a woman, and it is not thought necessary that a woman should understand Latin; nor can I explain to you, at your age, why it is expected that a gentleman should; but here are several gentlemen present—ask them whether it be not necessary that a gentleman should."

Charles gathered all the opinions, and especially that of the entertaining traveller.

Mrs. Holloway, the silly lady, during that part of the conversation from which she might have acquired some knowledge, had retired to the further end of the room to a game at trictrac with an obsequious chaplain. Her game being finished, she came up to hear what the crowd round the sofa could be talking about; and hearing Charles ask the opinions of the gentlemen about the necessity of learning Latin, she nodded sagaciously at Mrs. Howard, and, by way of making up for former errors, said to Charles, in the most authoritative tone,—

"Yes, I can assure you, Mr. Charles, I am quite of the gentlemen's opinion, and so is every body—and this is a point upon which I have some right to speak; for my Augustus, who is only a year and seven months older than you are, sir, is one of the best scholars of his age, I am told, in England. But then, to be sure, it was flogged into him well at first, at a public school, which, I understand, is the best way of making good scholars."

"And the best way of making boys love literature?" said Mrs. Howard.

"Certainly, certainly," said Mrs. Holloway, who mistook Mrs. Howard's tone of inquiry for a tone of assertion, a tone more familiar to her—"certainly, ma'am, I knew you would come round to my notions at last. I'm sure my Augustus must be fond of his Latin, for never in the vacations did I ever catch him with any English book in his hand!"

"Poor boy!" said Charles, with unfeigned compassion, "And when, my dear Mrs. Howard," continued Mrs. Holloway, laying her hand upon Mrs. Howard's arm, with a yet untasted pinch of snuff between her fingers, "when will you send Mr. Charles to school?"

"Oh, aunt, don't send me away from you—Oh, sir! Mr. Russell, try me—I will do my very, very best, without having it flogged into me, to learn Latin—only try me."

"Dear sir, I really beg your pardon," said Mrs. Holloway to Mr. Russell; "I absolutely only meant to support Mrs. Howard's opinion for the sweet boy's good; and I thought I saw you go out of the room, or somebody else went out, whilst I was at trictrac. But I'm convinced a private tutor may do wonders at the same time; and if my Augustus prejudiced me in favour of public education, you'll excuse a mother's partiality. Besides, I make it a rule never to interfere in the education of my boys. Mr. Holloway is answerable for them; and if he prefer public schools to a private tutor, you must be sensible, sir, it would be very wrong in me to set my poor judgment in opposition to Mr. Holloway's opinion."

Mr. Russell bowed; for, when a lady claims a gentleman's assent to a series of inconsistent propositions, what answer can he make but—a bow? Mrs. Holloway's carriage was now at the door, and, without troubling herself any further about the comparative merits of public and private education, she departed.

When Mrs. Howard was left alone with her nephew, she seized the moment, while his mind was yet warm, to make a lasting impression. Charles, instead of going to Buffon's account of the elephant, which he was very impatient to read, sat down resolutely to his Latin lesson. Mrs. Howard looked over his shoulder, and when he saw her smile of approbation, he said, "Then you won't send me away from you?"

"Not unless you oblige me to do so," said his aunt: "I love to have you with me, and I will try for one year whether you have energy enough to learn what is disagreeable to you, without—"

"Without its being flogged into me," said Charles: "you shall see."

This boy had a great deal of energy and application. The Latin lessons were learned very perfectly; and as he did not spend above an hour a day at them, he was not disgusted with application. His general taste for literature, and his fund of knowledge, increased rapidly from year to year, and the activity of his mind promised continual improvement. His attachment to Mrs. Howard increased as he grew up, for she never claimed any gratitude from her pupil, or exacted from him any of those little observances, which women sometimes consider as essential proofs of affection. She knew that these minute attentions are particularly irksome to boys, and that they are by no means the natural expressions of their feelings. She had sufficient strength of mind to be secure in the possession of those qualities which merit esteem and love, and to believe that the child whom she had educated had a heart and understanding that must feel and appreciate her value.

When Charles Howard was about thirteen, an event happened which changed his prospects in life. Mrs. Howard's large fortune was principally derived from an estate in the West Indies, which had been left to her by her grandfather. She did not particularly wish to be the proprietor of slaves; and from the time that she came to the management of her own affairs, she had been desirous to sell her West India property. Her agent represented to her that this could not be done without considerable loss. From year to year the business was delayed, till at length a gentleman, who had a plantation adjoining to hers, offered to purchase her estate. She was neither one of those ladies who, jealous of their free will, would rather act for themselves, that is to say, follow their own whims in matters of business, than consult men who possess the requisite information; nor was she so ignorant of business, or so indolent, as to be at the mercy of any designing agent or attorney. After consulting proper persons, and after exerting a just proportion of her own judgment, she concluded her bargain with the West Indian. Her plantation was sold to him, and all her property was shipped for her on board The Lively Peggy. Mr. Alderman Holloway, husband to the silly Mrs. Holloway, was one of the trustees appointed by her grandfather's will. The alderman, who was supposed to be very knowing in all worldly concerns, sanctioned the affair with his approbation. The lady was at this time rich; and Alderman Holloway applauded her humanity in having stipulated for the liberty and provision grounds of some old negroes upon her plantation; he even suggested to his son Augustus, that this would make a very pretty, proper subject for a copy of verses, to be addressed to Mrs. Howard. The verses were written in elegant Latin; and the young gentleman was proceeding with some difficulty in his English translation of them, when they were suppressed by parental authority. The alderman changed his opinion as to the propriety of the argument of this poem: the reasons which worked upon his mind were never distinctly expressed; they may, however, be deduced from the perusal of the following letter:—

"TO MRS. FRANCES HOWARD.

"DEAR MADAM,
"Sorry am I to be under the disagreeable necessity of communicating to you thus abruptly, the melancholy news of the loss of 'The Lively Peggy,' with your valuable consignment on board, viz. sundry puncheons of rum, and hogsheads of sugar, in which commodities (as usual) your agent received the purchase-money of your late fine West India estate. I must not, however reluctantly, omit to mention the casket of your grandmother's jewels, which I now regret was sent by this opportunity. 'Tis an additional loss—some thousands, I apprehend.

"The captain of the vessel I have just seen, who was set on shore, on the 15th ultimo, on the coast of Wales: his mate mutinied, and, in conspiracy with the crew, have run away with the vessel.

"I have only to add, that Mrs. Holloway and my daughter Angelina sincerely unite with me in compliments and condolence; and I shall be happy if I can be of any service in the settlement of your affairs.

"Mrs Holloway desires me to say, she would do herself the honour of waiting upon you to-morrow, but is setting out for Margate.

"I am, dear madam,

"Your most obedient and humble servant,

"A. T. Holloway.

"P.S. Your agent is much to blame for neglecting to insure."

Mrs. Howard, as soon as she had perused this epistle, gave it to her nephew, who was reading in the room with her when she received it. He showed more emotion on reading it than she had done. The coldness of the alderman's letter seemed to strike the boy more than the loss of a fortune—"And this is a friend!" he exclaimed with indignation.

"No, my love," said Mrs. Howard, with a calm smile, "I never thought Mr. Holloway any thing more than a common acquaintance: I hope—I am sure I have chosen my friends better."

Charles fixed an eager, inquiring eye upon his aunt, which seemed to say, "Did you mean to call me one of your friends?" and then he grew very thoughtful.

"My dear Charles," said the aunt, after nearly a quarter of an hour's silence, "may I know what you have been thinking of all this time?"

"Thinking of, ma'am!" said Charles, starting from his reverie—"of a great many things—of all you have done for me—of—of what I could do—I don't mean now; for I know I am a child, and can do nothing—I don't mean nothing.—I shall soon be a man, and then I can be a physician, or a lawyer, or something.—Mr. Russell told me the other day, that if I applied myself, I might be whatever I pleased. What would you wish me to be, ma'am?—because that's what I will be—if I can."

"Then I wish you to be what you are."

"O madam," said Charles, with a look of great mortification, "but that's nothing. Won't you make me of some use to you?—But I beg your pardon, I know you can't think about me just now. Good night," said he, and hurried out of the room.

The news of the loss of the Lively Peggy, with all the particulars mentioned in Alderman Holloway's letter, appeared in the next day's newspapers, and in the succeeding paper appeared an advertisement of Mrs. Howard's house in Portman-square, of her plate, china, furniture, books, &c.—She had never in affluence disdained economy. She had no debts; not a single tradesman was a sufferer by her loss. She had always lived within her annual income; and though her generous disposition had prevented her from hoarding money, she had a small sum in the funds, which she had prudently reserved for any unforeseen exigence. She had also a few diamonds, which had been her mother's, which Mr. Carat, the jeweller, who had new set them, was very willing to purchase. He waited upon Mrs. Howard, in Portman-square, to complete the bargain.

The want of sensibility which Charles showed when his aunt was parting with her jewels to Mr. Carat, would have infallibly ruined him in the opinion of most ladies. He took the trinkets up, one by one, without ceremony, and examined them, asking his aunt and the jeweller questions about the use and value of diamonds—about the working of the mines of Golconda—about the shining of diamonds in the dark, observed by the children of Cogi Hassan, the rope-maker, in the Arabian Tales—about the experiment of Francis the First upon melting of diamonds and rubies. Mr. Carat was a Jew, and, though extremely cunning, profoundly ignorant.

"Dat king wash very grand fool, beg his majesty's pardon," said the Jew, with a shrewd smile; "but kings know better nowadays. Heaven bless dere majesties."

Charles had a great mind to vindicate the philosophic fame of Francis the First, but a new idea suddenly started into his head.

"My dearest aunt," cried he, stopping her hand as she was giving her diamond ear-rings to Mr. Carat—"stay, my dearest aunt, one instant, till I have seen whether this is a good day for selling diamonds."

"O my dear young gentleman, no day in de Jewish calendar more proper for de purchase," said the Jew.

"For the purchase! yes," said Charles; "but for the sale?"

"My love," said his aunt, "surely you are not so foolish as to think there are lucky and unlucky days."

"No, I don't mean any thing about lucky and unlucky days," said Charles, running up to consult the barometer; "but what I mean is not foolish indeed: in some book I've read that the dealers in diamonds buy them when the air is light, and sell them when it is heavy, if they can; because their scales are so nice that they vary with the change in the atmosphere. Perhaps I may not remember exactly the words, but that's the sense, I know. I'll look for the words; I know whereabout to find them." He jumped upon a chair, to get down the book.

"But, Master Charles," said the Jew, with a show of deference, "I will not pretend to make a bargain with you—I see you know a great deal more than I of these traffics."

To this flattery Charles made no answer, but continued looking for the passage he wanted in his book. Whilst he was turning over the leaves, a gentleman, a friend of Mrs. Howard, who had promised her to meet Mr. Carat, came in. He was the gentleman formerly mentioned by the name of the traveller: he was a good judge of diamonds, and, what is better, he was a good judge of the human heart and understanding. He was much pleased with Charles's ready recollection of the little knowledge he possessed, with his eagerness to make that knowledge of use to his aunt, and more with his perfect simplicity and integrity; for Charles, after a moment's thought, turned to the Jew and said,—

"But the day that is good for my aunt must be bad for you. The buyers and sellers should each have fair play. Mr. Carat, your weights should be diamonds, and then the changes in the weight of the air would not signify one way or the other.(3)"

(Footnote 3: This observation was literally made by a boy of ten years of age.)

Mr. Carat smiled at this speech, but, suppressing his contempt for the young gentleman, only observed, that he should most certainly follow Mr. Charles's advice, whenever he wash rich enough to have diamonds for weights.

The traveller drew from his pocket a small book, took a pen, and wrote in the title-page of it, For one who will make a good use of it; and, with Mrs. Howard's permission, he gave the book to her nephew.

"I do not believe," said the gentleman, "that there is at present another copy in England: I have just got this from France by a private hand."

The sale of his aunt's books appeared to Charles a much more serious affair than the parting with her diamonds. He understood something of the value of books, and he took a sorrowful leave of many which he had read, and of many more which he had intended to read. Mrs. Howard selected a few for her own use, and she allowed her nephew to select as many for himself as she had done. He observed that there was a beautiful edition of Shakspeare, which he knew his aunt liked particularly, but which she did not keep, reserving instead of it Smith's Wealth of Nations, which would in a few years, she said, be very useful to him. He immediately offered his favourite Etudes de la Nature to redeem the Shakspeare; but Mrs. Howard would not accept of it, because she justly observed, that she could read Shakspeare almost as well without its being in such a beautiful binding. Her readiness to part with all the luxuries to which she had been for many years accustomed, and the freedom and openness with which she spoke of all her affairs to her nephew, made a great impression upon his mind.

Those are mistaken who think that young people cannot be interested in such things: if no mystery be made of the technical parts of business, young people easily learn them, and they early take an interest in the affairs of their parents, instead of learning to separate their own views from those of their friends. Charles, young as he was, at this time, was employed by his aunt frequently to copy, and sometimes to write, letters of business for her. He drew out a careful inventory of all the furniture before it was disposed of; he took lists of all the books and papers: and at this work, however tiresome, he was indefatigable, because he was encouraged by the hope of being useful. This ambition had been early excited in his mind.

When Mrs. Howard had settled her affairs, she took a small neat house near Westminster school(4), for the purpose of a boarding-house for some of the Westminster boys. This plan she preferred, because it secured an independent means of support, and at the same time enabled her, in some measure, to assist in her nephew's education, and to enjoy his company. She was no longer able to afford a sufficient salary to a well-informed private tutor; therefore she determined to send Charles to Westminster school; and, as he would board with her, she hoped to unite by this scheme, as much as possible, the advantages of a private and of a public education. Mr. Russell desired still to have the care of Mrs. Howard's nephew; he determined to offer himself as a tutor at Westminster school; and, as his acquirements were well known to the literary world, he was received with eagerness.

(Footnote 4: See the account of Mrs. C. Ponten, in Gibbon's Life.)

"My dear boy," said Mrs. Howard to her nephew, when he first went to Westminster, "I shall not trouble you with a long chapter of advice: do you remember that answer of the oracle, which seemed to strike you so much the other day, when you were reading the life of Cicero?"

"Yes," said Charles, "I recollect it—I shall never forget it. When Cicero asked how he should arrive at the height of glory, the oracle answered, 'By making his own genius, and not the opinion of the people, the guide of his life.'"

"Well," said Mrs. Howard, smiling, "if I were your oracle, and you were to put the same question to me, I think I should make you nearly the same answer; except that I should change the word genius into good sense; and, instead of the people, I should say the world, which, in general, I think, means all the silly people of one's acquaintance. Farewell: now go to the Westminster world."

Westminster was quite a new world to young Howard. The bustle and noise at first astonished his senses, and almost confounded his understanding; but he soon grew accustomed to the din, and familiarized to the sight of numbers. At first, he thought himself much inferior to all his companions, because practice had given them the power of doing many things with ease, which to him appeared difficult, merely because he had not been used to them. In all their games and plays, either of address or force, he found himself foiled. In a readiness of repartee, and a certain ease and volubility of conversation, he perceived his deficiency; and though he frequently was conscious that his ideas were more just, and his arguments better, than those of his companions, yet he could not at first bring out his ideas to advantage, or manage his arguments so as to stand his ground against the mixed raillery and sophistry of his school fellows. He had not yet the tone of his new society, and he was as much at a loss as a traveller in a foreign country, before he understands the language of a people who are vociferating round about him. As fast, however, as he learned to translate the language of his companions into his own, he discovered that there was not so much meaning in their expressions as he had been inclined to imagine whilst they had remained unintelligible: but he was good-humoured and good-natured, so that, upon the whole, he was much liked; and even his inferiority, in many little trials of skill, was, perhaps, in his favour. He laughed with those that laughed at him, let them triumph in his awkwardness, but still persisted in new trials, till at last, to the great surprise of the spectators, he succeeded.

The art of boxing cost him more than all the rest; but as he was neither deficient in courage of mind nor activity of body, he did not despair of acquiring the necessary skill in this noble science—necessary, we say, for Charles had not been a week at Westminster before he was made sensible of the necessity of practising this art in his own defence. He had yet a stronger motive; he found it necessary for the defence of one who looked up to him for protection.

There was at this time at Westminster, a little boy of the name of Oliver, a Creole, lively, intelligent, open-hearted, and affectionate in the extreme, but rather passionate in his temper, and adverse to application. His literary education had been strangely neglected before he came to school, so that his ignorance of the common rudiments of spelling, reading, grammar, and arithmetic, made him the laughing-stock of the school. The poor boy felt inexpressible shame and anguish; his cheek burned with blushes, when every day, in the public class, he was ridiculed and disgraced; but his dark complexion, perhaps, prevented those blushes from being noticed by his companions, otherwise they certainly would have suppressed, or would have endeavoured to repress, some of their insulting peals of laughter. He suffered no complaint or tear to escape him in public; but his book was sometimes blistered with the tears that fell when nobody saw them: what was worse than all the rest he found insurmountable difficulties, at every step, in his grammar. He was unwilling to apply to any of his more learned companions for explanations or assistance. He began to sink into despair of his own abilities, and to imagine that he must for ever remain, what indeed he was every day called, a dunce. He was usually flogged three times a week. Day after day brought no relief, either to his bodily or mental sufferings: at length his honest pride yielded, and he applied to one of the elder scholars for help. The boy to whom he applied was Augustus Holloway, Alderman Holloway's son, who was acknowledged to be one of the best Latin scholars at Westminster. He readily helped Oliver in his exercises, but he made him pay most severely for this assistance, by the most tyrannical usage; and, in all his tyranny, he thought himself fully justifiable, because little Oliver, beside his other misfortunes, had the misfortune to be a fag.

There may be—though many schoolboys will, perhaps, think it scarcely possible—there may be, in the compass of the civilised world, some persons so barbarously ignorant as not to know what is meant by the term fag. To these it may be necessary to explain, that at some English schools it is the custom, that all little boys, when they first go to school, should be under the dominion of the elder boys. These little boys are called fags, and are forced to wait upon and obey their master-companions. Their duties vary in different schools. I have heard of its being customary in some places, to make use of a fag regularly in the depth of winter instead of a warming-pan, and to send the shivering urchin through ten or twenty beds successively to take off the chill of cold for their luxurious masters. They are expected, in most schools, to run of all the elder boys' errands, to be ready at their call, and to do all their high behests. They must never complain of being tired, or their complaints will, at least, never be regarded, because, as the etymology of the word implies, it is their business to be tired. The substantive fag is not to be found in Dr. Johnson's Dictionary; but the verb to fag is there a verb neuter, from fatigo, Latin, and is there explained to mean, "to grow weary, to faint with weariness." This is all the satisfaction we can, after the most diligent research, afford the curious and learned reader upon the subject of fags in general.

In particular, Mr. Augustus Holloway took great delight in teasing his fag, little Oliver. One day it happened that young Howard and Holloway were playing at nine-pins together, and little Oliver was within a few yards of them, sitting under a tree, with a book upon his knees, anxiously trying to make out his lesson. Holloway, whenever the nine-pins were thrown down, called to Oliver, and made him come from his book and set them up again: this he repeatedly did, in spite of Howard's remonstrances, who always offered to set up the nine-pins, and who said it teased the poor little fellow to call him every minute from what he was about.

"Yes," said Holloway, "I know it teases him—that I see plain enough, by his running so fast back to his form, like a hare—there he is, squatting again: halloo! halloo! come, start again here," cried Holloway; "you have not done yet: bring me the bowl, halloo!"

Howard did not at all enjoy the diversion of hunting the poor boy about in this manner, and he said, with some indignation,

"How is it possible, Holloway, that the boy can get his lesson, if you interrupt him every instant?"

"Pooh! what signifies his foolish lesson?"

"It signifies a great deal to him," replied Howard: "you know what he suffered this morning because he had not learned it."

"Suffered! why, what did he suffer?" said Holloway, upon whose memory the sufferings of others made no very deep impression. "Oh, ay, true—you mean he was flogged: more shame for him!—why did not he mind and get his lesson better?"

"I had not time to understand it rightly," said Oliver, with a deep sigh; "and I don't think I shall have time to-day either."

"More shame for you," repeated Holloway: "I'll lay any bet on earth, I get all you have to get in three minutes."

"Ah, you, to be sure," said Oliver, in a tone of great humiliation; "but then you know what a difference there is between you and me."

Holloway misunderstood him; and, thinking he meant to allude to the difference in their age, instead of the difference of their abilities, answered sharply,

"When I was your age, do you think I was such a dunce as you are, pray?"

"No, that I am sure you never were," said Oliver; "but perhaps you had some good father or mother, or somebody, who taught you a little before you came to school."

"I don't remember any thing about that," replied Holloway; "I don't know who was so good as to teach me, but I know I was so good as to learn fast enough, which is a goodness, I've a notion, some folks will never have to boast of—so trot, and fetch the bowl for me, do you hear, and set up the nine-pins. You've sense enough to do that, have not you? and as for your lesson, I'll drive that into your head by and by, if I can," added he, rapping with his knuckles upon the little boy's head.

"As to my lesson," said the boy, putting aside his head from the insulting knuckles, "I had rather try and make it out by myself, if I can."

"If you can!" repeated Holloway, sneering; "but we all know you can't."

"Why can't he, Holloway?" exclaimed Howard, with a raised voice, for he was no longer master of his indignation.

"Why can't he?" repeated Holloway, looking round upon Howard, with a mixture of surprise and insolence. "You must answer that question yourself, Howard: I say he can't."

"And I say he can, and he shall," replied Howard; "and he shall have time to learn: he's willing, and, I'll answer for it, able to learn; and he shall not be called a dunce; and he shall have time; and he shall have justice."

"Shall! shall! shall!" retorted Holloway, vociferating with a passion of a different sort from Howard's. "Pray, sir, who allowed you to say shall to me? and how dare you to talk in this here style to me about justice?—and what business have you, I should be glad to know, to interfere between me and my fag? What right have you to him, or his time either? And if I choose to call him a dunce forty times a day, what then? he is a dunce, and he will be a dunce to the end of his days, I say, and who is there thinks proper to contradict me?"

"I," said Howard, firmly; "and I'll do more than contradict you—I'll prove that you are mistaken. Oliver, bring your book to me."

"Oliver, stir at your peril!" cried Holloway, clinching his fist with a menacing gesture: "nobody shall give any help to my fag but myself, sir," added he to Howard.

"I am not going to help him, I am only going to prove to him that he may do it without your help," said Howard.

The little boy sprang forward, at these words, for his book; but his tormentor caught hold of him, and pulling him back, said, "He's my fag! do you recollect, sir, he's my fag?"

"Fag or no fag," cried Howard, "you shall not make a slave of him."

"I will! I shall! I will!" cried Holloway, worked up to the height of tyrannical fury: "I will make a slave of him, if I choose it—a negro-slave, if I please!"

At the sound of negro-slave, the little Creole burst into tears. Howard sprang forward to free him from his tyrant's grasp: Holloway struck Howard a furious blow, which made him stagger backwards.

"Ay," said Holloway, "learn to stand your ground, and fight, before you meddle with me, I advise you."

Holloway was an experienced pugilist, and he knew that Howard was not; but before his defiance had escaped his lips, he felt his blow returned, and a battle ensued. Howard fought with all his soul; but the body has something to do, as well as the soul, in the art of boxing, and his body was not yet a match for his adversary's. After receiving more blows than Holloway, perhaps, could have borne, Howard was brought to the ground.

"Beg my pardon, and promise never to interfere between me and my fag any more," said Holloway, standing over him triumphant: "ask my pardon."

"Never," said the fallen hero: "I'll fight you again, in the same cause, whenever you please; I can't have a better;" and he struggled to rise.

Several boys had, by this time, gathered round the combatants, and many admired the fortitude and spirit of the vanquished, though it is extremely difficult to boys, if not to men, to sympathize with the beaten. Every body called out that Howard had had enough for that night; and though he was willing to have renewed the battle, his adversary was withheld by the omnipotence of public opinion. As to the cause of the combat, some few inquired into its merits, but many more were content with seeing the fray, and with hearing, vaguely, that it began about Howard's having interfered with Holloway's fag in an impertinent manner.

Howard's face was so much disfigured, and his clothes were so much stained with blood, that he did not wish to present himself such a deplorable spectacle before his aunt; besides, no man likes to be seen, especially by a woman, immediately after he has been beaten; therefore, he went directly to bed as soon as he got home, but desired that one of his companions, who boarded at Mrs. Howard's, would, if his aunt inquired for him at supper, tell her "that he had been beaten in a boxing match, but hoped to be more expert after another lesson or two." This lady did not show her tenderness to her nephew by wailing over his disaster: on the contrary, she was pleased to hear that he had fought in so good a cause.

The next morning, as soon as Howard went to school, he saw little Oliver watching eagerly for him.

"Mr. Howard—Charles," said he, catching hold of him, "I've one word to say: let him call me dunce, or slave, or negro, or what he will, don't you mind any more about me—I can't bear to see it," said the affectionate child: "I'd rather have the blows myself, only I know I could not bear them as you did."

Oliver turned aside his head, and Howard, in a playful voice, said, "Why, my little Oliver, I did not think you were such a coward: you must not make a coward of me."

No sooner did the boys go out to play in the evening, than Howard called to Oliver, in Holloway's hearing, and said, "If you want any assistance from me, remember, I'm ready."

"You may be ready, but you are not able," cried Holloway, "to give him any assistance—therefore, you'd better be quiet: remember last night."

"I do remember it perfectly," said Howard, calmly.

"And do you want any more?—Come, then, I'll tell you what, I'll box with you every day, if you please, and when you have conquered me, you shall have my fag all to yourself, if you please; but, till then, you shall have nothing to do with him."

"I take you at your word," said Howard, and a second battle began. As we do not delight in fields of battle, or hope to excel, like Homer, in describing variety of wounds, we shall content ourselves with relating, that after five pitched battles, in which Oliver's champion received bruises of all shapes and sizes, and of every shade of black, blue, green, and yellow, his unconquered spirit still maintained the justice of his cause, and with as firm a voice as at first he challenged his constantly victorious antagonist to a sixth combat.

"I thought you had learned by this time," said the successful pugilist, "that Augustus Holloway is not to be conquered by one of woman breed." To this taunt Howard made no reply; but whether it urged him to superior exertion, or whether the dear-bought experience of the five preceding days had taught him all the caution that experience only can teach, we cannot determine; but, to the surprise of all the spectators, and to the lively joy of Oliver, the redoubted Holloway was brought, after an obstinate struggle, fairly to the ground. Every body sympathized with the generous victor, who immediately assisted his fallen adversary to rise, and offered his hand in token of reconciliation. Augustus Holloway, stunned by his fall, and more by his defeat, returned from the field of battle as fast as the crowd would let him, who stopped him continually with their impertinent astonishment and curiosity; for though the boasted unconquerable hero had pretty evidently received a black eye, not one person would believe it without looking close in his face; and many would not trust the information of their own senses, but pressed to hear the news confirmed by the reluctant lips of the unfortunate Augustus. In the meantime, little Oliver, a fag no longer, exulting in his liberty, clapped his joyful hands, sang, and capered round his deliverer.—"And now," said he, fixing his grateful, affectionate eyes upon Howard, "you will suffer no more for me; and if you'll let me, I'll be your fag. Do, will you? pray let me! I'll run of your errands before you can say one, two, three, and away: only whistle for me," said he, whistling, "and I'll hear you, wherever I am. If you only hold up your finger when you want me, I'm sure I shall see it; and I'll always set up your nine-pins, and fly for your ball, let me be doing what I will. May I be your fag?"

"Be my friend!" said Howard, taking Oliver in his arms, with emotion which prevented him from articulating any other words. The word friend went to the little Creole's heart, and he clung to Howard in silence. To complete his happiness, little Oliver this day obtained permission to board at Mrs. Howard's, so that he was now constantly to be with his protector. Howard's friendship was not merely the sudden enthusiasm of a moment; it was the steady persevering choice of a manly mind, not the caprice of a school-boy. Regularly, every evening, Oliver brought his books to his friend, who never was too busy to attend to him. Oliver was delighted to find that he understood Howard's manner of explaining: his own opinion of himself rose with the opinion which he saw his instructor had of his abilities. He was convinced that he was not doomed to be a dunce for life; his ambition was rekindled; his industry was encouraged by hope, and rewarded by success. He no longer expected daily punishment, and that worst of all punishments, disgrace. His heart was light, his spirits rose, his countenance brightened with intelligence, and resumed its natural vivacity: to his masters and his companions he appeared a new creature. "What has inspired you?" said one of his masters to him one day, surprised at the rapid development of his understanding—"what has inspired you?"

"My good genius," said the little boy, pointing to Howard. Howard had some merit in giving up a good deal of his time to Oliver, because he knew the value of time, and he had not quite so much as he wished for himself. The day was always too short for him; every moment was employed; his active mind went from one thing to another as if it did not know the possibility of idleness, and as if he had no idea of any recreation but in a change of employment. Not that he was always poring over books, but his mind was active, let him be about what he would; and, as his exertions were always voluntary, there was not that opposition in his opinion between the ideas of play and work, which exists so strongly in the imaginations of those school-boys who are driven to their tasks by fear, and who escape from them to that delicious exercise of their free-will which they call play.

"Constraint, that sweetens liberty,"

often gives a false value to its charms, or rather a false idea to its nature. Idleness, ennui, noise, mischief, riot, and a nameless train of mistaken notions of pleasure, are often classed, in a young man's mind, under the general head of liberty.

Mr. Augustus Holloway, who is necessarily recalled to our notice, when we want to personify an ill-educated young man, was, in the strictest sense of the word, a school-boy—a clever school-boy—a good scholar—a good historian: he wrote a good hand—read with fluency—declaimed at a public exhibition of Westminster orators with no bad grace and emphasis, and had always extempore words, if not extempore sense, at command. But still he was but a school-boy. His father thought him a man, and more than a man. Alderman Holloway prophesied to his friends that his son Augustus would be one of the first orators in England. He was in a hurry to have him ready to enter college, and had a borough secure for him at the proper age. The proper age, he regretted, that parliament had fixed to twenty-one; for the alderman was impatient to introduce his young statesman to the house, especially as he saw honours, perhaps a title, in the distant perspective of his son's advancement.

Whilst this vision occupied the father's imagination, a vision of another sort played upon the juvenile fancy of his son—a vision of a gig; for, though Augustus was but a school-boy, he had very manly ideas—if those ideas be manly which most young men have. Lord Rawson, the son of the Earl of Marryborough, had lately appeared to Augustus in a gig. The young Lord Rawson had lately been a school-boy at Westminster like Augustus: he was now master of himself and three horses at College. Alderman Holloway had lent the Earl of Marryborough certain monies, the interest of which the earl scrupulously paid in civility. The alderman valued himself upon being a shrewd man; he looked to one of the earl's boroughs as a security for his principal, and, from long-sighted political motives, encouraged an intimacy between the young nobleman and his son. It was one of those useful friendships, one of those fortunate connexions, which some parents consider as the peculiar advantage of a public school. Lord Rawson's example already powerfully operated upon his young friend's mind, and this intimacy was most likely to have a decisive influence upon the future destiny of Augustus. Augustus was the son of an alderman. Lord Rawson was two years older than Holloway—had left school—had been at college—had driven both a curricle and a barouche, and had gone through all the gradations of coachmanship—was a man, and had seen the world. How many things to excite the ambition of a schoolboy! Augustus was impatient for the moment when he might "be what he admired." The drudgery of Westminster, the confinement, the ignominious appellation of a boy, were all insupportable to this young man. He had obtained from his father a promise, that he should leave school in a few months; but these months appeared to him an age. It was rather a misfortune to Holloway that he was so far advanced in his Latin and Greek studies, for he had the less to do at school; his school business quickly despatched, his time hung upon his hands. He never thought of literature as an amusement for his leisure hours; he had no idea of improving himself further in general science and knowledge. He was told that his education was nearly at an end; he believed it was quite finished, and he was glad of it, and glad it was so well over. In the idle time that hung upon his hands, during this intermediate state at Westminster, he heartily regretted that he could not commence his manly career by learning to drive—to drive a curricle. Lord Rawson had carried him down to the country, the last summer vacation, in his dog-cart, driven randem-tandem. The reins had touched his fingers. The whip had been committed to his hand, and he longed for a repetition of these pleasures. From the windows of the house in Westminster, where he boarded, Holloway at every idle moment lolled, to enjoy a view of every carriage, and of every coachman that passed.

Mr. Supine, Mr. Holloway's tutor, used, at these leisure moments, to employ himself with practising upon the German flute, and was not sorry to be relieved from his pupil's conversation. Sometimes it was provoking to the amateur in music to be interrupted by the exclamations of his pupil; but he kept his eyes steadily upon his music-book, and contented himself with recommending a difficult passage, when Mr. Holloway's raptures about horses, and coachmanship, and driving well in hand, offended his musical ear. Mr. Supine was, both from nature and fashion, indolent; the trouble of reproving or of guiding his pupil was too much for him; besides, he was sensible that the task of watching, contradicting, and thwarting a young gentleman, at Mr. Holloway's time of life, would have been productive of the most disagreeable scenes of altercation, and could possibly have no effect upon the gentleman's character, which he presumed was perfectly well formed at this time. Mr. and Mrs. Holloway were well satisfied with his improvements. Mr. Supine was on the best terms imaginable with the whole family, and thought it his business to keep himself well with his pupil; especially as he had some secret hope that, through Mr. Holloway's interest with Lord Rawson, and through Lord Rawson's influence with a young nobleman, who was just going abroad, he might be invited as a travelling companion in a tour upon the continent. His taste for music and painting had almost raised him to the rank of a connoisseur: an amateur he modestly professed himself, and he was frequently stretched, in elegant ease, upon a sofa, already in reverie in Italy, whilst his pupil was conversing out of the window, in no very elegant dialect, with the driver of a stagecoach in the neighbourhood. Young Holloway was almost as familiar with this coachman as with his father's groom, who, during his visits at home, supplied the place of Mr. Supine, in advancing his education. The stage-coachman so effectually wrought upon the ambition of Augustus, that his desire to learn to drive became uncontrollable. The coachman, partly by entreaties, and partly by the mute eloquence of a crown, was prevailed upon to promise, that, if Holloway could manage it without his tutor's knowledge, he should ascend to the honours of the box, and at least have the satisfaction of seeing some good driving.

Mr. Supine was soon invited to a private concert, at which Mrs. Holloway was expected, and at which her daughter, Miss Angelina Holloway, was engaged to perform. Mr. Supine's judicious applause of this young lady's execution was one of his greatest recommendations to the whole family, at least to the female part of it; he could not, therefore, decline an invitation to this concert. Holloway complained of a sore throat, and desired to be excused from accompanying his tutor, adding, with his usual politeness, that "music was the greatest bore in nature, and especially Angelina's music." For the night of the concert Holloway had arranged his plan with the stage-coachman. Mr. Supine dressed, and then practised upon the German flute, till towards nine o'clock in the evening. Holloway heard the stage-coach rattling through the street, whilst his tutor was yet in the middle of a long concerto: the coachman was to stop at the public-house, about ten doors off, to take up parcels and passengers, and there he was to wait for Holloway; but he had given him notice that he could not wait many minutes.

"You may practise the rest without book, in the chair, as you are going to — street, quite at your ease, Mr. Supine," said Holloway to his tutor.

"Faith, so I can, and I'll adopt your idea, for it's quite a novel thing, and may take, if the fellows will only carry one steady. Good night: I'll mention your sore throat properly to Mrs. Holloway."

No sooner were the tutor and his German flute safely raised upon the chairmen's shoulders, than his pupil recovered from his sore throat, ran down to the place where the stage was waiting, seized the stage-coachman's down-stretched hand, sprang up, and seated himself triumphantly upon the coach-box.

"Never saw a cleverer fellow," said the coachman: "now we are off."

"Give me the reins, then," said Holloway.

"Not till we are out o'town," said the coachman: "when we get off the stones, we'll see a little of your driving."

When they got on the turnpike road, Holloway impatiently seized the reins, and was as much gratified by this coachman's praises of his driving as ever he had been by the applauses he had received for his Latin verses. A taste for vulgar praise is the most dangerous taste a young man can have; it not only leads him into vulgar company, but it puts him entirely in the power of his companions, whoever they may happen to be. Augustus Holloway, seated beside a coachman, became, to all intents and purposes, a coachman himself; he caught, and gloried in catching, all his companion's slang, and with his language caught all his ideas. The coachman talked with rapture of some young gentleman's horses which he had lately seen; and said that, if he was a gentleman, there was nothing he should pride himself so much upon as his horses. Holloway, as he was a gentleman, determined to have the finest horses that could be had for money, as soon as he should become his own master.

"And then," continued the coachman, "if I was a gentleman born, I'd never be shabby in the matters of wages and perquisites to them that be to look after my horses, seeing that horses can't be properly looked after for nothing."

"Certainly not," agreed the young gentleman:—"my friend, lord Rawson, I know, has a prodigious smart groom, and so will I, all in good time."

"To be sure," said the coachman; "but it was not in regard to grooms I was meaning, so much as in regard to a coachman, which, I take it, is one of the first persons to be considered in a really grand family, seeing how great a trust is placed in him—(mind, sir, if you please, the turn at the corner, it's rather sharp)—seeing how great a trust is placed in him, as I was observing, a good coachman is worth his weight in gold."

Holloway had not leisure to weigh the solidity of this observation, for the conversation was now interrupted by the sound of a postchaise, which drove rapidly by.

"The job and four!" exclaimed the coachman, with as many oaths "as the occasion required."

"Why did you let it pass us?" And with enthusiasm which forgot all ceremony, he snatched the whip from his young companion, and, seizing the reins, drove at a furious rate. One of the chaise postilions luckily dropped his whip. They passed the job and four; and the coachman, having redeemed his honour, resigned once more the reins to Holloway, upon his promising not to let the job and four get a head of them. The postilions were not without ambition: the men called to each other, and to their horses; the horses caught some portion of their masters' spirit, and began to gain upon the coach. The passengers in the coach put out their heads, and female voices screamed in vain. All these terrors increased the sport; till at length, at a narrow part of the road, the rival coachman and postilions hazarded every thing for precedency. Holloway was desperate in proportion to his ignorance. The coachman attempted to snatch the reins, but, missing his grasp, he shortened those of the off-hand horse, and drew them the wrong way: the coach ran upon a bank, and was overturned. Holloway was dismayed and silent; the coachman poured forth a torrent of abuse, sparing neither friend nor foe; the complaints of the female passengers were so incoherent, and their fears operated so much upon their imagination, that in the first moments of confusion, each asserted that she had broken either an arm or a leg, or fractured her skull.

The moon, which had shone bright in the beginning of the evening, was now under a cloud, and the darkness increased the impatience of the various complainers; at length a lantern was brought from the turnpike-house, which was near the spot where the accident happened. As soon as the light came, the ladies looked at each other, and after they had satisfied themselves that no material injury had been done to their clothes, and that their faces were in no way disfigured, they began to recover from their terrors, and were brought to allow that all their limbs were in good preservation, and that they had been too hasty in declaring that their skulls were fractured. Holloway laughed loudly at all this, and joined in all the wit of the coachman upon the occasion. The coach was lifted up; the passengers got in; the coachman and Holloway mounted the box, when, just as they were setting off, the coachman heard a voice crying to him to stop. He listened, and the voice, which seemed to be that of a person in great pain, again called for assistance.

"It's the mulatto woman," said the coachman: "we forgot her in the bustle. Lend me hold of the lantern, and stand at the horses' heads, whilst I see after her," added the coachman, addressing himself to the man who had come from the turnpike-house.

"I shan't stir for a mulatto, I promise you," said Holloway, brutally: "she was on the top of the coach, wasn't she? She must have had a fine hoist!"

The poor woman was found to be much hurt: she had been thrown from the top of the coach into a ditch, which had stones at the bottom of it. She had not been able to make herself heard by any body, whilst the ladies' loud complaints continued; nor had she been able long to call for any assistance, for she had been stunned by her fall, and had not recovered her senses for many minutes. She was not able to stand; but when the coachman held her up, she put her hand to her head, and, in broken English, said she felt too ill to travel farther that night.

"You shall have an inside place, if you'll pluck up your heart; and you'll find yourself better with the motion of the coach."

"What, is she hurt—the mulatto woman?—I say, coachy, make haste," cried Holloway; "I want to be off."

"So do I," said the coachman; "but we are not likely to be off yet: here's this here poor woman can't stand, and is all over bruises, and won't get into the inside of the coach, though I offered her a place."

Holloway, who imagined that the sufferings of all who were not so rich as himself could be bought off for money, pulled out a handful of silver, and leaning from the coach-box, held it towards the fainting woman:—"Here's a shilling for every bruise at least, my good woman:"—but the woman did not hear him, for she was very faint. The coachman was forced to carry her to the turnpike-house, where he left her, telling the people of the house that a return chaise would call for her in an hour's time, and would carry her either to the next stage, or back to town, whichever she pleased. Holloway's diversion for the rest of the night was spoiled, not because he had too much sympathy with the poor woman that was hurt, but because he had been delayed so long by the accident, that he lost the pleasure of driving into the town of —. He had intended to have gone the whole stage, and to have returned in the job and four. This scheme had been arranged before he set out by his friend the coachman; but the postilions in the job and four having won the race, and made the best of their way, had now returned, and met the coach about two miles from the turnpike-house. "So," said Holloway, "I must descend, and get home before Mr. Supine wakens from his first sleep."

Holloway called at the turnpike-house, to inquire after the mulatto; or, rather, one of the postilions stopped as he had been desired by the coachman, to take her up to town, if she was able to go that night.

The postilion, after he had spoken to the woman, came to the chaise-door, and told Holloway "that he could hardly understand what she said, she talked such outlandish English; and that he could not make out where she wanted to be carried to."

"Ask the name of some of her friends in town," cried Holloway, "and don't let her keep us here all night."

"She has no friends, as I can find," replied the postilion, "nor acquaintance neither."

"Well, whom does she belong to, then?"

"She belongs to nobody—she's quite a stranger in these parts, and doesn't know no more than a child where to go in all London; she only knows the Christian name of an old gardener, where she lodged, she says."

"What would she have us to do with her, then?" said Holloway. "Drive on, for I shall be late."

The postilion, more humane than Holloway, exclaimed, "No, master, no!—it's a sin to leave her upon the road this ways, though she's no Christian, as we are, poor copper-coloured soul! I was once a stranger myself in Lon'on, without a six-pence to bless myself; so I know what it is, master."

The good-natured postilion returned to the mulatto woman. "Mistress," said he, "I'd fain see ye safe home, if you could but think of the t'other name of that gardener that you mentioned lodging with; because there be so many Pauls in London town, that I should never find your Paul, as you don't know neither the name of his street—But I'll tell ye now all the streets I'm acquainted with, and that's a many: do you stop me, mistress, when I come to the right; for you're sadly bruised, and I won't see ye left this ways on the road."

He then named several streets: the mulatto woman stopped him at one name, which she recollected to be the name of the street in which the gardener lived. The woman at the turnpike-house, as soon as she heard the street in which he lived named, said she knew this gardener; that he had a large garden about a mile off, and that he came from London early almost every morning with his cart, for garden-stuff for the market: she advised the mulatto woman to stay where she was that night, and to send to ask the gardener to come on to the turnpike-house for her in the morning. The postilion promised to go to the gardener's "by the first break of day." The woman raised her head to bless him; and the impatient Holloway loudly called to him to return to his horses, swearing that he would not give him one farthing for himself if he did not.

The anxiety which Holloway felt to escape detection kept him in pain; but Holloway never measured or estimated his pleasures and his pains; therefore he never discovered that, even upon the most selfish calculation, he had paid too dear for the pleasure of sitting upon a coach-box for one hour.

It was two o'clock in the morning before the chaise arrived in town, when he was set down at the house at which the stage-coach put up, walked home, got in at his bedchamber window—his bedchamber was upon the ground-floor. Mr. Supine was fast asleep, and his pupil triumphed in his successful frolic. Whilst Holloway, in his dreams, was driving again, and again overturning stage-coaches, young Howard, in his less manly dreams, saw Dr. B., the head master of Westminster school, advancing towards him, at a public examination, with a prize medal in his hand, which turned, Howard thought, as he looked upon it, first into the face of his aunt, smiling upon him; then into a striking likeness of his tutor, Mr. Russell, who also smiled upon him; and then changed into the head of little Oliver, whose eyes seemed to sparkle with joy. Just at the instant, Howard awoke, and, opening his eyes, saw Oliver's face close to him, laughing heartily.

"Why," exclaimed Oliver, "you seized my head with both your hands when I came to waken you: what could you be dreaming of, Charles?"

"I dreamed I took you for a medal, and I was right glad to have hold of you," said Howard, laughing; "but I shall not get my medal by dreaming about it. What o'clock is it? I shall be ready in half a second."

"Ay," said Oliver, "I wont tell you what o'clock it is till you're dressed: make haste; I have been up this half hour, and I've got every thing ready, and I've carried the little table, and all your books, and the pen and ink, and all the things, out to our seat; and the sun shines upon it, and every thing looks cheerful, and you'll have a full hour to work, for it's only half after five."

At the back of Mrs. Howard's house there was a little garden; at the end of the garden was a sort of root-house, which Oliver had cleaned out, and which he dignified by the title of the seat. There were some pots of geraniums and myrtles kept in it, with Mrs. Howard's permission, by a gardener, who lived next door to her, and who frequently came to work in her garden. Oliver watered the geraniums, and picked off the dead leaves, whilst Howard was writing at the little table which had been prepared for him. Howard had at this time two grand works in hand, on which he was enthusiastically intent: he was translating the little French book which the traveller had given to him; and he was writing an essay for a prize. The young gentlemen at Westminster were engaged in writing essays for a periodical paper; and Dr. B. had promised to give a prize medal as the reward for that essay, which he, and a jury of critics, to be chosen from among the boys themselves, should pronounce to be the best composition.

"I won't talk to you, I won't interrupt you," said Oliver to Howard; "but only answer me one question: what is your essay about?"

Howard put his finger upon his lips, and shook his head.

"I assure you I did not look, though I longed to peep at it this morning before you were up. Pray, Charles, do you think I shall ever be able to write essays?"

"To be sure," said Howard; "why not?"

"Ah," said Oliver, with a sigh, "because I've no genius, you know."

"But," said Howard, "have not you found out that you could do a great many things that you thought you could not do?"

"Ay, thank you for that: but then you know, those are the sort of things which can be done without genius."

"And what are the things," replied Howard, "which cannot be done without genius?"

"Oh, a great, great many, I believe," said Oliver: "you know Holloway said so."

"But we are not forced to believe it, because Holloway said so, are we? Besides, a great many things may mean any thing, buckling your shoes, or putting on your hat, for instance."

Oliver laughed at this, and said, "These, to be sure, are not the sort of things that can't be done without genius."

"What are the sort of things?" repeated Howard. "Let us, now I've the pen in my hand, make a list of them."

"Take a longer bit of paper."

"No, no, the list will not be so very long as you think it will. What shall I put first?—make haste, for I'm in a hurry."

"Well—writing, then—writing, I am sure, requires genius."

"Why?"

"Because I never could write, and I've often tried and tried to write something, but I never could; because I've no genius for it."

"What did you try to write?" said Howard.

"Why, letters," said Oliver: "my uncle, and my aunt, and my two cousins, desired I would write to them regularly once a fortnight; but I never can make out a letter, and I'm always sorry when letter-writing day comes; and if I sit thinking and thinking for ever so long I can find nothing to say. I used always to beg a beginning from somebody; but then, when I've got over the beginning, that's only three or four lines; and if I stretch it out ever so much, it won't make a whole letter; and what can I put in the middle? There's nothing but that I am well, and hope they are all well; or else, that I am learning Latin, as you desired, dear uncle, and am forward in my English. The end I can manage well enough, because there's duty and love to send to every body; and about the post is just going out, and believe me to be, in haste, your dutiful and affectionate nephew. But then," continued little Oliver, "this is all nonsense, I know, and I'm ashamed to write such bad letters. Now your pen goes on, scratch, scratch, scratch, the moment you sit down to it; and you can write three pages of a nice, long, good letter, whilst I am writing 'My dear uncle John,' and that's what I call having a genius for writing. I wonder how you came by it: could you write good letters when you were of my age?"

"I never wrote any letters at your age," said Howard.

"Oh, how happy you must have been! But then, if you never learned, how comes it that you can write them now? How can you always find something to say?"

"I never write but when I have something to say; and you know, when you had something to say last post about Easter holidays, your pen, Oliver, went scratch, scratch, scratch, as fast as any body's."

"So it did," cried Oliver; "but then the thing is, I'm forced to write when I've nothing about the holidays to say."

"Forced?"

"Yes, because I'm afraid my uncle and cousins should be angry if I didn't write."

"I'm sure I'm much obliged," said Howard, "to my dear aunt, who never forced me to write: she always said, 'Never write, Charles, but when you like it;' and I never did. When I had any thing to say, that is, any thing to describe, or any reasons to give upon any subject, or any questions to ask, which I very much wished to have answered, then, you know, I could easily write, because I had nothing to do but to write down just the words which I should have said, if I had been speaking."

"But I thought writing was quite a different thing from speaking, because, in writing, there must be sentences, and long sentences, and fine sentences, such as there are in books."

"In some books," said Howard; "but not in all."

"Besides," continued Oliver, "one person's speaking is quite different from another person's speaking. Now I believe I make use of a great number of odd words, and vulgar expressions, and bad English, which I learned from being with the servants, I believe, at home. You have never talked to servants, Charles, I dare say, for you have not one of their words."

"No," said Charles, "never; and my aunt took a great deal of pains to prevent me from hearing any of their conversation; therefore it was impossible that I should catch—"

Here the conversation was interrupted by the appearance of old Paul, the gardener.

"So, Paul," cried little Oliver, "I've been doing your work for you this morning; I've watered all the geraniums, and put the Indian corn in the sun; what kept you so late in your bed this fine morning, Paul?—fie, Paul!"

"You would not say fie, master," replied Paul, "if you knew how early I had been out of my bed, this morning: I was abroad afore sunrise, so I was, master."

"And why didn't you come to work then, Paul? You shall not have the watering-pot till you tell me: don't look so grave about it; you know you must smile when I please, Paul."

"I can't smile, just now, master," said old Paul; but he smiled, and then told Oliver, that "the reason he could not smile was, that he was a little sick at heart, with just coming from the sight of a poor soul who had been sadly bruised by a fall from the top of the stage, which was overturned last night. She was left all night at the pike, and as she had no other friends, she sent for me by a return chay-boy, and I went for her, and brought her home in my covered cart, to my good woman, which she liked, with good reason, better ten to one than the stage. And she's terribly black and blue, and does not seem quite right in her head, to my fancy."

"I wish we could do something for her," said Howard. "As soon as Mr. Russell is up, I'll ask him to go with us to see her. We will call as we go by to school this morning."

"But, master," said the gardener, "I should warn ye beforehand, that mayhap you mayn't pity her so much, for she's rather past her best days; and bad must have been her best, for she's swarthy, and not like one of this country: she comes from over the seas, and they call her a—a—not quite a negro."

"A mulatto!—I like her the better," cried Oliver; "for my nurse was a mulatto. I'll go and waken Mr. Russell this instant, for I'm sure he'll not be angry." He ran away to Mr. Russell, who was not angry at being awakened, but dressed himself almost as expeditiously as Oliver wished, and set out immediately with his pupils, delighted to be the companion of their benevolent schemes, instead of being the object of their fear and hatred. Tutors may inspire affection, even though they have the misfortune to be obliged to teach Greek and Latin.(5)

(Footnote 5: Vide Dr. Johnson's assertions to the contrary, in Mrs. Piozzi's Anecdotes.)

When the boys arrived at the gardener's, they found the poor mulatto woman lying upon a bed, in a small close room, which was so full of smoke, when they came in, that they could hardly breathe: the little window, that let in but a glimmering light, could not, without difficulty, be opened. The poor woman made but few complaints; she appeared to be most concerned at the thoughts of being a burden to the good old gardener and his wife. She said that she had not been long in England; that she came to London in hopes of finding a family who had been very kind to her in her youth; but that, after inquiry at the house where they formerly lived, she could hear nothing of them. After a great deal of trouble, she discovered that a West India gentleman, who had known her abroad, was now at Bath; but she had spent the last farthing of her money, and she was, therefore, unable to undertake the journey. She had brought over with her, she said, some foreign seeds of flowers, which her young mistress used to be fond of when she was a child, which she had kept till hunger obliged her to offer them to a gardener for a loaf of bread. The gardener to whom she offered them was old Paul, who took compassion upon her distress, lodged her for a week, and at last paid for an outside place for her upon the Bath coach. There was such an air of truth and simplicity in this woman, that Mr. Russell, more experienced than his pupils, believed her story, at once, as implicitly as they did. "Oh," exclaimed little Oliver, "I have but this half-crown for her: I wish Holloway had but paid me my half-guinea; I'll ask him for it again to-day; and will you come with us here again, this evening, Mr. Russell, that I may bring it then?"

Mr. Russell and Howard hired the room for a fortnight in which the mulatto woman was now lying, and paid old Paul, the gardener, for it, promising, at the same time, to supply her with food. The gardener's wife, at the poor woman's earnest request, promised that, as soon as she was able to sit up, she would get her some coarse plain work to do.

"But," said Oliver, "how can she see to work in this smoke? I'm sure it makes my eyes water so that I can hardly bear it, though I have been in it scarcely ten minutes."

"I wish," exclaimed Howard, turning to Mr. Russell, "that this chimney could be cured of smoking."

"Oh, well-a-day," said the gardener, "we must put up with it as it is, for I've had doctors to it, at one time or another, that have cost me a power of money; but, after all, it's as bad as ever, and my good dame never lights a fire in it this fine spring weather; howsomever, she (pointing to the mulatto woman) is so chilly, coming from a country that, by all accounts, is a hot-house, compared with ours, that she can't sleep o' nights, or live o' days without a small matter of fire, which she's welcome to, though, you see, it almost fills the house with smoke."

Howard, during the gardener's speech, had been trying to recollect where it was that he had lately seen some essay upon smoky chimneys; and he suddenly exclaimed, "It was in Dr. Franklin's works—was it not, Mr. Russell?"

"What?" said Mr. Russell, smiling.

"That essay upon smoky chimneys which I said I would skip over, the other day, because I had nothing to do with it, and I thought I should not understand. Don't you remember telling me, sir, that I had better not skip it, because it might, some time or other, be useful to me? I wish I could get the book now; I would take pains to understand it, because, perhaps, I might find out how this poor man's chimney might be cured of smoking. As for his window, I know how that can be easily mended, because I once watched a man who was hanging some windows for my aunt—I'll get some sash line."

"Do you recollect what o'clock it is, my good friend?" said Mr. Russell, holding out his watch to Howard. "We cannot wait till you are perfect master of the theory of smoky chimneys, and the practice of hanging windows; it is time that we should be gone." Mr. Russell spoke this with an air of raillery, as he usually did, when he was particularly pleased.

As they were going away, Oliver earnestly repeated his request, that Mr. Russell would come again in the evening, that he might have an opportunity of giving the poor woman his half-guinea. Mr. Russell promised him that he would; but he at the same time added, "All charity, my dear Oliver, does not consist in giving money: it is easy for a man to put his hand in his pocket, and take out a few shillings, to give any person in distress."

"I wish," said Oliver, "I was able to do more! what can I do? I'll think of something. Howard, will you think of something that I can do? But I must see about my Latin lesson first, for I had not time to look it over this morning, before I came out."

When they got back, the business of the day, for some hours, suspended all thoughts of the mulatto woman; but, in the first interval of leisure, Oliver went in search of Mr. Holloway, to ask for his half-guinea. Holloway had a crowd of his companions round him, whom he seemed to be entertaining with some very diverting story, for they were laughing violently when little Oliver first came up to them; but they no sooner perceived him than all their merriment suddenly ceased. Holloway first lowered his voice into a whisper, and then observing that Oliver still stood his ground, he asked him, in his usual peremptory tone, what might be his business? Oliver drew him aside, and asked him to pay him the half-guinea. "The half-guinea?" repeated Holloway: "man, you talk of the half-guinea as if there was but one half-guinea in the world: you shall have the half-guinea, for I hate to be dunned—Stay, I believe I have no half-a-guinea about me: you can't give me two half-guineas for a guinea, can ye?"

"Me!"

"Well, then, you must wait till I can get change."

"Must I wait? but I really want it for a particular reason, this evening: I wish you could give it me now—you know you promised; but I don't like putting people in mind of their promises, and I would not ask you about the money, only that I really want it."

"Want it!—nonsense: what can you want money for, such a little chap as you? I'll lay you any wager, your particular reason, if the truth was told, is, that you can't resist the tart-woman."

"I can resist the tart-woman," cried Oliver proudly; "I have a much better use for my money: but I don't want to boast, neither; only, Holloway, do give me the half-guinea: shall I run and ask somebody to give you two half-guineas for a guinea?"

"No, no, I'll not be dunned into paying you. If you had not asked me for it, I should have given it you to-night: but since you could not trust to my honour, you'll please to wait till to-morrow morning."

"But I did trust to your honour for a whole month."

"A month!—a great while, indeed; then trust to it a day longer; and if you ask me for the money to-morrow, you shan't have it till the next day. I'll teach you not to be such a little dun: nobody, that has any spirit, can bear to be dunned, particularly for such small sums. I thought you had been above such meanness, or, I promise you, I should never have borrowed your half-guinea," added Holloway; and he left his unfortunate creditor to reflect upon the new ideas of meanness and spirit, which had been thus artfully thrown out.

Oliver was roused from his reflections by his friend Howard. "Mr. Russell is ready to go with us to the gardener's again," said Howard: "have you a mind to come?"

"A great mind; but I am ashamed, for I've not got my half-guinea which I lent." Here his newly acquired fear of meanness checked Oliver, and without complaining of his creditor's want of punctuality, he added, "but I should like to see the poor woman though, for all that."

They set out, but stopped in their way at a bookseller's, where Howard inquired for that essay of Dr. Franklin on smoky chimneys, which he was impatient to see. This bookseller was well acquainted with Mr. Russell. Howard had promised to give the bookseller the translation of the little French book which we formerly mentioned; and the bookseller, on his part, was very obliging in furnishing Howard with any books he wanted.

Howard was deep in the essay on smoky chimneys, and examining the references in the print belonging to it, whilst Mr. Russell was looking over the prints in the Encyclopedia, with little Oliver. They were all so intent upon what they were about, that they did not perceive the entrance of Holloway and Mr. Supine. Mr. Supine called in merely to see what Mr. Russell could be looking at, with so much appearance of interest. The indolent are always curious, though they will not always exert themselves, even to gratify their curiosity.

"Only the Encyclopaedia prints," said Supine, looking over Mr. Russell's shoulder: "I thought you had got something new."

"Only smoky chimneys," exclaimed Holloway, looking over Howard's shoulder: "what upon earth, Howard, can you find so entertaining in smoky chimneys? Are you turned chimney-doctor, or chimney-sweeper? This will be an excellent thing for Lord Rawson, won't it, Mr. Supine? We'll tell it to him on Thursday; it will be a good joke for us, for half the day. Pray, doctor Charles Howard," continued the wit, with mock solemnity, "do you go up the chimneys yourself?"

Howard took this raillery with so much good-humour, that Holloway looked quite disappointed; and Mr. Supine, in a careless tone, cried, "I take it, reading such things as these will scarcely improve your style, sir—will they, think ye, Mr. Russell?"

"I am not sure," replied Mr. Russell, "that Mr. Howard's first object in reading is to improve his style; but," added he, turning to the title-page, and pointing to Franklin's name, "you, perhaps, did not know—"

"Oh, Dr. Franklin's works," interrupted Supine: "I did not see the name before—to be sure I must bow down to that."

Having thus easily satisfied Mr. Supine's critical scruples by the authority of a name, Mr. Russell rose to depart, as he perceived that there was no chance of getting rid of the idlers.

"What are you going to do with yourself, Russell?" said Mr. Supine; "we'll walk with you, if you are for walking, this fine evening; only don't let's walk like penny postmen."

"But he's in a hurry," said Oliver; "he's going to see a poor woman."

"A poor woman!" said Supine; "down this close lane too!"

"Oh, let's see all that's to be seen," whispered Holloway; "ten to one we shall get some diversion out of it: Russell's a quiz worth studying, and Howard's his ditto."

They came to the gardener's house. Holloway's high spirits suddenly subsided when he beheld the figure of the mulatto woman.

"What's the matter?" said Oliver, observing that he started; "why did you start so?"

"Tell Howard I want to speak one word with him, this instant, in the street; bid him come out to me," whispered Holloway; and he hastily retreated before the poor woman saw his face.

"Howard," cried Holloway, "I sent for you to tell you a great secret."

"I'm sorry for it," said Charles; "for I hate secrets."

"But you can keep a secret, man, can't you?"

"If it were necessary, I hope I could; but I'd rather not hear—"

"Pooh, nonsense," interrupted Holloway, "you must hear it; I'll trust to your honour; and, besides, I have not a moment to stand shilly shally: I've got a promise from my father to let me go down, this Easter, with Lord Rawson, to Marryborough, in his dog-cart, randem-tandem, you know."

"I did not know it, indeed," said Charles; "but what then?"

"Why, then, you see, I must be upon my good behaviour; and you would not do such an ill-natured trick as to betray me?"

"Betray you! I don't know what you mean," said Howard, astonished.

Holloway now briefly told him his stage-coach adventure, and concluded by saying, he was afraid that the mulatto woman should recollect either his face or voice, and should blow him.

"And what," said Howard, shocked at the selfishness which Holloway showed—"and what do you want me to do? why do you tell me all this?"

"Because," said Holloway, "I thought if you heard what the woman said, when she saw me, you would have got it all out of her to be sure; therefore I thought it best to trust you with my secret, and so put you upon honour with me. All I ask of you is, to hold your tongue about my—my—my—frolic, and just make some excuse for my not going into the room again where the mulatto woman is: you may tell Supine, if he asks what's become of me, that I'm gone to the music-shop, to get some new music for him: that will keep him quiet. Good by."

When Howard returned to the room where the mulatto woman lay, he expected to be questioned by Mr. Supine about Holloway's sudden departure; but this gentleman was not in the habit of paying great attention to his pupil's motions. He took it for granted that Holloway had escaped, because he did not wish to be called upon for a charitable subscription. From the same fear, Mr. Supine affected unusual absence of mind whilst Mr. Russell talked to the mulatto woman, and at length, professing himself unable to endure any longer the smell of smoke, he pushed his way into the street. "Mr. Holloway, I suppose," said he, "has taken himself home, very wisely, and I shall follow him: we make it a rule, I think, to miss one another; but to keep a young man in leading-strings would be a great bore. We're upon the best footing in the world together: as to the rest—"

New difficulties awaited Holloway. He got home some time before Mr. Supine, and found his friend, the stage-coachman, waiting for him with a rueful face.

"Master," said he, "here's a sad job: there was a parcel lost last night, in the confusion of the overturn of the coach; and I must make it good; for it's booked, and it's booked to the value of five guineas, for it was a gold muslin gown that a lady was very particular about; and, master, I won't peach if you'll pay: but as for losing my place, or making up five guineas afore Saturday, it's what I can't take upon me to do."

Holloway was much dismayed at this news; he now began to think he should pay too dear for his frolic. The coachman persisted in his demand. Mr. Supine appeared at the corner of the street; and his pupil was forced to get rid immediately of the coachman, by a promise, that the money should be ready on Saturday. When Holloway made this promise, he was not master of two guineas in the world; how to procure the whole sum was now the question. Alderman Holloway, with the hope of exciting in his son's mind a love for literature, made it a practice to reward him with solid gold, whenever he brought home any certificate of his scholarship. Holloway had lately received five guineas from his father, for an approved copy of Latin verses; and the alderman had promised to give him five guineas more if he brought home the medal which was to be the reward for the best essay in the periodical paper, which the Westminster boys were now writing. Holloway, though he could write elegant Latin verses, had not any great facility in English composition; he, consequently, according to the usual practice of little minds, undervalued a talent which he did not possess. He had ridiculed the scheme of writing an English essay, and had loudly declared, that he did not think it worth his while to write English. His opinion was, however, somewhat changed by his father's promised reward; and the stage-coachman's impatience for his money now impelled Holloway to exertion. He began to write his essay late on Friday evening—the medal was to be given on Saturday morning—so that there could not be much time for revisal and corrections. Corrections he affected to disdain, and piqued himself upon the rapidity with which he wrote. "Howard," said he, when they met to deliver in their compositions, "you have been three weeks writing your essay; I ran mine off in three hours and a quarter."

Mr. Holloway had not considered, that what is written with ease is not always read with ease. His essay was written with such a careless superfluity of words, and such a lack of ideas appeared in the performance, that the judges unanimously threw it aside, as unworthy of their notice. "Gentlemen," cried Dr. B., coming forward among the anxious crowd of expectants, "which of you owns this motto?—

"'Hear it, ye Senates, hear this truth sublime,
He who allows oppression shares the crime(6).'"

(Footnote 6: Botanic Garden, vol. ii.)

"It's his!—it's his!—it's his!" exclaimed little Oliver, clapping his hands—"it's Howard's, sir."

Dr. B., pleased with this grateful little boy's honest joy, put the medal into his hands, without speaking, and Oliver ran with it to his friend. "Only," said he, "only let me be by, when you show it to your aunt."

How much the pleasure of success is increased by the sympathy of our friends! The triumph of a school-boy over his competitors is sometimes despicable; but Howard's joy was not of this selfish and puerile sort. All the good passions had stimulated him to exertion, and he was rewarded by his own generous feelings. He would not have exchanged the delight which he saw in his little friend Oliver's face, the approving smile of his aunt, and the proud satisfaction Mr. Russell expressed at the sight of his medal, for all the solid gold which Alderman Holloway deemed the highest reward of literature.

Alderman Holloway was filled with indignation when he heard from Mr. Supine that his son's essay had been rejected with contempt. The young gentleman was also much surprised at the decision of the judges; and his tutor, by way of pleasing his pupil's friends, hesitated not to hint, that there "certainly was great injustice done to Mr. Augustus Holloway's talents." The subject was canvassed at a turtle dinner at the alderman's. "There shall not be injustice done to my Augustus," said the irritated father, wisely encouraging his Augustus in all his mean feelings. "Never mind 'em all, my boy; you have a father, you may thank Heaven, who can judge for himself, and will: you shall not be the loser by Dr. B.'s or doctor any body's injustice; I'll make it up to you, my boy; in the meantime, join us in a bumper of port. Here's to Dr. B.'s better judgment; wishing him health and happiness these Easter holidays, and a new pair of spectacles,—hey, Mr. Supine?"

This well-chosen toast was drunk with much applause and laughter by the company. The alderman insisted upon having his Augustus's essay produced in the evening. Holloway had now ample satisfaction, for the whole company were unanimous in their plaudits, after Mr. Supine had read two or three sentences: the alderman, to confirm his own critical judgment, drew out his purse, and counting out ten bright guineas, presented them, with a look of high self-satisfaction, to his son. "Here, Augustus, my boy," said he; "I promised you five guineas if you brought me home the prize medal; but I now present you with ten, to make you the amends you so richly deserve, for not having got their medal. Thank God, I am able to afford it; and I hope," added the alderman, looking round, and laughing, "I hope I'm as good a patron of the belles lettres as the head doctor of Westminster himself."

Holloway's eyes sparkled with joy at the sight of the glittering bribe. He began some speech in reply, in which he compared his father to Maecenas; but being entangled in a sentence, in which the nominative case had been too long separated from the verb, he was compelled to pause abruptly. Nevertheless, the alderman rubbed his hands with exultation; and "Hear him! hear him!—hear your member!" was vociferated by all the friends of the young orator. "Well, really," concluded his mother to the ladies, who were complimenting her upon her son's performance, "it was not a bad speech, considering he had nothing to say!"

Lord Rawson, who was one of the company, now congratulated his friend in a whisper—"You've made a good job of it to-day, Augustus," said he: "solid pudding's better than empty praise. We're going," continued his lordship to the alderman, "to try my new horses this evening;" and he pulled Augustus with him out of the room.

"There they go," said the prudent father, delighted with his own son's being the chosen friend of a nobleman—"there they go, arm in arm, a couple of rare ones: we shall have fine work with them, I foresee, when Augustus gets to college—but young men of spirit must not be curbed like common boys—we must make allowances—I have been young myself,—hey, Mr. Supine?"

"Certainly, sir," said the obsequious tutor; "and you still have all the sprightliness of youth; and my ideas of education square completely with yours."

According to Alderman Holloway's ideas of education, the holy days were always to be made a season of complete idleness and dissipation, to relieve his son from his school studies. It was his great delight to contrast the pleasures of home with the hardships of school, and to make his son compare the indulgence of a father with the severity of a schoolmaster. How he could expect an education to succeed which he sedulously endeavoured to counteract, it may be difficult for any rational person to conceive.

After Lord Rawson and Holloway had enjoyed the pleasures of driving the new horses, tandem, in a dog-cart, and had conversed about dogs and horses till they had nothing left to say to each other, his lordship proposed stepping in to Mr. Carat, the jeweller's shop, to look at some new watches: his lordship said he was tired of his own, for he had had it six months. Mr. Carat was not in the way when they first went in. One of the young men who attended in the shop said, "that his master was extremely busy, in settling some accounts with a captain of a ship, who was to leave England in a few days."

"Don't tell me of settling accounts," cried Lord Ramon—"I hate the sound of settling accounts: run and tell Mr. Carat that Lord Rawson is here, and must speak to him this instant, for I'm in a desperate hurry."

A quarter of an hour elapsed before the impatient lord could be obeyed; during this time, his lordship and Holloway rummaged over every thing in the shop. A pretty bauble to hang to his watch caught his lordship's fancy. His lordship happened to have no money in his pocket. "Holloway," said he, "my good fellow, you've ten guineas in your pocket, I know; do lend me them here." Holloway, rather proud of his riches, lent his ten guineas to his noble friend with alacrity; but a few minutes afterward recollected that he should want five of them that very night, to pay the poor stage-coachman. His recollection came too late, for after Lord Rawson had paid three or four guineas for his trinket, he let the remainder of the money down with an absent nonchalance, into his pocket. "We'll settle—I'll pay you, Holloway, to-morrow morning, you know."

Holloway, from false shame, replied, "Oh, very well." And at this instant Mr. Carat entered the shop, bowing and apologizing to his lordship for having been busy.

"I'm always, to be sure, in a very great hurry," cried Lord Rawson; "I never have a minute that I can call my own. All I wanted though, just now, was to tell you, that I could not settle any thing—you understand—till we come back from Marryborough. I go down there to-morrow."

The Jew bowed with unlimited acquiescence, assuring his lordship that he should ever wait his perfect convenience. As he spoke, he glanced an inquiring eye upon Holloway.

"Mr. Holloway, the eldest, the only son of Alderman Holloway—rich as a Jew! and he'll soon leave Westminster," whispered Lord Rawson to the Jew. "Holloway," continued he, turning to his friend, "give me leave to introduce Mr. Carat to you. You may," added his lordship, lowering his voice, "find this Jew a useful friend some time or other, my lad. He's my man in all money jobs."

The Jew and the school-boy seemed equally flattered and pleased by this introduction; they were quickly upon familiar terms with one another; and Mr. Carat, who was willing that such an acquaintance should begin in the most advantageous and agreeable manner on his part, took the young gentleman, with an air of mystery and confidence, into a little room behind the shop; there he produced a box full of old-fashioned secondhand trinkets, and, without giving Holloway time to examine them, said that he was going to make a lottery of these things. "If I had any young favourite friends," continued the wily Jew, "I should give them a little whisper in the ear, and bid them try their fortune; they never will have a finer opportunity." He then presented a hand-bill, drawn up in a style which even Messrs. Goodluck and Co. need not have disdained to admire. The youth was charmed with the composition. The Jew made him a present of a couple of tickets for himself, and gave him a dozen more, to distribute amongst his companions at Westminster. Holloway readily undertook to distribute the tickets upon condition that he might have a list of the prizes in the lottery. "If they don't see a list of the prizes," said he, "not a soul will put in."

The Jew took a pen immediately, and drew up a captivating list of prizes.

Holloway promised to copy it, because Mr. Carat said his hand must not appear in the business, and it must be conducted with the strictest secrecy; because "the law," added the Jew, "has a little jealousy of these sort of things—government likes none but licensed lotteries, young gentleman."

"The law! I don't care what the law likes," replied the school-boy; "if I break the law, I hope I'm rich enough to pay the forfeit, or my father will pay for me, which is better still."

To this doctrine the Jew readily assented, and they parted, mutually satisfied with each other.

It was agreed that Lord Rawson should drive his friend to Marryborough the next Tuesday, and that he should return on Wednesday, with Holloway, to Westminster, on purpose that he might meet Mr. Carat there, who was then to deliver the prizes.

"I'll lay you a bet," cried Lord Rawson, as he left the Jew's, "that you'll have a prize yourself. Now are you not obliged to me for introducing you to Carat?"

"Yes, that I am," replied Holloway; "it's easier to put into the lottery than to write Latin verses and English essays. I'll puzzle and bore myself no more with those things, I promise my father."

"Who does, after they've once left school, I want to know?" said his noble friend. "I'm sure I've forgot all I ever learned from Latin and Greek fellows; you know they tell just for nothing when one gets into the world. I make it a principle never to talk of books, for nobody does, you know, that has any thing else to talk of. None but quizzes and quozzes ever came out with any thing of that sort. Now, how they'd stare at Marryborough, Holloway, if you were to begin sporting some of your Horace and Virgil!"

The dashing, yet bashful school-boy, with much emotion, swore that he cared as little for Horace and Virgil as his lordship did. Holloway was really an excellent scholar, but he began to be heartily ashamed of it in his lordship's company, and prudently resolved to adopt the principles he had just heard; to forget as fast as possible all he had learned: never to talk of books; and to conceal both his knowledge and his abilities, lest they should stare at him at Maryborough.

The lottery tickets were easily disposed of amongst the young gentlemen at Westminster. As young men can seldom calculate, they are always ready to trust to their individual good fortune, and they are, consequently, ever ready to put into any species of lottery.

"Look here!" cried little Oliver, showing a lottery ticket to Howard; "look what Holloway has just offered to give me, instead of half-a-guinea, which he owes me. I told him I would just run and ask your advice. Shall I accept of it?"

"I would advise you not," answered Howard; "you are sure of your half-guinea, and you have only a chance of getting any thing in the lottery."

"Oh, but then I've a chance of such a number of fine things! You have not seen the list of prizes. Do you know there's a watch amongst them? Now, suppose my ticket should come up a prize, and that I should get a watch for my half-guinea!—a real watch!—a watch that would go!—a watch that I should wind up myself every night! O Charles! would not that be a good bargain for my half-guinea? I'm sure you have not read the list of prizes, have you?"

"No, I have not," said Howard: "have you seen the list of blanks?"

"Of blanks! No," said Oliver, with a changed countenance; "I never thought of the blanks."

"And yet in most lotteries there are many more blanks than prizes, you know."

"Are there? Well, but I hope I shall not have a blank," said Oliver.

"So every body hopes, but some people must be disappointed."

"Yes," said the little boy, pausing—"but then some people must win, and I have as good a chance as another, have not I?"

"And do you know what the chance against your winning is? Once I had a great mind, as you have now, Oliver, to put into a lottery. It was just after my aunt lost all her fortune, and I thought that if I were to get the twenty thousand pound prize, I could give it to her."

"I'll give my watch (if I get it, I mean) to somebody. I'll give it to the mulatto woman, because she is poor. No; I'll give it to you, because you are the best, and I love you the best, and I am more obliged to you than to any body in the world, for you have taught me more; and you have taught me as I was never taught before, without laughing at, or scolding, or frightening, or calling me blockhead or dunce; and you have made me think a great deal better of myself; and I am always happy when I'm with you; and I'm quite another creature since you came to school. I hope you'll never leave school whilst I am here," cried Oliver.

"But you have quite forgot the lottery," said Howard, smiling, and much touched by his little friend's simplicity and enthusiasm.

"Oh, the lottery! ay," said Oliver, "you were telling me something about yourself; do go on."

"I once thought, as you do now, that it would be a charming thing to put into a lottery."

"Well, and did you win?"

"No."

"Did you lose?"

"No."

"How then?"

"I did not put into the lottery, for I was convinced that it was a foolish way of spending money."

"If you think it's foolish or wrong," said Oliver, "I'll have nothing to do with this lottery."

"I don't want to govern you by my opinion," said Howard; "but if you have patience to attend to all the reasons that convinced me, you will be able to judge, and form an opinion for yourself. You know I must leave school some time or other, and then—"

"Well, don't talk of that, but tell me all the reasons, quick."

"I can't tell them so very quickly," said Howard, laughing: "when we go home this evening I'll ask my aunt to look for the passage in Smith's Wealth of Nations, which she showed me."

"Oh!" interrupted Oliver, with a sigh, "Smith's Wealth of what? That's a book, I'm sure, I shall never be able to understand; is it not that great large book that Mr. Russell reads?"

"Yes."

"But I shall never understand it."

"Because it's a large book?"

"No," said Oliver, smiling, "but because I suppose it's very difficult to understand."

"Not what I've read of it: but I have only read passages here and there. That passage about lotteries, I think, you would understand, because it is so plainly written."

"I'll read it, then," said Oliver, "and try; and in the meantime I'll go and tell Holloway that I had rather not put into the lottery, till I know whether it's right or not."

Holloway flew into a violent passion with little Oliver when he went to return his lottery ticket. He abused and ridiculed Howard for his interference, and succeeded so well in raising a popular cry, that the moment Howard appeared on the playground, a general hiss, succeeded by a deep groan, was heard.—Howard recollected the oracle's answer to Cicero, and was not dismayed by the voice of the multitude. Holloway threw down half-a-guinea, to pay Oliver, and muttered to himself, "I'll make you remember this, Mr. Oliver."

"I'll give this half-guinea to the mulatto woman, and that's much better than putting it into a lottery, Charles," said the little boy; and, as soon as the business of the day was done, Oliver, Howard, and Mr. Russell, took their usual evening's walk towards the gardener's house.

"Ay, come in," cried old Paul, "come in! God bless you all! I don't know which is the best of you. I've been looking out of my door this quarter of an hour for ye," said he, as soon as he saw them; "and I don't know when I've been idle a quarter of an hour afore. But I've put on my best coat, though it's not Sunday, and wife has treated her to a dish of tea, and she's up and dressed—the mulatto woman, I mean—and quite hearty again. Walk in, walk in; it will do your hearts good to see her; she's so grateful too, though she can't speak good English, which is her only fault, poor soul; but we can't be born what we like, or she would have been as good an Englishman as the best of us. Walk in, walk in.—And the chimney does not smoke, master, no more than I do; and the window opens too; and the paper's up, and looks beautiful. God bless ye, God bless ye—walk in." Old Paul, whilst he spoke, had stopped the way into the room; but at length he recollected that they could not walk in whilst he stood in the door-way, and he let them pass.

The little room was no longer the smoky, dismal, miserable place which it was formerly. It was neatly papered; it was swept clean; there was a cheerful fire, which burnt quite clearly: the mulatto woman was cleanly dressed, and, rising from her work, she clasped her hands together with an emotion of joyful gratitude, which said more than any words could have expressed.

This room was not papered, nor was the chimney cured of smoking, nor was the woman clad in new clothes, by magic. It was all done by human means—by the industry and abilities of a benevolent boy.

The translation of the little French book, which Howard had completed, procured him the means of doing good. The book-seller to whom he offered it was both an honest man, and a good judge of literary productions. Mr. Russell's name also operated in his pupil's favour, and Howard received ten guineas for his translation.

Oliver was impatient for an opportunity to give his half-guinea, which he had held in his hand, till it was quite warm. "Let me look at that pretty thimble of yours," said he, going up to the mulatto woman, who had now taken up her work again; and, as he playfully pulled off the thimble, he slipped his half-guinea into her hand; then he stopped her thanks, by running on to a hundred questions about her thimble. "What a strange thimble! How came you by such a thimble? Was it given to you? Did you buy it? What's the use of this screw round the inside of the rim of it? Do look at it, Charles!"

The thimble was, indeed, remarkable; and it seemed extraordinary that such a one should belong to a poor woman, who had lately been in great distress.

"It is gold," said Mr. Russell, examining it, "and very old gold."

The mulatto woman sighed; and as she put the thimble upon her finger again, said, that she did not know whether it was gold or not; but she had a great value for it; that she had had it a great many years; that it had been given to her by the best friend she had ever had.

"Tell me about that best friend," said Oliver; "I like to hear about best friends."

"She was a very good friend indeed; though she was but young, scarcely bigger than yourself, at the time she gave me this thimble: she was my young mistress; I came all the way from Jamaica on purpose to find her out, and in hopes to live with her in my elder days."

"Jamaica!" cried Howard; "Jamaica!" cried Oliver, in the same breath; "what was her name?"

"Frances Howard."

"My aunt," exclaimed Howard.

"I'll run and tell her; I'll run and bring her here, this instant!" said Oliver. But Mr. Russell caught hold of him, and detained him, whilst they further questioned the woman. Her answers were perfectly consistent and satisfactory. She said, that her mistress's estate in Jamaica had been sold just before she left the island; that some of the old slaves had been set at liberty, by orders, which came, she understood, in her mistress's last letter; and that, amongst the rest, she had been freed: that she had heard say that her good mistress had desired the agent to give her also some little provision ground, upon the plantation, but that this had never been done; and that she had sold all the clothes and little things she possessed, to raise money to pay for her passage to England, hoping to find her mistress in London. She added, that the agent had given her a direction to her mistress; but that she had, in vain, applied at at the house, and at every house in the same street. "Show us the direction, if you have it," said Mr. Russell. The woman said she had kept it very carefully; but now it was almost worn out. The direction was, however, still legible upon the ragged bit of paper which she produced—To Mrs. Frances Howard, Portman Square, London. The instant Mr. Russell was satisfied, he was as expeditious as Oliver himself; they all three went home immediately to Mrs. Howard: she had, some time before, been confined to her room by a severe toothache.

"You promised me, aunt," said her nephew, "that as soon as you were well enough, you would go to old Paul's with us, to see our poor woman; can you go this evening?"

"Oh do! do, pray; I'm sure you won't catch cold," said Oliver; "for we have a very particular reason for wishing you to go."

"There is a sedan chair at the door," said Mr. Russell, "if you are afraid, madam, of catching cold."

"I am not rich enough to go out in sedan chairs," interrupted Mrs. Howard, "nor prudent enough, I am afraid, to stay at home."

"Oh! thank you," said Oliver, who had her clogs ready in his hands; "now you'll see something that will surprise you."

"Then take care you don't tell me what it is, before I see it," said Mrs. Howard.

Oliver, with some difficulty, held his tongue during the walk, and contented himself with working off his superfluous animation, by jumping over every obstacle in his way.

The meeting between the poor mulatto woman and her mistress was as full of joy and surprise as little Oliver had expected; and this is saying a great deal, for where much is expected, there is usually much disappointment; and very sympathetic people are often angry with others, for not being as much astonished, or as much delighted, as they think the occasion requires.

The day which Mr. Augustus Holloway imagined would bring him such complete felicity—the day on which Lord Rawson had promised to call for him in his dog-cart, and to drive him down random-tandem, to Marryborough—was now arrived. His lordship, in his dog-cart, was at the door; and Holloway, in high spirits, was just going to get into the carriage, when some one pulled his coat, and begged to speak a few words with him. It was the stage-coachman, who was absolutely in distress for the value of the lost parcel, which Holloway had promised him should be punctually paid: but Holloway, now that his excursion to Marryborough was perfectly secure, thought but very little of the poor coachman's difficulties; and though he had the money, which he had raised by the lottery tickets, in his pocket, he determined to keep that for his amusements during the Easter holidays. "You must wait till I come back from Marryborough; I can't possibly speak to you now; I can't possibly, you see, keep Lord Rawson waiting. Why didn't you call sooner? I am not at all convinced that any parcel was lost."

"I'll show you the books—it's book'd, sir," said the man, eagerly.

"Well, well, this is not a time to talk of booking. I'll be with you in an instant, my lord," cried Holloway to Lord Rawson, who was all impatience to be off. But the coachman would not quit his hold. "I'm sorry to come to that, master," said he: "as long as we were both upon honour together, it was very well; but, if you break squares with me, being a gentleman, and rich, you can't take it ill, I being a poor man and my place and all at stake, if I take the shortest way to get my own: I must go to Dr. B. for justice, if you won't give it me without my peaching," said the coachman.

"I'll see you again to-morrow morning," said Holloway, alarmed: "we come up to town again to-morrow."

"To-morrow won't do," said the coachman; "I shall lose my place and my bread to-day. I know how to trust to young gentlemen's to-morrows."

A volley of oaths from Lord Rawson again summoned his companion. At this instant, Mr. Russell, young Howard, and little Oliver, came up the street, and were passing on to Mrs. Howard's, when Holloway stopped Howard, who was the last of the party. "For Heaven's sake," said he, in a whisper, "do settle for me with this confounded coachman! I know you are rich; your bookseller told me so; pay five guineas for me to him, and you shall have them again to-morrow, there's a good fellow. Lord Rawson's waiting; good by."

"Stay, stay," said Howard, who was not so easily to be drawn into difficulties by a moment's weakness, or by the want of a moment's presence of mind: "I know nothing of this business; I have other uses for my money; I cannot pay five guineas for you, Holloway."

"Then let it alone," cried Holloway, with a brutal execration; and he forcibly broke from the coachman, shook hands with his tutor, Mr. Supine, who was talking to Lord Rawson about the varnish of his gig, jumped into the carriage, and was whirled away from all reflection in a moment, by his noble companion.

The poor coachman entreated Howard to stay one instant, to hear him. He explained the business to him, and reproached himself bitterly for his folly. "I'm sure I thought," said he, "I was sure of a gentleman's honour; and young gentlemen ought to be above not paying handsome for their frolics, if they must have frolics; and a frolic's one thing, and cheating a poor man like me is another; and he had liked to have killed a poor mulatto woman, too, by the overturn of the coach, which was all his doings."

"The woman is got very well, and is very well off now," interrupted Howard; "you need say nothing about that."

"Well, but my money, I must say about that," said the coachman. Here Howard observed, that Mr. Supine had remained at the door in a lounging attitude, and was quite near enough to overhear their conversation. Howard, therefore, to avoid exciting his attention by any mysterious whispers, walked away from the coachman; but in vain; he followed: "I'll peach," said he; "I must in my own defence."

"Stay till to-morrow morning," said Howard: "perhaps you'll be paid then."

The coachman, who was a good-natured fellow, said, "Well, I don't like making mischief among young gentlemen; I will wait till to-morrow, but not a day more, master, if you'd go down on your knees to me."

Mr. Supine, whose curiosity was fully awake, called to the coachman the moment Howard was out of hearing, and tried, by various questions, to draw the secret from him. The words, "overturn of the coach—mulatto woman," and the sentence, which the irritated coachman had pronounced in a raised voice, that "young gentlemen should be above not paying handsome for their frolics," had reached Mr. Supine's attentive ear, before Howard had been aware that the tutor was a listener. Nothing more could Mr. Supine draw, however, from the coachman, who now felt himself upon honour, having promised Howard not to peach till the next morning. Difficulties stimulated Mr. Supine's curiosity; but he remained for the present satisfied in the persuasion that he had discovered a fine frolic of the immaculate Mr. Charles Howard; his own pupil he did not suspect upon this occasion. Holloway's whisperings with the coachman had ended the moment Mr. Supine appeared at the door, and the tutor had in the same moment been so struck with the beautiful varnish of Lord Rawson's dog-cart, that his pupil might have whispered longer, without rousing his attention. Mr. Supine was further confirmed in his mistake about Howard, from the recollection of the mulatto woman, whom he had seen at the gardener's: he knew that she had been hurt by a fall from a stage-coach. He saw Howard much interested about her. All this he joined with what he had just overheard about a frolic, and he was rejoiced at the idea of implicating in this business Mr. Russell, whom he disliked.

Mr. Supine, having got rid of his pupil, went immediately to Alderman Holloway's, where he had a general invitation to dinner. Mrs. Holloway approved of her son's tutor, full as much for his love of gossiping, as for his musical talents: Mr. Supine constantly supplied her with news and anecdotes; upon the present occasion, he thought that his story, however imperfect, would be eagerly received, because it concerned Howard.

Since the affair of the prize essay, and the medal, Mrs. Holloway had taken a dislike to young Howard, whom she considered as the enemy of her dear Augustus. No sooner had she heard Mr. Supine's blundering information, than, without any farther examination, she took the whole for granted: eager to repeat the anecdote to Mrs. Howard, she instantly wrote a note to her, saying that she would drink tea with her that evening.

When Mrs. Holloway, attended by Mr. Supine, went, in the evening, to Mrs. Howard's, they found with her Mrs. B., the lady of Dr. B., the master of Westminster School.

"Is not this an odd rencontre?" whispered Mrs. Holloway to Mr. Supine, as she drew him to a recessed window, commodious for gossiping: "I shall be called a tell-tale, I know, at Westminster; but I shall tell our story, notwithstanding. I would keep any other boy's secret; but Howard is such a saint: and I hate saints."

A knock at the door interrupted Mrs. Holloway; she looked out of the window. "Oh, here he comes, up the steps," continued she, "after his sober evening promenade, and his Mr. Russell with—and, I declare, the mulatto woman with him. Now for it!"

Howard entered the room, went up to his aunt, and said, in a low voice,—

"Ma'am, poor Cuba is come; she is rather tired with walking, and she is gone to rest herself in the front parlour."

"Her lameness, though," pursued little Oliver, who followed Howard into the room, "is almost well. I just asked her how high she thought the coach was from which she was—"

A look from Howard made Oliver stop short; for though he did not understand the full meaning of it, he saw it was designed to silence him. Howard was afraid of betraying Holloway's secret to Mr. Supine or to Mrs. Holloway: his aunt sent him out of the room with some message to Cuba, which gave Mrs. Holloway an opportunity of opening her business.

"Pray," said she, "might I presume to ask—for I perceive the young gentleman has some secret to keep from me, which he may have good reasons for—may I, just to satisfy my own mind, presume to ask whether, as her name leads one to guess, your Cuba, Mrs. Howard, is a mulatto woman?"

Surprised by the manner of the question, Mrs. Howard coldly replied, "Yes, madam—a mulatto woman."

"And she is lame, I think, sir, you mentioned?" persisted the curious lady, turning to little Oliver.

"Yes, she's a little lame still; but she will soon be quite well."

"Oh! then, her lameness came, I presume, from an accident, sir, and not from her birth?"

"From an accident, ma'am."

"Oh! an accident—a fall—a fall from a coach—from a stage-coach, perhaps," continued Mrs. Holloway, smiling significantly at Mr. Supine: "you take me for a conjuror, young gentleman, I see by your astonishment," continued she to Oliver; "but a little bird told me the whole story; and I see Mrs. Howard knows how to keep a secret as well as myself."

Mrs. Howard looked for an explanation.

"Nay," said Mrs. Holloway, "you know best, Mrs. Howard; but as we're all out of school now, I shall not be afraid to mention such a little affair, even before the doctor's lady; for, to be sure, she would never let it reach the doctor's ears."

"Really, ma'am," said Mrs. Howard, "you puzzle me a little; I wish you would explain yourself: I don't know what it is that you would not have reach the doctor's ears."

"You don't?—well, then, your nephew must have been very clever, to have kept you in the dark; mustn't he, Mr. Supine?"

"I always, you know, thought the young gentleman very clever, ma'am," said Mr. Supine, with a malicious emphasis.

Mrs. Howard's colour now rose, and with a mixture of indignation and anxiety she pressed both Mr. Supine and Mrs. Holloway to be explicit. "I hate mysteries!" said she. Mrs. Holloway still hung back, saying it was a tender point; and hinting, that it would lessen her esteem and confidence in one most dear to her, to hear the whole truth.

"Do you mean Howard, ma'am?" exclaimed little Oliver: "oh, speak! speak! it's impossible Charles Howard can have done any thing wrong."

"Go for him, my dear," said Mrs. Howard, resuming her composure; "let him be present. I hate mysteries."

"But, my dear Mrs. Howard," whispered Mrs. Holloway, "you don't consider; you'll get your nephew into a shocking scrape; the story will infallibly go from Mrs. B. to Dr. B. You are warm, and don't consider consequences."

"Charles," said Mrs. Howard to her nephew, the moment he appeared, "from the time you were five years old, till this instant, I have never known you tell a falsehood; I should, therefore, be very absurd, as well as very unjust, if I were to doubt your integrity. Tell me—have you got into any difficulties? I would rather hear of them from yourself, than from any body else. Is there any mystery about overturning a stage-coach, that you know of, and that you have concealed from me?"

"There is a mystery, ma'am, about overturning a stage-coach," replied Howard, in a firm tone of voice; "but when I assure you that it is no mystery of mine—nothing in which I have myself any concern—I am sure that you will believe me, my dear aunt, and that you will press me no further."

"Not a word further, not a frown further," said his aunt, with a smile of entire confidence; in which Mr. Russell joined, but which appeared incomprehensible to Mr. Supine.

"Very satisfactory indeed!" said that gentleman, leaning back in the chair; "I never heard any thing more satisfactory to my mind!"

"Perfectly satisfactory, upon my word!" echoed Mrs. Holloway; but no looks, no inuendoes, could now disturb Mrs. Howard's security, or disconcert the resolute simplicity which appeared in her nephew's countenance. Mrs. Holloway, internally devoured by curiosity, was compelled to submit in silence. This restraint soon became so irksome to her, that she shortened her visit as much as she decently could.

In crossing the passage, to go to her carriage, she caught a glimpse of the mulatto woman, who was going into a parlour. Resolute, at all hazards, to satisfy herself, Mrs. Holloway called to the retreating Cuba—began by asking some civil questions about her health; then spoke of the accident she had lately met with; and, in short, by a skilful cross-examination, drew her whole story from her. The gratitude with which the poor woman spoke of Howard's humanity was by no means pleasing to Mr. Supine.

"Then it was not he who overturned the coach?" said Mrs. Holloway.

The woman eagerly replied, "Oh no, madam!" and proceeded to draw, as well as she could, a description of the youth who had been mounted upon the coach-box: she had seen him only by the light of the moon, and afterwards by the light of a lantern; but she recollected his figure so well, and described him so accurately, that Mr. Supine knew the picture instantly, and Mrs. Holloway whispered to him, "Can it be Augustus?"

"Mr. Holloway!—Impossible!—I suppose—"

But the woman interrupted him by saying that she recollected to have heard the young gentleman called by that name by the coachman.

The mother and the tutor were nearly alike confounded by this discovery. Mrs. Holloway got into her carriage, and, in their way home, Mr. Supine represented, that he should be ruined for ever with the alderman, if this transaction came to his knowledge; that, in fact, it was a mere boyish frolic; but that the alderman might not consider it in that light, and would, perhaps, make Mr. Augustus feel his serious displeasure. The foolish mother, out of mistaken good-nature, at length promised to be silent upon the subject. But, before he slept, Alderman Holloway heard the whole story. The footman, who had attended the carriage, was at the door when Mrs. Holloway was speaking to the mulatto woman, and had listened to every word that was said. This footman was in the habit of telling his master, when he attended him at night, all the news which he had been able to collect in the day. Mr. Supine was no favourite of his; because, whenever the tutor came to the house, he gave a great deal of trouble, being too indolent to do any thing for himself, and yet not sufficiently rich, or sufficiently generous, to pay the usual premiums for the active civility of servants. This footman was not sorry to have an opportunity of repeating any story that might injure Mr. Supine with his master. Alderman Holloway heard it under the promise of concealing the name of the person who had given him the information, and resolved to discover the truth of the affair the next day, when he was to visit his son at Westminster.

But we must now return to Mrs. Howard's. We mentioned that Mrs. B. spent the evening with her. Dr. B., soon after Mrs. Holloway went away, called to take his lady home: he had been engaged to spend the evening at a card assembly; but, as he was a man who liked agreeable conversation better than cards, he had made his escape from a rout, to spend half an hour with Mrs. Howard and Mr. Russell. The doctor was a man of various literature; able to appreciate others, he was not insensible to the pleasure of seeing himself appreciated. Half an hour passes quickly in agreeable conversation: the doctor got into an argument, concerning the propriety of the distinction made by some late metaphysical writers, between imagination and fancy. Thence he was led to some critical remarks upon Warton's beautiful Ode to Fancy; then to the never-ending debate upon original genius; including also the doctrine of hereditary temper and dispositions, which the doctor warmly supported, and which Mrs. Howard coolly questioned.

In the midst of their conversation, they were suddenly interrupted by a groan. They all looked round to see whence it came. It came from little Oliver: he was sitting at a little table at the farther end of the room, reading so intently in a large book that he saw nothing else: a long unsnuffed candle, with a perilous fiery summit to its black wick, stood before him, and his left arm embraced a thick china jar, against which he leaned his head. There was, by common consent, a general silence in the room, whilst every one looked at Oliver, as at a picture. Mrs. Howard moved gently round behind his chair, to see what he was reading: the doctor followed her. It was the account of the execution of two rebel Koromantyn negroes, related in Edwards's History of the West Indies(7). To try whether it would interrupt Oliver's deep attention, Mrs. Howard leaned over him, and snuffed his dim candle; but the light was lost upon him—he did not feel the obligation. Dr. B. then put his hand upon the jar, which he pulled from Oliver's embrace. "Be quiet! I must finish this!" cried Oliver, still holding fast the jar, and keeping his eyes upon the book. The doctor gave a second pull at the jar, and the little boy made an impatient push with his elbow; then casting his eye upon the large hand which pulled the jar, he looked up, surprised, in the doctor's face.

(Footnote 7: Vol. ii. p. 57, second edition.)

The nice china jar, which Oliver had held so sturdily, was very precious to him. His uncle had just sent him two jars of fine West India sweetmeats. One of these he had shared with his companions: the other he had kept, to give to Mrs. Howard, who had once said, in his hearing, that she was fond of West India sweetmeats. She accepted Oliver's little present. Children sometimes feel as much pleasure in giving away sweetmeats as in eating them; and Mrs. Howard too well understood the art of education, even in trifles, to deny to grateful and generous feelings their natural and necessary exercise. A child can show gratitude and generosity only in trifles.

"Are these all the sweetmeats that you have left, Oliver?" said Mrs. Howard.

"Yes—all."

"Was not Rousseau wrong, Dr. B.," said Mrs. Howard, "when he asserted, that no child ever gives away his last mouthful of any thing good?"

"Of any thing good!" said the doctor, laughing; "when I have tasted these sweetmeats, I shall be a better judge."

"You shall taste them this minute, then," said Mrs. Howard; and she rang for a plate, whilst the doctor, to little Oliver's great amusement, exhibited various pretended signs of impatience, as Mrs. Howard deliberately untied the cover of the jar. One cover after another she slowly took off; at length the last transparent cover was lifted up: the doctor peeped in; but lo! instead of sweetmeats there appeared nothing but paper. One crumpled roll of paper after another Mrs. Howard pulled out; still no sweetmeats. The jar was entirely stuffed with paper, to the very bottom. Oliver was silent with amazement.

"The sides of the jar are quite clean," said Howard.

"But the inside of the paper that covered it is stained with sweetmeats," said Dr. B.

"There must have been sweetmeats in it lately," said Mrs. Howard, "because the jar smells so strongly of them."

Amongst the pieces of crumpled paper which had been pulled out of the jar, Dr. B. espied one, on which there appeared some writing: he looked it over.

"Humph! What have we here? What's this? What can this he about a lottery?—tickets, price half a guinea—prizes-gold watch!—silver ditto—chased tooth-pick case—buckles—knee-buckles. What is all this?—April 10th, 1797—the drawing to begin—prizes to be delivered at Westminster school, by Aaron Carat, jeweller? Hey, young gentlemen," cried Dr. B., looking at Oliver and Charles, "do you know any thing of this lottery?"

"I have no concern in it, sir, I assure you," said Howard.

"Nor I, thank goodness—I mean, thank you, Charles," exclaimed Oliver; "for you hindered me from putting into the lottery: how very lucky I was to take your advice!"

"How very wise, you should say, Oliver," said Dr. B. "I must inquire into this business; I must find out who ordered these things from Mr. Aaron Carat. There shall be no lotteries, no gaming at Westminster school, whilst I have power to prevent it. To-morrow morning I'll inquire into this affair; and to-morrow morning we shall also know, my little fellow, what became of your sweetmeats."

"Oh, never mind that," cried the good-natured Oliver; "don't say any thing, pray, sir, about my sweetmeats: I don't mind about them; I know already—I guess now, who took them; therefore you need not ask; I dare say it was only meant for a joke."

Dr. B. made no reply; but folded up the paper which he had been reading, put it into his pocket, and soon after took his leave.

Lord Rawson was one of those young men who measure their own merit and felicity by the number of miles which their horses can go in a day; he undertook to drive his friend up from Marryborough to Westminster, a distance of forty miles, in five hours. The arrival of his lordship's gig was a signal, for which several people were in waiting at Westminster school. The stage-coachman was impatiently waiting to demand his money from Holloway. Mr. Carat, the jeweller, was arrived, and eager to settle with Mr. Holloway about the lottery: he had brought the prizes in a small case, to be delivered, upon receiving from Holloway the money for all the tickets of which he had disposed. Dr. B. was waiting for the arrival of Mr. Holloway, as he had determined to collect all his pupils together, and to examine into the lottery business. Little Oliver was also watching for Holloway, to prevent mischief, and to assure him of forgiveness about the sweetmeats.

Lord Rawson's dog-cart arrived. Holloway saw the stage-coachman as he alighted, and, abruptly turning from him, shook hands with little Oliver, saying, "You look as if you had been waiting for me."

"Yes," said Oliver: "but I can't say what I want to say before every body."

"I'll wait upon you presently," said Holloway, escaping from the coachman. As he crossed the hall, he descried Mr. Carat, and a crowd of boys surrounding him, crying, "Mr. Carat's come—he has brought the prizes!—he has brought the prizes! he'll show them all as soon as you've settled with him." Holloway called to the Jew; but little Oliver insisted upon being heard first.

"You must hear me: I have something to say to you about the prizes—about the lottery."

The words arrested Holloway's attention: he followed Oliver; heard with surprise and consternation the history of the paper which had been found in the jar, by Dr. B. "I've done for myself, now, faith!" he exclaimed; "I suppose the doctor knows all about the hand I have in the lottery."

"No," replied Oliver, "he does not."

"Why, you must have known it; and did not he question you and Howard?"

"Yes; but when we told him that we had nothing to do with it, he did not press us farther."

"You are really a noble little fellow," exclaimed Holloway, "to bear me no malice for the many ill turns I have done you: this last has fallen upon myself, as ill-luck would have it: but before we go any farther—

your sweetmeats are safe in the press, in my room; I didn't mean to steal them; only to plague you, child:—but you have your revenge now."

"I don't want any revenge, indeed," said Oliver, "for I'm never happy when I've quarrelled with any body: and even when people quarrel with me, I don't feel quite sure that I'm in the right, which makes me uncomfortable; and, besides, I don't want to find out that they are quite in the wrong; and that makes me uncomfortable the other way. After all, quarrelling and bearing malice are very disagreeable things, somehow or other. Don't you, when you have made it up with people, and shaken hands, Holloway—don't you feel quite light, and ready to jump again? So shake hands, if you are not above shaking hands with such a little boy as I am; and I shall never think again about the sweetmeats, or old fag times."

Holloway could not help feeling touched. "Here's my hand," cried he, "I'm sorry I've tormented you so often; I'll never plague you any more. But now—I don't know what upon earth to do. Where's Charles Howard? If he can't help me, I'm undone. I have got into more scrapes than I can get out of, I know. I wish I could see Howard."

"I'll run and bring him to you; he's the best person at knowing what should be done—at least for me, I know—that ever I saw."

Holloway abruptly began, as soon as Howard came up to him: "Howard," said he, "you know this plaguy lottery business—but you don't know half yet: here's Carat come to be paid for his tickets; and here's that dunning stage-coachman sticks close to me for his five guineas; and not one farthing have I upon earth."

"Not a farthing! but you don't mean that you have not the money for Mr. Carat?"

"But I do though."

"Why, you cannot have spent it since yesterday morning?"

"No; but I have lost half and lent half; and the half that I have lent is gone for ever, I am afraid, as much as that which I lost."

"Whom did you lend the money to? How did you lose it?"

"I lost part to Sir John O'Shannon, last night, at billiards—more fool I to play, only because I wanted to cut a figure amongst those fine people at Marryborough. I wonder my father lets me go there; I know I sha'n't go back there this Easter, unless Lord Rawson makes me an apology, I can tell him. I've as good a right to be upon my high horse as he has; for though his father's an earl, my father's a great deal richer, I know; and has lent him a great deal of money, too, and that's the only reason he's civil to us; but I can tell him—"

Here Howard brought the angry Holloway from his high horse, by asking what all this had to do with Mr. Carat, who was waiting to be paid?

"Why, don't I explain to you," said Holloway, "that I lent him—Lord Rawson, I mean—all the money I had left yesterday, and I couldn't get it out of him again, though I told him my distress about the stage-coachman? Did you ever know any thing so selfish? Did you ever know any thing so shabby, so shameful? And then to make me his butt, as he did last night at supper, because there were two or three dashing young men by; I think more of that than all the rest. Do you know, he asked me to eat custard with my apple-pie, just to point me out for an alderman's son; and when I only differed from him about Captain Shouldham's puppy's ears, Lord Rawson said, to be sure, I must know about dog's ears, just to put me in mind that I was a school-boy; but I'll never go to Marryborough any more, unless he begs my pardon. I've no notion of being a humble friend; but it does not signify being in a passion about it now," continued Holloway. "What I want you, Howard, to do for me is, just to think; for I can't think at present, I'm in such a hurry, with all these things coming across me at once. What can I do to find money for the stage-coachman and for Mr. Carat? Why both together come to fifteen guineas. And what can I do about Dr. B.? And, do you know, my father is coming here this very morning. How shall I manage? He'd never forgive me: at least he'd not give me any money for I don't know how long, if these things were to come out. What would you advise me to do?"

Howard, with his usual honest policy, advised Holloway at once to tell all the circumstances to his father. Holloway was at first much alarmed at this proposal, and insisted upon it that this method would not do at all with the alderman, though it might do very well with such a woman as Mrs. Howard. At length, however, overcome, partly by the arguments, and partly by the persuasion of his new adviser, Holloway determined upon his confession.

Alderman Holloway arrived, and was beginning to talk to Dr. B. of his son's proficiency in his studies, when the young gentleman made his appearance, with a countenance extremely embarrassed and agitated. The sight of Dr. B. deprived Holloway of courage to speak. The doctor fixed his penetrating eye upon the pale culprit, who immediately stopped short in the middle of the room, stammering out, "I came to speak, sir—I had something to say to my father, sir—I came, if you please, to speak to my father, sir." To Holloway's utter astonishment, Dr. B.'s countenance and manner suddenly changed at these words; all his severity vanished; and, with a look and voice the most encouraging, he led the abashed youth towards his father.

"You came to speak to your father, sir? Speak to him then without fear, without reserve: you will certainly find in a father your most indulgent friend. I'll leave you together."

This opening of the case by Dr. B. was of equal advantage both to the father and to the son. Alderman Holloway, though without literature, was not without understanding: his affection for his son made him quickly comprehend the good sense of the doctor's hint. The alderman was not surprised by the story of the overturn of the stage-coach, because he had heard it before from his footman. But the lottery transaction with the Jew—and, above all, with the loss and loan of so much money to his friend, Lord Rawson—struck him with some astonishment; yet he commanded his temper, which was naturally violent; and, after a constrained silence, he begged his son to summon Mr. Supine. "At least," cried the alderman, "I've a right to be in a passion with that careless, indolent, dilettanti puppy, whom I've been paying all this while for taking such care of you. I wish I had hold of his German flute at this instant. You are very right, Augustus, to come like a man, and tell me all these things; and now I must tell you, that some of them I had heard of before. I wish I had that Jew, that Mr. Carat of yours, here! and that stage-coachman, who had the impertinence to take you out with him at night. But it's all Mr. Supine's fault—and mine, for not choosing a better tutor for you. As to Lord Rawson, I can't blame you either much for that, for I encouraged the connexion, I must own. I'm glad you have quarrelled with him, however; and pray look out for a better friend as fast as possible. You were very right to tell me all these things; on that consideration, and that only, I'll lend my hand to getting you out of these scrapes."

"For that," cried Holloway, "I may thank Howard, then; for he advised and urged me to tell you all this at once."

"Call him; let me thank him," said the alderman; "he's an excellent young man then—call him."

Dr. B. now entered the room with little Oliver.

When Holloway returned with Howard, he beheld the stage-coachman standing silent on one side of his father; Mr. Carat, the Jew, on the other side, jabbering an unintelligible vindication of himself; whilst Dr. B. was contemplating the box of lottery prizes, which lay open upon the table. Mr. Supine, leaning against the chimney-piece, appeared in the attitude of an Antinous in despair.

"Come, my little friend," said Dr. B. to Oliver, "you did not put into the lottery, I understand. Choose from amongst these things whatever you please. It is better to trust to prudence than fortune, you see. Mr. Howard, I know that I am rewarding you, at this instant, in the manner you best like, and best deserve."

There was a large old-fashioned chased gold toothpick-case, on which Oliver immediately fixed his eye. After examining it very carefully, he drew the doctor aside, and, after some consultation, Oliver left the room hastily; whilst the alderman, with all the eloquence of which he was master, expressed his gratitude to Howard for the advice which he had given his son. "Cultivate this young gentleman's friendship," added he, turning to Holloway: "he has not a title; but even I, Augustus, am now ready to acknowledge he is worth twenty Lord Rawsons. Had he a title, he would grace it; and that's as much as I can say for any man."

The Jew, all this time, stood in the greatest trepidation; he trembled lest the alderman should have him taken up and committed to gaol for his illegal, unlicensed lottery. He poured forth as many protestations as his knowledge of the English language could afford of the purity of his intentions; and, to demonstrate his disinterestedness, began to display the trinkets in his prize-box, with a panegyric upon each. Dr. B. interrupted him, by paying for the toothpick-case, which he had bought for Oliver.

"Now, Mr. Carat," said the doctor, "you will please to return, in the first place, the money you have received for your illegal lottery tickets."

The word illegal, pronounced in a tremendous tone, operated instantaneously upon the Jew; his hand, which had closed upon Holloway's guineas, opened; he laid the money down upon the table, but mechanically seized his box of trinkets, which he seemed to fear would be the next seized, as forfeits. No persons are so apprehensive of injustice and fraud as those who are themselves dishonest. Mr. Carat, bowing repeatedly to Alderman Holloway, shuffled toward the door, asking if he might now depart; when the door opened with such a force, as almost to push the retreating Jew upon his face.

Little Oliver, out of breath, burst into the room, whispered a few words to Dr. B. and Alderman Holloway, who answered, "He may come in;" and a tall, stout man, an officer from Bow-street, immediately entered. "There's your man, sir," said the alderman, pointing to the Jew; "there is Mr. Carat." The man instantly seized Mr. Carat, producing a warrant from Justice—for apprehending the Jew upon suspicion of his having in his possession certain valuable jewels, the property of Mrs. Frances Howard.

Oliver was eager to explain. "Do you know, Howard," said he, "how all this came about? Do you know your aunt's gone to Bow-street, and has taken the mulatto woman with her, and Mr. Russell is gone with her? and she thinks—and I think—she'll certainly have her jewels, her grandmother's jewels, that were left in Jamaica."

"How? but how?" exclaimed Howard.

"Why," said Oliver, "by the toothpick-case. The reason I chose that toothpick-case out of the Jew's box was, because it came into my head, the minute I saw it, that the mulatto woman's curious thimble—you remember her thimble, Howard—would just fit one end of it. I ran home and tried it, and the thimble screwed on as nicely as possible; and the chasing, as Mr. Russell said, and the colour of the gold, matched exactly. Oh! Mrs. Howard was so surprised when we showed it to her—so astonished to see this toothpick-case in England; for it had been left, she said, with all her grandmother's diamonds and things, in Jamaica."

"Yes," interrupted Howard; "I remember my aunt told us, when you asked her about Cuba's thimble, that she gave it to Cuba when she was a child, and that it belonged to some old trinket.—Go on."

"Well, where was I?—Oh, then, as soon as she saw the toothpick-case, she asked how it had been found; and I told her all about the lottery and Mr. Carat; then she and Mr. Russell consulted, and away they went, with Cuba, in a coach; and all the rest you know; and I wish I could hear the end of it!"

"And so you shall, my good little fellow; we'll all go together to hear the Jew's examination: you shall go with me in my coach to Bow-street," said Alderman Holloway.

In the midst of their bustle, the poor stage-coachman, who had waited with uncommon patience in the hope that Alderman Holloway would at last recollect him, pressed forward, and petitioned to be paid his five guineas for the lost parcel.—"I have lost my place already," said he, "and the little goods I have will be seized this day, for the value of that unlucky parcel, master."

The alderman put his hand slowly into his purse; but just when he had pulled out five guineas, a servant came into the room, to inform Dr. B. that a sailor was waiting in the hall, who desired to speak, directly, about something of consequence, to the stage-coachman.

Dr. B., who imagined that the sailor might have something to do with the business in question, ordered that he might be shown into the room.

"I wants one Gregory Giles, a stage-coachman, if such a one be here amongst ye, gentlefolks, and nobody else," cried the sailor, producing a parcel, wrapped up in brown paper.

"It's my very parcel!" exclaimed the stage-coachman. "I am Gregory Giles! God bless your honest heart!—Where did ye find it?—Give it me!"

The sailor said he had found it in a dry ditch on the Bath road, a little beyond the first turnpike, going out of town; that he had inquired at the turnpike-house; had heard that the stage had been overturned a few days before, and that a parcel had been lost, about which the coachman had been in great trouble;

that he had gone directly to the inn where the coach put up; had traced the coachman from place to place; and was heartily glad he had found him at last.

"Thank'ee, with all my heart," said the coachman, "for all the trouble you've been at; and here's the crown reward that I offered for it, and my thanks into the bargain."

"No, no," said the honest sailor, pushing back the money; "I won't take any thing from a poor fellow like myself: put your silver into your pocket: I hear you lost your place already by that parcel. There was a great talk at the turnpike-house about your losing your place, for giving some young gentleman a lift.— Put up your money."

All present were eager in rewarding the honest sailor.

A hackney-coach was now come to the door for Mr. Carat, and every body hurried off as fast as possible.

"Where are they all steering to?" said the sailor. The stage-coachman told him all that he had heard of the matter. "I'll be in their wake, then," cried the sailor; "I shall like to see the Jew upon his court-martial; I was choused once by a Jew myself." He got to Bow-street as soon as they did.

The first thing Howard learned was, that the jewels, which had been all found at Mr. Carat's, precisely answered the description which his aunt had given of them. The Jew was in the utmost consternation: finding that the jewels were positively sworn to, he declared, upon his examination, that he had bought them from a captain of a ship; that he had paid the full value for them; and that, at the time he purchased them, he had no suspicion of their having been fraudulently obtained. This defence appearing evidently evasive, the magistrates who examined Mr. Carat informed him, that, unless he could produce the person from whom he had bought the jewels, he must be committed to Newgate for receiving stolen goods. Terrified at this sentence, the Jew, though he had at first asserted that he knew nothing of the captain from whom he had received the diamonds, now acknowledged that he actually lodged at his house.

"Hah!" exclaimed Holloway: "I remember, the day that I and Lord Rawson called at your house, you were settling accounts, your foreman told us, with a captain of a ship, who was to leave England in a few days: it's well he's not off."

An officer was immediately sent to Mr. Carat's in quest of this captain; but there were great apprehensions that he might have escaped at the first alarm of the search for the jewels. Fortunately, however, he had not been able to get off, as two constables had been stationed at Mr. Carat's house. The officer from Bow-street found him in his own bed-chamber, rummaging a portmanteau for some papers, which he wanted to burn. His papers were seized, and carried along with him before the magistrate.

Alderman Holloway knew the captain the moment he was brought into the room, though his dress and whole appearance were very different from what they had been when he had waited upon the alderman some months before this time, with a dismal, plausible story of his own poverty and misfortunes. He had then told him that his mate and he had had a quarrel, upon the voyage from Jamaica; that the mate knew what a valuable cargo he had on board; that just when they got in sight of land, the crew rose upon him; the mate seized him, and by force put him into a boat, and set him ashore.

The discovery of the jewels at Mr. Carat's at once overturned the captain's whole story: cunning people often insert something in their narration to make it better, which ultimately tends to convict them of falsehood. The captain having now no other resource, and having the horrors of imprisonment, and the certainty of condemnation upon a public trial, full before him, threw himself, as the only chance that remained for him, upon Mrs. Howard's mercy; confessed that all that he had told her before was false; that his mate and he had acted in concert; that the rising of the crew against him had been contrived between them; that he had received the jewels, when he was set ashore, for his immediate share of the booty; and that the mate had run the ship off to Charlestown, to sell her cargo. According to agreement, the captain added, he was to have had a share in the cargo; but the mate had cheated him of that; he had never heard from him, or of him, he would take his oath, from the day he was set ashore, and knew nothing of him or the cargo.

"Avast, friend, by your leave," cried the honest sailor who had found the stage-coachman's parcel—"avast, friend, by your leave," said he, elbowing his way between Alderman Holloway and his next neighbour, and getting clear into the middle of the circle—"I know more of this matter, my lord, or please your worship, which is much the same thing, than any body here; and I'm glad on't, mistress," continued the tar, pulling a quid of tobacco out of his mouth, and addressing himself to Mrs. Howard: then turning to the captain, "Wasn't she the Lively Peggy, pray?—it's no use tacking. Wasn't your mate one John Matthews, pray? Captain, your face tells truth, in spite of your teeth."

The captain instantly grew pale, and trembled: on which the sailor turned abruptly from him, and went on with his story. "Mistress," said he, "though I'm a loser by it, no matter. The Lively Peggy and her cargo are safe and sound in Plymouth, at this very time being, and we have her mate in limbo, curse him. We made a prize of him, coming from America, for he was under French colours, and a fine prize we thought we'd made. But her cargo belongs to a British subject; and there's an end to our prize money: no matter for that. There was an ugly look with Matthews from the first; and I found, the day we took her, something odd in the look of her stern. The rascals had done their best to paint over her name; but I, though no great scholar, made a shift to spell the Lively Peggy through it all. We have the mate in limbo at Plymouth: but it's all come out, without any more to do; and, mistress, I'll get you her bill of lading in a trice, and I give ye joy with all my heart."

Alderman Holloway, a man used to business, would not indulge himself in a single compliment upon this occasion, till he had cautiously searched the captain's papers. The bill of lading which had been sent with the Lively Peggy from Jamaica, was found amongst them; it was an exact list, corresponding precisely with that which Mrs. Howard's agent had sent her by post, of the consignment shipped after the sale of her plantation. The alderman, satisfied, after counting the puncheons of rum and hogsheads of sugar, turned to Mrs. Howard, and shook hands with her, with a face of mercantile congratulation, declaring that "she was now as good a woman as ever she had been, and need never desire to be better."

"My dear Oliver," cried Howard, "this is all owing to you: you discovered—"

"No, no, no!" interrupted Oliver, precipitately: "all that I did was accident; all that you did was not accident. You first made me love you, by teaching me that I was not a blockhead, and by freeing me from—"

"A tyrant, you were going to say," cried Holloway, colouring deeply; "and, if you had, you'd have said the truth. I thought; Howard, afterwards, that you were a brave fellow for taking his part, I confess. But, Oliver, I thought you had forgiven me for all these things."

"Forgiven! Oh yes, to be sure," cried little Oliver; "I wasn't thinking of myself, or you either; I was only thinking of Howard's good nature; and then," continued he, "Howard was just as good to the mulatto woman as he was to me—wasn't he, Cuba?"

"That he was!" replied the poor woman; and, looking at Mrs. Howard, added, "Massa's heart as good as hers."

"And his head's as good as his heart, which makes it all better still," continued Oliver, with enthusiasm. "Mr. Russell, you know how hard he worked at that translation, to earn money to support poor Cuba, and to paper the room, and to pay the bricklayer for the smoky chimney: these things were not done by accident, were they? though it was by accident that I happened to observe Cuba's curious thimble."

"There are some people," interrupted Mr. Russell, "who, by accident, never observe any thing. We will not allow you, Oliver, to call your quick habit of observation accident; your excellent capacity will—"

"My excellent capacity," repeated Oliver, with unfeigned surprise: "why, you know, I get by rote slower than any body in the world."

"You may," said Dr. B., "notwithstanding, have an excellent capacity: much may be learned without books; much more with books, Oliver; but, for your comfort, you need not learn them by rote."

"I'm glad of it, heartily," cried Oliver; "but this put something out of my head that I was in a great hurry to say—O, one other thing about accident. It was not accident, but it was Howard's sense, in persuading me not to put into the lottery, that was the very cause of Dr. B.'s giving me the choice of all the things in the Jew's box—was it not?"

"Well, Oliver, we are ready to allow all you want us to perceive, in one word, that your friend Howard has not been educated by accident," said Dr. B., looking at Mrs. Howard.

The Jew and the captain of the Lively Peggy were now left in the hands of the law. The sailor was properly rewarded. Mr. Russell was engaged to superintend the education of Holloway. He succeeded, and was presented by the alderman with a living in Surrey. Mr. Supine never visited Italy, and did not meet with any consolation but in his German flute. Howard continued eager to improve himself; nor did he imagine that, the moment he left school, and parted from his tutor, his education was finished, and that his books were, "like past misfortunes," good for nothing but to be forgotten. His love for literature he found one of the first pleasures of his life; nor did he, after he came into the possession of a large fortune, find that his habits of constant occupation lessened his enjoyments, for he was never known to yawn at a window upon a rainy morning!

Little Oliver's understanding rapidly improved; his affection for his friend Howard increased as he grew up, for he always remembered that Howard was the first person who discovered that he was not a dunce. Mrs. Howard had the calm satisfaction of seeing an education well finished, which she had well begun; and she enjoyed, in her nephew's friendship, esteem, and unconstrained gratitude, all the rewards which her good sense, firmness, and benevolence had so well deserved.

CHAPTER I

"But, my dear Lady Di., indeed you should not let this affair prey so continually upon your spirits," said Miss Burrage, in the condoling tone of a humble companion—"you really have almost fretted yourself into a nervous fever. I was in hopes that change of air, and change of scene, would have done every thing for you, or I never would have consented to your leaving London; for you know your ladyship's always better in London than any where else. And I'm sure your ladyship has thought and talked of nothing but this sad affair since you came to Clifton."

"I confess," said Lady Diana Chillingworth, "I deserve the reproaches of my friends for giving way to my sensibility, as I do, upon this occasion: but I own I cannot help it.—Oh, what will the world say! What will the world say!—The world will lay all the blame upon me; yet I'm sure I'm the last, the very last person that ought to be blamed."

"Assuredly," replied Miss Burrage, "nobody can blame your ladyship; and nobody will, I am persuaded. The blame will all be thrown, where it ought to be, upon the young lady herself."

"If I could but be convinced of that," said her ladyship, in a tone of great feeling; "such a young creature, scarcely sixteen, to take such a step!—I am sure I wish to Heaven her father had never made me her guardian. I confess, I was most exceedingly imprudent, out of regard to her family, to take under my protection such a self-willed, unaccountable, romantic girl. Indeed, my dear," continued Lady Diana Chillingworth, turning to her sister, Lady Frances Somerset, "it was you that misled me. You remember you used to tell me, that Anne Warwick had such great abilities!"—

"That I thought it a pity they had not been well directed," said Lady Frances.

"And such generosity of temper, and such warm affections!" said Lady Di.—

"That I regretted their not having been properly cultivated."

"I confess, Miss Warwick was never a great favourite of mine," said Miss Barrage; "but now that she has lost her best friend—"

"She is likely to find a great number of enemies," said Lady Frances.

"She has been her own enemy, poor girl! I am sure I pity her," replied Miss Burrage; "but, at the same time, I must say, that ever since she came to my Lady Di. Chillingworth's, she has had good advice enough."

"Too much, perhaps; which is worse than too little," thought Lady Frances.

"Advice!" repeated Lady Di. Chillingworth: "why, as to that, my conscience, I own, acquits me there; for, to be sure, no young person, of her age, or of any age, had ever more advice, or more good advice, than

Miss Warwick had from me; I thought it my duty to advise her, and advise her I did from morning till night, as Miss Burrage very well knows, and will do me the justice, I hope, to say in all companies."

"That I shall certainly make it a principle to do," said Miss Burrage. "I am sure it would surprise and grieve you, Lady Frances, to hear the sort of foolish, imprudent things that Miss. Warwick, with all her abilities, used to say. I recollect—"

"Very possibly," replied Lady Frances; "but why should we trouble ourselves to recollect all the foolish, imprudent things which this poor girl may have said?—This unfortunate elopement is a sufficient proof of her folly and imprudence. With whom did she go off?"

"With nobody," cried Lady Diana—"there's the wonder."

"With nobody!—Incredible.—She had certainly some admirer, some lover, and she was afraid, I suppose, to mention the business to you."

"No such thing, my dear: there is no love at all in the case: indeed, for my part, I cannot in the least comprehend Miss Warwick, nor ever could. She used, every now and then, to begin and talk to me some nonsense about her hatred of the forms of the world, and her love of liberty, and I know not what; and then she had some female correspondent, to whom she used to write folio sheets, twice a week, I believe; but I could never see any of these letters. Indeed, in town, you know, I could not possibly have leisure for such things; but Miss Burrage, I fancy, has one of the letters, if you have any curiosity to see it. Miss Burrage can tell you a great deal more of the whole business than I can; for you know, in London, engaged as I always was, with scarcely a moment ever to myself, how could I attend to all Anne Warwick's oddities? I protest I know nothing of the matter, but that, one morning, Miss Warwick was nowhere to be found, and my maid brought me a letter, of one word of which I could not make sense: the letter was found on the young lady's dressing-table, according to the usual custom of eloping heroines. Miss Burrage, do show Lady Frances the letters—you have them somewhere; and tell my sister all you know of the matter, for I declare, I'm quite tired of it; besides, I shall be wanted at the card-table."

Lady Diana Chillingworth went to calm her sensibility at the card-table; and Lady Frances turned to Miss Burrage, for further information.

"All I know," said Miss Burrage, "is, that one night I saw Miss Warwick putting a lock of frightful hair into a locket, and I asked her whose it was.—'My amiable Araminta's,' said Miss Warwick, 'Is she pretty?' said I. 'I have never seen her,' said Miss Warwick; 'but I will show you a charming picture of her mind!'—and she put this long letter into my hand. I'll leave it with your ladyship, if you please; it is a good, or rather a bad hour's work to read it."

"Araminta!" exclaimed Lady Frances, looking at the signature of the letter—"this is only a nom de guerre, I suppose."

"Heaven knows!" answered Miss Burrage; "but Miss Warwick always signed her epistles Angelina, and her unknown friend's were always signed Araminta. I do suspect that Araminta, whoever she is, was the instigator of this elopement."

"I wish," said Lady Frances, examining the post-mark of the letter, "I wish that we could find out where Araminta lives; we might then, perhaps, recover this poor Miss Warwick, before the affair is talked of in the world—before her reputation is injured."

"It would certainly be a most desirable thing," said Miss Burrage; "but Miss Warwick has such odd notions, that I question whether she will ever behave like other people; and, for my part, I cannot blame Lady Diana Chillingworth for giving her up. She is one of those young ladies whom it is scarcely possible to manage by common sense."

"It is certainly true," said Lady Frances, "that young women of Miss Warwick's superior abilities require something more than common sense to direct them properly. Young ladies who think of nothing but dress, public amusements, and forming what they call high connexions, are undoubtedly most easily managed, by the fear of what the world will say of them; but Miss Warwick appeared to me to have higher ideas of excellence; and I therefore regret that she should be totally given up by her friends."

"It is Miss Warwick who has given up her friends," said Miss Burrage, with a mixture of embarrassment and sarcasm in her manner; "it is Miss Warwick who has given up her friends; not Miss Warwick's friends who have given up Miss Warwick."

The letter from the "amiable Araminta," which Miss Burrage left for the perusal of Lady Frances Somerset, contained three folio sheets, of which, it is hoped, the following abridgment will be sufficiently ample to satisfy the curiosity even of those who are lovers of long letters:—

"Yes, my Angelina! our hearts are formed for that higher species of friendship, of which common souls are inadequate to form an idea, however their fashionable puerile lips may, in the intellectual inanity of their conversation, profane the term. Yes, my Angelina, you are right—every fibre of my frame, every energy of my intellect, tells me so. I read your letter by moonlight! The air balmy and pure as my Angelina's thoughts! The river silently meandering!—The rocks!—The woods!—Nature in all her majesty. Sublime confidante! Sympathizing with my supreme felicity. And shall I confess to you, friend of my soul! that I could not refuse myself the pleasure of reading to my Orlando some of those passages in your last, which evince so powerfully the superiority of that understanding, which, if I mistake not strangely, is formed to combat, in all its Proteus forms, the system of social slavery? With what soul-rending eloquence does my Angelina describe the solitariness, the isolation of the heart she experiences in a crowded metropolis! With what emphatic energy of inborn independence does she exclaim against the family phalanx of her aristocratic persecutors!—Surely—surely she will not be intimidated from 'the settled purpose of her soul' by the phantom-fear of worldly censure!—The garnish-tinselled wand of fashion has waved in vain in the illuminated halls of folly-painted pleasure; my Angelina's eyes have withstood, yes, without a blink, the dazzling enchantment.—And will she—no, I cannot, I will not think so for an instant—will she now submit her understanding, spell-bound, to the soporific charm of nonsensical words, uttered in an awful tone by that potent enchantress, Prejudice?—The declamation, the remonstrances of self-elected judges of right and wrong, should be treated with deserved contempt by superior minds, who claim the privilege of thinking and acting for themselves. The words ward and guardian appal my Angelina! but what are legal technical formalities, what are human institutions, to the view of shackle-scorning Reason! Oppressed, degraded, enslaved, must our unfortunate sex for ever submit to sacrifice their rights, their pleasures, their will, at the altar of public opinion; whilst the shouts of interested priests, and idle spectators, raise the senseless enthusiasm of the self-devoted victim, or drown her cries in the truth-extorting moment of agonizing nature!—You will not perfectly understand, perhaps, to what these last exclamations of your Araminta allude:—But, chosen friend of my heart!—

when we meet—and oh, let that be quickly!—my cottage longs for the arrival of my unsophisticated Angelina!—when we meet you shall know all—your Araminta, too, has had her sorrows—Enough of this!—But her Orlando has a heart, pure as the infantine god of love could, in his most perfect mood, delight at once to wound, and own—joined to an understanding—shall I say it?—worthy to judge of your Araminta's—And will not my sober-minded Angelina prefer, to all that palaces can afford, such society in a cottage?—I shall reserve for my next the description of a cottage, which I have in my eye, within view of—; but I will not anticipate.—Adieu, my amiable Angelina.—I enclose, as you desire, a lock of my hair.—Ever, unalterably, your affectionate, though almost heart-broken,

"ARAMINTA.

"April, 1800.—Angelina Bower!

"So let me christen my cottage!"

What effect this letter may have on sober-minded readers in general can easily be guessed; but Miss Warwick, who was little deserving of this epithet, was so charmed with the sound of it, that it made her totally to forget to judge of her amiable Araminta's mode of reasoning. "Garnish-tinselled wands"—"shackle-scorning Reason"—"isolation of the heart"—"soul-rending eloquence"—with "rocks and woods, and a meandering river—balmy air—moonlight—Orlando—energy of intellect—a cottage—and a heart-broken friend," made, when all mixed together, strange confusion in Angelina's imagination. She neglected to observe, that her Araminta was in the course of two pages—"almost heart-broken"—and in the possession of—"supreme felicity."—Yet Miss Warwick, though she judged so like a simpleton, was a young woman of considerable abilities: her want of what the world calls common sense arose from certain mistakes in her education.—She had passed her childhood with a father and mother, who cultivated her literary taste, but who neglected to cultivate her judgment: her reading was confined to works of imagination; and the conversation which she heard was not calculated to give her any knowledge of realities. Her parents died when she was about fourteen, and she then went to reside with Lady Diana Chillingworth, a lady who placed her whole happiness in living in a certain circle of high company in London. Miss Warwick saw the follies of the society with which she now mixed; she felt insupportable ennui from the want of books and conversation suited to her taste; she heard with impatience Lady Diana's dogmatical advice; observed, with disgust, the meanness of her companion, Miss Burrage, and felt with triumph the superiority of her own abilities. It was in this situation of her mind that Miss Warwick happened, at a circulating library, to meet with a new novel, called "The Woman of Genius."—The character of Araminta, the heroine, charmed her beyond measure; and having been informed, by the preface, that the story was founded on facts in the life of the authoress herself, she longed to become acquainted with her; and addressed a letter to "The Woman of Genius," at her publisher's. The letter was answered in a highly flattering, and consequently, very agreeable style, and the correspondence continued for nearly two years; till, at length, Miss W. formed a strong desire to see her unknown friend. The ridicule with which Miss Burrage treated every thing, and every idea, that was not sanctioned by fashion, and her total want of any taste for literature, were continually contrasted in Miss Warwick's mind, with the picture she had formed of her Araminta.—Miss Burrage, who dreaded, though certainly without reason, that she might be supplanted in the good graces of Lady Diana, endeavoured by every petty means in her power, to disgust her young rival with the situation in which she was placed. She succeeded beyond her hopes. Miss Warwick determined to accept of her unknown friend's invitation to Angelina Bower—a charming romantic cottage in South Wales, where, according to Araminta's description, she might pass her halcyon days in tranquil, elegant retirement. It was not difficult for our heroine, though unused to deception, to conceal her project from Lady Diana

Chillingworth, who was much more observant of the appearance of her protégée in public, than interested about what passed in her mind in private. Miss Warwick quitted her ladyship's house without the least difficulty, and the following is the letter which our heroine left upon her dressing-table. Under all the emphatic words, according to the custom of some letter-writers, were drawn emphatic lines.

"Averse as I am to every thing that may have the appearance of a clandestine transaction, I have, however, found myself under the necessity of leaving your ladyship's house, without imparting to you my intentions. Confidence and sympathy go hand in hand, nor can either be commanded by the voice of authority. Your ladyship's opinions and mine, upon all subjects, differ so essentially, that I could never hope for your approbation, either of my sentiments or my conduct. It is my unalterable determination to act and think upon every occasion for myself; though I am well aware, that they who start out of the common track, either in words or action, are exposed to the ridicule and persecution of vulgar or illiberal minds. They who venture to carry the first torch into unexplored or unfrequented passages in the mine of truth are exposed to the most imminent danger. Rich, however, are the treasures of the place, and cowardly the soul that hesitates! But I forget myself.

"It may be necessary to inform your ladyship, that, disgusted with the frivolity of what is called fashionable life, and unable to live without the higher pleasures of friendship, I have chosen for my asylum the humble, tranquil cottage of a female friend, whose tastes, whose principles have long been known to me: whose genius I admire! whose virtues I revere! whose example I emulate!

"Though I do not condescend to use the fulsome language of a mean dependant, I am not forgetful of the kindness I have received from your ladyship. It has not been without a painful struggle that I have broken my bonds asunder—the bonds of what is falsely called duty: spontaneous gratitude ever will have full, indisputable, undisputed power over the heart and understanding of

"ANNE-ANGELINA WARWICK.

"P.S. It will be in vain to attempt to discover the place of my retreat. All I ask is to be left in peace, to enjoy, in my retirement, perfect felicity."

CHAPTER II

Full of her hopes of finding "perfect felicity" in her retreat at Angelina Bower, exulting in the idea of the courage and magnanimity with which she had escaped from her "aristocratic persecutors," our heroine pursued her journey to South Wales.

She had the misfortune—and it is a great misfortune to a young lady of her way of thinking—to meet with no difficulties or adventures, nothing interesting upon her journey. She arrived, with inglorious safety, at Cardiffe. The inn at Cardiffe was kept by a landlady of the name of Hoel. "Not high-born Hoel. Alas!" said Angelina to herself, when the name was screamed in her hearing by a waiter, as she walked into the inn. "Vocal no more to high-born Hoel's harp, or soft Llewellynn's lay!" A harper was sitting in the passage, and he tuned his harp to catch her attention as she passed. "A harp!—O play for me some plaintive air!" The harper followed her into a small parlour.

"How delightful!" said Miss Warwick, who, in common with other heroines, had the habit of talking to herself; or, to use more dignified terms, who had the habit of indulging in soliloquy:—"how delightful to taste at last the air of Wales. But 'tis a pity 'tis not North instead of South Wales, and Conway instead of Cardiffe Castle."

The harper, after he had finished playing a melancholy air, exclaimed, "That was but a melancholy ditty, miss—we'll try a merrier." And he began—

"Of a noble race was Shenkin."

"No more," cried Angelina, stopping her ears; "no more, barbarous man!—you break the illusion."

"Break the what?" said the harper to himself; "I thought, miss, that tune would surely please you; for it is a favourite one in these parts."

"A favourite with Welsh squires, perhaps," said our heroine; "but, unfortunately, I am not a Welsh squire, and have no taste for your 'Bumper Squire Jones.'"

The man tuned his harp sullenly. "I'm sorry for it, miss," said he: "more's the pity, I can't please you better!"

Angelina cast upon him a look of contempt. "He no way fills my idea of a bard!—an ancient and immortal bard!—He has no soul—fingers without a soul!—No 'master's hand,' or 'prophet's fire!'—No 'deep sorrows!'—No 'sable garb of woe!'—No loose beard, or hoary hair, 'streaming like a meteor to the troubled air!'—'No haggard eyes!'—Heigho!"—"It is time for me to be going," said the harper, who began to think, by the young lady's looks and manners, that she was not in her right understanding. "It is time for me to be going; the gentlemen above in the Dolphin will be ready for me."

"A mere modern harper! He is not even blind," Angelina said to herself, as he examined the shilling which she gave him. "Begone, for Heaven's sake!" added she, aloud, as he left the room;—and "leave me, leave me to repose." She threw up the sash, to taste the evening air; but scarcely had she begun to repeat a sonnet to her Araminta—scarcely had she repeated the first two lines—

"Hail, far-famed, fairest, unknown friend,
Our sacred silent sympathy of soul,"

when a little ragged Welsh boy, who was playing with his companions, in a field at the back of Cardifie Inn, espied her, gave the signal to his playfellows, and immediately they all came running up to the window at which Angelina was standing, and with one loud shrill chorus of "Gi' me ha'penny!—Gi' me ha'penny!—Gi' me one ha'penny!" interrupted the sonnet, Angelina threw out some money to the boys, though she was provoked by their interruption: her donation was, in the true spirit of a heroine, much greater than the occasion required and the consequence was, that these urchins, by spreading the fame of her generosity through the town of Cardiffe, collected a Lilliputian mob of petitioners, who assailed Angelina with fresh vehemence. Not a moment's peace, not a moment for poetry or reverie would they allow her: so that she was impatient for her chaise to come to the door. Her Araminta's cottage was but six miles distant from Cardiffe; and to speak in due sentimental language, every moment that delayed her long-expected interview with her beloved unknown friend, appeared to her an age.

"And what would you be pleased to have for supper, ma'am?" said the landlady. "We have fine Tenby oysters, ma'am; and, if you'd like a Welsh rabbit—"

"Tenby oysters!—Welsh rabbits!" repeated Angelina, in a disdainful tone. "Oh, detain me not in this cruel manner!—I want no Tenby oysters, I want no Welsh rabbits; only let me be gone—I am all impatience to see a dear friend. Oh, if you have any feeling, any humanity, detain me not!" cried she, clasping her hands.

Miss Warwick had an ungovernable propensity to make a display of sensibility; a fine theatrical scene upon every occasion; a propensity which she had acquired from novel-reading. It was never more unluckily displayed than in the present instance; for her audience and spectators, consisting of the landlady, a waiter, and a Welsh boy, who just entered the room with a knife-tray in his hand, were all more inclined to burst into rude laughter than to join in gentle sympathy. The chaise did not come to the door one moment sooner than it would have done without this pathetic wringing of the hands. As soon as Angelina drove from the door, the landlady's curiosity broke forth—

"Pray tell me, Hugh Humphries," said Mrs. Hoel, turning to the postilion, who drove Angelina from Newport, "pray, now, does not this seem strange, that such a young lady as this should be travelling about in such wonderful haste? I believe, by her flighty airs, she is upon no good errand—and I would have her to know, at any rate, that she might have done better than to sneer, in that way, at Mrs. Hoel of Cardiffe, and her Tenby oysters, and her Welsh rabbit. Oh, I'll make her repent her pehaviour to Mrs. Hoel, of Cardiffe. 'Not high-born Hoel,' forsooth! How does she know that, I should be glad to hear? The Hoels are as high born, I'll venture to say, as my young miss herself, I've a notion! and would scorn, moreover, to have a runaway lady for a relation of theirs. Oh, she shall learn to repent her disrespects to Mrs. Hoel, of Cardiffe. I pelieve she shall soon meet herself in the public newspapers—her eyes, and her nose, and her hair, and her inches, and her description at full length she shall see—and her friends shall see it too—and maybe they shall thank, and maybe they shall reward handsomely Mrs. Hoel, of Cardiffe."

Whilst the angry Welsh landlady was thus forming projects of revenge for the contempt with which she imagined that her high birth and her Tenby oysters had been treated, Angelina pursued her journey towards the cottage of her unknown friend, forming charming pictures, in her imagination, of the manner in which her amiable Araminta would start, and weep, and faint, perhaps with joy and surprise, at the sight of her Angelina. It was a fine moonlight night—an unlucky circumstance; for the by-road which led to Angelina Bower was so narrow and bad, that if the night had been dark, our heroine must infallibly have been overturned, and this overturn would have been a delightful incident in the history of her journey; but Fate ordered it otherwise. Miss Warwick had nothing to lament, but that her delicious reveries were interrupted, for several miles, by the Welsh postilion's expostulations with his horses.

"Good Heavens!" exclaimed she, "cannot the man hold his tongue? His uncouth vociferations distract me! So fine a scene, so placid the moonlight—but there is always something that is not in perfect unison with one's feelings."

"Miss, if you please, you must light here, and walk for a matter of a quarter of a mile, for I can't drive up to the house door, because there is no carriage-road down the lane; but if you be pleased, I'll go on before you—my horses will stand quite quiet here—and I'll knock the folks up for you, miss."

"Folks!—Oh, don't talk to me of knocking folks up," cried Angelina, springing out of the carriage "stay with your horses, man, I beseech you. You shall be summoned when you are wanted—I choose to walk up to the cottage alone."

"As you please, miss," said the postilion; "only hur had better take care of the dogs."

This last piece of sage counsel was lost upon our heroine; she heard it not—she was "rapt into future times."

"By moonlight will be our first interview—just as I had pictured to myself—but can this be the cottage?—It does not look quite so romantic as I expected—but 'tis the dwelling of my Araminta—Happy, thrice happy moment!—Now for our secret signal—I am to sing the first, and my unknown friend the second part of the same air."

Angelina then began to sing the following stanza—

"O waly waly up the bank,
And waly waly down the brae,
And waly waly yon burn side,
Where I and my love were wont to gae."

She sung and paused, in expectation of hearing the second part from her amiable Araminta—but no voice was heard.

"All is hushed," said Angelina—"ever tranquil be her slumbers! Yet I must waken her—her surprise and joy at seeing me thus will be so great!—by moonlight too!"

She knocked at the cottage window—still no answer.

"All silent as night!" said she—

"'When not a breath disturbs the deep serene,
And not a cloud o'ercasts the solemn scene.'"

Angelina, as she repeated these lines, stood with her back to the cottage window: the window opened, and a Welsh servant girl put out her head; her night-cap, if cap it might be called which shape had none, was half off, her black hair streamed over her shoulders, and her face was the face of vulgar, superstitious amazement.

"Oh, 'tis our old ghost of Nelly Gwynn, all in white, walking and saying her prayers backwards—I heard 'em quite plain, as I hope to breathe," said the terrified girl to herself; and, shutting the window with a trembling hand, she hastened to waken an old woman, who slept in the same room with her.—Angelina, whose patience was by this time exhausted, went to the door of the cottage, and shook it with all her force.—It rattled loud, and a shrill scream was heard from within.

"A scream!" cried Angelina; "Oh, my Araminta!—All is hushed again."—Then raising her voice, she called as loudly as she could at the window—"My Araminta! my unknown friend! be not alarmed, 'tis your Angelina."

The door opened slowly and softly, and a slip-shod beldam peeped out, leaning upon a stick; the head of Betty Williams appeared over the shoulder of this sibyl; Angelina was standing, in a pensive attitude, listening at the cottage window. At this instant the postilion, who was tired of waiting, came whistling up the lane; he carried a trunk on his back, and a bag in his hand. As soon as the old woman saw him, she held up her stick, exclaiming—

"A man! a man!—a ropper and murterer!—Cot suve us! and keep the door fast polted."—They shut the door instantly.

"What is all this?" said Angelina, with dignified composure.

"A couple of fools, I take it, miss, who are afraid and in tred of roppers," said the postilion; "put I'll make 'em come out, I'll be pound, plockheads."—So saying, he went to the door of Angelina Bower, and thundered and kicked at it, speaking all the time very volubly in Welsh. In about a quarter of an hour he made them comprehend that Angelina was a young lady come to visit their mistress: then they came forth curtsying.

"My name's Betty Williams," said the girl, who was tying a clean cap under her chin. "Welcome to Llanwaetur, miss!—pe pleased to excuse our keeping hur waiting, and polting the toor, and taking hur for a ghost and a ropper—put we know who you are now—the young lady from London, that we have been told to expect."

"Oh, then, I have been expected; all's right—and my Araminta, where is she? where is she?"

"Welcome to Llanwaetur, welcome to Llanwaetur, and Cot pless hur pretty face," said the old woman, who followed Betty Williams out of the cottage.

"Hur's my grandmother, miss," said Betty.

"Very likely—but let me see my Araminta," cried Angelina: "cruel woman! where is she, I say?"

"Cot pless hur!—Cot pless hur pretty face," repeated the old woman, curtsying.

"My grandmother's as deaf as a post, miss—don't mind her; she can't tell Inglis well, put I can:—who would you pe pleased to have?"

"In plain English, then—the lady who lives in this cottage."

"Our Miss Hodges?"

This odious name of Hodges provoked Angelina, who was so used to call her friend Araminta, that she had almost forgotten her real name.

"Oh, miss," continued Betty Williams, "Miss Hodges has gone to Pristol for a few days."

"Gone! how unlucky! my Araminta gone!"

"Put Miss Hodges will pe pack on Tuesday—Miss Hodges did not expect hur till Thursday—put her ped is very well aired—pe pleased to walk in, and light hur a candle, and get hur a nightcap."

"Heigho! must I sleep again without seeing my Araminta!—Well, but I shall sleep in a cottage for the first time in my life—

"'The swallow twittering from the straw-built shed.'"

At this moment, Angelina, forgetting to stoop, hit herself a violent blow as she was entering Angelina Bower—the roof of which, indeed, "was too low for so lofty a head."—A headache came on, which kept her awake the greatest part of the night. In the morning she set about to explore the cottage; it was nothing like the species of elegant retirement, of which she had drawn such a charming picture in her imagination. It consisted of three small bedchambers, which were more like what she had been used to call closets; a parlour, the walls of which were, in many places, stained with damp; and a kitchen which smoked. The scanty, moth-eaten furniture of the rooms was very different from the luxury and elegance to which Angelina had been accustomed in the apartments of Lady Diana Chillingworth. Coarse and ill-dressed was the food which Betty Williams with great bustle and awkwardness served up to her guest; but Angelina was no epicure. The first dinner which she ate on wooden trenchers delighted her; the second, third, fourth, and fifth, appeared less and less delectable; so that by the time she had boarded one week at her cottage, she was completely convinced that

"A scrip with herbs and fruit supplied,
And water from the spring,"

though delightful to Goldsmith's Hermit, are not quite so satisfactory in actual practice as in poetic theory; at least to a young lady who had been habituated to all the luxuries of fashionable life. It was in vain that our heroine repeated

"Man wants but little here below:"

She found that even the want of double refined sugar, of green tea, and Mocha coffee, was sensibly felt. Hour after hour, and day after day, passed with Angelina, in anxious expectation of her Araminta's return home. Her time hung heavy upon her hands, for she had no companion with whom she could converse; and one odd volume of Rousseau's Eloise, and a few well-thumbed German plays, were the only books which she could find in the house. There was, according to Betty Williams's report, "a vast sight of books in a press, along with some table-cloths," but Miss Hodges had the key of this press in her pocket. Deprived of the pleasures both of reading and conversation, Angelina endeavoured to amuse herself by contemplating the beauties of nature. There were some wild, solitary walks in the neighbourhood of Angelina Bower; but though our heroine was delighted with these, she wanted, in her rambles, some kindred soul, to whom she might exclaim—"How charming is solitude(1)!"—The day after her arrival in Wales, she wrote a long letter to Araminta, which Betty Williams undertook to send by a careful lad, a particular friend of her own, who would deliver it, without fail, into Miss Hodges's own hands, and who would engage to bring an answer by three o'clock the next day. The careful lad did not return till four days afterward, and he then could give no account of his mission, except that he had left the letter at Bristol, with a particular friend of his own, who would deliver it, without fail, into Miss Hodges's own hands, if he could meet with her. The post seems to be the last expedient which a heroine ever thinks of for the conveyance of her letters; so that, if we were to judge from the annals of romance, we should infallibly conclude there was no such thing as a post-office in England. On the sixth day of her abode at this comfortless cottage, the possibility of sending a letter to her friend by the post occurred to Angelina, and she actually discovered that there was a post-office at Cardiffe. Before she could receive an answer to this epistle, a circumstance happened, which made her determine to abandon her present retreat. One evening she rambled out to a considerable distance from the cottage, and it was long after sunset ere she recollected that it would be necessary to return homewards before it grew dark. She mistook her way at last, and following a sheep-path, down the steep side of a mountain, she came to a point, at which she, apparently, could neither advance nor recede. A stout Welsh farmer who was counting his sheep in a field, at the top of the mountain, happened to look down its steep side in search of one of his flock that was missing: the farmer saw something white at a distance below him, but there was a mist—it was dusk in the evening—and whether it were a woman, or a sheep, he could not he certain. In the hope that Angelina was his lost sheep, he went to her assistance, and though, upon a nearer view, he was disappointed, in finding that she was a woman, yet he had the humanity to hold out his stick to her, and he helped her up by it, with some difficulty. One of her slippers fell off as she scrambled up the hill—there was no recovering it; her other slipper, which was of the thinnest kid leather, was cut through by the stones; her silk stockings were soon stained with the blood of her tender feet; and it was with real gratitude that she accepted the farmer's offer, to let her pass the night at his farmhouse, which was within view. Angelina Bower was, according to his computation, about four miles distant, as well, he said, as he could judge of the place she meant by her description: she had unluckily forgotten that the common name of it was Llanwaetur. At the farmer's house, she was, at first, hospitably received, by a tight-looking woman; but she had not been many minutes seated, before she found herself the object of much curiosity and suspicion. In one corner of the room, at a small round table, with a jug of ale before him, sat a man, who looked like the picture of a Welsh squire: a candle had just been lighted for his worship, for he was a magistrate, and a great man, in those parts, for he could read the newspaper, and his company was, therefore, always welcome to the farmer, who loved to hear the news, and the reader was paid for his trouble with good ale, which he loved even better than literature.

(Footnote 1: Voltaire.)

"What news, Mr. Evans?" said the farmer.

"What news?" repeated Mr. Evans, looking up from his paper, with a sarcastic smile. "Why, news that might not be altogether so agreeable to the whole of this good company; so 'tis best to keep it to ourselves."

"Every thing's agreeable to me, I'm sure," said the farmer—"every thing's agreeable to me in the way of news."

"And to me, not excepting politics, which you gentlemen always think so polite," said the farmer's wife, "to keep to yourselves; but, you recollect, I was used to politics when I lived with my uncle at Cardiffe; not having, though a farmer's wife, always lived in the country, as you see, ma'am—nor being quite illiterate.—Well, Mr. Evans, let us have it. What news of the fleets?"

Mr. Evans made no reply, but pointed out a passage in the newspaper to the farmer, who leant over his shoulder, in vain endeavouring to spell and put it together: his smart wife, whose curiosity was at least equal to her husband's, ran immediately to peep at the wonderful paragraph, and she read aloud the beginning of an advertisement:—

"Suspected to have strayed, or eloped, from her friends or relations, a young lady, seemingly not more than sixteen years of age, dressed in white, with a straw hat: blue eyes, light hair."

Angelina coloured so deeply whilst this was reading, and the description so exactly suited with her appearance, that the farmer's wife stopped short; the farmer fixed his eyes upon her; and Mr. Evans cleared his throat several times with much significance.—A general silence ensued; at last the three heads nodded to one another across the round table; the farmer whistled and walked out of the room; his wife fidgeted at a buffet, in which she began to arrange some cups and saucers; and, after a few minutes, she followed her husband. Angelina took up the newspaper, to read the remainder of the advertisement. She could not doubt that it was meant for her, when she saw that it was dated the very day of her arrival at the inn at Cardiffe, and signed by the landlady of the inn, Mrs. Hoel. Mr. Evans swallowed the remainder of his ale, and then addressed Angelina in these words:—

"Young lady, it is plain to see you know when the cap fits: now, if you'll take my advice, you'll not make the match you have in your eye; for, though a lord's son, he is a great gambler. I dined with one that has dined with him not long ago. My son, who has a living near Bristol, knows a great deal—more about you than you'd think; and 'tis my advice to you, which I wouldn't be at the trouble of giving, if you were not as pretty as you are, to go back to your relations; for he'll never marry you, and marriage to be sure is your object. I have no more to say, but only this—I shall think it my duty, as a magistrate, to let your friends know as soon as possible where you are, coming under my cognizance as you do; for a vagabond, in the eye of the law, is a person—"

Angelina had not patience to listen to any more of this speech; she interrupted Mr. Evans with a look of indignation, assured him that he was perfectly unintelligible to her, and walked out of the room with great dignity. Her dignity made no impression upon the farmer or his wife, who now repented having offered her a night's lodging in their house: in the morning they were as eager to get rid of her as she was impatient to depart. Mr. Evans insisted upon seeing her safe home, evidently for the purpose of discovering precisely where she lived. Angelina saw that she could no longer remain undisturbed in her retreat, and determined to set out immediately in quest of her unknown friend at Bristol.—Betty Williams, who had a strong desire to have a jaunt to Bristol, a town which she had never seen but once in her life, offered to attend Miss Warwick, assuring her that she perfectly well knew the house where Miss Hodges always lodged. Her offer was accepted; and what adventures our heroine met with in Bristol, and what difficulties she encountered before she discovered her Araminta, will be seen in the next chapter.

CHAPTER III

Angelina went by water from Cardiff to Bristol; the water was rather rough, and, as she was unused to the motion of a vessel, she was both frightened and sick. She spent some hours very disagreeably, and without even the sense of acting like a heroine, to support her spirits. It was late in the evening before she arrived at the end of her voyage: she was landed on the quay at Bristol. No hackney-coach was to be had, and she was obliged to walk to the Bush. To find herself in the midst of a bustling, vulgar crowd, by whom she was unknown, but not unnoticed, was new to Miss Warwick. Whilst she was with Lady Diana Chillingworth, she had always been used to see crowds make way for her; she was now surprised to feel herself jostled in the streets by passengers, who were all full of their own affairs, hurrying different ways, in pursuit of objects which probably seemed to them as important as the search for an unknown friend appeared to Angelina.

Betty Williams's friend's friend, the careful lad, who was to deliver the letter to Miss Hodges, was a waiter at the Bush. Upon inquiry, it was found that he had totally forgotten his promise: Angelina's letter was, after much search, found in a bottle-drainer, so much stained with port wine, that it was illegible. The man answered with the most provoking nonchalance, when Angelina reproached him for his carelessness—"That, indeed, no such person as Miss Hodges was to be found: that nobody he could meet with had ever heard the name." They who are extremely enthusiastic suffer continually from the total indifference of others to their feelings; and young people can scarcely conceive the extent of this indifference until they have seen something of the world. Seeing the world does not always mean seeing a certain set of company in London.

Angelina, the morning after her arrival at the Bush, took a hackney-coach, and left the care of directing the coachman to Betty Williams, who professed to have a perfect knowledge of Bristol. Betty desired the man to drive to the drawbridge; and, at the sound of the word drawbridge, various associations of ideas with the drawbridges of ancient times were called up in Miss Warwick's imagination. How different was the reality from her castles in the air! She was roused from her reverie by the voices of Betty Williams and the coachman.

"Where will I drive ye to, I ask you?" said the coachman, who was an Irishman: "Will I stand all day upon the drawbridge stopping the passage?"

"Trive on a step, and I will get out and see apout me," said Betty: "I know the look of the house, as well as I know any thing."

Betty got out of the coach, and walked up and down the street, looking at the houses like one bewildered.

"Bad luck to you! for a Welsh woman as you are," exclaimed the coachman, jumping down from the box, "will I lave the young lady standing in the streets all day alone for you to be making a fool this way of us both?—Sorrow take me now! If I do—"

"Pless us, pe not in a pet or a pucker, or how shall I recollect any body or any thing.—Cood! Cood!— Stand you there while I just say over my alphabet: a, p, c, t, e, f, g, h, i, k, l, m, n, o, b.—It was some name which begins with p, and ends with a t, I pelieve."

"Here's a pretty direction, upon my troth; some name which begins with a p, and ends with a t," cried the coachman; and after he had uttered half a score of Hibernian execrations upon the Welsh woman's folly, he with much good nature went along with her to read the names on the street doors.—"Here's a name now that's the very thing for you—here's Pushit now.—Was the name Pushit?—Ricollict yourself, my good girl, was that your name?"

"Pushit!—Oh, yes, I am sure, and pelieve it was Pushit—Mrs. Pushit's house, Pristol, where our Miss Hodges lodges alway."

"Mrs. Pushit—but this is quite another man; I tell you this is Sir John—Faith now we are in luck," continued the coachman—"here's another p just at hand; here's Mrs. Puffit; sure she begins with a p, and ends with a t, and is a milliner into the bargain? so sure enough I'll engage the young lady lodges here.—Puffit—Hey?—Ricollict now, and don't be looking as if you'd just been pulled out of your sleep, and had never been in a Christian town before now."

"Pless us, Cot pless us!" said the Welsh girl, who was quite overpowered by the Irishman's flow of words—and she was on the point of having recourse, in her own defence, to her native tongue, in which she could have matched either male or female in fluency; but, to Angelina's great relief, the dialogue between the coachman and Betty Williams ceased. The coachman drew up to Mrs. Puffit's; but, as there was a handsome carriage at the door, Miss Warwick was obliged to wait in her hackney-coach some time longer. The handsome carriage belonged to Lady Frances Somerset.—By one of those extraordinary coincidences which sometimes occur in real life, but which are scarcely believed to be natural when they are related in books, Miss Warwick happened to come to this shop at the very moment when the persons she most wished to avoid were there. Whilst the dialogue between Betty Williams and the hackney-coachman was passing, Lady Diana Chillingworth and Miss Burrage were seated in Mrs. Puffit's shop: Lady Diana was extremely busy bargaining with the milliner; for, though rich, and a woman of quality, her ladyship piqued herself upon making the cheapest bargains in the world.

"Your la'ship did not look at this eight and twenty shilling lace," said Mrs. Puffit; "'tis positively the cheapest thing your la'ship ever saw. Jessie! the laces in the little blue band-box. Quick! for my Ladi Di.—Quick!"

"But it is out of my power to stay to look at any thing more now," said Lady Diana; "and yet," whispered she to Miss Burrage, "when one does go out a shopping, one certainly likes to bring home a bargain."

"Certainly; but Bristol's not the place for bargains," said Miss Burrage; "you will find nothing tolerable, I assure you, my dear Lady Di., at Bristol."

"Why, my dear," said her ladyship, "were you ever at Bristol before? How comes it that I never heard that you were at Bristol before? Where were you, child?"

"At the Wells, at the Wells, ma'am," replied Miss Burrage, and she turned pale and red in the space of a few seconds; but Lady Diana, who was very near-sighted, was holding her head so close to the blue band-box full of lace, that she could not see the changes in her companion's countenance. The fact was, that Miss Burrage was born and bred in Bristol, where she had several relations, who were not in high life, and by whom she consequently dreaded to be claimed. When she first met Lady Diana Chillingworth at Buxton, she had passed herself upon her for one of the Burrages of Dorsetshire, and she knew that, if her ladyship was to discover the truth, she would cast her off with horror. For this reason, she had done every thing in her power to prevent Lady Di. from coming to Clifton; and for this reason she now endeavoured to persuade her that nothing tolerable could be met with at Bristol.

"I am afraid, Lady Di., you will be late at Lady Mary's," said she.

"Look at this lace, child, and give me your opinion—eight and twenty shillings, Mrs. Puffit, did you say?"

"Eight and twenty, my lady—and I lose by every yard I sell at that price. Ma'am, you see," said Mrs. Puffit, appealing to Miss Burrage, "'tis real Valenciennes, you see."

"I see 'tis horrid dear," said Miss Burrage: then in a whisper to Lady Di. she added, "at Miss Trentham's at the Wells, your ladyship will meet with such bargains!"

Mrs. Puffit put her lace upon the alabaster neck of the large doll which stood in the middle of her shop. "Only look, my lady—only see, ma'am, how beautiful becoming 'tis to the neck, and sets off a dress too, you know, ma'am. And (turning to Miss Burrage) eight and twenty, you know, ma'am, is really nothing for any lace you'd wear; but more particularly for real Valenciennes, which can scarce be had real, for love or money, since the French Revolution. Real Valenciennes!—and will wear and wash, and wash and wear—not that your ladyship minds that—for ever and ever,—and is such a bargain, and so becoming to the neck, especially to ladies of your la'ship's complexion."

"Well, I protest, I believe, Burrage, I don't know what to say, my dear—hey?"

"I'm told," whispered Miss Burrage, "that Miss Trentham's to have a lace raffle at the Wells next week."

"A raffle?" cried Lady Di., turning her back immediately upon the doll and the lace.

"Well," cried Mrs. Puffit, "instead of eight say seven and twenty shillings, Miss Burrage, for old acquaintance sake."

"Old acquaintance!" exclaimed Miss Burrage: "la! Mrs. Puffit, I don't remember ever being twice in your shop all the time I was at the Wells before."

"No, ma'am," replied Mrs. Puffit, with a malicious smile—"but when you was living on Saint Augustin's Back."

"Saint Augustin's Back, my dear!" exclaimed Lady Diana Chillingworth, with a look of horror and amazement.

Miss Burrage, laying down a bank-note on the counter, made a quick and expressive sign to the milliner to hold her tongue.

"Dear Mrs. Puffit," cried she, "you certainly mistake me for some other strange person. Lady Di., now I look at it with my glass, this lace is very fine, I must agree with you, and not dear, by any means, for real Valenciennes: cut me off three yards of this lace—I protest there's no withstanding it, Lady Di."

"Three yards at eight and twenty—here, Jesse," said Mrs. Puffit. "I beg your pardon, ma'am, for my mistake; I supposed it was some other lady of the same name; there are so many Burrages. Only three yards did you say, ma'am?"

"Nay, I don't care if you give me four. I'm of the Burrages of Dorsetshire."

"A very good family, those Burrages of Dorsetshire, as any in England," said Lady Di.—"and put up twelve yards of this for me, Mrs. Puffit."

"Twelve at eight and twenty—yes, my lady—very much obliged to your ladyship—much obliged to you, Miss Burrage. Here, Jesse, this to my Lady Di. Chillingworth's carriage." Jesse called at the shop-door, in a shrill voice, to a black servant of Lady Frances Somerset—"Mr. Hector, Mr. Hector! Sir, pray put this parcel into the carriage for Lady Diana Chillingworth."

Angelina, who was waiting in her hackney-coach, started; she could scarcely believe that she heard the name rightly:—but, an instant afterwards, the voice of Lady Diana struck her ear, and she sunk back in great agitation. However, neither Miss Burrage nor Lady Di. saw her; they got into their carriage, and drove away.

Angelina was so much alarmed, that she could scarcely believe that the danger was past when she saw the carriage at the furthest end of the street.

"Wouldn't you be pleased to 'light, ma'am?" said Jesse.

"We don't bring things to the door."

"Who have we here?" cried Mrs. Puffit; "who have we here?"

"Only some folks out of a hack, that was kept waiting, and couldn't draw up whilst my Lady Di.'s carriage was at the door," said Jesse.

"A good pretty girl, the foremost," said Mrs. Puffit. "But, in the name of wonder, what's that odd fish coming behind her?"

"A queer-looking pair, in good truth!" said Jesse.

Angelina seated herself, and gave a deep sigh. "Ribands, if you please, ma'am," said she to Mrs. Puffit. "I must," thought she, "ask for something before I ask for my Araminta."

"Ribands—yes, ma'am—what sort? Keep an eye upon the glass," whispered the milliner to her shop girl, as she stooped behind the counter for a drawer of ribands—"keep an eye on the glass, Jesse—a girl of the town, I take it. What colour, ma'am?"

"Blue—'cerulean blue.' Here, child," said Angelina, turning to Betty Williams, "here's a riband for you."

Betty Williams did not hear, for Betty was fascinated by the eyes of the great doll, opposite to which she stood fixed.

"Lord, what a fine lady! and how hur stares at Betty Williams!" thought she: "I wish hur would take her eyes off me."

"Betty! Betty Williams!—a riband for you," cried Angelina, in a louder tone.

Betty started—"Miss!—a riband!" She ran forward, and, in pushing by the doll, threw it backward: Mrs. Puffit caught it in her arms, and Betty, stopping short, curtsied, and said to the doll—"Peg pardon, miss—peg pardon, miss—tit I hurt you?—peg pardon. Pless us! 'tis a toll, and no woman, I teclare."

The milliner and Jesse now burst into uncontrollable, and, as Angelina feared, "unextinguishable laughter." Nothing is so distressing to a sentimental heroine as ridicule: Miss Warwick perceived that she had her share of that which Betty Williams excited; and she who imagined herself to be capable of "combating, in all its Proteus forms, the system of social slavery," was unable to withstand the laughter of a milliner and her 'prentice.

"Do you please to want any thing else, ma'am?" said Mrs. Puffit, in a saucy tone—"Rouge, perhaps?"

"I wish to know, madam," said Angelina, "whether a lady of the name of Hodges does not lodge here?"

"A lady of the name of Hodges!—no, ma'am—I'm very particular about lodgers—no such lady ever lodged with me.—Jesse! to the door—quick!—Lady Mary Tasselton's carriage."

Angelina hastily rose and departed. Whilst Jesse ran to the door, and whilst Mrs. Puffit's attention was fixed upon Lady Mary Tasselton's carriage, Betty Williams twitched from off the doll's shoulders the remainder of the piece of Valenciennes lace which had been left there. "Since hur's only wood, I'll make free," said she to herself, and she carried off the lace unobserved.

Angelina's impatience to find her Araminta was increased, by the dread of meeting Lady Di. Chillingworth in every carriage that passed, and in every shop where she might call. At the next house at which the coachman stopped, the words, Dinah Plait, relict of Jonas Plait, cheesemonger, were written in large letters over the shop-door. Angelina thought she was in no danger of meeting her ladyship here, and she alighted. There was no one in the shop but a child of seven years old; he could not understand well what Angelina or Betty said, but he ran to call his aunt. Dinah Plait was at dinner; and when the child opened the door of the parlour, there came forth such a savoury smell, that Betty Williams, who was extremely hungry, could not forbear putting her head in, to see what was upon the table.

"Pless hur! heggs and pacon and toasted cheese—Cot pless hur!" exclaimed Betty.

"Aunt Dinah," said the child, "here are two women in some great distress, they told me—and astray and hungry."

"In some great distress, and astray and hungry?—then let them in here, child, this minute."

There was seated at a small table, in a perfectly neat parlour, a quaker, whose benevolent countenance charmed Angelina the moment she entered the room.

"Pardon this intrusion," said she.

"Friend, thou art welcome," said Dinah Plait, and her looks said so more expressively than her words. An elderly man rose, and leaving the cork-screw in the half-drawn cork of a bottle of cider, he set a chair for Angelina, and withdrew to the window.

"Be seated, and eat, for verily thou seemest to be hungry," said Mrs. Plait to Betty Williams, who instantly obeyed, and began to eat like one that had been half famished.

"And now, friend, thy business, thy distress—what is it?" said Dinah, turning to Angelina: "so young to have sorrows."

"I had best take myself away," said the elderly gentleman, who stood at the window—"I had best take myself away, for miss may not like to speak before me—though she might, for that matter."

"Where is the gentleman going?" said Miss Warwick; "I have but one short question to ask, and I have nothing to say that need—"

"I dare say, young lady, you can have nothing to say that you need be ashamed of, only people in distress don't like so well to speak before third folks, I guess—though, to say the truth, I have never known, by my own experience, what it was to be in much distress since I came into the world—but I hope I am not the more hard-hearted for that—for I can guess, I say, pretty well, how those in distress feel when they come to speak. Do as you would be done by is my maxim till I can find a better—so I take myself away, leaving my better part behind me, if it will be of any service to you, madam."

As he passed by Miss Warwick, he dropped his purse into her lap, and he was gone before she could recover from her surprise.

"Sir!—madam!" cried she, rising hastily, "here has been some strange mistake—I am not a beggar—I am much, very much obliged to you, but—"

"Nay, keep it, friend, keep it," said Dinah Plait, pressing the purse upon Angelina; "John Barker is as rich as a Jew, and as generous as a prince. Keep it, friend, and you'll oblige both him and me—'tis dangerous in this world for one so young and so pretty as you are to be in great distress; so be not proud."

"I am not proud," said Miss Warwick, drawing her purse from her pocket; "but my distress is not of a pecuniary nature—Convince yourself—I am in distress only for a friend, an unknown friend."

"Touched in her brain, I doubt," thought Dinah.

"Coot ale!" exclaimed Betty Williams—"Coot heggs and pacon."

"Does a lady of the name of Araminta—Miss Hodges, I mean—lodge here?" said Miss Warwick.

"Friend, I do not let lodgings; and I know of no such person as Miss Hodges."

"Well, I swear hur name, the coachman told me, did begin with a p, and end with a t," cried Betty Williams, "or I would never have let him knock at hur toor."

"Oh, my Araminta! my Araminta!" exclaimed Angelina, turning up her eyes towards heaven—"when, oh when shall I find thee? I am the most unfortunate person upon earth."

"Had not hur petter eat a hegg, and a pit of pacon? here's one pit left," said Betty: "hur must be hungry, for 'tis two o'clock past, and we preakfasted at nine—hur must be hungry;" and Betty pressed her to try the pacon; but Angelina put it away, or, in the proper style, motioned the bacon from her.

"I am in no want of food," cried she, rising: "happy they who have no conception of any but corporeal sufferings. Farewell, madam!—may the sensibility, of which your countenance is so strongly expressive, never be a source of misery to you!"—and with that depth of sigh which suited the close of such a speech, Angelina withdrew.

"If I could but have felt her pulse," said Dinah Plait to herself, "I could have prescribed something that, maybe, would have done her good, poor distracted thing! Now it was well done of John Barker to leave this purse for her—but how is this?—poor thing! she's not fit to be trusted with money—here she has left her own purse full of guineas."

Dinah ran immediately to the house-door, in hopes of being able to catch Angelina; but the coach had turned down into another street, and was out of sight. Mrs. Plait sent for her constant counsellor, John Barker, to deliberate on the means of returning the purse. It should be mentioned, to the credit of Dinah's benevolence, that, at the moment when she was interrupted by the entrance of Betty Williams and Angelina, she was hearing the most flattering things from a person who was not disagreeable to her: her friend, John Barker, was a rich hosier, who had retired from business; and who, without any ostentation, had a great deal of real feeling and generosity. But the fastidious taste of fine, or sentimental readers, will probably be disgusted by our talking of the feelings and generosity of a hosier and a cheesemonger's widow. It belongs to a certain class of people to indulge in the luxury of sentiment: we shall follow our heroine, therefore, who, both from her birth and education, is properly qualified to have—"exquisite feelings."

The next house at which Angelina stopped, to search for her amiable Araminta, was at Mrs. Porett's academy for young ladies.

"Yes, ma'am, Miss Hodges is here—Pray walk into this room, and you shall see the young lady immediately." Angelina burst into the room instantly, exclaiming—

"Oh, my Araminta! have I found you at last?"

She stopped short, a little confounded at finding herself in a large room full of young ladies, who were dancing reels, and who all stood still at one and the same instant, and fixed their eyes upon her, struck with astonishment at her theatrical entrée and exclamation.

"Miss Hodges!" said Mrs. Porett—and a little girl of seven years old came forward:—"Here, ma'am," said Mrs. Porett to Angelina, "here is Miss Hodges."

"Not my Miss Hodges! not my Araminta! alas!"

"No, ma'am," said the little girl; "I am only Letty Hodges."

Several of her companions now began to titter.

"These girls," said Angelina to herself, "take me for a fool;" and, turning to Mrs. Porett, she apologized for the trouble she had given, in language as little romantic as she could condescend to use.

"Tid you bid me, miss, wait in the coach, or the passage?" cried Betty Williams, forcing her way in at the door, so as almost to push down the dancing-master, who stood with his back to it. Betty stared round, and dropped curtsy after curtsy, whilst the young ladies laughed and whispered, and whispered and laughed; and the words, odd—vulgar—strange—who is she?—what is she?—reached Miss Warwick.

"This Welsh girl," thought she, "is my torment. Wherever I go she makes me share the ridicule of her folly."

Clara Hope, one of the young ladies, saw and pitied Angelina's confusion.

"Gif over, an ye have any gude nature—gif over your whispering and laughing," said Clara to her companions: "ken ye not ye make her so bashful, she'd fain hide her face wi' her twa hands."

But it was in vain that the good-natured Clara Hope remonstrated: her companions could not forbear tittering, as Betty Williams, upon Miss Warwick's laying the blame of the mistake on her, replied in a strong Welsh accent—"I will swear almost the name was Porett or Plait, where our Miss Hodges tid always lodge in Pristol. Porett, or Plait, or Puffit, or some of her names that pekin with a p and ent with at."

Angelina, quite overpowered, shrunk back, as Betty bawled out her vindication, and she was yet more confused, when Monsieur Richelet, the dancing-master, at this unlucky instant, came up to her, and with an elegant bow, said, "It is not difficult to see by her air, that mademoiselle dances superiorly. Mademoiselle vould she do me de plaisir—de honneur to dance one minuet?"

"Oh, if she would but dance!" whispered some of the group of young ladies.

"Excuse me, sir," said Miss Warwick.

"Not a minuet?—den a minuet de la cour, a cotillon, or contredanse, or reel; vatever mademoiselle please vill do us honneur."

Angelina, with a mixture of impatience and confusion, repeated, "Excuse me, sir—I am going—I interrupt—I beg I may not interrupt."

"A coot morrow to you all, creat and small," said Betty Williams, curtsying awkwardly at the door as she went out before Miss Warwick.

The young ladies were now diverted so much beyond the bounds of decorum, that Mrs. Porett was obliged to call them to order.

"Oh, my Araminta, what scenes have I gone through! to what derision have I exposed myself for your sake!" said our heroine to herself.

Just as she was leaving the dancing-room, she was stopped short by Betty Williams, who, with a face of terror, exclaimed, "'Tis a poy in the hall, that I tare not pass for my lifes; he has a pasket full of pees in his hand, and I cannot apide pees, ever since one tay when I was a chilt, and was stung on the nose by a pee. The poy in the hall has a pasketful of pees, ma'am," said Betty, with an imploring accent, to Mrs. Porett.

"A basketful of bees!" said Mrs. Porett, laughing: "Oh, you are mistaken: I know what the boy has in his basket—they are only flowers; they are not bees: you may safely go by them."

"Put I saw pees with my own eyes," persisted Betty.

"Only a basketful of the bee orchis, which I commissioned a little boy to bring from St. Vincent's rocks for my young botanists," said Mrs. Porett to Angelina: "you know the flower is so like a bee, that at first sight you might easily mistake it." Mrs. Porett, to convince Betty Williams that she had no cause for fear, went on before her into the hall; but Betty still hung back, crying—

"It is a pasket full of pees! I saw the pees with my own eyes."

The noise she made excited the curiosity of the young ladies in the dancing-room: they looked out to see what was the matter.

"Oh, 'tis the wee-wee French prisoner boy, with the bee orchises for us—there, I see him standing in the hall," cried Clara Hope, and instantly she ran, followed by several of her companions, into the hall.

"You see that they are not bees," said Mrs. Porett to Betty Williams, as she took several of the flowers in her hand. Betty, half convinced, yet half afraid, moved a few steps into the hall.

"You have no cause for dread," said Clara Hope; "poor boy, he has nought in his basket that can hurt any body."

Betty Williams's heavy foot was now set upon the train of Clara's gown, and, as the young lady sprang forwards, her gown, which was of thin muslin, was torn so as to excite the commiseration of all her young companions.

"What a terrible rent! and her best gown!" said they. "Poor Clara Hope!"

"Pless us! peg pardon, miss!" cried the awkward, terrified Betty; "peg pardon, miss!"

"Pardon's granted," said Clara; and whilst her companions stretched out her train, deploring the length and breadth of her misfortune, she went on speaking to the little French boy. "Poor wee boy! 'tis a sad thing to be in a strange country, far away from one's ane ane kin and happy hame—poor wee thing," said she, slipping some money into his hand.

"What a heavenly countenance!" thought Angelina, as she looked at Clara Hope: "Oh, that my Araminta may resemble her!"

"Plait il—take vat you vant—tank you," said the little boy, offering to Clara Hope his basket of flowers, and a small box of trinkets, which he held in his hand.

"Here's a many pretty toys—who'll buy?" cried Clara, turning to her companions.

The young ladies crowded round the box and the basket.

"Is he in distress?" said Angelina; "perhaps I can be of some use to him!" and she put her hand into her pocket, to feel for her purse.

"He's a very honest, industrious little boy," said Mrs. Porett, "and he supports his parents by his active ingenuity."

"And, Louis, is your father sick still?" continued Clara Hope to the poor boy.

"Bien malade! bien malade! very sick! very sick!" said he. The unaffected language of real feeling and benevolence is easily understood, and is never ridiculous; even in the broken English of little Louis, and the broad Scotch tone of Clara, it was both intelligible and agreeable.

Angelina had been for some time past feeling in her pocket for her purse.

"'Tis gone—certainly gone!" she exclaimed: "I've lost it! lost my purse! Betty, do you know any thing of it? I had it at Mrs. Plait's!—What shall I do for this poor little fellow?—This trinket is of gold!" said she, taking from her neck a locket—"Here, my little fellow, I have no money to give you, take this—nay, you must, indeed."

"Tanks! tanks! bread for my poor fader! joy! joy!—too much joy! too much!"

"You see you were wrong to laugh at her," whispered Clara Hope to her companions: "I liked her lukes from the first."

Natural feeling, at this moment, so entirely occupied and satisfied Angelina, that she forgot her sensibility for her unknown friend; and it was not till one of the children observed the lock of hair in her locket that she recollected her accustomed cant of—"Oh, my Araminta! my amiable Araminta! could I part with that hair, more precious than gold?"

"Pless us!" said Betty; "put, if she has lost her purse, who shall pay for the coach, and what will become of our tinners?"

Angelina silenced Betty Williams with peremptory dignity.

Mrs. Porett, who was a good and sensible woman, and who had been interested for our heroine, by her good-nature to the little French boy, followed Miss Warwick as she left the room. "Let me detain you but for a few minutes," said she, opening the door of a little study. "You have nothing to fear from any impertinent curiosity on my part; but, perhaps, I may be of some assistance to you."—Miss Warwick could not refuse to be detained a few minutes by so friendly a voice.

"Madam, you have mentioned the name of Araminta several times since you came into this house," said Mrs. Porett, with something of embarrassment in her manner, for she was afraid of appearing impertinent. "I know, or at least I knew, a lady who writes under that name, and whose real name is Hodges."

"Oh, a thousand, thousand thanks!" cried Angelina: "tell me, where can I find her?"

"Are you acquainted with her? You seem to be a stranger, young lady, in Bristol. Are you acquainted with Miss Hodges's whole history?"

"Yes, her whole history; every feeling of her soul; every thought of her mind!" cried Angelina, with enthusiasm. "We have corresponded for two years past."

Mrs. Porett smiled. "It is not always possible," said she, "to judge of ladies by their letters. I am not inclined to believe above half what the world says, according to Lord Chesterfield's allowance for scandalous stories; but it may be necessary to warn you, as you seem very young, that—"

"Madam," cried Angelina, "young as I am, I know that superior genius and virtue are the inevitable objects of scandal. It is in vain to detain me further."

"I am truly sorry for it," said Mrs. Porett; "but, perhaps, you will allow me to tell you, that—"

"No, not a word; not a word more will I hear," cried our heroine; and she hurried out of the house, and threw herself into the coach. Mrs. Porett contrived, however, to make Betty Williams hear, that the most probable means of gaining any intelligence of Miss Hodges, would be to inquire for her at the shop of Mr. Beatson, who was her printer. To Mr. Beatson's they drove—though Betty professed that she was half unwilling to inquire for Miss Hodges from any one whose name did not begin with a p, and end with a t.

"What a pity it is," said Mrs. Porett, when she returned to her pupils—"what a pity it is that this young lady's friends should permit her to go about in a hackney-coach, with such a strange, vulgar servant girl as that! She is too young to know how quickly, and often how severely, the world judges by appearances. Miss Hope, now we talk of appearances, you forget that your gown is torn, and you do not know, perhaps, that your friend, Lady Frances Somerset—"

"Lady Frances Somerset!" cried Clara Hope—"I love to hear her very name."

"For which reason you interrupt me the moment I mention it—I have a great mind not to tell you—that Lady Frances Somerset has invited you to go to the play with her to-night:—'The Merchant of Venice, and the Adopted Child.'"

"Gude-natured Lady Frances Somerset, I'm sure an' if Clara Hope had been your adopted child twenty times over, you could not have been more kind to her nor you have been.—No, not had she been your are countrywoman, and of your are clan—and all for the same reasons that make some neglect and look down upon her—because Clara is not meikle rich, and is far away from her ane ane friends.—Gude Lady Frances Somerset! Clara Hope luves you in her heart, and she's as blythe wi' the thought o' ganging to see you as if she were going to dear Inverary."

It is a pity, for the sake of our story, that Miss Warwick did not stay a few minutes longer at Mrs. Porett's, that she might have heard this eulogium on Lady Frances Somerset, and might have, a second time in one day, discovered that she was on the very brink of meeting with the persons she most dreaded to see; but, however temptingly romantic such an incident would have been, we must, according to our duty as faithful historians, deliver a plain unvarnished tale.

Miss Warwick arrived at Mr. Beatson's, and as soon as she had pronounced the name of Hodges, the printer called to his devil for a parcel of advertisements, which he put into her hand; they were proposals for printing by subscription a new novel—"The Sorrows of Araminta."

"Oh, my Araminta! my amiable Araminta! have I found you at last?—The Sorrows of Araminta, a novel, in nine volumes—Oh, charming!—together with a tragedy on the same plan—Delightful!—Subscriptions received at Joseph Beatson's, printer and bookseller; and by Rachael Hodges—Odious name!—at Mrs. Bertrand's."

"Bartrand!—There now you, do ye hear that? the lady lives at Mrs. Bartrand's: how will you make out now that Bartrand begins with a p, and ends with a t, now?" said the hackney-coachman to Betty, who was standing at the door.

"Pertrant! why," cried Betty, "what would you have?"

"Silence! O silence!" said Miss Warwick; and she continued reading—"Subscriptions received at Mrs. Bertrand's."

"Pertrant, you hear, plockhead, you Irishman!" cried Betty Williams.

"Bartrand—you have no ears, Welshwoman as you are!" retorted Terence O'Grady.

"Subscription two guineas, for the Sorrows of Araminta," continued our heroine; but, looking up, she saw Betty Williams and the hackney-coachman making menacing faces and gestures at one another.

"Fight it out in the passage, for Heaven's sake!" said Angelina; "if you must fight, fight out of my sight."

"For shame, before the young lady!" said Mr. Beatson, holding the hackney-coachman: "have done disputing so loud."

"I've done, but she is wrong," cried Terence.

"I've done, put he is wrong," said Betty.

Terence was so much provoked by the Welshwoman, that he declared he would not carry her a step further in his coach—that his beasts were tired, and that he must be paid his fare, for that he neither could nor would wait any longer. Betty Williams was desired by Angelina to pay him. She hesitated; but after being assured by Miss Warwick that the debt should be punctually discharged in a few hours, she acknowledged that she had silver enough "in a little box at the bottom of her pocket;" and, after much fumbling, she pulled out a snuff-box, which, she said, had been given to her by her "creat crandmother."—Whilst she was paying the coachman, the printer's devil observed one end of a piece of lace hanging out of her pocket; she had, by accident, pulled it out along with the snuff-box.

"And was this your great grandmother's too?" said the printer's devil, taking hold of the lace.

Betty started. Angelina was busy, making inquiries from the printer, and she did not see or hear what was passing close to her: the coachman was intent upon the examination of his shillings. Betty, with great assurance, reproved the printer's devil for touching such lace with his plack fingers.

"'Twas not my Grandmother's—'tis the young lady's," said she: "let it pe, pray—look how you have placked it, and marked it, with plack fingers."

She put the stolen lace hastily into her pocket, and immediately went out, as Miss Warwick desired, to call another coach.

Before we follow our heroine to Mrs. Bertrand's, we must beg leave to go, and, if we can, to transport our readers with us, to Lady Frances Somerset's house, at Clifton.

CHAPTER IV

"Well, how I am to get up this hill again, Heaven knows!" said Lady Diana Chillingworth, who had been prevailed upon to walk down Clifton Hill to the Wells. "Heigho! that sister of mine, Lady Frances, walks, and talks, and laughs, and admires the beauties of nature till I'm half dead."

"Why, indeed, Lady Frances Somerset, I must allow," said Miss Burrage, "is not the fittest companion in the world for a person of your ladyship's nerves; but then it is to be hoped that the glass of water which you have just taken fresh at the pump will be of service, provided the racketing to Bristol to the play don't counteract it, and undo all again."

"How I dread going into that Bristol playhouse!" said Miss Burrage to herself—"some of my precious relations may be there to claim me. My aunt Dinah—God bless her for a starched quaker—wouldn't be seen at a play, I'm sure—so she's safe;—but the odious sugar-baker's daughters might be there, dizened out; and between the acts, their great tall figures might rise in judgment against me—spy me out—stare and curtsy—pop—pop—pop at me without mercy, or bawl out across the benches, 'Cousin Burrage! Cousin Burrage!' And Lady Diana Chillingworth to hear it!—oh, I should sink into the earth."

"What amusement," continued Miss Burrage, addressing herself to Lady Di., "what amusement Lady Frances Somerset can find at a Bristol playhouse, and at this time of the year too, is to me really unaccountable."

"I do suppose," replied Lady Diana, "that my sister goes only to please that child—(Clara Hope, I think they call her)—not to please me, I'm sure;—but what is she doing all this time in the pump-room? does she know we are waiting for her?—oh, here she comes.—Frances, I am half dead."

"Half dead, my dear! well, here is something to bring you to life again," said Lady Frances: "I do believe I have found out Miss Warwick."

"I am sure, my dear, that does not revive me—I've been almost plagued to death with her already," said Lady Diana.

"There's no living in this world without plagues of some sort or other—but the pleasure of doing good makes one forget them all: here, look at this advertisement, my dear," said Lady Frances: "a gentleman, whom I have just met with in the pump-room, was reading it in the newspaper when I came in, and a whole knot of scandal-mongers were settling who it could possibly be. One snug little man, a Welsh curate, I believe, was certain it was the bar-maid of an inn at Bath, who is said to have inveigled a young nobleman into matrimony. I left the Welshman in the midst of a long story, about his father and a young lady, who lost her shoe on the Welsh mountains, and I ran away with the paper to bring it to you."

Lady Diana received the paper with an air of reluctance.

"Was not I very fortunate to meet with it?" said Lady Frances.

"I protest I see no good fortune in the business, from beginning to end."

"Ah, because you are not come to the end yet—look—'tis from Mrs. Hoel, of the inn at Cardiffe, and by the date, she must have been there last week."

"Who—Mrs. Hoel?"

"Miss Warwick, my dear—I beg pardon for my pronoun—but do read this—eyes—hair—complexion—age—size—it certainly must be Miss Warwick."

"And what then?" said Lady Di, with provoking coldness, walking on towards home.

"Why, then, my dear, you know we can go to Cardiffe to-morrow morning, find the poor girl, and, before any body knows any thing of the matter, before her reputation is hurt, or you blamed, before any harm can happen, convince the girl of her folly and imprudence, and bring her back to you and common sense."

"To common sense, and welcome, if you can; but not to me."

"Not to you!—Nay; but, my dear, what will become of her?"

"Nay; but, my dear Frances, what will the world say?"

"Of her?"

"Of me."

"My dear Di., shall I tell you what the world would say?"

"No, Lady Frances, I'll tell you what the world would say—that Lady Diana Chillingworth's house was an asylum for runaways."

"An asylum for nonsense!—I beg your pardon, sister—but it always provokes me to see a person afraid to do what they think right, because, truly, 'the world will say it is wrong.' What signifies the uneasiness we may suffer from the idle blame or tittle-tattle of the day, compared with the happiness of a young girl's whole life, which is at stake?"

"Oh, Lady Frances, that is spoken like yourself—I love you in my heart—that's right! that's right!" thought Clara Hope.

Lady Diana fell back a few paces, that she might consult one whose advice she always found agreeable to her own opinions.

"In my opinion," whispered Miss Burrage to Lady Diana, "you are right, quite right, to have nothing more to do with the happiness of a young lady who has taken such a step."

They were just leaving St. Vincent's parade, when they heard the sound of music upon the walk by the river side, and they saw a little boy there, seated at the foot of a tree, playing on the guitar, and singing—

"J'ai quitté mon pays et mes amis, Pour jouer de la guitare, Qui va clin, clin, qui va clin, clin, Qui va clin, clin, clin, clin."

"Ha! my wee wee friend," said Clara Hope, "are you here?—I was just thinking of you, just wishing for you. By gude luck, have you the weeny locket about you that the young lady gave you this morning?— the weeny locket, my bonny boy?"

"Plait-il?" said little Louis.

"He don't understand one word," said Miss Burrage, laughing sarcastically, "he don't understand one word of all your bonnys, and wee wees and weenies, Miss Hope; he, unfortunately, don't understand broad Scotch, and maybe he mayn't be so great a proficient as you are in boarding-school French; but I'll try if he can understand me, if you'll tell me what you want."

"Such a trinket as this," said Clara, showing a locket which hung from her neck.

"Ah oui—yes, I comprehend now," cried the boy, taking from his coat-pocket a small case of trinkets— "la voilà!—here is vat de young lady did give me—good young lady!" said Louis, and he produced the locket.

"I declare," exclaimed Miss Burrage, catching hold of it, "'tis Miss Warwick's locket! I'm sure of it— here's the motto—I've read it, and laughed at it twenty times—L'Amie Inconnue."

"When I heard you all talking just now about that description of the young lady in the newspaper, I cude not but fancy," said Clara Hope, "that the lady whom I saw this morning must be Miss Warwick."

"Saw—where?" cried Lady Frances, eagerly.

"At Bristol—at our academy—at Mrs. Porett's," said Clara; "but mark me, she is not there now—I do not ken where she may be now."

"Moi je sais!—I do know de demoiselle did stop in a coach at one house; I was in de street—I can show you de house."

"Can you so, my good little fellow? then let us begone directly," said Lady Frances.

"You'll excuse me, sister," said Lady Di.

"Excuse you!—I will, but the world will not. You'll be abused, sister, shockingly abused."

This assertion made more impression upon Lady Di. Chillingworth than could have been made either by argument or entreaty.

"One really does not know how to act—people take so much notice of every thing that is said and done by persons of a certain rank: if you think that I shall be so much abused—I absolutely do not know what to say."

"But I thought," interposed Miss Burrage, "that Lady Frances was going to take you to the play to-night, Miss Hope?"

"Oh, never heed the play—never heed the play, or Clara Hope—never heed taking me to the play: Lady Frances is going to do a better thing.—Come on, my bonny boy," said she to the little French boy, who was following them.

We must now return to our heroine, whom we left on her way to Mrs. Bertrand's. Mrs. Bertrand kept a large confectionary and fruit shop in Bristol.

"Please to walk through this way, ma'am—Miss Hodges is above stairs—she shall be apprized directly—Jenny! run up stairs," said Mrs. Bertrand to her maid—"run up stairs, and tell Miss Hodges here's a young lady wants to see her in a great hurry—You'd best sit down, ma'am," continued Mrs. Bertrand to Angelina, "till the girl has been up with the message."

"Oh, my Araminta! how my heart beats!" exclaimed Miss Warwick.

"How my mouth waters!" cried Betty Williams, looking round at the fruit and confectionaries.

"Would you, ma'am, be pleased," said Mrs. Bertrand, "to take a glass of ice this warm evening? cream-ice, or water-ice, ma'am? pine-apple or strawberry ice?" As she spoke, Mrs. Bertrand held a salver, covered with ices, toward Miss Warwick: but, apparently, she thought that it was not consistent with the delicacy of friendship to think of eating or drinking when she was thus upon the eve of her first interview with her Araminta. Betty Williams, who was of a different nature from our heroine, saw the salver recede with excessive surprise and regret; she stretched out her hand after it, and seized a glass of raspberry-ice; but no sooner had she tasted it than she made a frightful face, and let the glass fall, exclaiming—

"Pless us! 'tis not as good as cooseherry fool."

Mrs. Bertrand next offered her a cheesecake, which Betty ate voraciously.

"She's actually a female Sancho Panza!" thought Angelina: her own more striking resemblance to the female Quixote never occurred to our heroine—so blind are we to our own failings.

"Who is the young lady?" whispered the mistress of the fruit shop to Betty Williams, whilst Miss Warwick was walking—we should say pacing—up and down the room, in anxious solicitude, and evident agitation.

"Hur's a young lady," replied Betty, stopping to take a mouthful of cheesecake between every member of her sentence, "a young lady—that has—lost hur—"

"Her heart—so I thought."

"Hur purse!" said Betty, with an accent, which showed that she thought this the more serious loss of the two.

"Her purse!—that's bad indeed:—you pay for your own cheesecake and raspberry-ice, and for the glass that you broke," said Mrs. Bertrand.

"Put hur has a great deal of money in hur trunk, I pelieve, at Llanwaetur," said Betty.

"Surely Miss Hodges does not know I am here," cried Miss Warwick—"her Angelina!"

"Ma'am, she'll be down immediately, I do suppose," said Mrs. Bertrand. "What was it you pleased called for—angelica, ma'am, did you say? At present we are quite out, I'm ashamed to say, of angelica, ma'am—Well, child," continued Mrs. Bertrand to her maid, who was at this moment seen passing by the back door of the shop in great haste.

"Ma'am—anan," said the maid, turning back her cap from off her ear.

"Anan! deaf doll! didn't you hear me tell you to tell Miss Hodges a lady wanted to speak to her in a great hurry?"

"No, mam," replied the girl, who spoke in the broad Somersetshire dialect: "I heard you zay, up to Miss Hodges; zoo I thought it was the bottle o'brandy, and zoo I took alung with the tea-kettle—but I'll go up again now, and zay miss bes in a hurry, az she zays."

"Brandy!" repeated Miss Warwick, on whom the word seemed to make a great impression.

"Pranty, ay, pranty," repeated Betty Williams—"our Miss Hodges always takes pranty in her teas at Llanwaetur."

"Brandy!—then she can't be my Araminta."

"Oh, the very same, and no other; you are quite right, ma'am," said Mrs. Bertrand, "if you mean the same that is publishing the novel, ma'am,—'The Sorrows of Araminta'—for the reason I know so much about it is, that I take in the subscriptions, and distributed the purposals."

Angelina had scarcely time to believe or disbelieve what she heard, before the maid returned, with "Mam, Mizz Hodges haz hur best love to you, mizz—and please to walk up—There be two steps; please to have a care, or you'll break your neck."

Before we introduce Angelina to her "unknown friend," we must relate the conversation which was actually passing between the amiable Araminta and her Orlando, whilst Miss Warwick was waiting in the fruit shop. Our readers will be so good as to picture to themselves a woman, with a face and figure which seemed to have been intended for a man, with a voice and gesture capable of setting even man, "imperial man," at defiance—such was Araminta. She was, at this time, sitting cross-legged in an arm-chair at a tea-table, on which, beside the tea equipage, was a medley of things of which no prudent tongue or pen would undertake to give a correct inventory. At the feet of this fair lady, kneeling on one knee, was a thin, subdued, simple-looking quaker, of the name of Nathaniel Gazabo.

"But now, Natty," said Miss Hodges, in a voice more masculine than her looks, "you understand the conditions—If I give you my hand, and make you my husband, it is upon condition that you never contradict any of my opinions: do you promise me that?"

"Yea, verily," replied Nat.

"And you promise to leave me entirely at liberty to act, as well as to think, in all things as my own independent understanding shall suggest?"

"Yea, verily," was the man's response.

"And you will be guided by me in all things?"

"Yea, verily."

"And you will love and admire me all your life, as much as you do now?"

"Yea, verily."

"Swear," said the unconscionable woman.

"Nay, verily," replied the meekest of men, "I cannot swear, my Rachel, being a quaker; but I will affirm."

"Swear, swear," cried the lady, in an imperious tone, "or I will never be your Araminta."

"I swear," said Nat Gazabo, in a timid voice.

"Then, Natty, I consent to be Mrs. Hodges Gazabo. Only remember always to call me your dear Araminta."

"My dear Araminta! thus," said he, embracing her, "thus let me thank thee, my dear Araminta!"

It was in the midst of these thanks that the maid interrupted the well-matched pair, with the news that a young lady was below, who was in a great hurry to see Miss Hodges.

"Let her come," said Miss Hodges; "I suppose it is only one of the Miss Carvers—Don't stir, Nat; it will vex her to see you kneeling to me—don't stir, I say—"

"Where is she? Where is my Araminta?" cried Miss Warwick, as the maid was trying to open the outer passage-door for her, which had a bad lock.

"Get up, get up, Natty; and get some fresh water in the tea-kettle—quick!" cried Miss Hodges, and she began to clear away some of the varieties of literature, &c., which lay scattered about the room. Nat, in obedience to her commands, was making his exit with all possible speed, when Angelina entered, exclaiming—

"My amiable Araminta!—My unknown friend!"

"My Angelina!—My charming Angelina!" cried Miss Hodges.

Miss Hodges was not the sort of person our heroine expected to see;—and to conceal the panic, with which the first sight of her unknown friend struck her disappointed imagination, she turned back to listen to the apologies which Nat Gazabo was pouring forth about his awkwardness and the tea-kettle.

"Turn, Angelina, ever dear!" cried Miss Hodges, with the tone and action of a bad actress who is rehearsing an embrace—"Turn, Angelina, ever dear!—thus, thus let us meet, to part no more."

"But her voice is so loud," said Angelina to herself, "and her looks so vulgar, and there is such a smell of brandy!—How unlike the elegant delicacy I had expected in my unknown friend!" Miss Warwick involuntarily shrunk from the stifling embrace.

"You are overpowered, my Angelina—lean on me," said her Araminta.

Nat Gazabo re-entered with the tea-kettle—

"Here's boiling water, and we'll have fresh tea in a trice—the young lady's over-tired, seemingly—Here's a chair, miss, here's a chair," cried Nat. Miss Warwick sunk upon the chair: Miss Hodges seated herself beside her, continuing to address her in a theatrical tone.

"This moment is bliss unutterable! my kind, my noble-minded Angelina, thus to leave all your friends for your Araminta!"—Suddenly changing her voice—"Set the tea-kettle, Nat!"

"Who is this Nat, I wonder?" thought Miss Warwick.

"Well, and tell me," said Miss Hodges, whose attention was awkwardly divided between the ceremonies of making tea and making speeches—"and tell me, my Angelina—That's water enough, Nat—and tell me, my Angelina, how did you find me out?"

"With some difficulty, indeed, my Araminta." Miss Warwick could hardly pronounce the words.

"So kind, so noble-minded," continued Miss Hodges—"and did you receive my last letter—three sheets?—And how did you contrive—Stoop the kettle, do, Nat."

"Oh, this odious Nat! how I wish she would send him away!" thought Miss Warwick.

"And tell me, my Araminta—my Angelina I mean—how did you contrive your elopement—and how did you escape from the eye of your aristocratic Argus—how did you escape from all your unfeeling persecutors?—Tell me, tell me all your adventures, my Angelina!—Butter the toast, Nat," said Miss Hodges who was cutting bread and butter, which she did not do with the celebrated grace of Charlotte, in the Sorrows of Werter.

"I'll tell you all, my Araminta," whispered Miss Warwick, "when we are by ourselves."

"Oh, never mind Nat," whispered Miss Hodges.

"Couldn't you tell him," rejoined Miss Warwick, "that he need not wait any longer?"

"Wait, my dear! why, what do you take him for?"

"Why, is not he your footman?" whispered Angelina.

"My footman!—Nat!" exclaimed Miss Hodges, bursting out a laughing, "my Angelina took you for my footman."

"Good heavens! what is he?" said Angelina, in a low voice.

"Verily," said Nat Gazabo, with a sort of bashful simple laugh, "verily, I am the humblest of her servants."

"And does my Angelina—spare my delicacy," said Miss Hodges—"does my Angelina not remember, in any of my long letters, the name of—Orlando!—There he stands."

"Orlando!—Is this gentleman your Orlando, of whom I have heard so much?"

"He! he! he!" simpered Nat. "I am Orlando, of whom you have heard so much; and she—(pointing to Miss Hodges)—she is, to-morrow morning, God willing, to be Mistress Hodges Gazabo."

"Mrs. Hodges Gazabo, my Araminta!" said Angelina, with astonishment, which she could not suppress.

"Yes, my Angelina: so end 'The Sorrows of Araminta'—Another cup?—do I make the tea too sweet?" said Miss Hodges, whilst Nat handed the bread and butter to the ladies officiously.

"The man looks like a fool," thought Miss Warwick.

"Set down the bread and butter, and be quiet, Nat—Then, as soon as the wedding is over, we fly, my Angelina, to our charming cottage in Wales:—there may we bid defiance to the storms of fate—

"'The world forgetting, by the world forgot.'"

"That," said Angelina, "'is the blameless vestal's lot:'—but you forget that you are to be married, my Araminta; and you forget that, in your letter of three folio sheets, you said not one word to me of this intended marriage."

"Nay, my dear, blame me not for a want of confidence, that my heart disclaims," said Miss Hodges: "from the context of my letters, you must have suspected the progress my Orlando had made in my affections; but, indeed, I should not have brought myself to decide apparently so precipitately, had it not been for the opposition, the persecution of my friends—I was determined to show them that I know, and can assert, my right to think and act, upon all occasions, for myself."

Longer, much longer, Miss Hodges, spoke in the most peremptory voice; but whilst she was declaiming on her favourite topic, her Angelina was "revolving in her altered mind" the strange things which she had seen and heard in the course of the last half-hour; every thing appeared to her in a new light; when she compared the conversation and conduct of Miss Hodges with the sentimental letters of her Araminta; when she compared Orlando in description to Orlando in reality, she could scarcely believe her senses: accustomed as she had been to elegance of manners, the vulgarity and awkwardness of Miss Hodges shocked and disgusted her beyond measure. The disorder, and—for the words must be said—slatternly dirty appearance of her Araminta's dress, and of every thing in her apartment, were such as would have made a hell of heaven; and the idea of spending her life in a cottage with Mrs. Hodges Gazabo and Nat overwhelmed our heroine with the double fear of wretchedness and ridicule.

"Another cup of tea, my Angelina?" said Miss Hodges, when she had finished her tirade against her persecutors, that is to say, her friends, "another cup, my Angelina?—do, after your journey and fatigue, take another cup."

"No more, I thank you."

"Then reach me that tragedy, Nat—you know—"

"Your own tragedy, is it, my dear?" said he.

"Ah, Nat, now! you never can keep a secret," said Miss Hodges. "I wanted to have surprised my Angelina."

"I am surprised!" thought Angelina—"oh, how much surprised!"

"I have a motto for our cottage here somewhere," said Miss Hodges, turning over the leaves of her tragedy—"but I'll keep that till to-morrow—since to-morrow's the day sacred to love and friendship."

Nat, by way of showing his joy in a becoming manner, rubbed his hands, and hummed a tune. His mistress frowned, and bit her lips; but the signals were lost upon him, and he sung out, in an exulting tone—

"When the lads of the village so merrily, ah! Sound their tabours, I'll hand thee along."

"Fool! Dolt! Idiot!" cried his Araminta, rising furious—"out of my sight!" Then, sinking down upon the chair, she burst into tears, and threw herself into the arms of her pale, astonished Angelina. "Oh, my Angelina!" she exclaimed, "I am the most ill-matched! most unfortunate! most wretched of women!"

"Don't be frighted, miss," said Nat; "she'll come to again presently—'tis only her way." As he spoke, he poured out a bumper of brandy, and kneeling, presented it to his mistress. "'Tis the only thing in life does her good," continued he, "in this sort of fits."

"Heavens, what a scene!" said Miss Warwick to herself—"and the woman so heavy, I can scarce support her weight—and is this my unknown friend?"

How long Miss Hodges would willingly have continued to sob upon Miss Warwick's shoulder, or how long that shoulder could possibly have sustained her weight, is a mixed problem in physics and metaphysics, which must for ever remain unsolved: but suddenly a loud scream was heard. Miss Hodges started up—the door was thrown open, and Betty Williams rushed in, crying loudly—"Oh, shave me! shave me! for the love of Cot, shave me, miss!" and, pushing by the swain, who held the unfinished glass of brandy in his hand, she threw herself on her knees at the feet of Angelina.

"Gracious me!" exclaimed Nat, "whatever you are, you need not push one so."

"What now, Betty Williams? is the wench mad or drunk?" cried Miss Hodges.

"We are to have a mad scene next, I suppose," said Miss Warwick, calmly—"I am prepared for every thing, after what I have seen."

Betty Williams continued crying bitterly, and wringing her hands—"Oh, shave me this once, miss! 'tis the first thing of the kind I ever tid, inteet, inteet! Oh, shave me this once—I tid not know it was worth so much as a shilling, and that I could be hanged, inteet—and I—"

Here Betty was interrupted by the entrance of Mrs. Puffit, the milliner, the printer's devil, and a stern-looking man, to whom Mrs. Puffit, as she came in, said, pointing to Betty Williams and Miss Warwick, "There they are—do your duty, Mr. Constable: I'll swear to my lace."

"And I'll swear to my black thumbs," said the printer's devil.

"I saw the lace hanging out of her pocket, and there's the marks of my fingers upon it, Mr. Constable."

"Fellow!" cried Miss Hodges, taking the constable by the arm, "this is my apartment, into which no minion of the law has a right to enter; for, in England, every man's house is his castle."

"I know that as well as you do, madam!" said the constable; "but I make it a principle to do nothing without a warrant: here's my warrant."

"Oh, shave me! the lace is hers inteet!" cried Betty Williams, pointing to Miss Warwick. "Oh, miss is my mistress inteet—"

"Come, mistress or miss, then, you'll be pleased to come along with me," said the constable, seizing hold of Angelina—"like mistress, like maid."

"Villain! unfeeling villain! oh, unhand my Angelina, or I shall die! I shall die!" exclaimed Araminta, falling into the arms of Nat Gazabo, who immediately held the replenished glass of brandy to her lips—"Oh, my Angelina, my Angelina!"

Struck with horror at her situation, Miss Warwick shrunk from the grasp of the constable, and leaned motionless on the back of a chair.

"Come, my angel, as they call you, I think—the lady there has brandy enough, if you want spirits—all the fits and faintings in Christendom won't serve you now. I'm used to the tricks o' the trade.—The law must take its course; and if you can't walk, I must carry you."

"Touch me at your peril! I am innocent," said Angelina.

"Innocent—innocence itself! pure, spotless, injured innocence!" cried Miss Hodges. "I shall die! I shall die! I shall die on the spot! barbarous, barbarous villain!"

Whilst Miss Hodges spoke, the ready Nat poured out a fresh glass of that restorative, which he always had ready for cases of life and death; and she screamed and sipped, and sipped and screamed, as the constable took up Angelina in his arms, and carried her towards the door.

"Mrs. Innocence," said the man, "you shall see whom you shall see."

Mrs. Puffit opened the door; and, to the utter astonishment of every body present, Lady Diana Chillingworth entered the room, followed by Lady Frances Somerset and Mrs. Bertrand. The constable set down Angelina. Miss Hodges set down the glass of brandy. Mrs. Puffit curtsied. Betty Williams stretched out her arms to Lady Diana, crying, "Shave me! shave me this once!" Miss Warwick hid her face with her hands.

"Only my Valenciennes lace, that has been found in that girl's pocket, and—" said Mrs. Puffit.

Lady Diana Chillingworth turned away with indescribable haughtiness, and, addressing herself to her sister, said, "Lady Frances Somerset, you would not, I presume, have Lady Diana Chillingworth lend her countenance to such a scene as this—I hope, sister, that you are satisfied now." As she said these words, her ladyship walked out of the room.

"Never was further from being satisfied in my life," said Lady Frances.

"If you look at this, my lady," said the constable, holding out the lace, "you'll soon be satisfied as to what sort of a young lady that is."

"Oh, you mistake the young lady," said Mrs. Bertrand, and she whispered to the constable. "Come away: you may be sure you'll be satisfied—we shall all be satisfied, handsomely, all in good time. Don't let the delinquency there on her knees," added she aloud, pointing to Betty Williams—"don't let the delinquency there on her knees escape."

"Come along, mistress," said the constable, pulling up Betty Williams from her knees. "But I say the law must have its course, if I am not satisfied."

"Oh, I am confident," said Mrs. Puffit, the milliner, "we shall all be satisfied, no doubt; but Lady Di. Chillingworth knows my Valenciennes lace, and Miss Burrage too, for they did me this morning the honour—"

"Will you do me the favour," interrupted Lady Frances Somerset, "to leave us, good Mrs. Puffit, for the present? Here is some mistake—the less noise we make about it the better. You shall be satisfied."

"Oh, your ladyship—I'm sure, I'm confident—I shan't utter another syllable—nor never would have articulated a syllable about the lace (though Valenciennes, and worth thirty guineas, if it is worth a farthing), had I had the least intimacy or suspicion the young lady was your la'ship's protégée. I shan't, at any rate, utter another syllable."

Mrs. Puffit, having glibly run off this speech, left the room, and carried in her train the constable and Betty Williams, the printer's devil, and Mrs. Bertrand, the woman of the house.

Miss Warwick, whose confusion during this whole scene was excessive, stood without power to speak or move.

"Thank God, they are gone!" said Lady Frances; and she went to Angelina, and taking her hands gently from before her face, said, in a soothing tone, "Miss Warwick, your friend, Lady Frances Somerset, you cannot think that she suspects—"

"La, dear, no!" cried Nat Gazabo, who had now sufficiently recovered from his fright and amazement to be able to speak: "Dear heart! who could go for to suspect such a thing? but they made such a bustle and noise, they quite flabbergasted me, so many on them in this small room. Please to sit down, my lady.—Is there any thing I can do?"

"If you could have the goodness, sir, to leave us for a few minutes," said Lady Frances, in a polite, persuasive manner—"you could have the goodness, sir, to leave us for a few minutes."

Nat, who was not always spoken to by so gentle a voice, smiled, bowed, and was retiring, when Miss Hodges came forward with an air of defiance: "Aristocratic insolence!" exclaimed she: "Stop, Nat—stir not a foot, at your peril, at the word of command of any of the privileged orders upon earth—stir not a foot, at your peril, at the behest of any titled She in the universe!—Madam, or my lady—or by whatever other name more high, more low, you choose to be addressed—this is my husband."

"Very probably, madam," said Lady Frances, with an easy calmness, which provoked Miss Hodges to a louder tone of indignation.

"Stir not a foot, at your peril, Nat," cried she. "I will defend him, I say, madam, against every shadow, every penumbra of aristocratic insolence."

"As you and he think proper, madam," replied Lady Frances. "'Tis easy to defend the gentleman against shadows."

Miss Hodges marched up and down the room with her arms folded. Nat stood stock still.

"The woman," whispered Lady Frances to Miss Warwick, "is either mad or drunk—or both; at all events we shall be better in another room." As she spoke, she drew Miss Warwick's arm within hers.—"Will you allow aristocratic insolence to pass by you, sir?" said she to Nat Gazabo, who stood like a statue in the doorway—he edged himself aside.

"And is this your independence of soul, my Angelina?" cried Araminta, setting her back to the door, so as effectually to prevent her from passing—"and is this your independence of soul, my Angelina—thus, thus tamely to submit, to resign yourself again to your unfeeling, proud, prejudiced, intellect-lacking persecutors?"

"This lady is my friend, madam," said Angelina, in as firm and tranquil a tone as she could command, for she was quite terrified by her Araminta's violence.

"Take your choice, my dear; stay or follow me, as you think best," said Lady Frances.

"Your friend!" pursued the oratorical lady, detaining Miss Warwick with a heavy hand: "Do you feel the force of the word? Can you feel it, as I once thought you could? Your friend! am not I your friend, your best friend, my Angelina? your own Araminta, your amiable Araminta, your unknown friend?"

"My unknown friend, indeed!" said Angelina. Miss Hodges let go her struggling hand, and Miss Warwick that instant followed Lady Frances, who, having effected her retreat, had by this time gained the staircase.

"Gone!" cried Miss Hodges; "then never will I see or speak to her more. Thus I whistle her off, and let her down the wind to prey at fortune."

"Gracious heart! what quarrels," said Nat, "and doings, the night before our wedding-day!"

We leave this well-matched pair to their happy prospects of conjugal union and equality.

Lady Frances, who perceived that Miss Warwick was scarcely able to support herself, led her to a sofa, which she luckily saw through the half-open door of a drawing-room, at the head of the staircase.

"To be taken for a thief!—Oh, to what have I exposed myself!" said Miss Warwick.

"Sit down, my dear, now we are in a room where we need not fear interruption—sit down, and don't tremble like an aspen leaf," said Lady Frances Somerset, who saw that at this moment, reproaches would have been equally unnecessary and cruel.

Unused to be treated with judicious kindness, Angelina's heart was deeply touched by it, and she opened her whole mind to Lady Frances, with the frankness of a young person conscious of her own folly, not desirous to apologize or extenuate, but anxious to regain the esteem of a friend.

"To be sure, my dear, it was, as you say, rather foolish to set out in quest of an unknown friend," said Lady Frances, after listening to the confessions of Angelina. "And why, after all, was it necessary to have an elopement?"

"Oh, madam, I am sensible of my folly—I had long formed a project of living in a cottage in Wales—and Miss Burrage described Wales to me as a terrestrial paradise."

"Miss Burrage! then why did she not go to paradise along with you?" said Lady Frances.

"I don't know—she was was so much attached to Lady Di. Chillingworth, she said, she could never think of leaving her: she charged me never to mention the cottage scheme to Lady Di., who would only laugh at it. Indeed, Lady Di. was almost always out whilst we were in London, or dressing, or at cards, and I could seldom speak to her, especially about cottages; and I wished for a friend, to whom I could open my whole heart, and whom I could love and esteem, and who should have the same tastes and notions with myself."

"I am sorry that last condition is part of your definition of a friend," said Lady Frances, smiling; "for I will not swear that my notions are the same as yours, but yet I think you would have found me as good a friend as this Araminta of yours. Was it necessary to perfect felicity to have an unknown friend?"

"Ah! there was my mistake," said Miss Warwick. "I had read Araminta's writings, and they speak so charmingly of friendship and felicity, that I thought

'Those best can paint them who can feel them most.'"
"No uncommon mistake," said Lady Frances.

"But I am fully sensible of my folly," said Angelina.

"Then there is no occasion to say any more about it at present—to-morrow, as you like romances, we'll read Arabella, or the Female Quixote; and you shall tell me which, of all your acquaintance, the heroine resembles most. And in the mean time, as you seem to have satisfied your curiosity about your unknown friend, will you come home with me?"

"Oh, madam," said Angelina, with emotion, "your goodness—"

"But we have not time to talk of my goodness yet—stay—let me see—yes, it will be best that it should be known that you are with us as soon as possible—for there is a thing, my dear, of which, perhaps, you are not fully sensible—of which you are too young to be fully sensible—that, to people who have nothing to do or to say, scandal is a necessary luxury of life; and that, by such a step as you have taken, you have given room enough for scandal-mongers to make you and your friends completely miserable."

Angelina burst into tears—though a sentimental lady, she had not yet acquired the art of bursting into tears upon every trifling occasion. Hers were tears of real feeling. Lady Frances was glad to see that she had made a sufficient impression upon her mind; but she assured Angelina that she did not intend to torment her with useless lectures and reproaches. Lady Frances Somerset understood the art of giving advice rather better than Lady Diana Chillingworth.

"I do not mean, my dear," said Lady Frances, "to make you miserable for life—but I mean to make an impression upon you that may make you prudent and happy for life. So don't cry till you make your eyes so red as not to be fit to be seen at the play to-night, where they must—positively—be seen."

"But Lady Diana is below," said Miss Warwick: "I am ashamed and afraid to see her again."

"It will be difficult, but I hope not impossible, to convince my sister," said Lady Frances, "that you clearly understand that you have been a simpleton; but that a simpleton of sixteen is more an object of mercy than a simpleton of sixty—so my verdict is—Guilty;—but recommended to mercy."

By this mercy Angelina was more touched than she could have been by the most severe reproaches.

CHAPTER V

Whilst the preceding conversation was passing, Lady Diana Chillingworth was in Mrs. Bertrand's fruit-shop, occupied with her smelling-bottle and Miss Burrage. Clara Hope was there also, and Mrs. Puffit, the milliner, and Mrs. Bertrand, who was assuring her ladyship that not a word of the affair about the young lady and the lace should go out of her house.

"Your la'ship need not be in the least uneasy," said Mrs. Bertrand, "for I have satisfied the constable, and satisfied every body; and the constable allows Miss Warwick's name was not mentioned in the warrant; and as to the servant girl, she's gone before the magistrate, who, of course, will send her to the house of correction; but that will no ways implicate the young lady, and nothing shall transpire from this house detrimental to the young lady, who is under your la'ship's protection. And I'll tell your la'ship how Mrs. Puffit and I have settled to tell the story: with your ladyship's approbation, I shall say—"

"Nothing, if you please," said her ladyship, with more than her usual haughtiness. "The young lady to whom you allude is under Lady Frances Somerset's protection, not mine; and whatever you do or say, I beg that in this affair the name of Lady Diana Chillingworth may not be used."

She turned her back upon the disconcerted milliner as she finished this speech, and walked to the furthest end of the long room, followed by the constant flatterer of all her humours, Miss Burrage.

The milliner and Mrs. Bertrand now began to console themselves for the mortification they had received from her ladyship's pride, and for the insolent forgetfulness of her companion, by abusing them both in a low voice. Mrs. Bertrand began with, "Her ladyship's so touchy and so proud; she's as high as the moon, and higher."

"Oh, all the Chillingworths, by all accounts, are so," said Mrs. Puffit; "but then, to be sure, they have a right to be so if any body has, for they certainly are real high-horn people. But I can't tolerate to see some people, that aren't no ways born nor entitled to it, give themselves such airs as some people do. Now, there's that Miss Burrage, that pretends not to know me, ma'am."

"And me, ma'am,—just the same: such provoking assurance—I that knew her from this high."

"On St. Augustin's Back, you know," said Mrs. Puffit.

"On St. Augustin's Back, you know," echoed Mrs. Bertrand.

"So I told her this morning, ma'am," said Mrs. Puffit.

"And so I told her this evening, ma'am, when the three Miss Herrings came in to give me a call in their way to the play; girls that she used to walk with, ma'am, for ever and ever in the green, you know."

"Yes; and that she was always glad to drink tea with, ma'am, when asked, you know," said Mrs. Puffit.

"Well, ma'am," pursued Mrs. Bertrand, "here she had the impudence to pretend not to know them. She takes up her glass—my Lady Di. herself couldn't have done it better, and squeezes up her ugly face this way, pretending to be near-sighted, though she can see as well as you or I can."

"Such airs! she near-sighted!" said Mrs. Puffit: "what will the world come to!"

"Oh, I wish her pride may have a fall," resumed the provoked milliner, as soon as she had breath. "I dare to say now she wouldn't know her own relations if she was to meet them; I'd lay any wager she would not vouchsafe a curtsy to that good old John Barker, the friend of her father, you know, who gave up to this Miss Burrage I don't know how many hundreds of pounds, that were due to him, or else miss wouldn't have had a farthing in the world; yet now, I'll be bound, she'd forget this as well as St.

Augustin's Back, and wouldn't know John Barker from Abraham; and I don't doubt that she'd pull out her glass at her aunt Dinah, because she is a cheesemonger's widow."

"Oh no," said Mrs. Bertrand, "she couldn't have the baseness to be near-sighted to good Dinah Plait, that bred her up, and was all in all to her."

Just as Mrs. Bertrand finished speaking, into the fruit-shop walked the very persons of whom she had been talking—Dinah Plait and Mr. Barker.

"Mrs. Dinah Plait, I declare!" exclaimed Mrs. Bertrand.

"I never was so glad to see you, Mrs. Plait and Mr. Barker, in all my days," said Mrs. Puffit.

"Why you should be so particularly glad to see me, Mrs. Puffit, I don't know," said Mr. Barker, laughing; "but I'm not surprised Dinah Plait should be a welcome guest wherever she goes, especially with a purse full of guineas in her hand."

"Friend Bertrand," said Dinah Plait, producing a purse which she held under her cloak, "I am come to restore this purse to its rightful owner: after a great deal of trouble, John Barker (who never thinks it a trouble to do good) hath traced her to your house."

"There is a young lady here, to be sure," said Mrs. Bertrand, "but you can't see her just at present, for she is talking on petticlar business with my Lady Frances Somerset above stairs."

"Tis well," said Dinah Plait: "I would willingly restore this purse, not to the young creature herself, but to some of her friends,—for I fear she is not quite in a right state of mind. If I could see any of the young lady's friends."

"Miss Burrage," cried Mrs. Bertrand, in a tone of voice so loud that she could not avoid hearing it, "are not you one of the young lady's friends?"

"What young lady's friend?" replied Miss Burrage, without stirring from her seat.

"Miss Burrage, here's a purse for a young lady," said Mrs. Puffit.

"A purse for whom? Where?" said Miss Burrage, at last deigning to rise, and come out of her recess.

"There, ma'am," said the milliner. "Now for her glass!" whispered Mrs. Puffit to Mrs. Bertrand. And, exactly as it had been predicted, Miss Burrage eyed her aunt Dinah through her glass, pretending not to know her. "The purse is not mine," said she, coolly: "I know nothing of it—nothing."

"Hetty!" exclaimed her aunt; but as Miss Burrage still eyed her through her glass with unmoved invincible assurance, Dinah thought that, however strong the resemblance, she was mistaken. "No, it can't be Hetty. I beg pardon, madam," said she, "but I took you for—Did not I hear you say the name of Burrage, friend Puffit?"

"Yes, Burrage; one of the Burrages of Dorsetshire," said the milliner, with malicious archness.

"One of the Burrages of Dorsetshire: I beg pardon. But did you ever see such a likeness, friend Barker, to my poor niece, Hetty Burrage?"

Miss Burrage, who overheard these words, immediately turned her back upon her aunt. "A grotesque statue of starch,—one of your quakers, I think, they call themselves: Bristol is full of such primitive figures," said Miss Burrage to Clara Hope, and she walked back to the recess and to Lady Di.

"So like, voice and all, to my poor Hester," said Dinah Plait, and she wiped the tears from her eyes. "Though Hetty has neglected me so of late, I have a tenderness for her; we cannot but have some for our own relations."

"Grotesque or not, 'tis a statue that seems to have a heart, and a gude one," said Clara Hope.

"I wish we could say the same of every body," said Mrs. Bertrand.

All this time, old Mr. Barker, leaning on his cane, had been silent: "Burrage of Dorsetshire!" said he; "I'll soon see whether she be or no; for Hetty has a wart on her chin that I cannot forget, let her forget whom and what she pleases."

Mr. Barker, who was a plain-spoken, determined man, followed the young lady to the recess; and, after looking her full in the face, exclaimed in a loud voice, "Here's the wart!—'tis Hetty!"

"Sir!—wart!—man!—Lady Di.!" cried Miss Burrage, in accents of the utmost distress and vexation.

Mr. Barker, regardless of her frowns and struggles, would by no means relinquish her hand; but leading, or rather pulling her forwards, he went on with barbarous steadiness: "Dinah," said he, "'tis your own niece. Hetty, 'tis your own aunt, that bred you up! What, struggle—Burrage of Dorsetshire!"

"There certainly," said Lady Diana Chillingworth, in a solemn tone, "is a conspiracy, this night, against my poor nerves. These people, amongst them, will infallibly surprise me to death. What is the matter now?—why do you drag the young lady, sir? She came here with me, sir,—with Lady Diana Chillingworth; and, consequently, she is not a person to be insulted."

"Insult her!" said Mr. Barker, whose sturdy simplicity was not to be baffled or disconcerted either by the cunning of Miss Burrage, or by the imposing manner and awful name of Lady Diana Chillingworth. "Insult her! why, 'tis she insults us; she won't know us."

"How should Miss Burrage know you, sir, or any body here?" said Lady Diana, looking round, as if upon beings of a species different from her own.

"How should she know her own aunt that bred her up?" said the invincible John Barker, "and me who have had her on my knee a hundred times, giving her barley-sugar till she was sick?"

"Sick! I am sure you make me sick," said Lady Diana. "Sir, that young lady is one of the Burrages of Dorsetshire, as good a family as any in England."

"Madam," said John Barker, replying in a solemnity of tone equal to her ladyship's, "that young lady is one of the Burrages of Bristol, drysalters; niece to Dinah Plait, who is widow to a man, who was, in his time, as honest a cheesemonger as any in England."

"Miss Burrage!—My God!—don't you speak!" cried Lady Diana, in a voice of terror.

"The young lady is bashful, my lady, among strangers," said Mrs. Bertrand.

"Oh, Hester Burrage, is this kind of thee?" said Dinah Plait, with in accent of mixed sorrow and affection; "but thou art my niece, and I forgive thee."

"A cheesemonger's niece!" cried Lady Diana, with horror; "how have I been deceived! But this is the consequence of making acquaintance at Buxton, and those watering-places: I've done with her, however. Lord bless me! here comes my sister, Lady Frances! Good heavens! my dear," continued her ladyship, going to meet her sister, and drawing her into the recess at the farthest end of the room, "here are more misfortunes—misfortunes without end. What will the world say? Here's this Miss Burrage,— take no more notice of her, sister; she's an impostor; who do you think she turns out to be? Daughter to a drysalter, niece to a cheesemonger! Only conceive!—a person that has been going about with me every where!—What will the world say?"

"That it is very imprudent to have unknown friends, my dear," replied Lady Frances. "The best thing you can possibly do is to say nothing about the matter, and to receive this penitent ward of yours without reproaches; for if you talk of her unknown friends, the world will certainly talk of yours."

Lady Diana drew back with haughtiness when her sister offered to put Miss Warwick's hands into hers; but she condescended to say, after an apparent struggle with herself, "I am happy to hear, Miss Warwick, that you have returned to your senses. Lady Frances takes you under her protection, I understand; at which, for all our sakes, I rejoice; and I have only one piece of advice, Miss Warwick, to give you—"

"Keep it till after the play, my dear Diana," whispered Lady Frances; "it will have more effect."

"The play!—Bless me!" said Lady Diana, "why, you have contrived to make Miss Warwick fit to be seen, I protest. But, after all I have gone through to-night, how can I appear in public? My dear, this Miss Burrage's business has given me such a shock,—such nervous affections!"

"Nervous affections!—Some people, I do believe, have none but nervous affections," thought Lady Frances.

"Permit me," said Mrs. Dinah Plait, coming up to Lady Frances, and presenting Miss Warwick's purse— "permit me, as thou seemest to be a friend to this young lady, to restore to thee her purse, which she left by mistake at my house this forenoon. I hope she is better, poor thing!"

"She is better, and I thank you for her, madam," said Lady Frances, who was struck with the obliging manner and benevolent countenance of Dinah Plait, and who did not think herself contaminated by standing in the same room with the widow of a cheesemonger.

"Let me thank you myself, madam," said Angelina; "I am perfectly in my senses now, I can assure you; and I shall never forget the kindness which you and this benevolent gentleman showed me when you thought I was in real distress."

"Some people are more grateful than other people," said Mrs. Puffit, looking at Miss Burrage, who in mortified, sullen silence, followed the aunt and the benefactor of whom she was ashamed, and who had reason to be ashamed of her.

We do not imagine that our readers can be much interested for a young lady who was such a compound of pride and meanness; we shall therefore only add, that her future life was spent on St. Augustin's Back, where she made herself at once as ridiculous and as unhappy as she deserved to be.

As for our heroine, under the friendly and judicious care of Lady Frances Somerset, she acquired that which is more useful to the possessor than genius—good sense. Instead of rambling over the world in search of an unknown friend, she attached herself to those of whose worth she received proofs more convincing than a letter of three folio sheets, stuffed with sentimental nonsense. In short, we have now, in the name of Angelina Warwick, the pleasure to assure all those whom it may concern, that it is possible for a young lady of sixteen to cure herself of the affectation of sensibility, and the folly of romance.

THE GOOD FRENCH GOVERNESS

Among the sufferers during the bloody reign of Robespierre, was Mad. de Rosier, a lady of good family, excellent understanding, and most amiable character. Her husband, and her only son, a promising young man of about fourteen, were dragged to the horrid prison of the Conciergerie, and their names, soon afterward, appeared in the list of those who fell a sacrifice to the tyrant's cruelty. By the assistance of a faithful domestic, Mad. de Rosier, who was destined to be the next victim, escaped from France, and took refuge in England—England!—that generous country, which, in favour of the unfortunate, forgets her national prejudices, and to whom, in their utmost need, even her "natural enemies" fly for protection. English travellers have sometimes been accused of forgetting the civilities which they receive in foreign countries; but their conduct towards the French emigrants has sufficiently demonstrated the injustice of this reproach.

Mad. de Rosier had reason to be pleased by the delicacy of several families of distinction in London, who offered her their services under the name of gratitude; but she was incapable of encroaching upon the kindness of her friends. Misfortune had not extinguished the energy of her mind, and she still possessed the power of maintaining herself honourably by her own exertions. Her character and her abilities being well known, she easily procured recommendations as a preceptress. Many ladies anxiously desired to engage such a governess for their children, but Mrs. Harcourt had the good fortune to obtain the preference.

Mrs. Harcourt was a widow, who had been a very fine woman, and continued to be a very fine lady; she had good abilities, but, as she lived in a constant round of dissipation, she had not time to cultivate her understanding, or to attend to the education of her family; and she had satisfied her conscience by procuring for her daughters a fashionable governess and expensive masters. The governess whose place Mad. de Rosier was now to supply, had quitted her pupils, to go abroad with a lady of quality, and Mrs.

Harcourt knew enough of the world to bear her loss without emotion;—she, however, stayed at home one whole evening, to receive Mad. de Rosier, and to introduce her to her pupils. Mrs. Harcourt had three daughters and a son—Isabella, Matilda, Favoretta, and Herbert. Isabella was about fourteen; her countenance was intelligent, but rather too expressive of confidence in her own capacity, for she had, from her infancy, been taught to believe that she was a genius. Her memory had been too much cultivated; she had learned languages with facility, and had been taught to set a very high value upon her knowledge of history and chronology. Her temper had been hurt by flattery, yet she was capable of feeling all the generous passions.

Matilda was a year younger than Isabella; she was handsome, but her countenance, at first view, gave the idea of hopeless indolence; she did not learn the French and Italian irregular verbs by rote as expeditiously as her sister, and her impatient preceptress pronounced, with an irrevocable nod, that Miss Matilda was no genius. The phrase was quickly caught by her masters, so that Matilda, undervalued even by her sister, lost all confidence in herself, and with the hope of success, lost the wish for exertion. Her attention gradually turned to dress and personal accomplishments; not that she was vain of her beauty, but she had more hopes of pleasing by the graces of her person than of her mind. The timid, anxious blush, which Mad. De Rosier observed to vary in Matilda's countenance, when she spoke to those for whom she felt affection, convinced this lady that, if Matilda were no genius, it must have been the fault of her education. On sensibility, all that is called genius, perhaps, originally depends: those who are capable of feeling a strong degree of pain and pleasure may surely be excited to great and persevering exertion, by calling the proper motives into action.

Favoretta, the youngest daughter, was about six years old. At this age, the habits that constitute character are not formed, and it is, therefore, absurd to speak of the character of a child six years old. Favoretta had been, from her birth, the plaything of her mother and of her mother's waiting-maid. She was always produced, when Mrs. Harcourt had company, to be admired and caressed by the fashionable circle; her ringlets and her lively nonsense were the never-failing means of attracting attention from visitors. In the drawing-room, Favoretta, consequently, was happy, always in high spirits, and the picture of good humour; but, change the scene, and Favoretta no longer appeared the same person: when alone, she was idle and spiritless; when with her maid or with her brother and sisters, pettish and capricious. Her usual play-fellow was Herbert, but their plays regularly ended in quarrels—quarrels in which both parties were commonly in the wrong, though the whole of the blame necessarily fell upon Herbert, for Herbert was neither caressing nor caressed. Mrs. Grace, the waiting-maid, pronounced him to be the plague of her life, and prophesied evil of him, because, as she averred, if she combed his hair a hundred times a day, it would never be fit to be seen; besides this, she declared "there was no managing to keep him out of mischief," and he was so "thick-headed at his book," that Mrs. Grace, on whom the task of teaching him his alphabet had, during the negligent reign of the late governess, devolved, affirmed that he never would learn to read like any other young gentleman. Whether the zeal of Mrs. Grace for his literary progress were of service to his understanding, may be doubted; there could be no doubt of its effect upon his temper; a sullen gloom overspread Herbert's countenance, whenever the shrill call of "Come and say your task, Master Herbert!" was heard; and the continual use of the imperative mood—"Let that alone, do, Master Herbert!"—"Don't make a racket, Master Herbert!"—"Do hold your tongue and sit still where I bid you, Master Herbert!" operated so powerfully upon this young gentleman, that, at eight years old, he partly fulfilled his tormentor's prophecies, for he became a little surly rebel, who took pleasure in doing exactly the contrary to every thing that he was desired to do, and who took pride in opposing his powers of endurance to the force of punishment. His situation was scarcely more agreeable in the drawing-room than in the nursery, for his mother usually announced him to the company by the appropriate appellation of Roughhead; and Herbert Roughhead being assailed, at his entrance into the room, by a variety of petty reproaches and maternal witticisms upon his uncouth appearance, became bashful and awkward, averse from polite society, and prone to the less fastidious company of servants in the stable and the kitchen. Mrs. Harcourt absolutely forbade his intercourse with the postilions, though she did not think it necessary to be so strict in her injunctions as to the butler and footman; because, argued she, "children will get to the servants when one's from home, and it is best that they should be with such of them as one can trust. Now Stephen is quite a person one can entirely depend upon, and he has been so long in the family, the children are quite used to him, and safe with him."

How many mothers have a Stephen, on whom they can entirely depend!

Mrs. Harcourt, with politeness, which in this instance supplied the place of good sense, invested Mad. de Rosier with full powers, as the preceptress of her children, except as to their religious education; she stipulated that Catholic tenets should not be instilled into them. To this Mad. de Rosier replied—"that children usually follow the religion of their parents, and that proselytes seldom do honour to their conversion; that were she, on the other hand, to attempt to promote her pupils' belief in the religion of their country, her utmost powers could add nothing to the force of public religious instruction, and to the arguments of those books which are necessarily put into the hands of every well-educated person."

With these opinions, Mad. de Rosier readily promised to abstain from all direct or indirect interference in the religious instruction of her pupils. Mrs. Harcourt then introduced her to them as "a friend, in whom she had entire confidence, and whom she hoped and believed they would make it their study to please."

Whilst the ceremonies of the introduction were going on, Herbert kept himself aloof, and, with his whip suspended over the stick on which he was riding, eyed Mad. de Rosier with no friendly aspect: however, when she held out her hand to him, and when he heard the encouraging tone of her voice, he approached, held his whip fast in his right hand, but very cordially gave the lady his left to shake.

"Are you to be my governess?" said he: "you won't give me very long tasks, will you?"

"Favoretta, my dear, what has detained you so long?" cried Mrs. Harcourt, as the door opened, and as Favoretta, with her hair in nice order, was ushered into the room by Mrs. Grace. The little girl ran up to Mad. de Rosier, and, with the most caressing freedom, cried,—

"Will you love me? I have not my red shoes on to-day!"

Whilst Mad. de Rosier assured Favoretta that the want of the red shoes would not diminish her merit, Matilda whispered to Isabella—"Mourning is very becoming to her, though she is not fair;" and Isabella, with a look of absence, replied—"But she speaks English amazingly well for a French woman."

Mad. de Rosier did speak English remarkably well; she had spent some years in England, in her early youth, and, perhaps, the effect of her conversation was heightened by an air of foreign novelty. As she was not hackneyed in the common language of conversation, her ideas were expressed in select and accurate terms, so that her thoughts appeared original, as well as just.

Isabella, who was fond of talents, and yet fonder of novelty, was charmed, the first evening, with her new friend, more especially as she perceived that her abilities had not escaped Mad. de Rosier. She displayed all her little treasures of literature, but was surprised to observe that, though every shining thing she said was taken notice of, nothing dazzled the eyes of her judge; gradually her desire to talk subsided, and she felt some curiosity to hear. She experienced the new pleasure of conversing with a person whom she perceived to be her superior in understanding, and whose superiority she could admire, without any mixture of envy.

"Then," said she, pausing, one day, after having successfully enumerated the dates of the reigns of all the English kings, "I suppose you have something in French, like our Gray's Memoria Technica, or else you never could have such a prodigious quantity of dates in your head. Had you as much knowledge of chronology and history, when you were of my age, as—as—"

"As you have?" said Mad. de Rosier: "I do not know whether I had at your age, but I can assure you that I have not now."

"Nay," replied Isabella, with an incredulous smile, "but you only say that from modesty."

"From vanity, more likely."

"Vanity! impossible—you don't understand me."

"Pardon me, but you do not understand me."

"A person," cried Isabella, "can't, surely, be vain—what we, in English, call vain—of not remembering any thing."

"Is it, then, impossible that a person should be what you, in English, call vain, of not remembering what is useless? I dare say you can tell me the name of that wise man who prayed for the art of forgetting."

"No, indeed, I don't know his name; I never heard of him before: was he a Grecian, or a Roman, or an Englishman? can't you recollect his name? what does it begin with?"

"I do not wish either for your sake or my own, to remember the name; let us content ourselves with the wise man's sense, whether he were a Grecian, a Roman, or an Englishman: even the first letter of his name might be left among the useless things—might it not?"

"But," replied Isabella, a little piqued, "I do not know what you call useless."

"Those of which you can make no use," said Mad. de Rosier, with simplicity.

"You don't mean, though, all the names, and dates, and kings, and Roman emperors, and all the remarkable events that I have learned by heart?"

"It is useful, I allow," replied Mad. de Rosier, "to know by heart the names of the English kings and Roman emperors, and to remember the dates of their reigns, otherwise we should be obliged, whenever we wanted them, to search in the books in which they are to be found, and that wastes time."

"Wastes time—yes; but what's worse," said Isabella, "a person looks so awkward and foolish in company, who does not know these things—things that every body knows."

"And that every body is supposed to know," added Mad. de Rosier.

"That never struck me before," said Isabella, ingenuously; "I only remembered these things to repeat in conversation."

Here Mad. de Rosier, pleased to observe that her pupil had caught an idea that was new to her, dropped the conversation, and left Isabella to apply what had passed. Active and ingenious young people should have much left to their own intelligent exertions, and to their own candour.

Matilda, the second daughter, was at first pleased with Mad. de Rosier, because she looked well in mourning; and afterwards she became interested for her, from hearing the history of her misfortunes, of which Mad. de Rosier, one evening, gave her a simple, pathetic account. Matilda was particularly touched by the account of the early death of this lady's beautiful and accomplished daughter; she dwelt upon every circumstance, and, with anxious curiosity, asked a variety of questions.

"I think I can form a perfect idea of her now," said Matilda, after she had inquired concerning the colour of her hair, of her eyes, her complexion, her height, her voice, her manners, and her dress—"I think I have a perfect idea of her now!"

"Oh no!" said Mad. de Rosier, with a sigh, "you cannot form a perfect idea of my Rosalie from any of these things; she was handsome and graceful; but it was not her person—it was her mind," said the mother, with a faltering voice: her voice had, till this instant, been steady and composed.

"I beg your pardon—I will ask you no more questions," said Matilda.

"My love," said Mad. de Rosier, "ask me as many as you please—I like to think of her—I may now speak of her without vanity—her character would have pleased you."

"I am sure it would," said Matilda: "do you think she would have liked me or Isabella the best?"

"She would have liked each of you for your different good qualities, I think: she would not have made her love an object of competition, or the cause of jealousy between two sisters; she could make herself sufficiently beloved, without stooping to any such mean arts. She had two friends who loved her tenderly; they knew that she was perfectly sincere, and that she would not flatter either of them—you know that is only childish affection which is without esteem. Rosalie was esteemed autant qu'aimée."

"How I should have liked such a friend! but I am afraid she would have been so much my superior, she would have despised me—Isabella would have had all her conversation, because she knows so much, and I know nothing!"

"If you know that you know nothing," said Mad. de Rosier, with an encouraging smile, "you know as much as the wisest of men. When the oracle pronounced Socrates to be the wisest of men, he explained it by observing, 'that he knew himself to be ignorant, whilst other men,' said he, 'believing that they know every thing, are not likely to improve.'"

"Then you think I am likely to improve?" said Matilda, with a look of doubtful hope.

"Certainly," said Mad. de Rosier: "if you exert yourself, you may be any thing you please."

"Not any thing I please, for I should please to be as clever, and as good, and as amiable, and as estimable, too, as your Rosalie—but that's impossible. Tell me, however, what she was at my age—and what sort of things she used to do and say—and what books she read—and how she employed herself from morning till night."

"That must be for to-morrow," said Mad. de Rosier; "I must now show Herbert the book of prints that he wanted to see."

It was the first time that Herbert had ever asked to look into a book. Mad. de Rosier had taken him entirely out of the hands of Mrs. Grace, and finding that his painful associations with the sight of the syllables in his dog's-eared spelling-book could not immediately be conquered, she prudently resolved to cultivate his powers of attention upon other subjects, and not to return to syllabic difficulties, until the young gentleman should have forgotten his literary misfortunes, and acquired sufficient energy and patience to ensure success.

"It is of little consequence," said she, "whether the boy read a year sooner or later; but it is of great consequence that he should love literature."

"Certainly," said Mrs. Harcourt, to whom this observation was addressed; "I am sure you will manage all those things properly—I leave him entirely to you—Grace quite gives him up: if he read by the time we must think of sending him to school I shall be satisfied—only keep him out of my way," added she, laughing, "when he is stammering over that unfortunate spelling-book, for I don't pretend to be gifted with the patience of Job."

"Have you any objection," said Mad. de Rosier, "to my buying for him some new toys?"

"None in the world—buy any thing you will—do any thing you please—I give you carte blanche," said Mrs. Harcourt.

After Mad. de Rosier had been some time at Mrs. Harcourt's, and had carefully studied the characters, or, more properly speaking, the habits of all her pupils, she took them with her one morning to a large toy-shop, or rather warehouse for toys, which had been lately opened, under the direction of an ingenious gentleman, who had employed proper workmen to execute rational toys for the rising generation.

When Herbert entered "the rational toy-shop," he looked all around, and, with an air of disappointment, exclaimed, "Why, I see neither whips nor horses! nor phaetons, nor coaches!"—"Nor dressed dolls!" said Favoretta, in a reproachful tone—"nor baby houses!"—"Nor soldiers—nor a drum!" continued Herbert.—"I am sure I never saw such a toy-shop," said Favoretta; "I expected the finest things that ever were seen, because it was such a new great shop, and here are nothing but vulgar-looking things—great carts and wheel-barrows, and things fit for orange-women's daughters, I think."

This sally of wit was not admired as much as it would have been by Favoretta's flatterers in her mother's drawing-room:—her brother seized upon the very cart which she had abused, and dragging it about the room, with noisy joy, declared he had found out that it was better than a coach and six that would hold nothing; and he was even satisfied without horses, because he reflected that he could be the best horse himself; and that wooden horses, after all, cannot gallop, and they never mind if you whip them ever so much: "you must drag them along all the time, though you make believe," said Herbert, "that they draw the coach of themselves; if one gives them the least push, they tumble down on their sides, and one must turn back, for ever and ever, to set them up upon their wooden legs again. I don't like make-believe horses; I had rather be both man and horse for myself." Then, whipping himself, he galloped away, pleased with his centaur character.

When the little boy in Sacontala is offered for a plaything "a peacock of earthenware, painted with rich colours," he answers, "I shall like the peacock if it can run and fly—not else." The Indian drama of Sacontala was written many centuries ago. Notwithstanding it has so long been observed, that children dislike useless, motionless playthings, it is but of late that more rational toys have been devised for their amusements.

Whilst Herbert's cart rolled on, Favoretta viewed it with scornful eyes; but at length, cured by the neglect of the spectators of this fit of disdain, she condescended to be pleased, and spied a few things worthy of her notice. Bilboquets, battledores, and shuttlecocks, she acknowledged were no bad things— "And pray," said she, "what are those pretty little baskets, Mad. de Rosier? And those others, which look as if they were but just begun? And what are those strings, that look like mamma's bell cords?—and is that a thing for making laces, such as Grace laces me with? And what are those cabinets with little drawers for?"

Mad. de Rosier had taken notice of these little cabinets—they were for young mineralogists; she was also tempted by a botanical apparatus; but as her pupils were not immediately going into the country, where flowers could be procured, she was forced to content herself with such things as could afford them employment in town. The making of baskets, of bell-ropes, and of cords for window-curtains, were occupations in which, she thought, they might successfully employ themselves. The materials for these little manufactures were here ready prepared; and only such difficulties were left as children love to conquer. The materials for the baskets, and a little magnifying glass, which Favoretta wished to have, were just packed up in a basket, which was to serve for a model, when Herbert's voice was heard at the other end of the shop: he was exclaiming in an impatient tone, "I must and I will eat them, I say." He had crept under the counter, and, unperceived by the busy shopman, had dragged out of a pigeon-hole, near the ground, a parcel, wrapped up in brown paper: he had seated himself upon the ground, with his back to the company, and, with patience worthy of a better object, at length untied the difficult knot, pulled off the string, and opened the parcel. Within the brown paper there appeared a number of little packets, curiously folded in paper of a light brown. Herbert opened one of these, and finding that it contained a number of little round things which looked like comfits, he raised the paper to his mouth, which opened wide to receive them. The shopman stopping his arm, assured him that they were "not good to eat;" but Herbert replied in the angry tone, which caught Mad. de Rosier's ear. "They are the seeds of radishes, my dear," said she: "if they be sown in the ground, they will become radishes; then they will be fit to eat, but not till then. Taste them now, and try." He willingly obeyed; but put the seeds very quickly out of his mouth, when he found that they were not sweet. He then said "that he wished he might have them, that he might sow them in the little garden behind his mother's house, that they might be fit to eat some time or other."

Mad. de Rosier bought the radish-seeds, and ordered a little spade, a hoe, and a watering-pot, to be sent home for him. Herbert's face brightened with joy: he was surprised to find that any of his requests were granted, because Grace had regularly reproved him for being troublesome whenever he asked for any thing; hence he had learned to have recourse to force or fraud to obtain his objects. He ventured now to hold Mad. De Rosier by the gown: "Stay a little longer," said he; "I want to look at every thing:" his curiosity dilated with his hopes. When Mad. de Rosier complied with his request to "stay a little longer," he had even the politeness to push a stool towards her, saying, "You'd better sit down; you will be tired of standing, as some people say they are;—but I'm not one of them. Tell 'em to give me down that wonderful thing, that I may see what it is, will you?"

The wonderful thing which had caught Herbert's attention was a dry printing press. Mad. de Rosier was glad to procure this little machine for Herbert, for she hoped that the new associations of pleasure which he would form with the types in the little compositor's stick, would efface the painful remembrance of his early difficulties with the syllables in the spelling-book. She also purchased a box of models of common furniture, which were made to take to pieces, and to be put together again, and on which the names of all the parts were printed. A number of other useful toys tempted her, but she determined not to be too profuse: she did not wish to purchase the love of her little pupils by presents; her object was to provide them with independent occupations; to create a taste for industry, without the dangerous excitation of continual variety.

Isabella was delighted with the idea of filling up a small biographical chart, which resembled Priestley's; she was impatient also to draw the map of the world upon a small silk balloon, which could be filled with common air, or folded up flat at pleasure.

Matilda, after much hesitation, said she had decided in her mind, just as they were going out of the shop. She chose a small loom for weaving riband and tape, which Isabella admired, because she remembered to have seen it described in "Townsend's Travels:" but, before the man could put up the loom for Matilda, she begged to have a little machine for drawing in perspective, because the person who showed it assured her that it required no sort of genius to draw perfectly well in perspective with this instrument.

In their way home, Mad. de Rosier stopped the carriage at a circulating library. "Are you going to ask for the novel we were talking of yesterday?" cried Matilda.

"A novel!" said Isabella, contemptuously: "no, I dare say Mad. de Rosier is not a novel-reader."

"Zeluco, sir, if you please," said Mad. de Rosier. "You see, Isabella, notwithstanding the danger of forfeiting your good opinion, I have dared to ask for a novel."

"Well, I always understood, I am sure," replied Isabella, disdainfully, "that none but trifling, silly people were novel-readers."

"Were readers of trifling, silly novels, perhaps you mean," answered Mad. de Rosier, with temper; "but I flatter myself you will not find Zeluco either trifling or silly."

"No, not Zeluco, to be sure," said Isabella, recollecting herself; "for now I remember Mr. Gibbon, the great historian, mentions Zeluco in one of his letters; he says it is the best philosophical romance of the age. I particularly remember that, because somebody had been talking of Zeluco the very day I was reading that letter; and I asked my governess to get it for me, but she said it was a novel—however, Mr. Gibbon calls it a philosophical romance."

"The name," said Mad. de Rosier, "will not make such difference to us; but I agree with you in thinking, that as people who cannot judge for themselves are apt to be misled by names, it would be advantageous to invent some new name for philosophical novels, that they may no longer be contraband goods—that they may not be confounded with the trifling, silly productions, for which you have so just a disdain."

"Now, ma'am, will you ask," cried Herbert, as the carriage stopped at his mother's door—"will you ask whether the man has brought home my spade and the watering-pot? I know you don't like that I should go to the servants for what I want; but I'm in a great hurry for the spade, because I want to dig the bed for my radishes before night: I've got my seeds safe in my hand."

Mad. de Rosier, much pleased by this instance of obedience in her impatient pupil, instantly inquired for what he wanted, to convince him that it was possible he could have his wishes gratified by a person who was not an inhabitant of the stable or the kitchen. Isabella might have registered it in her list of remarkable events, that Herbert, this day, was not seen with the butler, the footman, or the coachman. Mad. de Rosier, who was aware of the force of habit, and who thought that no evil could be greater than that of hazarding the integrity of her little pupils, did not exact from them any promise of abstaining from the company of the servants, with whom they had been accustomed to converse; but she had provided the children with occupations, that they might not be tempted, by idleness, to seek for improper companions; and, by interesting herself with unaffected good-nature in their amusements, she endeavoured to give them a taste for the sympathy of their superiors in knowledge, instead of a desire for the flattery of inferiors. She arranged their occupations in such a manner, that, without watching them every instant, she might know what they were doing, and where they were; and she showed so much readiness to procure for them any thing that was reasonable, that they found it the shortest method to address their petitions to her in the first instance. Children will necessarily delight in the company of those who make them happy; Mad. de Rosier knew how to make her pupils contented, by exciting them to employments in which they felt that they were successful.

"Mamma! mamma! dear mamma!" cried Favoretta, running into the hall, and stopping Mrs. Harcourt, who was dressed, and going out to dinner, "do come into the parlour, to look at my basket, my beautiful basket, that I am making all myself."

"And do, mother, or some of ye, come out into the garden, and see the bed that I've dug, with my own hands, for my radishes—I'm as hot as fire, I know," said Herbert, pushing his hat back from his forehead.

"Oh! don't come near me with the watering-pot in your hand," said Mrs. Harcourt, shrinking back, and looking at Herbert's hands, which were not as white as her own.

"The carriage is but just come to the door, ma'am," said Isabella, who next appeared in the hall; "I only want you for one instant, to show you something that is to hang up in your dressing-room, when I have finished it, mamma; it is really beautiful."

"Well, don't keep me long," said Mrs. Harcourt, "for, indeed, I am too late already."

"Oh, no! indeed you will not be too late, mamma—only look at my basket," said Favoretta, gently pulling her mother by the hand into the parlour.—Isabella pointed to her silk globe, which was suspended in the window, and, taking up her camel-hair pencil, cried, "Only look, ma'am, how nicely I have traced the Rhine, the Po, the Elbe, and the Danube; you see I have not finished Europe; it will be quite another looking thing, when Asia, Africa, and America are done, and when the colours are quite dry."

"Now, Isabella, pray let her look at my basket," cried the eager Favoretta, holding up the scarcely begun basket—"I will do a row, to show you how it is done;" and the little girl, with busy fingers, began to weave. The ingenious and delicate appearance of the work, and the happy countenance of the little workwoman, fixed the mother's pleased attention, and she, for a moment, forgot that her carriage was waiting.

"The carriage is at the door, ma'am," said the footman.

"I must be gone!" cried Mrs. Harcourt, starting from her reverie. "What am I doing here? I ought to have been away this half-hour—Matilda!—why is not she amongst you?"

Matilda, apart from the busy company, was reading with so much earnestness, that her mother called twice before she looked up.

"How happy you all look," continued Mrs. Harcourt; "and I am going to one of those terrible great dinners—I shan't eat one morsel; then cards all night, which I hate as much as you do, Isabella—pity me, Mad. de Rosier!—Good bye, happy creatures!"—and with some real and some affected reluctance, Mrs. Harcourt departed.

It is easy to make children happy, for one evening, with new toys and new employments; but the difficulty is to continue the pleasure of occupation after it has lost its novelty: the power of habit may well supply the place of the charm of novelty. Mad. de Rosier exerted herself, for some weeks, to invent occupations for her pupils, that she might induce in their minds a love for industry; and when they had tasted the pleasure, and formed the habit of doing something, she now and then suffered them to experience the misery of having nothing to do. The state of ennui, when contrasted with that of pleasurable mental or bodily activity, becomes odious and insupportable to children.

Our readers must have remarked that Herbert, when he seized upon the radish-seeds in the rational toy-shop, had not then learned just notions of the nature of property. Mad. de Rosier did not, like Mrs. Grace, repeat ineffectually, fifty times a day—"Master Herbert, don't touch that!" "Master Herbert, for shame!" "Let that alone, sir!" "Master Herbert, how dare you, sir!" but she prudently began by putting forbidden goods entirely out of his reach: thus she, at least, prevented the necessity for perpetual, irritating prohibitions, and diminished with the temptation the desire to disobey; she gave him some things for his own use, and scrupulously refrained from encroaching upon his property: Isabella and Matilda followed her example, in this respect, and thus practically explained to Herbert the meaning of the words mine and yours. He was extremely desirous of going with Mad. de Rosier to different shops, but she coolly answered his entreaties by observing, "that she could not venture to take him into any one's house, till she was sure that he would not meddle with what was not his own." Herbert now felt the inconvenience of his lawless habits: to enjoy the pleasures, he perceived that it was necessary to submit to the duties of society; and he began to respect "the rights of things and persons(1)." When his new sense of right and wrong had been sufficiently exercised at home, Mad. de Rosier ventured to expose him to more dangerous trials abroad; she took him to a carpenter's workshop, and though the saw, the hammer, the chisel, the plane, and the vice, assailed him in various forms of temptation, his powers of forbearance came off victorious.

"To bear and forbear" has been said to be the sum of manly virtue: the virtue of forbearance in childhood must always be measured by the pupil's disposition to activity: a vivacious boy must often have occasion to forbear more, in a quarter of an hour, than a dull, indolent child in a quarter of a year.

"May I touch this?"—"May I meddle with that?" were questions which our prudent hero now failed not to ask, before he meddled with the property of others, and he found his advantage in this mode of proceeding. He observed that his governess was, in this respect, as scrupulous as she required that he should be, and he consequently believed in the truth and general utility of her precepts.

The coachmaker's, the cooper's, the turner's, the cabinet-maker's, even the black ironmonger's and noisy tinman's shop, afforded entertainment for many a morning; a trifling gratuity often purchased much instruction, and Mad. de Rosier always examined the countenance of the workman before she suffered her little pupils to attack him with questions. The eager curiosity of children is generally rather agreeable than tormenting to tradesmen, who are not too busy to be benevolent; and the care which Herbert took not to be troublesome pleased those to whom he addressed himself. He was delighted, at the upholsterer's, to observe that his little models of furniture had taught him how several things were put together, and he soon learned the workmen's names for his ideas. He readily understood the use of all that he saw, when he went to a bookbinder's, and to a printing-office, because, in his own printing and bookbinder's press, he had seen similar contrivances in miniature.

Prints, as well as models, were used to enlarge his ideas of visible objects. Mad. de Rosier borrowed the Dictionnaire des Arts et des Métiers, Buffon, and several books, which contained good prints of animals, machines, and architecture; these provided amusement on rainy days. At first she found it difficult to fix the attention of the boisterous Herbert and the capricious Favoretta. Before they had half examined one print, they wanted to turn over the leaf to see another; but this desultory, impatient curiosity she endeavoured to cure by steadily showing only one or two prints for each day's amusement. Herbert, who could but just spell words of one syllable, could not read what was written at the bottom of the prints, and he was sometimes ashamed of applying to Favoretta for assistance;—the names that were printed upon his little models of furniture he at length learned to make out. The press was obliged to stand still when Favoretta, or his friend, Mad. de Rosier, were not at hand, to tell him, letter by letter, how to spell the words that he wanted to print. He, one evening, went up to Mad. de Rosier, and, with a resolute face, said, "I must learn to read."

"If any body will be so good as to teach you, I suppose you mean," said she, smiling(2).

"Will you be so good?" said he: "perhaps you could teach me, though Grace says 'tis very difficult; I'll do my best."

"Then I'll do my best too," said Mad. de Rosier.

The consequences of these good resolutions were surprising to Mrs. Grace. Master Herbert was quite changed, she observed; and she wondered why he would never read when she took so much pains with him for an hour every day to hear him his task. "Madame de What d'ye call her," added Mrs. Grace, "need not boast much of the hand she has had in the business: for I've been by at odd times, and watched her ways, whilst I have been dressing Miss Favoretta, and she has been hearing you your task, Master Herbert."

"She doesn't call it my task—I hate that word."

"Well, I don't know what she calls it; for I don't pretend to be a French governess, for my part; but I can read English, Master Herbert, as well as another; and it's strange if I could not teach my mother tongue better than an emigrant. What I say is, that she never takes much pains one way or the other; for by the clock in mistress's dressing-room, I minuted her twice, and she was five minutes at one time, and not above seven the other. Easy earning money for governesses, nowadays. No tasks!—no, not she!—Nothing all day long but play—play—play, laughing and running, and walking, and going to see all the shops and sights, and going out in the coach to bring home radishes and tongue-grass, to be sure—and every thing in the house is to be as she pleases, to be sure. I am sure my mistress is too good to her, only because she was born a lady, they say. Do, pray, Master Herbert, stand still, whilst I comb your hair, unless that's against your new governess's commandments."

"I'll comb my own hair, Grace," said Herbert, manfully. "I don't like one word you have been saying; though I don't mind any thing you, or any body else, can say against my friend. She is my friend—and she has taught me to read, I say, without bouncing me about, and shaking me, and Master Herberting me for ever. And what harm did it do the coach to bring home my radishes? My radishes are come up, and she shall have some of them. And I like the sights and shops she shows me;—but she does not like that I should talk to you; therefore, I'll say no more; but good morning to you, Grace."

Herbert, red with generous passion, rushed out of the room, and Grace, pale with malicious rage, turned towards the other door that opened into Mrs. Harcourt's bedchamber, for Mad. de Rosier, at this moment, appeared.—"I thought I heard a great noise?"—"It was only Master Herbert, ma'am, that won't never stand still to have his hair combed—and says he'll comb it for himself—I am sure I wish he would."

Mad. de Rosier saw, by the embarrassed manner and stifled choler of Mrs. Grace, that the whole truth of the business had not been told, and she repented her indiscretion in having left Herbert with her even for a few minutes. She forbore, however, to question Herbert, who maintained a dignified silence upon the subject; and the same species of silence would also become the historian upon this occasion, were it not necessary that the character of an intriguing lady's maid should, for the sake both of parents and children, be fully delineated.

Mrs. Grace, offended by Mad. de Rosier's success in teaching her former pupil to read; jealous of this lady's favour with her mistress and with the young ladies; irritated by the bold defiance of the indignant champion who had stood forth in his friend's defence, formed a secret resolution to obtain revenge. This she imparted, the very same day, to her confidant, Mrs. Rebecca. Mrs. Rebecca was the favourite maid of Mrs. Fanshaw, an acquaintance of Mrs. Harcourt. Grace invited Mrs. Rebecca to drink tea with her. As soon as the preliminary ceremonies of the tea-table had been adjusted, she proceeded to state her grievances.

"In former times, as nobody knows better than you, Mrs. Rebecca, I had my mistress's ear, and was all in all in the house, with her and the young ladies, and the old governess; and it was I that was to teach Master Herbert to read; and Miss Favoretta was almost constantly from morning to night, except when she was called for by company, with me, and a sweet little well-dressed creature always, you know, she was."

"A sweet little creature, indeed, ma'am, and I was wondering, before you spoke, not to see her in your room, as usual, to-night," replied Mrs. Rebecca.

"Dear Mrs. Rebecca, you need not wonder at that, or any thing else that's wonderful, in our present government above stairs, I'll assure you; for we have a new French governess, and new measures. Do you know, ma'am, the coach is ordered to go about at all hours, whenever she pleases for to take the young ladies out, and she is quite like my mistress. But no one can bear two mistresses, you know, Mrs. Rebecca; wherefore, I'm come to a resolution, in short, that either she or I shall quit the house, and we shall presently see which of us it must be. Mrs. Harcourt, at the upshot of all things, must be conscious, at the bottom of her heart, that, if she is the elegantest dresser about town, it's not all her own merit."

"Very true indeed, Mrs. Grace," replied her complaisant friend; "and what sums of money her millinery might cost her, if she had no one clever at making up things at home! You are blamed by many, let me tell you, for doing so much as you do. Mrs. Private, the milliner, I know from the best authority, is not your friend: now, for my part, I think it is no bad thing to have friends abroad, if one comes to any difficulties at home. Indeed, my dear, your attachment to Mrs. Harcourt quite blinds you—but, to be sure, you know your own affairs best."

"Why, I am not for changing when I am well," replied Grace: "Mrs. Harcourt is abroad a great deal, and hers is, all things considered, a very eligible house. Now, what I build my hopes upon, my dear Mrs. Rebecca, is this—that ladies, like some people who have been beauties, and come to make themselves up, and wear pearl powder, and false auburn hair, and twenty things that are not to be advertised, you know, don't like quarrelling with those that are in the secret—and ladies who have never made a rout about governesses and edication, till lately, and now, perhaps, only for fashion's sake, would upon a pinch—don't you think—rather part with a French governess, when there are so many, than with a favourite maid who knows her ways, and has a good taste in dress, which so few can boast?"

"Oh, surely! surely!" said Mrs. Rebecca; and having tasted Mrs. Grace's crême-de-noyau, it was decided that war should be declared against the governess.

Mad. de Rosier, happily unconscious of the machinations of her enemies, and even unsuspicious of having any, was, during this important conference, employed in reading Marmontel's Silvain, with Isabella and Matilda. They were extremely interested in this little play; and Mrs. Harcourt, who came into the room whilst they were reading, actually sat down on the sofa beside Isabella, and, putting her arm round her daughter's waist, said—"Go on, love; let me have a share in some of your pleasures—lately, whenever I see you, you all look the picture of happiness—Go on, pray, Mad. de Rosier."

"It was I who was reading, mamma," said Isabella, pointing to the place over Mad. de Rosier's shoulder—

Une femme douce et sage
A toujours tant d'avantage!
Elle a pour elle en partage
L'agrément, et la raison.'"

"Isabella," said Mrs. Harcourt, from whom a scarcely audible sigh had escaped—"Isabella really reads French almost as well as she does English."

"I am improved very much since I have heard Mad. de Rosier read," said Isabella.

"I don't doubt that, in the least; you are, all of you, much improved, I think, in every thing;—I am sure I feel very much obliged to Mad. de Rosier."

Matilda looked pleased by this speech of her mother, and affectionately said, "I am glad, mamma, you like her as well as we do—Oh, I forgot that Mad, de Rosier was by—but it is not flattery, however."

"You see you have won all their hearts"—from me, Mrs. Harcourt was near saying, but she paused, and, with a faint laugh, added—"yet you see I am not jealous. Matilda! read those lines that your sister has just read; I want to hear them again."

Mrs. Harcourt sent for her work, and spent the evening at home. Mad. de Rosier, without effort or affectation, dissipated the slight feeling of jealousy which she observed in the mother's mind, and directed towards her the attention of her children, without disclaiming, however, the praise that was justly her due. She was aware that she could not increase her pupils' real affection for their mother, by urging them to sentimental hypocrisy.

Whether Mrs. Harcourt understood her conduct this evening, she could not discover—for politeness does not always speak the unqualified language of the heart—but she trusted to the effect of time, on which persons of integrity may always securely rely for their reward. Mrs. Harcourt gradually discovered that, as she became more interested in the occupations and amusements of her children, they became more and more grateful for her sympathy; she consequently grew fonder of domestic life, and of the person who had introduced its pleasures into her family.

That we may not be accused of attributing any miraculous power to our French governess, we shall explain the natural means by which she improved her pupils.

We have already pointed out how she discouraged, in Isabella, the vain desire to load her memory with historical and chronological facts, merely for the purpose of ostentation. She gradually excited her to read books of reasoning, and began with those in which reasoning and amusement are mixed. She also endeavoured to cultivate her imagination, by giving her a few well-chosen passages to read, from the best English, French, and Italian poets. It was an easier task to direct the activity of Isabella's mind, than to excite Matilda's dormant powers. Mad. de Rosier patiently waited till she discovered something which seemed to please Matilda more than usual. The first book that she appeared to like particularly was, "Les Conversations d'Emilie:" one passage she read with great delight aloud; and Mad. de Rosier, who perceived by the manner of reading it that she completely understood the elegance of the French, begged her to try if she could translate it into English: it was not more than half a page. Matilda was not terrified at the length of such an undertaking: she succeeded, and the praises that were bestowed upon her translation excited in her mind some portion of ambition.

Mad. de Rosier took the greatest care in conversing with Matilda, to make her feel her own powers: whenever she used good arguments, they were immediately attended to; and when Matilda perceived that a prodigious memory was not essential to success, she was inspired with courage to converse unreservedly.

An accident pointed out to Mad. de Rosier another resource in Matilda's education. One day Herbert called his sister Matilda to look at an ant, which was trying to crawl up a stick; he seemed scarcely able to carry his large white load in his little forceps, and he frequently fell back, when he had just reached the top of the stick. Mad. de Rosier, who knew how much of the art of instruction depends upon seizing the proper moments to introduce new ideas, asked Herbert whether he had ever heard of the poor snail, who, like this ant, slipped back continually, as he was endeavouring to climb a wall twenty feet high.

"I never heard of that snail; pray tell me the story," cried Herbert.

"It is not a story—it is a question in arithmetic," replied Mad. de Rosier. "This snail was to crawl up a wall twenty feet high; he crawled up five feet every day, and slipped back again four feet every night: in how many days did he reach the top of the wall?"

"I love questions in arithmetic," exclaimed Matilda, "when they are not too difficult!" and immediately she whispered to Mad. de Rosier the answer to this easy question.

Her exclamation was not lost;—Mad. de Rosier determined to cultivate her talents for arithmetic. Without fatiguing Matilda's attention by long exercises in the common rules, she gave her questions which obliged her to think, and which excited her to reason and to invent; she gradually explained to her pupil the relations of numbers, and gave her rather more clear ideas of the nature and use of the common rules of arithmetic than she had acquired from her writing-master, who had taught them only in a technical manner. Matilda's confidence in herself was thus increased. When she had answered a difficult question, she could not doubt that she had succeeded; this was not a matter that admitted of the uncertainty which alarms timid tempers. Mad. de Rosier began by asking her young arithmetician questions only when they were by themselves—but by and by she appealed to her before the rest of the family. Matilda coloured at first, and looked as if she knew nothing of the business; but a distinct answer was given at last, and Isabella's opinions of her sister's abilities rose with amazing rapidity, when she heard that Matilda understood decimal fractions.

"Now, my dear Matilda," said Mad. de Rosier, "since you understand what even Isabella thinks difficult, you will, I hope, have sufficient confidence in yourself to attempt things which Isabella does not think difficult."

Matilda shook her head—"I am not Isabella yet," said she.

"No!" cried Isabella, with generous, sincere warmth; "but you are much superior to Isabella: I am certain that I could not answer those difficult questions, though you think me so quick—and, when once you have learned any thing, you never forget it; the ideas are not superficial," continued Isabella, turning to Mad. de Rosier; "they have depth, like the pins in mosaic work."

Mad. de Rosier smiled at this allusion, and, encouraged by her smile, Isabella's active imagination immediately produced another simile.

"I did not know my sister's abilities till lately—till you drew them out, Mad. de Rosier, like your drawing upon the screen in sympathetic inks;—when you first produced it, I looked, and said there was nothing;

and when I looked again, after you had held it to the fire for a few moments, beautiful colours and figures appeared."

Mad. de Rosier, without using any artifice, succeeded in making Isabella and Matilda friends, instead of rivals, by placing them, as much as possible, in situations in which they could mutually sympathize, and by discouraging all painful competition.

With Herbert and Favoretta she pursued a similar plan. She scarcely ever left them alone together, that she might not run the hazard of their quarrelling in her absence. At this age children have not sufficient command of their tempers—they do not understand the nature of society and of justice: the less they are left together, when they are of unequal strength, and when they have not any employments in which they are mutually interested, the better. Favoretta and Herbert's petty, but loud and violent disputes, had nearly ceased since these precautions had been regularly attended to. As they had a great deal of amusement in the few hours which they spent together, they grew fond of each other's company: when Herbert was out in his little garden, he was impatient for the time when Favoretta was to come to visit his works; and Favoretta had equal pleasure in exhibiting to her brother her various manufactures.

Mad. de Rosier used to hear them read in Mrs. Barbauld's excellent little books, and in "Evenings at Home;" she generally told them some interesting story when they had finished reading, and they regularly seated themselves, side by side, on the carpet, opposite to her.

One day Herbert established himself in what he called his "happy corner," Favoretta placed herself close beside him, and Mad. de Rosier read to them that part of Sandford and Merton in which Squire Chace is represented beating Harry Sandford unmercifully because he refused to tell which way the hare was gone. Mad. de Rosier observed that this story made a great impression upon Herbert, and she thought it a good opportunity, whilst his mind was warm, to point out the difference between resolution and obstinacy. Herbert had been formerly disposed to obstinacy; but this defect in his temper never broke out towards Mad. de Rosier, because she carefully avoided urging him to do those things to which she knew him to be adverse; and she frequently desired him to do what she knew would be agreeable to him: she thought it best to suffer him gradually to forget his former bad habits and false associations, before she made any trial of his obedience; then she endeavoured to give him new habits, by placing him in new situations. She now resolved to address herself to his understanding, which she perceived had opened to reason.

He exclaimed with admiration, upon hearing the account of Harry Sandford's fortitude, "That's right!— that's right!—I am glad Harry did not tell that cruel Squire Chace which way the hare was gone. I like Harry for bearing to be beaten, rather than speak a word when he did not choose it. I love Harry, don't you?" said he, appealing to Mad. de Rosier.

"Yes, I like him very much," said Mad. de Rosier: "but not for the reason that you have just given."

"No!" said Herbert, starting up: "why, ma'am, don't you like Harry for saving the poor hare? don't you admire him for bearing all the hard blows, and for saying, when the man asked him afterward why he didn't tell which way the hare was gone, 'Because I don't choose to betray the unfortunate?'"

"Oh! don't you love him for that?" said Favoretta, rising from her seat; "I think Herbert himself would have given just such an answer, only not in such good words. I wonder, Mad. de Rosier, you don't like that answer!"

"I have never said that I did not like that answer," said Mad. de Rosier, as soon as she was permitted to speak.

"Then you do like it? then you do like Harry?" exclaimed Herbert and Favoretta, both at once.

"Yes, I like that answer, Herbert; I like your friend Harry for saying that he did not choose to betray the unfortunate. You did not do him justice or yourself, when you said just now that you liked Harry because he bore to be beaten rather than speak a word when he did not choose it."

Herbert looked puzzled.

"I mean," continued Mad. de Rosier, "that, before I can determine whether I like and admire any body for persisting in doing or in not doing any thing, I must hear their reasons for their resolution. 'I don't choose it,' is no reason; I must hear their reasons for choosing or not choosing it before I can judge."

"And I have told you the reason Harry gave for not choosing to speak when he was asked, and you said it was a good one; and you like him for his courage, don't you?" said Herbert.

"Yes," said Mad. de Rosier; "those who are resolute, when they have good reasons for their resolution, I admire; those who persist merely because they choose it, and who cannot, or will not, tell why they choose it, I despise."

"Oh, so do I!" said Favoretta: "you know, brother, whenever you say you don't choose it, I am always angry, and ask you why."

"And if you were not always angry," said Mad. de Rosier, "perhaps sometimes your brother would tell you why."

"Yes, that I should," said Herbert; "I always have a good reason to give Favoretta, though I don't always choose to give it."

"Then," said Mad. de Rosier, "you cannot always expect your sister to admire the justice of your decisions."

"No," replied Herbert; "but when I don't give her a reason, 'tis generally because it is not worth while. There can be no great wisdom, you know, in resolutions about trifles: such as, whether she should be my horse or I her horse, or whether I should water my radishes before breakfast or after."

"Certainly, you are right: there can be no great wisdom in resolutions about such trifles, therefore wise people never are obstinate about trifles."

"Do you know," cried Herbert, after a pause, "they used, before you came, to say that I was obstinate; but with you I have never been so, because you know how to manage me; you manage me a great deal more cunningly than Grace used to do."

"I would not manage you more cunningly than Grace used to do, if I could," replied Mad. de Rosier; "for then I should manage you worse than she did. It is no pleasure to me to govern you; I had much rather that you should use your reason to govern yourself."

Herbert pulled down his waistcoat, and, drawing up his head, looked with conscious dignity at Favoretta.

"You know," continued Mad. de Rosier, "that there are two ways of governing people—by reason and by force. Those who have no reason, or who do not use it, must be governed by force."

"I am not one of those," said Herbert; "for I hate force."

"But you must also love reason," said Mad. de Rosier, "if you would not be one of those."

"Well, so I do, when I hear it from you," replied Herbert, bluntly; "for you give me reasons that I can understand, when you ask me to do or not to do any thing: I wish people would always do so."

"But, Herbert," said Mad. de Rosier, "you must sometimes be contented to do as you are desired, even when I do not think it proper to give you my reasons;—you will, hereafter, find that I have good ones."

"I have found that already in a great many things," said Herbert; "especially about the caterpillar."

"What about the caterpillar?" said Favoretta.

"Don't you remember," said Herbert, "the day that I was going to tread upon what I thought was a little bit of black stick, and she desired me not to do it, and I did not, and afterwards I found out that it was a caterpillar;—ever since that day I have been more ready, you know," continued he, turning to Mad. de Rosier, "to believe that you might be in the right, and to do as you bid me—you don't think me obstinate, do you?"

"No," said Mad. de Rosier.

"No! no!—do you hear that, Favoretta?" cried Herbert joyfully: "Grace used to say I was as obstinate as a mule, and she used to call me an ass, too: but even poor asses are not obstinate when they are well treated. Where is the ass, in the Cabinet of Quadrupeds, Favoretta, which we were looking at the other day? Oh, let me read the account to you, Mad. de Rosier. It is towards the middle of the book, Favoretta; let me look, I can find it in a minute. It is not long—may I read it to you?"

Mad. de Rosier consented, and Herbert read as follows:—"Much has been said of the stupid and stubborn disposition of the ass, but we are greatly inclined to suspect that the aspersion is ill-founded: whatever bad qualities of this kind he may sometimes possess, they do not appear to be the consequences of any natural defect in his constitution or temper, but arise from the manner used in training him, and the bad treatment he receives. We are the rather led to this assertion, from having lately seen one which experiences a very different kind of treatment from his master than is the fate of the generality of asses. The humane owner of this individual is an old man, whose employment is the selling of vegetables, which he conveys from door to door on the back of his ass. He is constantly baiting the poor creature with handfuls of hay, pieces of bread, or greens, which he procures in his progress. It is with pleasure we relate, for we have often curiously observed the old man's demeanour towards his ass, that he seldom carries any instrument of incitement with him, nor did we ever see him lift his hand to drive it on.

"Upon our observing to him that he seemed to be very kind to his ass, and inquiring whether he were apt to be stubborn, how long he had had him, &c., he replied, 'Ah, master, it is no use to be cruel, and as for stubbornness, I cannot complain, for he is ready to do any thing, and will go any where; I bred him myself, and have had him these two years: he is sometimes skittish and playful, and once ran away from me: you will hardly believe it, but there were more than fifty people after him to stop him, and they were not able to effect it, yet he turned back of himself, and never stopped till he run his head kindly into my breast.'

"The countenance of this individual is open, lively, and cheerful; his pace nimble and regular; and the only inducement used to make him increase his speed is that of calling him by name, which he readily obeys."

"I am not an ass," said Herbert, laughing, as he finished this sentence, "but I think Mad. de Rosier is very like the good old man, and I always obey whenever she speaks to me. By the by," continued Herbert, who now seemed eager to recollect something by which he could show his readiness to obey—"by the by, Grace told me that my mother desired I should go to her, and have my hair combed every day; now I don't like it, but I will do it, because mamma desires it, and I will go this instant; will you come and see how still I can stand? I will show you that I am not obstinate."

Mad. de Rosier followed the little hero, to witness his triumph over himself. Grace happened to be with her mistress who was dressing.

"Mamma, I am come to do as you bid me," cried Herbert, walking stoutly into the room: "Grace, here's the comb;" and he turned to her the tangled locks at the back of his head. She pulled unmercifully, but he stood without moving a muscle of his countenance.

Mrs. Harcourt, who saw in her looking-glass what was passing, turned round, and said, "Gently, gently, Grace; indeed, Grace, you do pull that poor boy's hair as if you thought that his head had no feeling; I am sure, if you were to pull my hair in that manner, I could not bear it so well."

"Your hair!—Oh, dear ma'am, that's quite another thing—but Master Herbert's is always in such a tangle, there's no such thing as managing it." Again Mrs. Grace gave a desperate pull: Herbert bore it, looked up at Mad. de Rosier, and said, "Now, that was resolution, not obstinacy, you know."

"Here is your little obedient and patient boy," said Mad. de Rosier, leading Herbert to his mother, "who deserves to be rewarded with a kiss from you."

"That he shall have," said Mrs. Harcourt; "but why does Grace pull your hair so hard? and are not you almost able to comb your own hair?"

"Able! that I am. Oh, mother, I wish I might do it for myself."

"And has Mad. de Rosier any objection to it?" said Mrs. Harcourt.

"None in the least," said Mad. de Rosier; "on the contrary, I wish that he should do every thing that he can do for himself; but he told me that it was your desire that he should apply to Mrs. Grace, and I was pleased to see his ready obedience to your wishes: you may be very certain that, even in the slightest trifles, as well as in matters of consequence, it is our wish, as much as it is our duty, to do exactly as you desire."

"My dear madame," said Mrs. Harcourt, laying her hand upon Mad. de Rosier's, with an expression of real kindness, mixed with her habitual politeness, "I am sensible of your goodness, but you know that in the slightest trifles, as well as in matters of consequence, I leave every thing implicitly to your better judgment: as to this business between Herbert and Grace, I don't understand it."

"Mother—" said Herbert.

"Madam," said Grace, pushing forward, but not very well knowing what she intended to say, "if you recollect, you desired me to comb Master Herbert's hair, ma'am, and I told Master Herbert so, ma'am, that's all."

"I do not recollect any thing about it, indeed, Grace."

"Oh dear, ma'am! don't you recollect the last day there was company, and Master Herbert came to the top of the stairs, and you was looking at the organ's lamp, I said, 'Dear! Master Herbert's hair's as rough as a porcupine's;' and you said directly, ma'am, if you recollect, 'I wish you would make that boy's hair fit to be seen;' those was your very words, ma'am, and I thought you meant always, ma'am."

"You mistook me, Grace," said Mrs. Harcourt, smiling at her maid's eager volubility: "in future, you understand, that Herbert is to be entire master of his own hair."

"Thank you, mother," said Herbert.

"Nay, my dear Herbert, thank Mad. de Rosier: I only speak in her name. You understand, I am sure, Grace, now," said Mrs. Harcourt, calling to her maid, who seemed to be in haste to quit the room—"you, I hope, understand, Grace, that Mad. de Rosier and I are always of one mind about the children; therefore you need never be puzzled by contradictory orders—hers are to be obeyed."

Mrs. Harcourt was so much pleased when she looked at Herbert, as she concluded this sentence, to see an expression of great affection and gratitude, that she stooped instantly to kiss him.

"Another kiss! two kisses to-day from my mother, and one of her own accord!" exclaimed Herbert joyfully, running out of the room to tell the news to Favoretta.

"That boy has a heart," said Mrs. Harcourt, with some emotion; "you have found it out for me, Mad. de Rosier, and I thank you."

Mad. de Rosier seized the propitious moment to present a card of invitation, which Herbert, with much labour, had printed with his little printing-press.

"What have we here?" said Mrs. Harcourt, and she read aloud—

'Mr. Herbert Harcourt's love to his dear mother, and, if she be not engaged this evening, he should be exceedingly glad of her company, to meet Isabella, Matilda, Favoretta, and Mad. de Rosier, who have promised to sup with him upon his own radishes to-night. They are all very impatient for your answer.'"

"My answer they shall have in an instant," said Mrs. Harcourt:—"why, Mad. de Rosier, this is the boy who could neither read nor spell six months ago. Will you be my messenger?" added she, putting a card into Mad. de Rosier's hand, which she had written with rapidity:—

"Mrs. Harcourt's love to her dear little Herbert; if she had a hundred other invitations, she would accept of his."

"Bless me!" said Mrs. Grace, when she found the feathers, which she had placed with so much skill in her mistress's hair, lying upon the table half an hour afterward—"why, I thought my mistress was going out!"

Grace's surprise deprived her even of the power of exclamation, when she learned that her mistress stayed at home to sup with Master Herbert upon radishes. At night she listened with malignant curiosity, as she sat at work in her mistress's dressing-room, to the frequent bursts of laughter, and to the happy little voices of the festive company who were at supper in an adjoining apartment.

"This will never do!" thought Grace; but presently the laughter ceased, and listening attentively, she heard the voice of one of the young ladies reading. "Oh ho!" thought Grace, "if it comes to reading, Master Herbert will soon be asleep."—But though it had come to reading, Herbert was, at this instant, broad awake.

At supper, when the radishes were distributed, Favoretta was very impatient to taste them; the first which she tasted was hot, she said, and she did not quite like it.

"Hot!" cried Herbert, who criticized her language, in return for her criticism upon his radishes, "I don't think you can call a radish hot—it is cold, I think: I know what is meant by tasting sweet, or sour, or bitter."

"Well," interrupted Favoretta, "what is the name for the taste of this radish which bites my tongue?"

"Pungent," said Isabella, and she eagerly produced a quotation in support of her epithet—

"'And pungent radish biting infant's tongue.'"

"I know for once," said Matilda, smiling, "where you met with that line, I believe: is it not in Shenstone's Schoolmistress, in the description of the old woman's neat little garden?"

"Oh! I should like to hear about that old woman's neat little garden," cried Herbert.

"And so should I," said Mrs. Harcourt and Mad. de Rosier. Isabella quickly produced the book after supper, and read the poem.

Herbert and Favoretta liked the old woman and her garden, and they were much interested for the little boy, who was whipped for having been gazing at the pictures on the horn-book, instead of learning his lesson; but, to Isabella's great mortification, they did not understand above half of what she read—the old English expressions puzzled them.

"You would not be surprised at this, my dear Isabella," said Mad. de Rosier, "if you had made as many experiments upon children as I have. It is quite a new language to them; and what you have just been reading is scarcely intelligible to me, though you compliment me so much upon my knowledge of the English language." Mad. de Rosier took the book, and pointed to several words which she had not understood—such as "eftsoons," "Dan Phoebus," and "ne and y," which had made many lines incomprehensible.

Herbert, when he heard Mad. de Rosier confess her ignorance, began to take courage, and came forward with his confessions.

"Gingerbread y rare," he thought, was some particular kind of gingerbread; and "Apples with cabbage net y covered o'er" presented no delightful image to his mind, because, as he said, he did not know what the word netycovered could mean.

These mistakes occasioned some laughter; but as Herbert perceived that he was no longer thought stupid, he took all the laughter with good humour, and he determined to follow, in future, Mad. de Rosier's example, in pointing out the words which were puzzling.

Grace was astonished, at the conclusion of the evening, to find Master Herbert in such high spirits. The next day she heard sounds of woe, sounds agreeable to her wishes—Favoretta crying upon the stairs. It had been a rainy morning: Favoretta and Herbert had been disappointed in not being able to walk out; and after having been amused the preceding evening, they were less disposed to bear disappointment, and less inclined to employ themselves than usual. Favoretta had finished her little basket, and her mother had promised that it should appear at the dessert; but it wanted some hours of dinner-time; and between the making and the performance of a promise, how long the time appears to an impatient child! how many events happen which may change the mind of the promiser!

Mad. de Rosier had lent Favoretta and Herbert, for their amusement, the first number of "The Cabinet of Quadrupeds," in which there are beautiful prints; but, unfortunately, some dispute arose between the children. Favoretta thought her brother looked too long at the hunchbacked camel; he accused her of turning over leaves before she had half seen the prints; but she listened not to his just reproaches, for she had caught a glimpse of the royal tiger springing upon Mr. Munro, and she could no longer restrain her impatience. Each party began to pull at the book; and the camel and the royal tiger were both in imminent danger of being torn in pieces, when Mad. de Rosier interfered, parted the combatants, and sent them into separate rooms, as it was her custom to do, whenever they could not agree together.

Grace, the moment she heard Favoretta crying, went up to the room where she was, and made her tiptoe approaches, addressing Favoretta in a tone of compassion, which, to a child's unpractised ear, might appear, perhaps, the natural voice of sympathy. The sobbing child hid her face in Grace's lap; and when she had told her complaint against Mad. de Rosier, Grace comforted her for the loss of the royal tiger by the present of a queen-cake. Grace did not dare to stay long in the room, lest Mad. de Rosier should detect her; she therefore left the little girl, with a strict charge "not to say a word of the queen-cake to her governess."

Favoretta kept the queen-cake, that she might divide it with Herbert; for she now recollected that she had been most to blame in the dispute about the prints. Herbert absolutely refused, however, to have any share of the cake, and he strongly urged his sister to return it to Grace.

Herbert had, formerly, to use his own expression, been accused of being fond of eating, and so, perhaps, he was; but since he had acquired other pleasures, those of affection and employment, his love of eating had diminished so much, that he had eaten only one of his own radishes, because he felt more pleasure in distributing the rest to his mother and sisters.

It was with some difficulty that he prevailed upon Favoretta to restore the queen-cake: the arguments that he used we shall not detail, but he concluded with promising, that, if Favoretta would return the cake, he would ask Mad. de Rosier, the next time they passed by the pastrycook's shop, to give them some queen-cakes—"and I dare say she will give us some, for she is much more really good-natured than Grace."

Favoretta, with this hope of a future queen-cake, in addition to all her brother's arguments, at last determined to return Grace's present—"Herbert says I had better give it you back again," said she, "because Mad. de Rosier does not know it."

Grace was somewhat surprised by the effect of Herbert's oratory, and she saw that she must change her ground. The next day, when the children were walking with Mad. de Rosier by a pastrycook's shop, Herbert, with an honest countenance, asked Mad. de Rosier to give Favoretta and him a queen-cake. She complied, for she was glad to find that he always asked frankly for what he wanted; and yet that he bore refusals with good humour.

Just as Herbert was going to eat his queen-cake, he heard the sound of music in the street; he went to the door, and saw a poor man who was playing on the dulcimer—a little boy was with him, who looked extremely thin and hungry—he asked Herbert for some halfpence.

"I have no money of my own," said Herbert, "but I can give you this, which is my own."

Mad. de Rosier held his hand back, which he had just stretched out to offer his queen-cake; she advised him to exchange it for something more substantial; she told him that he might have two buns for one queen-cake. He immediately changed it for two buns, and gave them to the little boy, who thanked him heartily. The man who was playing on the dulcimer asked where Herbert lived, and promised to stop at his door to play a tune for him, which he seemed to like particularly.

Convinced by the affair of the queen-cake that Herbert's influence was a matter of some consequence in the family, Mrs. Grace began to repent that she had made him her enemy, and she resolved, upon the first convenient occasion, to make him overtures of peace—overtures which, she had no doubt, would be readily accepted.

One morning she heard him sighing and groaning, as she thought, over some difficult sum, which Mad. de Rosier had set for him; he cast up one row aloud several times, but could not bring the total twice to the same thing. When he took his sum to Mad. de Rosier, who was dressing, he was kept waiting a few minutes at the door, because Favoretta was not dressed. The young gentleman became a little impatient, and when he gained admittance his sum was wrong.

"Then I cannot make it right," said Herbert, passionately.

"Try," said Mad. de Rosier; "go into that closet by yourself, and try once more, and perhaps you will find that you can make it right."

Herbert knelt down in the closet, though rather unwillingly, to this provoking sum.

"Master Herbert, my dear," said Mrs. Grace, following him, "will you be so good as to go for Miss Favoretta's scissors, if you please, which she lent you yesterday?—she wants 'em, my dear."

Herbert, surprised by the unusually good-natured tone of this request, ran for the scissors, and at his return, found that his difficult sum had been cast up in his absence; the total was written at the bottom of it, and he read these words, which he knew to be Mrs. Grace's writing—"Rub out my figurs, and write them in your own." Herbert immediately rubbed out Mrs. Grace's figures with indignation, and determined to do the sum for himself. He carried it to Mad. de Rosier—it was wrong: Grace stared, and when she saw Herbert patiently stand beside Mad. de Rosier and repeat his efforts, she gave up all idea of obtaining any influence over him.

"Mad. de Rosier," said she to herself, "has bewitched 'em all; I think it's odd one can't find out her art!"

Mrs. Grace seemed to think that she could catch the knack of educating children, as she had surreptitiously learnt, from a fashionable hairdresser, the art of dressing hair. Ever since Mrs. Harcourt had spoken in such a decided manner respecting Mad. de Rosier, her maid had artfully maintained the greatest appearance of respect for that lady, in her mistress's presence, and had even been scrupulous, to a troublesome extreme, in obeying the governess's orders; and by a studied show of attachment to Mrs. Harcourt, and much alacrity at her toilette, she had, as she flattered herself, secured a fresh portion of favour.

One morning Mrs. Harcourt found, when she awoke, that she had a headache, and a slight feverish complaint. She had caught cold the night before in coming out of a warm assembly-room. Mrs. Grace affected to be much alarmed at her mistress's indisposition, and urged her to send immediately for Dr. X—. To this Mrs. Harcourt half consented, and a messenger was sent for him. In the meantime Mrs. Harcourt, who had been used to be much attended to in her slight indispositions, expressed some surprise that Mad. de Rosier, or some of her children, when they heard that she was ill, had not come to see her.

"Where is Isabella? where is Matilda? or Favoretta? what is become of them all? do they know I am ill, Grace?"

"Oh dear! yes, ma'am; but they're all gone out in the coach, with Mad. de Rosier."

"All?" said Mrs. Harcourt.

"All, I believe, ma'am," said Grace; "though, indeed, I can't pretend to be sure, since I make it my business not to scrutinize, and to know as little as possible of what's going on in the house, lest I should seem to be too particular."

"Did Mad. de Rosier leave any message for me before she went out?"

"Not with me, ma'am."

Here the prevaricating waiting-maid told barely the truth in words: Mad. de Rosier had left a message with the footman in Grace's hearing.

"I hope, ma'am," continued Grace, "you weren't disturbed with the noise in the house early this morning?"

"What noise?—I heard no noise," said Mrs. Harcourt.

"No noise! dear ma'am, I'm as glad as can possibly be of that, at any rate; but to be sure there was a great racket. I was really afraid, ma'am, it would do no good to your poor head."

"What was the matter?" said Mrs. Harcourt, drawing back the curtain.

"Oh! nothing, ma'am, that need alarm you—only music and dancing."

"Music and dancing so early in the morning!—Do, Grace, say all you have to say at once, for you keep me in suspense, which, I am sure, is not good for my head."

"La, ma'am, I was so afraid it would make you angry, ma'am—that was what made me so backward in mentioning it; but, to be sure, Mad. de Rosier, and the young ladies, and Master Herbert, I suppose, thought you couldn't hear, because it was in the back parlour, ma'am."

"Hear what? what was in the back parlour?"

"Only a dulcimer man, ma'am, playing for the young ladies."

"Did you tell them I was ill, Grace?"

It was the second time Mrs. Harcourt had asked this question. Grace was gratified by this symptom.

"Indeed, ma'am," she replied, "I did make bold to tell Master Herbert, that I was afraid you would hear him jumping and making such an uproar up and down the stairs; but to be sure, I did not say a word to the young ladies—as Mad. de Rosier was by, I thought she knew best."

A gentle knock at the door interrupted Mrs. Grace's charitable animadversions.

"Bless me, if it isn't the young ladies! I'm sure I thought they were gone out in the coach."

As Isabella and Matilda came up to the side of their mother's bed, she said, in a languid voice—

"I hope, Matilda, my dear, you did not stay at home on my account—Is Isabella there? What book has she in her hand?"

"Zeluco, mamma—I thought, perhaps, you would like to hear some more of it—you liked what I read to you the other day."

"But you forget that I have a terrible headache—Pray don't let me detain either of you, if you have any thing to do for Mad. de Rosier."

"Nothing in the world, mamma," said Matilda; "she is gone to take Herbert and Favoretta to Exeter Change."

No farther explanation could take place, for, at this instant, Mrs. Grace introduced Dr. X—. Now Dr. X— was not one of those complaisant physicians who flatter ladies that they are very ill when they have any desire to excite tender alarm.

After satisfying himself that his patient was not quite so ill as Mrs. Grace had affected to believe, Dr. X— insensibly led from medical inquiries to general conversation: he had much playful wit and knowledge of the human heart, mixed with a variety of information, so that he could with happy facility amuse and interest nervous patients, who were beyond the power of the solemn apothecary.

The doctor drew the young ladies into conversation by rallying Isabella upon her simplicity in reading a novel openly in her mother's presence; he observed that she did not follow the example of the famous Serena, in "The Triumphs of Temper." "Zeluco!" he exclaimed, in an ironical tone of disdain: "why not the charming 'Sorrows of Werter,' or some of our fashionable hobgoblin romances?"

Isabella undertook the defence of her book with much enthusiasm—and either her cause, or her defence, was so much to Dr. X.—'s taste, that he gradually gave up his feigned attack.

After the argument was over, and every body, not excepting Mrs. Harcourt, who had almost forgotten her headache, was pleased with the vanquished doctor, he drew from his pocket-book three or four small cards; they were tickets of admittance to Lady N—'s French reading parties.

Lady N— was an elderly lady, whose rank made literature fashionable amongst many, who aspired to the honour of being noticed by her. She was esteemed such an excellent judge of manners, abilities, and character, that her approbation was anxiously courted, more especially by mothers who were just introducing their daughters into the world. She was fond of encouraging youthful merit; but she was nice, some thought fastidious, in the choice of her young acquaintance.

Mrs. Harcourt had been very desirous that Isabella and Matilda should be early distinguished by a person, whose approving voice was of so much consequence in fashionable as well as in literary society; and she was highly flattered by Dr. X—'s prophecy, that Isabella would be a great favourite of this "nice judging" lady—"Provided," added he, turning to Isabella, "you have the prudence not to be always, as you have been this morning, victorious in argument."

"I think," said Mrs. Harcourt—after the doctor had taken his leave—"I think I am much better—ring for Grace, and I will get up."

"Mamma," said Matilda, "if you will give me leave, I will give my ticket for the reading party to Mad. de Rosier, because, I am sure, it is an entertainment she will like particularly—and, you know, she confines herself so much with us—"

"I do not wish her to confine herself so much, my dear, I am sure," said Mrs. Harcourt, coldly, for, at this instant, Grace's representations of the morning's music and dancing, and some remains of her former jealousy of Mad. de Rosier's influence over her children's affections, operated upon her mind. Pride prevented her from explaining herself further to Isabella or Matilda—and though they saw that she was displeased, they had no idea of the reason. As she was dressing, Mrs. Harcourt conversed with them about the books they were reading. Matilda was reading Hogarth's Analysis of Beauty; and she gave a distinct account of his theory.

Mrs. Harcourt, when she perceived her daughter's rapid improvement, felt a mixture of joy and sorrow.

"My dears," said she, "you will all of you be much superior to your mother—but girls were educated, in my days, quite in a different style from what they are now."

"Ah! there were no Mad. de Rosiers then," said Matilda, innocently.

"What sort of a woman was your mother, mamma?" said Isabella, "my grandmother, mamma?"

"She—she was a very good woman."

"Was she sensible?" said Isabella.

"Matilda, my dear," said Mrs. Harcourt, "I wish you would see if Mad. de Rosier has returned—I should be very glad to speak with her, for one moment, if she be not engaged."

Under the veil of politeness, Mrs. Harcourt concealed her real feelings, and declaring to Mad. de Rosier that she did not feel in spirits, or sufficiently well, to go out that evening, she requested that Mad. de Rosier would go, in her stead, to a dinner, where she knew her company would be particularly acceptable.—"You will trust me, will you, with your pupils for one evening?" added Mrs. Harcourt.

The tone and manner in which she pronounced these words revealed the real state of her mind to Mad. de Rosier, who immediately complied with her wishes.

Conscious of this lady's quick penetration, Mrs. Harcourt was abashed by this ready compliance, and she blamed herself for feelings which she could not suppress.

"I am sorry that you were not at home this morning," she continued, in a hurried manner—"you would have been delighted with Dr. X—; he is one of the most entertaining men I am acquainted with—and you would have been vastly proud of your pupil there," pointing to Isabella; "I assure you, she pleased me extremely."

In the evening, after Mad. de Rosier's departure, Mrs. Harcourt was not quite so happy as she had expected. They who have only seen children in picturesque situations, are not aware how much the duration of this domestic happiness depends upon those who have the care of them. People who, with the greatest abilities and the most anxious affection, are unexperienced in education, should not be surprised or mortified if their first attempts be not attended with success. Mrs. Harcourt thought that she was doing what was very useful in hearing Herbert read; he read with tolerable fluency, but he stopped at the end of almost every sentence to weigh the exact sense of the words. In this habit he had been indulged, or rather encouraged, by his preceptress; but his simple questions, and his desire to have every word precisely explained, were far from amusing to one who was little accustomed to the difficulties and misapprehensions of a young reader.

Herbert was reading a passage, which Mad. de Rosier had marked for him, in Xenophon's Cyropaedia. With her explanations, it might have been intelligible to him. Herbert read the account of Cyrus's judgment upon the two boys, who had quarrelled about their great and little coats, much to his mother's satisfaction, because he had understood every word of it, except the word constituted.

"Constituted judge—what does that mean, mamma?"

"Made a judge, my dear: go on."

"I saw a judge once, mamma, in a great wig—had Cyrus a wig, when he was con—const!—made a judge?"

Isabella and Mrs. Harcourt laughed at this question; and they endeavoured to explain the difference between a Persian and an English judge.

Herbert with some difficulty separated the ideas, which he had so firmly associated, of a judge and a great wig; and when he had, or thought he had, an abstract notion of a judge, he obeyed his mother's repeated injunctions of "Go on—go on." He went on, after observing that what came next was not marked by Mad. de Rosier for him to read.

Cyrus's mother says to him: "Child, the same things are not accounted just with your grandfather here, and yonder in Persia." At this sentence Herbert made a dead stop; and, after pondering for some time, said, "I don't understand what Cyrus's mother meant—what does she mean by accounted just?— Accounted, Matilda, I thought meant only about casting up sums?"

"It has another meaning, my dear," Matilda mildly began.

"Oh, for Heaven's sake, spare me!" exclaimed Mrs. Harcourt; "do not let me hear all the meanings of all the words in the English language. Herbert may look for the words that he does not understand, in the dictionary, when he has done reading. Go on, now, pray; for," added she, looking at her watch, "you have been half an hour reading half a page: this would tire the patience of Job."

Herbert, perceiving that his mother was displeased, began in the same instant to be frightened; he hurried on as fast as he could, without understanding one word more of what he was reading; his precipitation was worse than his slowness: he stumbled over the words, missed syllables, missed lines, made the most incomprehensible nonsense of the whole; till, at length, Mrs. Harcourt shut the book in despair, and soon afterward despatched Herbert, who was also in despair, to bed. At this catastrophe, Favoretta looked very grave, and a general gloom seemed to overspread the company.

Mrs. Harcourt was mortified at the silence that prevailed, and made several ineffectual attempts to revive the freedom and gaiety of conversation:—"Ah!" said she to herself, "I knew it would be so;—they cannot be happy without Mad. de Rosier."

Isabella had taken up a book. "Cannot you read for our entertainment, Isabella, my dear, as well as for your own?" said her mother: "I assure you, I am as much interested always in what you read to me, as Mad. de Rosier herself can be."

"I was just looking, mamma, for some lines, that we read the other day, which Mad. de Rosier said she was sure you would like. Can you find them, Matilda? You know Mad. de Rosier said that mamma would like them, because she has been at the opera."

"I have been at a great many operas," said Mrs. Harcourt, dryly; "but I like other things as well as operas—and I cannot precisely guess what you mean by the opera—has it no name?"

"Medea and Jason, ma'am."

"The ballet of Medea and Jason. It's a very fine thing, certainly; but one has seen it so often. Read on, my dear."

Isabella then read a passage, which, notwithstanding Mrs. Harcourt's inclination to be displeased, captivated her ear, and seized her imagination.

"Slow out of earth, before the festive crowds,
On wheels of fire, amid a night of clouds,
Drawn by fierce fiends, arose a magic car,
Received the queen, and, hov'ring, flamed in air.
As with raised hands the suppliant traitors kneel,
And fear the vengeance they deserved to feel;

"Thrice, with parch'd lips, her guiltless babes she press'd,
And thrice she clasp'd them to her tortured breast.
Awhile with white uplifted eyes she stood,
Then plunged her trembling poniards in their blood.
Go, kiss your sire! go, share the bridal mirth!
She cried, and hurl'd their quiv'ring limbs on earth.
Rebellowing thunders rock the marble tow'rs,
And red-tongucd lightnings shoot their arrowy show'rs:
Earth yawns!—the crashing ruin sinks!—o'er all
Death with black hands extends his mighty pall."

"They are admirable lines, indeed!" exclaimed Mrs. Harcourt.

"I knew, mamma, you would like them," said Isabella; "and I'm sure I wish I had seen the ballet too."

"You were never at an opera," said Mrs. Harcourt, after Isabella had finished reading; "should you, either of you, or both, like to go with me to-night to the opera?"

"To-night, ma'am!" cried Isabella, in a voice of joy.

"To-night, mamma!" cried Matilda, timidly; "but you were not well this morning."

"But I am very well, now, my love; at least quite well enough to go out with you—let me give you some pleasure. Ring for Grace, my dear Matilda," added Mrs. Harcourt, looking at her watch, "and do not let us be sentimental, for we have not a moment to lose—we must prevail upon Grace to be as quick as lightning in her operations."

Grace was well disposed to be quick—she was delighted with what she called the change of measures;—she repeated continually, in the midst of their hurried toilette—

"Well, I am so glad, young ladies, you're going out with your mamma, at last—I never saw my mistress look so well as she does to-night."

Triumphant, and feeling herself to be a person of consequence, Grace was indefatigably busy, and Mrs. Harcourt thought that her talkative zeal was the overflowing of an honest heart.

After Mrs. Harcourt, with Isabella and Matilda, were gone to the opera, Favoretta, who had been sent to bed by her mother, because she was in the way when they were dressing, called to Grace to beg that she would close the shutters in her room, for the moon shone upon her bed, and she could not go to sleep.

"I wish mamma would have let me sit up a little longer," said Favoretta, "for I am not at all sleepy."

"You always go to bed a great deal earlier, you know, miss," said Grace, "when your governess is at home; I would let you get up, and come down to tea with me, for I'm just going to take my late dish of tea, to rest myself, only I dare not let you, because—"

"Because what?"

"Because, miss, you remember how you served me about the queen-cake."

"But I do not want you to give me any queen-cake; I only want to get up for a little while," said Favoretta.

"Then get up," said Grace: "but don't make a noise, to waken Master Herbert."

"Do you think," said Favoretta, "that Herbert would think it wrong?"

"Indeed, I don't think at all about what he thinks," said Mrs. Grace, tossing back her head, as she adjusted her dress at the glass; "and, if you think so much about it, you'd better lie down again."

"Oh! I can't lie down again," said Favoretta; "I have got my shoes on—stay for me, Grace—I'm just ready."

Grace, who was pleased with an opportunity of indulging this little girl, and who flattered herself that she should regain her former power over Favoretta's undistinguishing affections, waited for her most willingly. Grace drank her late dish of tea in her mistress's dressing-room, and did every thing in her power to humour "her sweet Favoretta."

Mrs. Rebecca, Mrs. Fanshaw's maid, was summoned; she lived in the next street. She was quite overjoyed, she said, at entering the room, to see Miss Favoretta—it was an age since she had a sight or a glimpse of her.

We pass over the edifying conversation of those two ladies—Miss Favoretta was kept awake, and in such high spirits by flattery, that she did not perceive how late it was—she begged to stay up a little longer, and a little longer.

Mrs. Rebecca joined in these entreaties, and Mrs. Grace could not refuse them; especially as she knew that the coach would not go for Mad. de Rosier till after her mistress's return from the opera.

The coachman had made this arrangement for his own convenience, and had placed it entirely to the account of his horses.

Mrs. Grace depended, rather imprudently, upon the coachman's arrangement; for Mad. de Rosier, finding that the coach did not call for her at the hour she had appointed, sent for a chair, and returned home, whilst Grace, Mrs. Rebecca, and Favoretta, were yet in Mrs. Harcourt's dressing-room.

Favoretta was making a great noise, so that they did not hear the knock at the door.

One of the housemaids apprised Mrs. Grace of Mad. de Rosier's arrival. "She's getting out of her chair, Mrs. Grace, in the hall."

Grace started up, put Favoretta into a little closet, and charged her not to make the least noise for her life.—Then, with a candle in her hand, and a treacherous smile upon her countenance, she sallied forth to the head of the stairs, to light Mad. de Rosier.—"Dear ma'am! my mistress will be so sorry the coach didn't go for you in time;—she found herself better after you went—and the two young ladies are gone with her to the opera."

"And where are Herbert and Favoretta?"

"In bed, ma'am, and asleep, hours ago.—Shall I light you, ma'am, this way, to your room?"

"No," said Mad. de Rosier; "I have a letter to write: and I'll wait in Mrs. Harcourt's dressing-room till she comes home."

"Very well, ma'am. Mrs. Rebecca, it's only Mad. de Rosier.—Mad. de Rosier, it's only Rebecca, Mrs. Fanshaw's maid, ma'am, who's here very often when my mistress is at home, and just stepped out to look at the young ladies' drawings, which my mistress gave me leave to show her the first time she drank tea with me, ma'am."

Mad. de Rosier, who thought all this did not concern her in the least, listened to it with cold indifference, and sat down to write her letter.

Grace fidgeted about the room, as long as she could find any pretence for moving any thing into or out of its place; and, at length, in no small degree of anxiety for the prisoner she had left in the closet, quitted the dressing-room.

As Mad. de Rosier was writing, she once or twice thought that she heard some noise in the closet; she listened, but all was silent; and she continued to write, till Mrs. Harcourt, Isabella, and Matilda, came home.

Isabella was in high spirits, and began to talk, with considerable volubility, to Mad. de Rosier about the opera.

Mrs. Harcourt was full of apologies about the coach; and Matilda rather anxious to discover what it was that had made a change in her mother's manner towards Mad. de Rosier.

Grace, glad to see that they were all intent upon their own affairs, lighted their candles expeditiously, and stood waiting, in hopes that they would immediately leave the room, and that she should be able to release her prisoner.

Favoretta usually slept in a little closet within Mrs. Grace's room, so that she foresaw no difficulty in getting her to bed.

"I heard!—did not you hear a noise, Isabella?" said Matilda.

"A noise!—No; where?" said Isabella, and went on talking alternately to her mother and Mad. de Rosier, whom she held fast, though they seemed somewhat inclined to retire to rest.

"Indeed," said Matilda, "I did hear a noise in that closet."

"Oh dear, Miss Matilda," cried Grace, getting between Matilda and the closet, "it's nothing in life but a mouse."

"A mouse, where?" said Mrs. Harcourt.

"Nowhere, ma'am," said Grace; "only Miss Matilda was hearing noises, and I said they must be mice."

"There, mamma! there! that was not a mouse, surely!" said Matilda. "It was a noise louder, certainly, than any mouse could make."

"Grace is frightened," said Isabella, laughing.

Grace, indeed, looked pale and terribly frightened.

Mad. de Rosier took a candle, and walked directly to the closet.

"Ring for the men," said Mrs. Harcourt.

Matilda held back Mad. de Rosier; and Isabella, whose head was now just recovered from the opera, rang the bell with considerable energy.

"Dear Miss Isabella, don't ring so;—dear ma'am, don't be frightened, and I'll tell you the whole truth, ma'am," said Grace to her mistress; "it's nothing in the world to frighten any body—it's only Miss Favoretta, ma'am."

"Favoretta!" exclaimed every body at once, except Mad. de Rosier, who instantly opened the closet door, but no Favoretta appeared.

"Favoretta is not here," said Mad. de Rosier.

"Then I'm undone!" exclaimed Grace; "she must have got out upon the leads." The leads were, at this place, narrow, and very dangerous.

"Don't scream, or the child is lost," said Mad. de Rosier.

Mrs. Harcourt sank down into an arm-chair. Mad. de Rosier stopped Isabella, who pressed into the closet.

"Don't speak, Isabella—Grace, go into the closet—call Favoretta—hear me, quietly," said Mad. de Rosier, steadily, for Mrs. Grace was in such confusion of mind, that she was going to call upon the child, without waiting to hear what was said to her.—"Hear me," said Mad. de Rosier, "or you are undone—go into the closet without making any bustle—call Favoretta, gently; she will not be frightened, when she hears only your voice."

Grace did as she was ordered, and returned from the closet in a few instants, with Favoretta. Grace instantly began an exculpatory speech, but Mrs. Harcourt, though still trembling, had sufficient firmness to say, "Leave us, Grace, and let me hear the truth from the child."

Grace left the room. Favoretta related exactly what had happened, and said that when she heard all their voices in the dressing-room, and when she heard Matilda say there's a noise, she was afraid of being discovered in the closet, and had crept out through a little door, with which she was well acquainted, that opened upon the leads.

Mrs. Harcourt now broke forth into indignant exclamations against Grace. Mad. de Rosier gently pacified her, and hinted that it would be but just to give her a fair hearing in the morning.

"You are always yourself! always excellent!" cried Mrs. Harcourt; "you have saved my child—we none of us had any presence of mind, but yourself."

"Indeed, mamma, I did ring the bell, however," said Isabella.

With much difficulty those who had so much to say, submitted to Mad. de Rosier's entreaty of "Let us talk of it in the morning." She was afraid that Favoretta, who was present, would not draw any salutary moral from what might be said in the first emotions of joy for her safety. Mad. de Rosier undressed the little girl herself, and took care that she should not be treated as a heroine just escaped from imminent danger.

The morning came, and Mrs. Grace listened, with anxious ear, for the first sound of her mistress's bell—but no bell rang; and, when she heard Mrs. Harcourt walking in her bedchamber, Grace augured ill of her own fate, and foreboded the decline and fall of her empire.

"If my mistress can get up and dress herself without me, it's all over with me," said Grace; "but I'll make one trial." Then she knocked with her most obliging knock at her mistress's door, and presented herself with a Magdalen face—"Can I do any thing for you, ma'am?"

"Nothing, I thank you, Grace. Send Isabella and Matilda."

Isabella and Matilda came, but Mrs. Harcourt finished dressing herself in silence, and then said—

"Come with me, my dear girls, to Mad. de Rosier's room. I believe I had better ask her the question that I was going to ask you. Is she up?"

"Yes, but not dressed," said Matilda; "for we have been reading to her."

"And talking to her," added Isabella; "which, you know, hinders people very much, mamma, when they are dressing."

At Mad. de Rosier's door they found Herbert, with his slate in his hand, and his sum ready cast up.

"May I bring this little man in with me?" said Mrs. Harcourt to Mad. de Rosier—"Herbert, shake hands with me," continued his mother: "I believe I was a little impatient with you and your Cyrus last night; but you must not expect that every body should be as good to you as this lady has been;" leading him up to Mad. de Rosier.

"Set this gentleman's heart at ease, will you?" continued she, presenting the slate, upon which his sum was written, to Mad. de Rosier. "He looks the picture, or rather the reality, of honesty and good humour this morning, I think. I am sure that he has not done any thing that he is ashamed of."

Little Herbert's countenance glowed with pleasure at receiving such praise from his mother; but he soon checked his pride, for he discovered Favoretta, upon whom every eye had turned, as Mrs. Harcourt concluded her speech.

Favoretta was sitting in the furthest corner of the room, and she turned her face to the wall when Herbert looked at her; but Herbert saw that she was in disgrace. "Your sum is quite right, Herbert," said Mad. de Rosier.

"Herbert, take your slate," said Matilda; and the young gentleman had at length the politeness to relieve her outstretched arm.

"Send him out of the way," whispered Mrs. Harcourt.

"Go out of the room, Herbert, my dear," said Mad. de Rosier, who never made use of artifices upon any occasion to get rid of children—"go out of the room, Herbert, my dear: for we want to talk about something which we do not wish that you should hear."

Herbert, though he was anxious to know what could be the matter with Favoretta, instantly withdrew, saying, "Will you call me again when you've done talking?"

"We can speak French," added Mad. de Rosier, looking at Favoretta, "since we cannot trust that little girl in a room by herself; we must speak in a language which she does not understand, when we have any thing to say that we do not choose she should hear."

"After all this preparation," said Mrs. Harcourt, in French, "my little mouse will make you laugh; it will not surprise or frighten you, Matilda, quite so much as the mouse of last night. You must know that I have been much disturbed by certain noises."

"More noises!" said Matilda, drawing closer, to listen.

"More noises!" said Mrs. Harcourt, laughing; "but the noises which disturbed my repose were not heard in the dead of the night, just as the clock struck twelve—the charming hour for being frightened out of one's wits, Matilda: my noises were heard in broad daylight, about the time

'When lap-dogs give themselves the rousing shake.'

Was not there music and dancing here, early yesterday morning, when I had the headache, Isabella?"

"Yes, mamma," said Isabella: "Herbert's dulcimer-boy was here! We call him Herbert's dulcimer-boy, because Herbert gave him two buns the other day;—the boy and his father came from gratitude, to play a tune for Herbert, and we all ran and asked Mad. de Rosier to let him in."

"We did not know you had the headache, mamma," said Matilda, "till after they had played several tunes, and we heard Grace saying something to Herbert about racketing upon the stairs—he only ran up stairs once for my music-book; and the moment Grace spoke to him, he came to us, and said that you were not well; then Mad. de Rosier stopped the dulcimer, and we all left off dancing, and we were very sorry Grace had not told us sooner that you were ill: at that time it was ten—nearly eleven o'clock."

"Grace strangely misrepresented all this," said Mrs. Harcourt: "as she gave her advice so late, I am sorry she gave it at all; she prevented you and Isabella from the pleasure of going out with Mad. de Rosier."

"We prevented ourselves—Grace did not prevent us, I assure you, mamma," said Isabella, eagerly: "we wished to stay at home with you—Herbert and Favoretta were only going to see the royal tiger."

"Then you did not stay at home by Mad. de Rosier's desire."

"No, indeed, madam," said Mad. de Rosier, who had not appeared in any haste to justify herself; "your children always show you affection by their own desire, never by mine: your penetration would certainly discover the difference between attentions prompted by a governess, and those which are shown by artless affection."

"My dear madam, say no more," said Mrs. Harcourt, holding out her hand: "you are a real friend."

Mad. de Rosier now went to call Herbert, but on opening the door, Mrs. Grace fell forward upon her face into the room; she had been kneeling with her head close to the key-hole of the door; and, probably, the sound of her own name, and a few sentences now and then spoken in English, had so fixed her attention, that she did not prepare in time for her retreat.

"Get up, Grace, and walk in, if you please," said Mrs. Harcourt, with much calmness; "we have not the least objection to your hearing our conversation."

"Indeed, ma'am," said Grace, as soon as she had recovered her feet, "I'm above listening to any body's conversations, except that when one hears one's own name, and knows that one has enemies, it is but natural to listen in one's own defence."

"And is that all you can do, Grace, in your own defence?" said Mrs. Harcourt.

"It's not all I can say, ma'am," replied Grace, pushed to extremities; and still with a secret hope that her mistress, upon a pinch, would not part with a favourite maid: "I see I'm of no further use in the family, neither to young or old—and new comers have put me quite out of favour, and have your ear to themselves—so, if you please, ma'am, I had better look out for another situation."

"If you please, Grace," said Mrs. Harcourt.

"I will leave the house this instant, if you think proper, ma'am."

"If you think proper, Grace," said her mistress, with immovable philosophy.

Grace burst into tears: "I never thought it would come to this, Mrs. Harcourt—I, that have lived so long such a favourite!—but I don't blame you, madam; you have been the best and kindest of mistresses to me; and, whatever becomes of me, to my dying words, I shall always give you and the dear young ladies the best of characters."

"The character we may give you, Grace, is of rather more consequence."

"Every thing that I say and do," interrupted the sobbing Grace, "is vilified and misinterpreted by those who wish me ill. I—"

"You have desired to leave me, Grace; and my desire is that you should leave me," said Mrs. Harcourt, with firmness. "Mad. de Rosier and I strictly forbade you to interfere with any of the children in our absence; you have thought proper to disregard these orders; and were you to stay longer in my house, I perceive that you would teach my children first to disobey, and afterward to deceive me."

Grace, little prepared for this calm decision, now in a frightened, humble tone, began to make promises of reformation; but her promises and apologies were vain; she was compelled to depart, and every body was glad to have done with her.

Favoretta, young as she was, had already learned from this cunning waiting-maid habits of deceit which could not be suddenly changed. Mad. de Rosier attempted her cure, by making her feel, in the first place, the inconveniences and the disgrace of not being trusted. Favoretta was ashamed to perceive that she was the only person in the house who was watched: and she was heartily glad when, by degrees, she had opportunities allowed her of obtaining a character for truth, and all the pleasures and all the advantages of confidence.

Things went on much better after the gnome-like influence of Mrs Grace had ceased; but we must now hasten to introduce our readers to Mrs. Fanshaw. Mrs. Fanshaw was a card-playing lady, who had been educated at a time when it was not thought necessary for women to have any knowledge, or any taste for literature. As she advanced in life, she continually recurred to the maxims as well as to the fashions of her youth; and the improvements in modern female education she treated as dangerous innovations. She had placed her daughter at a boarding-school in London, the expense of which was its chief recommendation; and she saw her regularly at the Christmas and Midsummer holidays. At length, when Miss Fanshaw was about sixteen, her prudent mother began to think that it was time to take her from school, and to introduce her into the world. Miss Fanshaw had learned to speak French passably, to read a little Italian, to draw a little, to play tolerably well upon the piano-forte, and to dance as well as many other young ladies. She had been sedulously taught a sovereign contempt of whatever was called vulgar at the school where she was educated; but, as she was profoundly ignorant of every thing but the routine of that school, she had no precise idea of propriety; she only knew what was thought vulgar or genteel at Suxberry House; and the authority of Mrs. Suxberry (for that was the name of her schoolmistress) she quoted as incontrovertible upon all occasions. Without reflecting upon what was wrong or right, she decided with pert vivacity on all subjects; and firmly believed that no one could know or could learn any thing who had not been educated precisely as she had been. She considered her mother as an inferior personage, destitute of genteel accomplishments: her mother considered her as a model of perfection, that could only have been rendered thus thoroughly accomplished by the most expensive masters—her only fear was, that her dear Jane should be rather too learned.

Mrs. Harcourt, with Isabella and Matilda, paid Mrs. Fanshaw a visit, as soon as they heard that her daughter was come home.

Miss Fanshaw, an erect stiffened figure, made her entrée; and it was impossible not to perceive that her whole soul was intent upon her manner of holding her head and placing her elbows, as she came into the room. Her person had undergone all the ordinary and extraordinary tortures of back-boards, collars, stocks, dumbbells, &c. She looked at Isabella and Matilda with some surprise and contempt during the first ten minutes after her entrance; for they were neither of them seated in the exact posture which she had been instructed to think the only position in which a young lady should sit in company. Isabella got up to look at a drawing; Miss Fanshaw watched every step she took, and settled it in her own mind that Miss Harcourt did not walk as if she had ever been at Suxberry House. Matilda endeavoured to engage the figure that sat beside her in conversation; but the figure had no conversation, and the utmost that Matilda could obtain was a few monosyllables pronounced with affected gravity; for at Suxberry House this young lady had been taught to maintain an invincible silence when produced to strangers; but she made herself amends for this constraint, the moment she was with her companions, by a tittering, gossiping species of communication, which scarcely deserves the name of conversation.

Whilst the silent Miss Fanshaw sat so as to do her dancing-master strict justice, Mrs. Fanshaw was stating to Mrs. Harcourt the enormous expense to which she had gone in her daughter's education. Though firm to her original doctrine, that women had no occasion for learning—in which word of reproach she included all literature—she nevertheless had been convinced, by the unanimous voice of fashion, that accomplishments were most desirable for young ladies—desirable, merely because they were fashionable; she did not, in the least, consider them as sources of independent occupation.

Isabella was struck with sudden admiration at the sight of a head of Jupiter which Miss Fanshaw had just finished, and Mrs. Harcourt borrowed it for her to copy; though Miss Fanshaw was secretly but decidedly of opinion, that no one who had not learned from the drawing-master at Suxberry House could copy this head of Jupiter with any chance of success.

There was a pretty little netting-box upon the table which caught Matilda's eye, and she asked the silent figure what it was made of. The silent figure turned its head mechanically, but could give no information upon the subject. Mrs. Fanshaw, however, said that she had bought the box at the Repository for ingenious works, and that the reason she chose it was because Lady N— had recommended it to her.

"It is some kind of new manufacture, her ladyship tells me, invented by some poor little boy that she patronizes; her ladyship can tell you more of the matter, Miss Matilda, than I can," concluded Mrs. Fanshaw; and, producing her netting, she asked Mrs. Harcourt, "if she had not been vastly notable to have got forward so fast with her work."

The remainder of the visit was spent in recounting her losses at the card-table, and in exhortation to Mrs. Harcourt to send Miss Isabella and Matilda to finish their education at Suxberry House.

Mrs. Harcourt was somewhat alarmed by the idea that her daughters would not be equal to Miss Fanshaw in accomplishments but, fortunately for Mad. de Rosier and herself, she was soon induced to change her opinion by farther opportunities of comparison.

In a few days her visit was returned. Mrs. Harcourt happened to mention the globe that Isabella was painting: Miss Fanshaw begged to see it, and she went into Mrs. Harcourt's dressing-room, where it hung. The moment she found herself with Isabella and Matilda, out of company, the silent figure became talkative. The charm seemed to be broken, or rather reversed, and she began to chatter with pert incessant rapidity.

"Dear me," said she, casting a scornful glance at Matilda's globe, "this is vastly pretty, but we've no such thing at Suxberry House. I wonder Mrs. Harcourt didn't send both of you to Suxberry House—every body sends their daughters, who can afford it, now, to Suxberry House; but, to be sure, it's very expensive—we had all silver forks, and every thing in the highest style, and Mrs. Suxberry keeps a coach. I assure you she's not at all like a schoolmistress, and she thinks it very rude and vulgar of any body to call her a schoolmistress. Won't you ask your mamma to send you, if it's only for the name of it, for one year, to Suxberry House?"

"No," said Matilda; "we are so happy under the care of Mad. de Rosier."

"Ah, dear me! I forgot—mamma told me you'd got a new French governess lately—our French teacher, at Suxberry House, was so strict, and so cross, if one made a mistake in the tenses: it's very well for you your governess is not cross—does she give you very hard exercises?—let me look at your exercise book, and I'll tell you whether it's the right one—I mean that we used to have at Suxberry House."

Miss Fanshaw snatched up a book, in which she saw a paper, which she took for a French exercise.

"Come, show it me, and I'll correct the faults for you, before your governess sees it, and she'll be so surprised!"

"Mad. de Rosier has seen it," said Matilda;—but Miss Fanshaw, in a romping manner, pulled the paper out of her hands. It was the translation of a part of "Les Conversations d'Emilie," which we formerly mentioned.

"La!" said Miss Fanshaw, "we had no such book as this at Suxberry House."

Matilda's translation she was surprised to find correct.

"And do you write themes?" said she—"We always wrote themes once every week, at Suxberry House, which I used to hate of all things, for I never could find any thing to say—it made me hate writing, I know;—but that's all over now; thank goodness, I've done with themes, and French letters, and exercises, and translations, and all those plaguing things; and now I've left school for ever, I may do just as I please—that's the best of going to school; it's over some time or other, and there's an end of it; but you that have a governess and masters at home, you go on for ever and ever, and you have no holidays either; and you have no out-of-school hours; you are kept hard at it from morning till night: now I should hate that of all things. At Suxberry House, when we had got our task done, and finished with the writing-master and the drawing-master, and when we had practised for the music-master, and all that, we might be as idle as we pleased, and do what we liked out of school-hours—you know that was very pleasant: I assure you, you'd like being at Suxberry House amazingly."

Isabella and Matilda, to whom it did not appear the most delightful of all things to be idle, nor the most desirable thing in the world to have their education finished, and then to lay aside all thoughts of farther improvement, could not assent to Miss Fanshaw's concluding assertion. They declared that they did not feel any want of holidays; at which Miss Fanshaw stared: they said that they had no tasks, and that they liked to be employed rather better than to be idle; at which Miss Fanshaw laughed, and sarcastically said, "You need not talk to me as if your governess were by, for I'm not a tell-tale—I shan't repeat what you say."

Isabella and Matilda, who had not two methods of talking, looked rather displeased at this ill-bred speech.

"Nay," said Miss Fanshaw, "I hope you aren't affronted now at what I said; when we are by ourselves, you know, one says just what comes into one's head. Whose handsome coach is this, pray, with a coronet?" continued she, looking out of the window: "I declare it is stopping at your door; do let us go down. I'm never afraid of going into the room when there's company, for we were taught to go into a room at Suxberry House; and Mrs. Suxberry says it's very vulgar to be ashamed, and I assure you it's all custom. I used to colour, as Miss Matilda does, every minute; but I got over it before I had been long at Suxberry House."

Isabella, who had just been reading "A Father's Legacy to his Daughters," recollected at this instant Dr. Gregory's opinion, "that when a girl ceases to blush, she has lost the most powerful charm of beauty." She had not, however, time to quote this in Matilda's defence; for Miss Fanshaw ran down stairs, and Isabella recollected, before she overtook her, that it would not be polite to remind her of her early loss of charms.

Lady N— was in the coach which had excited Miss Fanshaw's admiration; and this young lady had a glorious opportunity of showing the graces that she had been taught at so much expense, for the room was full of company. Several morning visitors had called upon Mrs. Harcourt, and they formed a pretty large circle, which Miss Fanshaw viewed upon her entrance with a sort of studied assurance.

Mrs. Fanshaw watched Lady N—'s eye as her daughter came into the room; but Lady N— did not appear to be much struck with the second-hand graces of Suxberry House; her eye passed over Miss Fanshaw, in search of something less affected and more interesting.

Miss Fanshaw had now resumed her company face and attitude; she sat in prudent silence, whilst Lady N— addressed her conversation to Isabella and Matilda, whose thoughts did not seem to be totally engrossed by their own persons.

Dr. X— had prepared this lady to think favourably of Mad. de Rosier's pupils, by the account which he had given her of Isabella's remarks upon Zeluco.

A person of good sense, who has an encouraging countenance, can easily draw out the abilities of young people, and from their manner of listening, as well as from their manner of speaking, can soon form a judgment of their temper and understanding.

Miss Fanshaw, instead of attending with a desire to improve herself from sensible conversation, sat with a look as absent as that of an unskilful actress, whilst the other performers are engaged in their parts.

There was a small book-case, in a recess, at the farthest end of the room, and upon a little table there were some books, which Isabella and Matilda had been reading with Mad. de Rosier. Mrs. Fanshaw looked towards the table, with a sarcastic smile, and said—

"You are great readers, young ladies, I see: may we know what are your studies?"

Miss Fanshaw, to show how well she could walk, crossed the room, and took up one of the books.

"'Alison upon Taste'—that's a pretty book, I dare say—but la! what's this, Miss Isabella? 'A Smith's Theory of Moral Sentiments'—dear me! that must be a curious performance—by a smith! a common smith!"

Isabella, good-naturedly, stopped her from farther absurd exclamations by turning to the title-page of the book and showing her the words "Adam Smith."

"Ah! A stands for Adam! very true—I thought it was a smith," said Miss Fanshaw.

"Well, my dear," said her mother, who had quickness enough to perceive that her daughter had made some mistake, by the countenances of the company, but who had not sufficient erudition to know what the mistake could be—"well, my dear, and suppose it was a smith, there's nothing extraordinary in that—nothing extraordinary in a smith's writing a book nowadays,—why not a common blacksmith, as well as a common ploughman?—I was asked, I know, not long ago, to subscribe to the poems of a common ploughman."

"The Ayrshire ploughman?" said Lady N—.

"Yes, they called him so, as I recollect, and I really had a mind to put my name down, for I think I saw your ladyship's amongst the subscribers."

"Yes, they are beautiful poems," said Lady N—.

"So I understand—there are some vastly pretty things in his collection—but one hears of so many good things coming out every day," said Mrs. Fanshaw, in a plaintive voice. "In these days, I think, every body writes—"

"And reads," said Lady N—.

"And reads," said Mrs. Fanshaw. "We have learned ladies now, wherever one goes, who tell one they never play at cards—I am sure they are very bad company. Jane," said she, turning to her daughter, "I hope you won't take it into your head to turn out a reading lady!"

"Oh dear, no!" said Miss Fanshaw: "we had not much time for reading at Suxberry House, we were so busy with our masters;—we had a charming English master though, to teach us elocution, because it's so fashionable now to read loud well. Mrs. Harcourt, isn't it odd to read English books to a French governess?" continued this young lady, whose constrained taciturnity now gave way to a strong desire to show herself off before Lady N—. She had observed that Isabella and Matilda had been listened to with approbation, and she imagined that, when she spoke, she should certainly eclipse them. Mrs. Harcourt replied to her observation, that Mad. de Rosier not only read and spoke English remarkably well, but that she had also a general knowledge of English literature.

"Oh! here are some French books," said Miss Fanshaw, taking down one out of the book-case—"'Journal Étranger'—dear me! are you translating of this, Miss Isabella?"

"No," said Mrs. Harcourt; "Madame de Rosier brought it down stairs yesterday, to show us an essay of Hume's on the study of history, which is particularly addressed to women; and Mad. de Rosier says that it is not to be found in several of the late editions of Hume's Essays—she thought it singular that it should be preserved in a French translation."

"There is," said Isabella, "an entertaining account in that essay of a lady who asked Hume to lend her some novels! He lent her Plutarch's Lives, which she thought very amusing, till she found out that they were true. As soon as she came to the names of Caesar and Alexander, she returned the books."

Mrs. Fanshaw was surprised that Lady N— begged to look at this essay; and was much disappointed to observe that the graceful manner in which Miss Fanshaw presented the book to her ladyship escaped notice.

"Pray, Miss Matilda, is that a drawing?" said Mrs. Fanshaw, in hopes of leading to a more favourable subject.

"Oh, dear me! do pray favour us with a sight of it!" cried Miss Fanshaw, and she eagerly unrolled the paper, though Matilda assured her that it was not a drawing.

It was Hogarth's print of a country dance, which was prefixed to his "Analysis of Beauty."

"It is the oddest thing!" exclaimed Miss Fanshaw, who thought every thing odd or strange which she had not seen at Suxberry house. Without staying to observe the innumerable strokes of humour and of original genius in the print, she ran on—"La! its hardly worth any one's while, surely, to draw such a set of vulgar figures—one hates low humour." Then, in a hurry to show her taste for dress, she observed that "people, formerly, must have had no taste at all;—one can hardly believe such things were ever worn."

Mrs. Fanshaw, touched by this reflection upon the taste of former times, though she seldom presumed to oppose any of her daughter's opinions, could not here refrain from saying a few words in defence of sacks, long waists, and whalebone stays, and she pointed to a row of stays in the margin of one of these prints of Hogarth.

Miss Fanshaw, who did not consider that, with those who have a taste for propriety in manners, she could not gain any thing by a triumph over her mother, laughed in a disdainful manner at her mother's "partiality for stays," and wondered how any body could think long waists becoming.

"Surely, any body who knows any thing of drawing, or has any taste for an antique figure, must acknowledge the present fashion to be most graceful." She appealed to Isabella and Matilda.

They were so much struck with the impropriety of her manner towards her mother, that they did not immediately answer; Matilda at length said, "It is natural to like what we have been early used to;" and, from unaffected gentleness, eager to prevent Miss Fanshaw from further exposing her ignorance, she rolled up the print; and Lady N—, smiling at Mrs. Harcourt, said, "I never saw a print more gracefully rolled up in my life." Miss Fanshaw immediately rolled up another of the prints, but no applause ensued.

At the next pause in the conversation, Mrs. Fanshaw and her daughter took their leave, seemingly dissatisfied with their visit.

Matilda, just after Mrs. Fanshaw left the room, recollected her pretty netting-box, and asked Lady N— whether she knew any thing of the little boy by whom it was made.

Her ladyship gave such an interesting account of him, that Matilda determined to have her share in relieving his distress.

Matilda's benevolence was formerly rather passive than active; but from Mad. de Rosier she had learned that sensibility should not be suffered to evaporate in sighs, or in sentimental speeches. She had also learnt that economy is necessary to generosity; and she consequently sometimes denied herself the gratification of her own tastes, that she might be able to assist those who were in distress.

She had lately seen a beautiful print(3) of the king of France taking leave of his family; and, as Mad. de Rosier was struck with it, she wished to have bought it for her; but she now considered that a guinea, which was the price of the print, might be better bestowed on this poor, little, ingenious, industrious boy; so she begged her mother to send to the repository for one of his boxes. The servants were all busy, and Matilda did not receive her box till the next morning.

(Footnote 3: By Egginton.)

Herbert was reading to Mad. de Rosier when the servant brought the box into the room. Favoretta got up to look at it, and immediately Herbert's eye glanced from his book: in spite of all his endeavours to command his attention, he heard the exclamations of "Beautiful!—How smooth!—like tortoise-shell!—What can it be made of?"

"My dear Herbert, shut the book," said Mad. de Rosier, "if your head be in that box. Never read one moment after you have ceased to attend."

"It is my fault," said Matilda; "I will put the box out of the way till he has finished reading."

When Herbert had recalled his wandering thoughts, and had fixed his mind upon what he was about, Mad. de Rosier put her hand upon the book—he started—"Now let us see the beautiful box," said she.

After it had passed through Favoretta and Herbert's impatient hands, Matilda, who had scarcely looked at it herself, took it to the window, to give it a sober examination. "It is not made of paper, or pasteboard, and it is not the colour of tortoise-shell," said Matilda: "I never saw any thing like it before; I wonder what it can be made of?"

Herbert, at this question, unperceived by Matilda, who was examining the box very earnestly, seized the lid, which was lying upon the table, and ran out of the room; he returned in a few minutes, and presented the lid to Matilda. "I can tell you one thing, Matilda," said he, with an important face—"it is an animal—an animal substance, I mean."

"Oh, Herbert," cried Matilda, "what have you been doing?—you have blackened the corner of the box."

"Only the least bit in the world," said Herbert, "to try an experiment. I only put one corner to the candle that Isabella had lighted to seal her letter."

"My dear Herbert, how could you burn your sister's box?" expostulated Madame de Rosier: "I thought you did not love mischief."

"Mischief!—no, indeed; I thought you would be pleased that I remembered how to distinguish animal from vegetable substances. You know, the day that my hair was on fire, you told me how to do that; and Matilda wanted to know what the box was made of; so I tried."

"Well," said Matilda, good-naturedly, "you have not done me much harm."

"But another time," said Mad. de Rosier, "don't burn a box that costs a guinea to try an experiment; and, above all things, never, upon any account, take what is not your own."

The corner of the lid that had been held to the candle was a little warped, so that the lid did not slide into its groove as easily as it did before. Herbert was disposed to use force upon the occasion; but Matilda with difficulty rescued her box by an argument which fortunately reached his understanding in time enough to stop his hand.

"It was the heat of the candle that warped it," said she: "let us dip it into boiling water, which cannot be made too hot, and that will, perhaps, bring it back to its shape."

The lid of the box was dipped into boiling-water, and restored to its shape. Matilda, as she was wiping it dry, observed that some yellow paint, or varnish, came off, and in one spot, on the inside of the lid, she discovered something like writing.

"Who will lend me a magnifying glass?"

Favoretta produced hers.

"I have kept it," said she, "a great, great while, ever since we were at the Rational Toy-shop."

"Mad. de Rosier, do look at this!" exclaimed Matilda—"here are letters quite plain!—I have found the name, I do believe, of the boy who made the box!" and she spelled, letter by letter, as she looked through the magnifying glass, the words Henri-Montmorenci.

Mad. de Rosier started up; and Matilda, surprised at her sudden emotion, put the box and magnifying glass into her hand. Madame de Rosier's hand trembled so much that she could not fix the glass.

"Je ne vois rien—lisez—vite!—ma chère amie—un mot de plus!" said she, putting the glass again into Matilda's hand, and leaning over her shoulder with a look of agonizing expectation.

The word de was all Matilda could make out—Isabella tried—it was in vain—no other letters were visible.

"De what?—de Rosier!—it must be! my son is alive!" said the mother.

Henri-Montmorenci was the name of Mad. de Rosier's son; but when she reflected for an instant that this might also be the name of some other person, her transport of joy was checked, and seemed to be converted into despair.

Her first emotions over, the habitual firmness of her mind returned. She sent directly to the repository—no news of the boy could there be obtained. Lady N— was gone, for a few days, to Windsor; so no intelligence could be had from her. Mrs. Harcourt was out—no carriage at home—but Mad. de Rosier set out immediately, and walked to Golden-square, near which place she knew that a number of French emigrants resided. She stopped first at a bookseller's shop; she described the person of her son, and inquired if any such person had been seen in that neighbourhood.

The bookseller was making out a bill for one of his customers, but struck with Mad. de Rosier's anxiety, and perceiving that she was a foreigner by her accent, he put down his pen, and begged her to repeat, once more, the description of her son. He tried to recollect whether he had seen such a person—but he had not. He, however, with true English good-nature, told her that she had an excellent chance of finding him in this part of the town, if he were in London—he was sorry that his shopman was from home, or he would have sent him with her through the streets near the square, where he knew the emigrants chiefly lodged;—he gave her in writing a list of the names of these streets, and stood at his door to watch and speed her on her way.

She called at the neighbouring shops—she walked down several narrow streets, inquiring at every house, where she thought that there was any chance of success, in vain. At one a slip-shod maid-servant came to the door, who stared at seeing a well-dressed lady, and who was so bewildered, that she could not, for some time, answer any questions; at another house the master was out; at another, the master was at dinner. As it got towards four o'clock, Mad. de Rosier found it more difficult to obtain civil answers to her inquiries, for almost all the tradesmen were at dinner, and when they came to the door, looked out of humour, at being interrupted, and disappointed at not meeting with a customer. She walked on, her mind still indefatigable:—she heard a clock in the neighbourhood strike five—her strength was not equal to the energy of her mind—and the repeated answers of, "We know of no such person"—"No such boy lives here, ma'am," made her at length despair of success.

One street upon her list remained unsearched—it was narrow, dark, and dirty;—she stopped for a moment at the corner, but a porter, heavily laden, with a sudden "By your leave, ma'am!" pushed forwards, and she was forced into the doorway of a small ironmonger's shop. The master of the shop, who was weighing some iron goods, let the scale go up, and, after a look of surprise, said—

"You've lost your way, madam, I presume—be pleased to rest yourself—it is but a dark place;" and wiping a stool, on which some locks had been lying, he left Mad. de Rosier, who was, indeed, exhausted with fatigue, to rest herself, whilst, without any officious civility, after calling his wife from a back shop, to give the lady a glass of water, he went on weighing his iron and whistling.

The woman, as soon as Mad. de Rosier had drunk the water, inquired if she should send for a coach for her, or could do any thing to serve her.

The extreme good-nature of the tone in which this was spoken seemed to revive Mad. de Rosier; she told her that she was searching for an only son, whom she had for nearly two years believed to be dead: she showed the paper on which his name was written: the woman could not read—her husband read the name, but he shook his head—"he knew of no lad who answered to the description."

Whilst they were speaking, a little boy came into the shop with a bit of small iron wire in his hand, and, twitching the skirt of the ironmonger's coat to attract his attention, asked if he had any such wire as that in his shop. When the ironmonger went to get down a roll of wire, the little boy had a full view of Mad. de Rosier. Though she was naturally disposed to take notice of children, yet now she was so intent upon her own thoughts that she did not observe him till he had bowed several times just opposite to her.

"Are you bowing to me, my good boy?" said she—"you mistake me for somebody else; I don't know you;" and she looked down again upon the paper, on which she had written the name of her son.

"But, indeed, ma'am, I know you," said the little boy: "aren't you the lady that was with the good-natured young gentleman, who met me going out of the pastry-cook's shop, and gave me the two buns?"

Mad. de Rosier now looked in his face; the shop was so dark that she could not distinguish his features, but she recollected his voice, and knew him to be the little boy belonging to the dulcimer man.

"Father would have come again to your house," said the boy, who did not perceive her inattention— "Father would have come to your house again, to play the tune the young gentleman fancied so much, but our dulcimer is broken."

"Is it? I am sorry for it," said Mad. de Rosier. "But can you tell me," continued she to the ironmonger, "whether any emigrants lodge in the street to the left of your house?" The master of the shop tried to recollect: she again repeated the name and description of her son.

"I know a young French lad of that make," said the little dulcimer boy.

"Do you?—Where is he? Where does he lodge?" cried Mad. de Rosier.

"I am not speaking as to his name, for I never heard his name," said the little boy; "but I'll tell you how I came to know him. One day lately—"

Mad. de Rosier interrupted him with questions concerning the figure, height, age, eyes, of the French lad.

The little dulcimer boy, by his answers, sometimes made her doubt, and sometimes made her certain, that he was her son.

"Tell me," said she, "where he lodges; I must see him immediately."

"I am just come from him, and I'm going back to him with the wire; I'll show the way with pleasure; he is the best-natured lad in the world; he is mending my dulcimer; he deserves to be a great gentleman, and I thought he was not what he seemed," continued the little boy, as he walked on, scarcely able to keep before Mad. de Rosier.

"This way, ma'am—this way—he lives in the corner house, turning into Golden-square." It was a stationer's.

"I have called at this house already," said Mad. de Rosier; but she recollected that it was when the family were at dinner, and that a stupid maid had not understood her questions. She was unable to speak, through extreme agitation, when she came to the shop: the little dulcimer boy walked straight forward, and gently drew back the short curtain that hung before a glass door, opening into a back parlour. Mad. de Rosier sprang forward to the door, looked through the glass, and was alarmed to see a young man taller than her son; he was at work; his back was towards her.

When he heard the noise of some one trying to open the door, he turned and saw his mother's face! The tools dropped from his hands, and the dulcimer boy was the only person present who had strength enough to open the door.

How sudden! how powerful is the effect of joy! The mother, restored to her son, in a moment felt herself invigorated—and, forgetful of her fatigue, she felt herself another being. When she was left alone with her son, she looked round his little workshop with a mixture of pain and pleasure. She saw one of his unfinished boxes on the window-seat, which served him for a work-bench; his tools were upon the floor. "These have been my support," said her son, taking them up: "how much am I obliged to my dear father for teaching me early how to use them!"

"Your father!" said Mad. de Rosier—"I wish he could have lived to be rewarded as I am! But tell me your history, from the moment you were taken from me to prison: it is nearly two years ago,—how did you escape? how have you supported yourself since? Sit down, and speak again, that I may be sure that I hear your voice."

"You shall hear my voice, then, my dear mother," said her son, "for at least half an hour, if that will not tire you. I have a long story to tell you. In the first place, you know that I was taken to prison; three months I spent in the Conciergerie, expecting every day to be ordered out to the guillotine. The gaoler's son, a boy about my own age, who was sometimes employed to bring me food, seemed to look upon me with compassion; I had several opportunities of obliging him: his father often gave him long returns of the names of the prisoners, and various accounts, to copy into a large book; the young gentleman did not like this work; he was much fonder of exercising as a soldier with some boys in the neighbourhood, who were learning the national exercise; he frequently employed me to copy his lists for him, and this I performed to his satisfaction: but what completely won his heart was my mending the lock of his fusil. One evening he came to me in a new uniform, and in high spirits; he was just made a captain, by the unanimous voice of his corps; and he talked of his men, and his orders, with prodigious fluency; he then played his march upon his drum, and insisted upon teaching it to me; he was much pleased with my performance, and, suddenly embracing me, he exclaimed, 'I have thought of an excellent thing for you; stay till I have arranged the plan in my head, and you shall see if I am not a great general.' The next evening he did not come to me till it was nearly dusk; he was in his new uniform; but out of a bag which he brought in his hand, in which he used to carry his father's papers, he produced his old uniform, rolled up into a surprisingly small compass. 'I have arranged every thing,' said he; 'put on this old uniform of mine—we are just of a size—by this light, nobody will perceive any difference: take my drum and march out of the prison slowly; beat my march on the drum as you go out; turn to the left, down to the Place de —, where I exercise my men. You'll meet with one of my soldiers there, ready to forward your escape.' I hesitated; for I feared that I should endanger my young general; but he assured me that he had taken his precautions so 'admirably,' that even after my escape should be discovered, no suspicion would fall upon him. 'But, if you delay,' cried he, 'we are both of us undone.' I hesitated not a moment longer, and never did I change my clothes so expeditiously in my life: I obeyed my little captain exactly, marched out of the prison slowly, playing deliberately the march which I had been taught; turned to the left, according to orders, and saw my punctual guide waiting for me on the Place de —, just by the broken statue of Henry the Fourth.

"'Follow me, fellow-citizen,' said he, in a low voice; 'we are not all Robespierres.'"

Most joyfully I followed him. We walked on, in silence, till at length we came to a narrow street, where the crowd was so great that I thought we should both of us have been squeezed to death. I saw the guillotine at a distance, and I felt sick.

"'Come on,' said my guide, who kept fast hold of me; and he turned sharp into a yard, where I heard the noise of carts, and the voices of muleteers. 'This man,' said he, leading me up to a muleteer, who seemed to be just ready to depart, 'is my father; trust yourself to him.'

"I had nobody else to trust myself to. I got into the muleteer's covered cart; he began a loud song; we proceeded through the square where the crowd were assembled. The enthusiasm of the moment occupied them so entirely, that we were fortunately disregarded. We got out of Paris safely: I will not tire you with all my terrors and escapes. I, at length, got on board a neutral vessel, and landed at Bristol. Escaped from prison, and the fear of the guillotine, I thought myself happy; but my happiness was not very lasting. I began to apprehend that I should be starved to death; I had not eaten for many hours. I wandered through the bustling streets of Bristol, where every body I met seemed to be full of their own business, and brushed by me without seeing me. I was weak, and I sat down upon a stone by the door of a public-house.

"A woman was twirling a mop at the door. I wiped away the drops with which I was sprinkled by this operation. I was too weak to be angry; but a hairdresser, who was passing by, and who had a nicely powdered wig poised upon his hand, was furiously enraged, because a few drops of the shower which had sprinkled me reached the wig. He expressed his anger half in French and half in English; but at last I observed to him in French, that the wig was still 'bien poudrée'—this calmed his rage; and he remarked that I also had been horribly drenched by the shower. I assured him that this was a trifle in comparison with my other sufferings.

"He begged to hear my misfortunes, because I spoke French; and as I followed him to the place where he was going with the wig, I told him that I had not eaten for many hours; that I was a stranger in Bristol, and had no means of earning any food. He advised me to go to a tavern, which he pointed out to me— 'The Rummer;'—he told me a circumstance, which convinced me of the humanity of the master of the house.(4)

(Footnote 4: During Christmas week it is the custom in Bristol to keep a cheap ordinary in taverns: the master of the Rummer observed a stranger, meanly dressed, who constantly frequented the public table. It was suspected that he carried away some of the provision, and a waiter at length communicated his suspicions to the master of the house. He watched the stranger, and actually detected him putting a large mince-pie into his pocket. Instead of publicly exposing him, the landlord, who judged from the stranger's manner that he was not an ordinary pilferer, called the man aside as he was going away, and charged him with the fact, demanding of him what could tempt him to such meanness. The poor man immediately acknowledged that he had for several days carried off precisely what he would have eaten himself for his starving wife, but he had eaten nothing. The humane, considerate landlord gently reproved him for his conduct, and soon found means to have him usefully and profitably employed.)

"I resolved to apply to this benevolent man. When I first went into his kitchen, I saw his cook, a man with a very important face, serving out a large turtle. Several people were waiting with covered dishes, for turtle soup and turtle, which had been bespoken in different parts of the city. The dishes, as fast as they were filled, continually passed by me, tantalizing me by their savoury odours. I sat down upon a stool near the fire—I saw food within my reach that honesty forbade me to touch, though I was starving: how easy is it to the rich to be honest! I was at this time so weak, that my ideas began to be confused— my head grew dizzy—I felt the heat of the kitchen fire extremely disagreeable to me. I do not know what happened afterward; but when I came to myself, I found that I was leaning against some one who supported me near an open window: it was the master of the house. I do not know why I was ashamed to ask him for food; his humanity, however, prevented me. He first gave me a small basin of broth, and afterwards a little bit of bread, assuring me, with infinite good nature, that he gave me food in such small quantities, because he was afraid that it would hurt me to satisfy my hunger at once—a worthy, humane physician, he said, had told him, that persons in my situation should be treated in this manner. I thanked him for his kindness, adding, that I did not mean to encroach upon his hospitality. He pressed me to stay at his house for some days, but I could not think of being a burden to him, when I had strength enough to maintain myself.

"In the window of the little parlour, where I ate my broth, I saw a novel, which had been left there by the landlord's daughter, and in the beginning of this book was pasted a direction to the circulating library in Bristol. I was in hopes that I might earn my bread as a scribe. The landlord of the Rummer told me that he was acquainted with the master of the library, and that I might easily procure employment from him on reasonable terms.

"Mr. S—, for that was the name of the master of the library, received me with an air of encouraging benevolence, and finding that I could read and write English tolerably well, he gave me a manuscript to copy, which he was preparing for the press. I worked hard, and made, as I fancied, a beautiful copy; but the printers complained of my upright French hand, which they could not easily decipher:—I began to new-model my writing, to please the taste of my employers; and as I had sufficient motives to make me take pains, I at last succeeded. I found it a great advantage to be able to read and write the English language fluently; and when my employers perceived my education had not been neglected, and that I had some knowledge of literature, their confidence in my abilities increased. I hope you will not think me vain if I add, that I could perceive my manners were advantageous to me. I was known to be a gentleman's son; and even those who set but little value upon manners seemed to be influenced by them, without perceiving it. But, without pronouncing my own eulogium, let me content myself with telling you my history.

"I used often, in carrying my day's work to the printer's, to pass through a part of the town of Bristol which has been allotted to poor emigrants, and there I saw a variety of little ingenious toys, which were sold at a high price, or at a price which appeared to me to be high. I began to consider that I might earn money by invention, as well as by mere manual labour; but before I gave up any part of my time to my new schemes, I regularly wrote as much each day as was sufficient to maintain me. Now it was that I felt the advantage of having been taught, when I was a boy, the use of carpenters' tools, and some degree of mechanical dexterity. I made several clumsy toys, and I tried various unsuccessful experiments, but I was not discouraged. One day I heard a dispute near me about some trinket—a toothpick-case, I believe—which was thought by the purchaser to be too highly priced; the man who made it repeatedly said, in recommendation of the toy—'Why, sir, you could not know it from tortoise-shell.'

"I, at this instant, recollected to have seen, at the Rummer, a great heap of broken shells, which the cook had thrown aside, as if they were of no value. Upon inquiry, I found that there was part of the inside shell which was thought to be useless—it occurred to me that I might possibly make it useful. The good-natured landlord ordered that all this part of the shells should be carefully collected and given to me. I tried to polish it for many hours in vain. I was often tempted to abandon my project—there was a want of finish, as the workmen call it, in my manufacture, which made me despair of its being saleable. I will not weary you with a history of all my unsuccessful processes; it was fortunate for me, my dear mother, that I remembered one of the principles which you taught me when I was a child, that it is not genius, but perseverance, which brings things to perfection. I persevered, and though I did not bring my manufacture to perfection, I actually succeeded so far as to make a very neat-looking box out of my refuse shells. I offered it for sale—it was liked: I made several more, and they were quickly sold for me, most advantageously, by my good friend, Mr. S—. He advised me to make them in the shape of netting-boxes; I did so, and their sale extended rapidly.

"Some benevolent lady, about this time, raised a subscription for me; but as I had now an easy means of supporting myself, and as I every day beheld numbers of my countrymen, nearly in the condition in which I was when I first went to the Rummer, I thought it was not fit to accept of the charitable assistance, which could be so much better bestowed upon others. Mr. S— told me, that the lady who raised the contribution, so far from being offended, was pleased by my conduct in declining her bounty, and she undertook to dispose of as many of my netting-boxes as I could finish. She was one of the patronesses of a repository in London, which has lately been opened, called the 'Repository for Ingenious Works.' When she left Bristol, she desired Mr. S— to send my boxes thither.

"My little manufacture continued to prosper—by practice I grew more and more expert, and I had no longer any fears that I should not be able to maintain myself. It was fortunate for me that I was obliged to be constantly employed: whenever I was not actually at hard work, whenever I had leisure for reflection, I was unhappy.

"A friend of Mr. S—, who was going to London, offered to take me with him—I had some curiosity to see this celebrated metropolis, and I had hopes of meeting with some of my friends amongst the emigrants in this city—amongst all the emigrants at Bristol there was not one person with whom I had been acquainted in France.

"Impelled by these hopes, I quitted Bristol, and arrived a few weeks ago in London. Mr. S— gave me a direction to a cabinet-maker in Leicester Fields, and I was able to pay for a decent lodging, for I was now master of what appeared to me a large sum of money—seven guineas.

"Some time after I came to town, as I was returning from a visit to an emigrant, with whom I had become acquainted, I was stopped at the corner of a street by a crowd of people—a mob, as I have been taught to call it, since I came to England—who had gathered round a blind man, a little boy, and a virago of a woman, who stood upon the steps before a print-shop door. The woman accused the boy of being a thief. The boy protested that he was innocent, and his ingenuous countenance spoke strongly in his favour. He belonged to the blind man, who, as soon as he could make himself heard, complained bitterly of the damage which had been done to his dulcimer. The mob, in their first fury, had broken it. I was interested for the man but more for the boy. Perhaps, said I to myself, he has neither father nor mother!

"When the woman, who was standing yet furious at the shop-door, had no more words for utterance, the little boy was suffered to speak in his own defence. He said, that, as he was passing by the open window of the print-shop, he put his hand in to give part of a bun which he was eating to a little dog, who was sitting on the counter, near the window; and who looked thin and miserable, as if he was half-starved. 'But,' continued the little boy, 'when I put the bun to the dog's mouth, he did not eat it; I gave him a little push to make him mind me, and he fell out of the window into my hands; and then I found that it was not a real dog, but only the picture of a dog, painted upon pasteboard. The mistress of the shop saw the dog in my hand, and snatched it away, and accused me of being a thief; so then, with the noise she made, the chairmen, who were near the door, came up, and the mob gathered, and our dulcimer was broken, and I'm very sorry for it.' The mistress of the print-shop observed, in a loud and contemptuous tone, 'that all this must be a lie, for that such a one as he could not have buns to give away to dogs!'—Here the blind man vindicated his boy, by assuring us that 'he came honestly by the bun—that two buns had been given to him about an hour before this time by a young gentleman, who met him as he was coming out of a pastry-cook's shop.' When the mob heard this explanation, they were sorry for the mischief they had done to the blind man's dulcimer; and, after examining it with expressions of sorrow, they quietly dispersed. I thought that I could perhaps mend the dulcimer, and I offered my services; they were gladly accepted, and I desired the man to leave it at the cabinet-maker's, in Leicester Fields, where I lodged. In the meantime the little boy, whilst I had been examining the dulcimer, had been wiping the dirt from off the pasteboard dog, which, during the fray, had fallen into the street—'Is it not like a real dog?' said the boy, 'Was it not enough to deceive any body?'

"It was, indeed, extremely like a real dog—like my dog, Caesar, whom I had taken care of from the time I was five years old, and whom I was obliged to leave at our house in Paris, when I was dragged to prison. The more I looked at this pasteboard image, the more I was convinced that the picture must have been drawn from the life. Every streak, every spot, every shade of its brown coat I remembered. Its extreme thinness was the only circumstance in which the picture was unlike my Caesar. I inquired from the scolding woman of the shop how she came by this picture—'Honestly,' was her laconic answer; but when I asked whether it were to be sold, and when I paid its price, the lady changed her tone; no longer considering me as the partisan of the little boy, against whom she was enraged, but rather looking upon me as a customer, who had paid too much for her goods, she condescended to inform me that the dog was painted by one of the poor French emigrants, who lived in her neighbourhood. She directed me to the house, and I discovered the man to be my father's old servant Michael. He was overjoyed at the sight of me; he was infirm, and unequal to any laborious employment; he had supported himself with great difficulty by painting toys, and various figures of men, women, and animals, upon pasteboard. He showed me two excellent figures of French poissardes, and also a good cat, of his doing;—but my Caesar was the best of his works.

"My lodgings at the cabinet-maker's were too small to accommodate Michael; and yet I wished to have him with me, for he seemed so infirm as to want assistance. I consequently left my cabinet-maker, and took lodgings with this stationer; he and his wife are quiet people, and I hope poor Michael has been happier since he came to me; he has, however, been for some days confined to his bed, and I have been so busy, that I have not been able to stir from home. To-day the poor little boy called for his dulcimer; I must own that I found it a more difficult job to mend it than I had expected. I could not match the wire, and I sent the boy out to an ironmonger's a few hours ago. How little did I expect to see him return with—my mother!"

We shall not attempt to describe the alternate emotions of joy and sorrow which quickly succeeded each other in Mad. de Rosier's heart, while she listened to her son's little history. Impatient to communicate her happiness to her friends, she took leave hastily of her beloved son, promising to call for him early the next day. "Settle all your business to-night," said she, "and I will introduce you to my friends to-morrow. My friends, I say proudly—for I have made friends since I came to England; and England, amongst other commodities excellent in their kind, produces incomparable friends—friends in adversity. We know their value. Adieu: settle all your affairs here expeditiously."

"I have no affairs, no business, my dear mother," interrupted Henry, "except to mend the dulcimer, as I promised, and that I'll finish directly. Adieu, till to-morrow morning! What a delightful sound!"

With all the alacrity of benevolence he returned to his work, and his mother returned to Mrs. Harcourt's. It was nearly eight o'clock before she arrived at home. Mrs. Harcourt, Isabella, and Matilda, met her with inquiring eyes.

"She smiles," said Matilda; and Herbert, with a higher jump than he had ever been known to make before, exclaimed, "She has found her son!—I am sure of it!—I knew she would find him."

"Let her sit down," said Matilda, in a gentle voice.

Isabella brought her an excellent dish of coffee; and Mrs. Harcourt, with kind reproaches, asked why she had not brought her son home with her. She rang the bell with as much vivacity as she spoke, ordered her coach to be sent instantly to Golden-square, and wrote an order, as she called it, for his coming immediately to her, quitting all dulcimers and dulcimer boys, under pain of his mother's displeasure. "Here, Mad. de Rosier," said she, with peremptory playfulness, "countersign my order, that I may be sure of my prisoner."

Scarcely were the note and carriage despatched, before Herbert and Favoretta stationed themselves at the window, that they might be ready to give the first intelligence. Their notions of time and distance were not very accurate upon this occasion; for before the carriage had been out of sight ten minutes, they expected it to return; and they exclaimed, at the sight of every coach that appeared at the end of the street, "Here's the carriage!—Here he is!" But the carriages rolled by continually, and convinced them of their mistakes.

Herbert complained of the dull light of the lamps, though the street was remarkably well lighted; and he next quarrelled with the glare of the flambeaux, which footmen brandished behind carriages that were unknown to him. At length a flambeau appeared with which he did not quarrel. Herbert, as its light shone upon the footman, looked with an eager eye, then put his finger upon his own lips, and held his other hand forcibly before Favoretta's mouth, for now he was certain. The coach stopped at the door—Mad. de Rosier ran down stairs—Mrs. Harcourt and all the family followed her—Herbert was at the coach door before Henri de Rosier could leap out, and he seized his hand with the familiarity of an old acquaintance.

The sympathy of all her joyful pupils, the animated kindness with which Mrs. Harcourt received her son, touched Mad. de Rosier with the most exquisite pleasure. The happiness that we are conscious of having deserved is doubly grateful to the heart.

Mrs. Harcourt did not confine her attentions within the narrow limits of politeness—with generous eagerness she exerted herself to show her gratitude to the excellent governess of her children. She applied to the gentleman who was at the head of the academy for the education of the sons of French emigrants, and recommended Henri de Rosier to him in the strongest terms.

In the meantime Lady N—, who had been warmly interested in Mad. de Rosier's favour, and more by what she had seen of her pupils, wrote to her brother, who was at Paris, to request that he would make every possible inquiry concerning the property of the late Comte de Rosier. The answer to her letter informed her that Mad. de Rosier's property was restored to her and to her son by the new government of France.

Mrs. Harcourt, who now foresaw the probability of Mad. de Rosier's return to France, could not avoid feeling regret at the thoughts of parting with a friend to whom her whole family was sincerely attached. The plan of education which had been traced out remained yet unfinished, and she feared, she said, that Isabella and Matilda might feel the want of their accomplished preceptress. But these fears were the best omens for her future success: a sensible mother, in whom the desire to educate her family has once been excited, and who turns the energy of her mind to this interesting subject, seizes upon every useful idea, every practical principle, with avidity, and she may trust securely to her own persevering cares. Whatever a mother learns for the sake of her children, she never forgets.

The rapid improvement of Mrs. Harcourt's understanding since she had applied herself to literature, was her reward, and her excitement to fresh application. Isabella and Matilda were now of an age to be her companions, and her taste for domestic life was confirmed every day by the sweet experience of its pleasures.

"You have taught me your value, and now you are going to leave me," said she to Mad. de Rosier. "I quarrelled with the Duke de la Rochefoucault for his asserting, that in the misfortunes of our best friends there is always something that is not disagreeable to us; but I am afraid I must stand convicted of selfishness, for in the good fortune of my best friend there is something that I cannot feel to be perfectly agreeable."

MADEMOISELLE PANACHE.
SECOND PART(1)
(Footnote 1: The first part is in the Parent's Assistant, vol. iv.)

The tendency of any particular mode of education is not always perceived, before it is too late to change the habits or the character of the pupil. To superficial observers, children of nearly the same age often seem much alike in manners and disposition, who, in a few years afterward, appear in every respect strikingly different. We have given our readers some idea of the manner in which Mrs. Temple educated her daughters, and some notion of the mode in which Lady Augusta was managed by Mlle. Panache; the difference between the characters of Helen and Lady Augusta, though visible even at the early age of twelve or thirteen to an intelligent mother, was scarcely noticed by common acquaintance, who contented themselves with the usual phrases, as equally applicable to both the young ladies. "Upon my word, Lady Augusta and Miss Helen Temple are both of them very fine girls, and very highly accomplished, and vastly well educated, as I understand. I really cannot tell which to prefer. Lady Augusta, to be sure, is rather the taller of the two, and her manners are certainly more womanly and fashioned than Miss Helen's; but then, Miss Helen Temple has something of simplicity about her that some people think very engaging. For my part, I don't pretend to judge—girls alter so; there's no telling at twelve years old what they may turn out at sixteen."

From twelve to sixteen, Lady Augusta continued under the direction of Mlle. Panache; whilst her mother, content with her daughter's progress in external accomplishments, paid no attention to the cultivation of her temper or her understanding. Lady S— lived much in what is called the world; was fond of company, and fonder of cards, sentimentally anxious to be thought a good mother, but indolently willing to leave her daughter wholly to the care of a French governess, whose character she had never taken the trouble to investigate. Not that Lady S— could be ignorant that, however well qualified to teach the true French pronunciation, she could not be a perfectly eligible companion for her daughter as she grew up: her ladyship intended to part with the governess when Lady Augusta was fifteen; but from day to day, and from year to year, this was put off: sometimes Lady S— thought it a pity to dismiss mademoiselle, because "she was the best creature in the world;" sometimes she rested content with the idea, that six months more or less could not signify; till at length family reasons obliged her to postpone mademoiselle's dismission: part of the money intended for the payment of the governess's salary had been unfortunately lost by the mother at the card-table. Lady Augusta consequently continued under the auspices of Mlle. Panache till her ladyship was eighteen, and till her education was supposed to be entirely completed.

In the meantime Mlle. Panache endeavoured, by all the vulgar arts of flattery, to ingratiate herself with her pupil, in hopes that from a governess she might become a companion. The summer months seemed unusually long to the impatient young lady, whose imagination daily anticipated the glories of her next winter's campaign. Towards the end of July, however, a reinforcement of visitors came to her mother's, and the present began to engage some attention, as well as the future. Amongst these visitors was Lord George —, a young nobleman, near twenty-one, who was heir to a very considerable fortune. We mention his fortune first, because it was his first merit, even in his own opinion. Cold, silent, selfish, supercilious, and silly, there appeared nothing in him to engage the affections, or to strike the fancy of a fair lady; but Lady Augusta's fancy was not fixed upon his lordship's character or manners, and much that might have disgusted consequently escaped her observation. Her mother had not considered the matter very attentively; but she thought that this young nobleman might be no bad match for her Augusta, and she trusted that her daughter's charms would make their due impression on his heart. Some weeks passed away in fashionable negligence of the lady on his part, and alternate pique and coquetry on hers, whilst, during these operations, her confidante and governess was too much occupied with her own manoeuvres to attend to those of her pupil. Lord George had with him upon this visit a Mr. Dashwood, who was engaged to accompany him upon his travels, and who had had the honour of being his lordship's tutor. At the name of a tutor, let no one picture to himself a gloomy pedant; or yet a man whose knowledge, virtue, and benevolence, would command the respect, or win the affections, of youth. Mr. Dashwood could not be mistaken for a pedant, unless a coxcomb be a sort of pedant. Dashwood pretended neither to win affection nor to command respect; but he was, as his pupil emphatically swore, "the best fellow in the world." Upon this best fellow in the world, Mlle. Panache fixed her sagacious hopes; she began to think that it would be infinitely better to be the wife of the gallant Mr. Dashwood, than the humble companion or the slighted governess of the capricious Lady Augusta. Having thus far opened the views and characters of these various personages, we shall now give our readers an opportunity of judging of them by their words and actions.

"You go with us, my lord, to the archery-meeting this evening?" said Lady S—, as she rose from breakfast—his lordship gave a negligent assent.

"Ah!" exclaimed Mlle. Panache, turning eagerly to Dashwood, "have you seen de uniforme?—C'est charmant; and I have no small hand in it."

Dashwood paid the expected compliment to her taste. "Ah! non," said she, "you are too good, too flattering; but you must tell me your judgment without flattery! Vous êtes homme de goût, though an Englishman—you see I have got no préjugés." Dashwood bowed. "Allons!" said she, starting up with vast gaiety: "we have got no time to lose. I have de rubans to put to de bow; I must go and attend my Diane."

"Attend her Diane!" repeated Dashwood, the moment the door was shut, and he was left alone with Lord George. "Attend her Diane! a very proper attendant." Lord George was wholly indifferent to propriety or impropriety upon this, as upon all other subjects. "What are we to do with ourselves, I wonder, this morning!" said he, with his customary yawn; and he walked towards the window. The labour of finding employment for his lordship always devolved upon his companion. "I thought, my lord," said Dashwood, "you talked yesterday of going upon the water; the river is very smooth, and I hope we shall have a fine day."

"I hope so too; but over the hill yonder it looks confounded black, hey? Well, at any rate we may go down and make some of them get ready to go with us. I'll take my black Tom—he's a handy fellow."

"But if you take black Tom," said Dashwood, laughing, "we must not expect to have the ladies of our party; for you know mademoiselle has an unconquerable antipaty, as she calls it, to a negro."

Lord George declared that, for this very reason, he would order black Tom down to the water-side, and that he should enjoy her affectation, or her terror, whichever it was, of all things. "I suppose," said he, "she'll scream as loud as Lady Augusta screamed at a frog the other day."

"I'll lay you a wager I spoil your sport, my lord; I'll lay you a guinea I get mademoiselle into the boat without a single scream," said Dashwood.

"Done!" said Lord George. "Two to one she screams."

"Done!" said Dashwood; and he hoped that, by proposing this bet, he had provided his pupil with an object for the whole morning. But Lord George was not so easily roused immediately after breakfast. "It looks terribly like rain," said he, going back and forward irresolutely between the door and the window. "Do you think it will rain, hey?"

"No, no; I'm sure it will not rain."

"I wouldn't lay two to one of that, however: look at this great cloud that's coming."

"Oh! it will blow over."

"I don't know that," said Lord George, shaking his head with great solemnity. "Which way is the wind?" opening the window. "Well, I believe it may hold up, hey?"

"Certainly—I think so."

"Then I'll call black Tom, hey?—though I think one grows tired of going upon the water," muttered his lordship, as he left the room. "Couldn't one find something better?"

"Nothing better," thought Dashwood, "but to hang yourself, my lord, which, I'll be bound, you'll do before you are forty, for want of something better. But that's not my affair."

"Where's mademoiselle?" cried Lady Augusta, entering hastily, with a bow and arrow in her hand: "I've lost my quiver: where's mademoiselle?"

"Upon my word I don't know," said Dashwood, assuming an air of interest.

"You don't know, Mr. Dashwood!" said Lady Augusta, sarcastically; "that's rather extraordinary. I make it a rule, whenever I want mademoiselle, to ask where you are, and I never found myself disappointed before."

"I am sorry, madam, you should ever be disappointed," said Dashwood, laughing. "Is this your ladyship's own taste?" added he, taking the painted bow out of her hand. "It's uncommonly pretty."

"Pretty or not, Lord George did not think it worth while to look at it last night. His lordship will go through the world mighty easily, don't you think so, Mr. Dashwood?" Dashwood attempted an apology for his pupil, but in such a sort, as if he did not mean it to be accepted, and then, returning the bow to her ladyship's hand, paused, sighed, and observed, that, upon the whole, it was happy for his lordship that he possessed so much nonchalance. "Persons of a different cast," continued he, "cannot, as your ladyship justly observes, expect to pass through life so easily." This speech was pronounced in a tone so different from Dashwood's usual careless gaiety, that Lady Augusta could not help being struck with it; and by her vanity, it was interpreted precisely as the gentleman wished. Rank and fortune were her serious objects, but she had no objection to amusing herself with romance. The idea of seeing the gay, witty Mr. Dashwood metamorphosed, by the power of her charms, into a despairing, sighing swain, played upon her imagination, and she heard his first sigh with a look which plainly showed how well she understood its meaning.

"Why now, was there ever any thing so provoking!" cried Lord George, swinging himself into the room.

"What's the matter, my lord?" said Dashwood.

"Why, don't you see, it's raining as hard as it can rain?" replied his lordship, with the true pathos of a man whose happiness is dependent upon the weather. His scheme of going upon the water being now impracticable, he lounged about the room all the rest of the morning, supporting that miserable kind of existence, which idle gentlemen are doomed to support, they know not how, upon a rainy day. Neither Lady Augusta nor her mother, in calculating the advantages and disadvantages of an alliance with his lordship, ever once considered his habits of listless idleness as any objection in a companion for life.

After dinner the day cleared up—the ladies were dressed in their archery uniform—the carriages came to the door, and Lord George was happy in the prospect of driving his new phaeton. Dashwood handed the ladies to their coach; for his lordship was too much engaged in confabulation with his groom, on the merits of his off-leader, to pay attention to any thing else upon earth.

His phaeton was presently out of sight, for he gloried in driving as fast as possible; and, to reward his exertions, he had the satisfaction of hearing two strangers, as he passed them, say—"Ha! upon my word, those horses go well!" A postilion at a turnpike gate, moreover, exclaimed to a farmer, who stood with his mouth wide open—"There goes Lord George! he cuts as fine a figure on the road as e'er a man in England." Such was the style of praise of which this young nobleman was silly enough to be vain.

"I've been in these three quarters of an hour!" cried he, exultingly, as Lady S— got out of her coach.

"There has been no shooting yet though, I hope?" said Lady Augusta.

"No, no, ma'am," replied Dashwood; "but the ladies are all upon the green—a crowd of fair competitors; but I'd bet a thousand pounds upon your ladyship's arrows. Make way there—make way," cried the man of gallantry, in an imperious tone, to some poor people, who crowded round the carriage; and talking and laughing loud, he pushed forward, making as much bustle in seating the ladies as they could have wished. Being seated, they began to bow and nod to their acquaintance. "There's Mrs. Temple and her daughters," said Lady S—.

"Where, ma'am?" said Lady Augusta: "I'm sure I did not expect to meet them here. Where are they?"

"Just opposite to us. Pray, Mr. Dashwood, who is that gentleman in brown, who is talking to Miss Helen Temple?" "Upon my word I don't know, madam; he bowed just now to Lord George."

"Did he?" said Lady Augusta. "I wonder who he is!"

Lord George soon satisfied her curiosity, for, coming up to them, he said negligently, "Dashwood, there's young Mountague yonder."

"Ha! is that young Mountague? Well, is his father dead? What has he done with that old quiz?"

"Ask him yourself," said Lord George sullenly: "I asked him just now, and he looked as black as November."

"He was so fond of his father—it is quite a bore," said Dashwood. "I think he'll be a quiz himself in due time."

"No," said Lord George; "he knows better than that too in some things. He has a monstrous fine horse with him here; and that's a good pretty girl that he's going to marry."

"Is he going to be married to Miss Helen Temple?" said Lady S—. "Who is he, pray? I hope a suitable match."

"That I can't tell, for I don't know what she has," replied Lord George. "But Mountague can afford to do as he pleases—very good family—fine fortune."

"Yes; old quiz made an excellent nurse to his estate," observed Dashwood; "he owes him some gratitude for that."

"Is not he very young to settle in the world?" said Lady S—.

"Young—yes—only a year older than I am," said Lord George; "but I knew he'd never be quiet till he got himself noosed."

"I suppose he'll be at the ball to-night," said Lady Augusta, "and then we shall see something of him, perhaps. It's an age since we've seen the Miss Temples any where. I wonder whether there's any thing more than report, my lord, in this conquest of Miss Helen Temple? Had you the thing from good authority?"

"Authority!" said Lord George; "I don't recollect my authority, faith!—somebody said so to me, I think. It's nothing to me, at any rate." Lady Augusta's curiosity, however, was not quite so easily satisfied as his lordship's; she was resolved to study Mr. Mountague thoroughly at the ball; and her habitual disposition to coquetry, joined to a dislike of poor Helen, which originated whilst they were children, made her form a strong desire to rival Helen in the admiration of this young gentleman of—"very good family and fine fortune." Her ladyship was just falling into a reverie upon this subject, when she was summoned to join the archeresses.

The prize was a silver arrow. The ladies were impatient to begin—the green was cleared. Some of the spectators took their seats on benches under the trees, whilst a party of gentlemen stood by, to supply the ladies with arrows. Three ladies shot, but widely from the mark; a fourth tried her skill, but no applause ensued; a fifth came forward, a striking figure, elegantly dressed, who, after a prelude of very becoming diffidence, drew her bow, and took aim in the most graceful attitude imaginable.

"Who is that beautiful creature?" exclaimed Mr. Mountague, with enthusiasm; and as the arrow flew from the bow, he started up, wishing it success.

"The nearest, by six inches, that has been shot yet," cried Dashwood. "Here, sir! here!" said he to Mr. Mountague, who went up to examine the target, "this is Lady Augusta S—'s arrow, within the second circle, almost put out the bull's eye!" The clamour of applause at length subsiding, several other arrows were shot, but none came near to Lady Augusta's, and the prize was unanimously acknowledged to be hers.

The silver arrow was placed on high over the mark, and several gentlemen tried to reach it in vain: Mr. Mountague sprung from the ground with great activity, brought down the arrow, and presented it, with an air of gallantry, to the fair victor.

"My dear Helen," said Emma to her sister, in a low voice, "you are not well."

"I!" replied Helen, turning quickly: "why! can you think me so mean as to—"

"Hush, hush! you don't consider how loud you are speaking."

"Am I?" said Helen, alarmed, and lowering her tone; "but then, why did you say I was not well?"

"Because you looked so pale."

"Pale! I'm sure I don't look pale," said Helen—"do I?"

"Not now, indeed," said Emma, smiling.

"Was not it an excellent shot?" said Mr. Mountague, returning to them; "but you were not near enough to see it; do come and look at it." Mrs. Temple rose and followed him.—"I can't say," continued he, "that I particularly admire lady archeresses; but this really is a surprising shot."

"It really is a surprising shot," said Helen, looking at it quite at ease. But a moment afterwards she observed that Mr. Mountague's eyes were not intent upon the surprising shot, but were eagerly turned to another side of the green, where, illuminated by the rays of the setting sun, stood a beautiful figure, playing with a silver arrow, totally unconscious, as he imagined, either of her own charms or his admiration.—"Are you acquainted with Lady Augusta?" said Mr. Mountague.

"Yes," said Mrs. Temple. "Are you?"

"Not yet; but I have met her mother often in town—a silly, card-playing woman. I hope her daughter is as little like her in her mind as in her person." Here Mr. Mountague paused, for they had walked up quite close to the seemingly unconscious beauty.—"Oh, Mrs. Temple!" said she, starting, and then recovering herself, with an innocent smile—"is it you? I beg ten thousand pardons," and, offering a hand to Helen and Emma, seemed delighted to see them. Helen involuntarily drew back her hand, with as much coldness as she could without being absolutely rude.

It was now late in the evening, and as the ball was to begin at ten, the ladies called for their carriages, that they might drive to their lodgings, in an adjacent town, to change their dress. In the crowd, Helen happened to be pretty close behind Lady S—, so close, that she could not avoid hearing her conversation.

"Dear ma'am!" an elderly lady in black was saying to her, "I can assure you, your ladyship has been misinformed. I assure you, it is no such thing. He's a relation of the family—he has paid a long visit in this country, but then it is a parting visit to his uncle: he sets out immediately for Italy, I'm told. I assure you, your ladyship has been misinformed; he and his uncle are often at Mrs. Temple's; but depend upon it he has no thoughts of Miss Helen."

These words struck Helen to the heart: she walked on, leaning upon her sister's arm, who fortunately happened to know where she was going. Emma helped her sister to recollect that it was necessary to get into the carriage when the step was let down. The carriage presently stopped with them at the inn, and they were shown to their rooms. Helen sat down, the moment she got up stairs, without thinking of dressing; and her mother's hair was half finished, when she turned round and said, "Why, Helen, my dear! you certainly will not be ready."

"Shan't I, ma'am?" said Helen, starting up. "Is there any occasion that we should dress any more?"

"Nay, my dear," said Mrs. Temple, laughing, "look in the glass at your hair; it has been blown all over your face by the wind."

"It is a great deal of useless trouble," said Helen, as she began the duties of the toilette.

"Why, Helen, this is a sudden fit of laziness," said her mother.

"No, indeed, mamma; I'm not lazy. But I really don't think it signifies. Nobody will take notice how I am dressed, I dare say."

"A sudden fit of humility, then?" said Mrs. Temple, still laughing.

"No, ma'am; but you have often told us how little it signifies. When the ball is over, every thing about it is forgotten in a few hours."

"Oh, a sudden fit of philosophy, Helen?"

"No, indeed, mother," said Helen, sighing; "I'm sure I don't pretend to any philosophy."

"Well, then, a sudden fit of caprice, Helen?"

"No, indeed, ma'am!"

"No, indeed, ma'am!" said Mrs. Temple, still rallying her.—Why, Helen, my dear, you have answered 'No, indeed, ma'am,' to every thing I've said this half hour."

"No, indeed, mother," said Helen; "but I assure you, ma'am," continued she, in a hurried manner, "if you would only give me leave to explain—"

"My dear child," said Mrs. Temple, "this is no time for explanations: make haste and dress yourself, and follow me down to tea." Mr. Mountague was engaged to drink tea with Mrs. Temple.

How many reflections sometimes pass rapidly in the mind in the course of a few minutes!

"I am weak, ridiculous, and unjust," said Helen to herself. "Because Lady Augusta won a silver arrow, am I vexed? Why should I be displeased with Mr. Mountague's admiring her? I will appear no more like a fool; and Heaven forbid I should become envious."

As this last thought took possession of her mind, she finished dressing herself, and went with Emma down to tea. The well-wrought-up dignity with which Helen entered the parlour was, however, thrown away upon this occasion; for opposite to her mother at the tea-table there appeared, instead of Mr. Mountague, only an empty chair, and an empty teacup and saucer, with a spoon in it. He was gone to the ball; and when Mrs. Temple and her daughters arrived there, they found him at the bottom of the country dance, talking in high spirits to his partner, Lady Augusta, who, in the course of the evening, cast many looks of triumph upon Helen. But Helen kept to her resolution of commanding her own mind, and maintained an easy serenity of manner, which the consciousness of superior temper never fails to bestow. Towards the end of the night, she danced one dance with Mr. Mountague, and as he was leading her to her place, Lady Augusta, and two or three of her companions, came up, all seemingly stifling a laugh. "What is the matter?" said Helen. "Why, my dear creature," said Lady Augusta, who still apparently laboured under a violent inclination to laugh, and whispering to Helen, but so loud that she could distinctly be overheard—"you must certainly be in love."

"Madam!" said Helen, colouring, and much distressed.

"Yes; you certainly must," pursued Lady Augusta, rudely; for ladies of quality can be as rude, sometimes ruder, than other people. "Must not she, Lady Di.," appealing to one of her companions, and laughing affectedly—"must not she be either in love, or out of her senses? Pray, Miss Temple, put out your foot." Helen put out her foot.

"Ay, that's the black one—well, the other." Now the other was white. The ill-bred raillery commenced. Helen, though somewhat abashed, smiled with great good humour, and walked on towards her seat. "What is the matter, my dear?" said her mother.

"Nothing, madam," answered Mr. Mountague, "but that Miss Helen Temple's shoes are odd, and her temper—even." These few words, which might pass in a ball-room, were accompanied with a look of approbation, which made her ample amends for the pain she had felt. He then sat down by Mrs. Temple, and, without immediately adverting to any one, spoke with indignation of coquetry, and lamented that so many beautiful girls should be spoiled by affectation.

"If they be spoiled, should they bear all the blame?" said Mrs. Temple. "If young women were not deceived into a belief that affectation pleases, they would scarcely trouble themselves to practise it so much."

"Deceived!" said Mr. Mountague—"but is any body deceived by a person's saying, 'I have the honour to be, madam, your obedient, humble servant?' Besides, as to pleasing—what do we mean? pleasing for a moment, for a day, or for life?"

"Pleasing for a moment," said Helen, smiling, "is of some consequence; for, if we take care of the moments, the years will take care of themselves, you know."

"Pleasing for one moment, though," said Mr. Mountague, "is very different, as you must perceive, from pleasing every moment."

Here the country dance suddenly stopped, and three or four couple were thrown into confusion. The gentlemen were stooping down, as if looking for something on the floor. "Oh, I beg, I insist upon it; you can't think how much you distress me!" cried a voice which sounded like Lady Augusta's. Mr. Mountague immediately went to see what was the matter. "It is only my bracelet," said she, turning to him. "Don't, pray don't trouble yourself," cried she, as he stooped to assist in collecting the scattered pearls, which she received with grace in the whitest hand imaginable. "Nay, now I must insist upon it," said she to Mr. Mountague, as he stooped again—"you shall not plague yourself any longer." And in her anxiety to prevent him from plaguing himself any longer, she laid upon his arm the white hand, which he had an instant before so much admired. Whether all Mr. Mountague's sober contempt of coquetry was, at this moment, the prevalent feeling in his mind, we cannot presume to determine; we must only remark, that the remainder of the evening was devoted to Lady Augusta; he sat beside her at supper, and paid her a thousand compliments, which Helen in vain endeavoured to persuade herself meant nothing more than—"I am, madam, your obedient, humble servant."

"It is half after two," said Mrs. Temple, when she rose to go.

"Half after two!" said Mr. Mountague, as he handed Mrs. Temple to her carriage—"bless me! can it be so late?"

All the way home Emma and Mrs. Temple were obliged to support the conversation; for Helen was so extremely entertained with watching the clouds passing over the moon, that nothing else could engage her attention.

The gossiping old lady's information respecting Mr. Mountague was as accurate as the information of gossips usually is found to be. Mr. Mountague, notwithstanding her opinion and sagacity, had thoughts of Miss Helen Temple. During some months which he had spent at his uncle's, who lived very near Mrs. Temple, he had had opportunities of studying Helen's character and temper, which he found perfectly well suited to his own; but he had never yet declared his attachment to her. Things were in this undecided situation, when he saw, and was struck with the beauty of Lady Augusta —, at this archery-ball. Lord George — introduced him to Lady S—; and, in consequence of a pressing invitation he received from her ladyship, he went to spend a few days at S— Hall.

"So Mr. Mountague is going to spend a week at S— Hall, I find," said Mrs. Temple, as she and her daughters were sitting at work the morning after the archery-ball. To this simple observation of Mrs. Temple a silence, which seemed as if it never would be broken, ensued.

"Helen, my dear!" said Mrs. Temple, in a soft voice.

"Ma'am!" said Helen, starting.

"You need not start so, my dear; I am not going to say any thing very tremendous. When you and your sister were children, if you remember, I often used to tell you that I looked forward, with pleasure, to the time when I should live with you as friends and equals. That time is come; and I hope, now that your own reason is sufficiently matured to be the guide of your conduct, that you do not think I any longer desire you to be governed by my will. Indeed," continued she, "I consider you as my equals in every respect but in age; and I wish to make that inequality useful to you, by giving you, as far as I can, that advantage, which only age can give—experience."

"You are very kind, dear mother," said Helen.

"But you must be sensible," said Mrs. Temple, in a graver tone, "that it will depend upon yourselves, in a great measure, whether I can be so much your friend as I shall wish."

"Oh, mother," said Helen, "be my friend! I shall never have a better; and, indeed, I want a friend," added she, the tears starting from her eyes. "You'll think me very silly, very vain. He never gave me any reason, I'm sure, to think so; but I did fancy that Mr. Mountague liked me."

"And," said Mrs. Temple, taking her daughter's hand, "without being very silly or very vain, may not one sometimes be mistaken? Then you thought you had won Mr. Mountague's heart? But what did you think about your own? Take care you don't make another mistake (smiling). Perhaps you thought he never could win yours?"

"I never thought much about that," replied Helen, "till yesterday."

"And to-day," said Mrs. Temple—"what do you think about it to-day?"

"Why," said Helen, "don't you think, mother, that Mr. Mountague has a great many good qualities?"

"Yes; a great many good qualities, a great many advantages, and, amongst them, the power of pleasing you."

"He would not think that any advantage," said Helen; "therefore I should be sorry that he had it."

"And so should I," said Mrs. Temple, "be very sorry that my daughter's happiness should be out of her own power."

"It is the uncertainty that torments me," resumed Helen, after a pause. "One moment I fancy that he prefers me, the next moment I am certain he prefers another. Yesterday, when we were coming away from the green, I heard Mrs. Hargrave say to Lady S— but why, mother, should I take up your time with these minute circumstances? I ought not to think any more about it."

"Ought not!" repeated Mrs. Temple; "my dear, it is a matter of prudence, rather than duty. By speaking to your mother with so much openness, you secure her esteem and affection; and, amongst the goods of this life, you will find the esteem and affection of a mother worth having," concluded Mrs. Temple, with a smile; and Helen parted from her mother with a feeling of gratitude, which may securely be expected from an ingenuous well-educated daughter, who is treated with similar kindness.

No one was ready for breakfast the morning that Mr. Mountague arrived at S— Hall, and he spent an hour alone in the breakfast-room. At length the silence was interrupted by a shrill female voice, which, as it approached nearer, he perceived to be the voice of a foreigner half suffocated with ineffectual desire to make her anger intelligible. He could only distinguish the words—"I ring, ring, ring, ay, twenty time, and nobody mind my bell nor me, no more dan noting at all." With a violent push, the breakfast-room door flew open, and Mlle. Panache, little expecting to find any body there, entered, volubly repeating—"Dey let me ring, ring, ring!" Surprised at the sight of a gentleman, and a young gentleman, she repented having been so loud in her anger. However, upon the second reconnoitring glance at Mr.

Mountague, she felt much in doubt how to behave towards him. Mademoiselle boasted often of the well-bred instinct, by which she could immediately distinguish "un homme comme il faut" from any other; yet sometimes, like Falstaff's, her instinct was fallacious. Recollecting that Lady S— had sent for an apothecary, she took it into her head that Mr. Mountague was this apothecary. "Miladi is not visible yet, sir," said she; "does she know you are here?"

"I hope not, ma'am; for I should be very sorry she were to be disturbed, after sitting up so late last night."

"Oh, dat will do her no harm, for I gave her, pardonnez, some excellent white wine whey out of my own head last night, when she got into her bed. I hope you don't make no objection to white wine whey, sir?"

"I!—not in the least, ma'am."

"Oh, I'm glad you don't disapprove of what I've done! You attend many family in dis country, sir?"

"Madam!" said Mr. Mountague, taking an instant's time to consider what she could mean by attend.

"You visit many family in dis country, sir?" persisted mademoiselle.

"Very few, ma'am; I am a stranger in this part of the world, except at Mrs. Temple's."

"Madame Temple, ah, oui! I know her very well; she has two fine daughters—I mean when dey have seen more of de world. It's a great pity, too, dey have never had de advantage of a native, to teach de good pronunciation de la langue Francaise. Madame Temple will repent herself of dat when it is too late, as I tell her always. But, sir, you have been at her house. I am sorry we did not hear none of de family had been indisposed."

"They are all now perfectly well, ma'am," replied Mr. Mountague, "except, indeed, that Mrs. Temple had a slight cold last week."

"But she is re-establish by your advise, I suppose? and she—did she recommend you to miladi?"

"No, madam," said Mr. Mountague, not a little puzzled by mademoiselle's phraseology: "Lord George — did me the honour to introduce me to Lady S—."

"Ah, Milord George! are you a long time acquainted wid milord?"

"Yes, ma'am, I have known Lord George many years."

"Ah, many year!—you be de family physician, apparemment?"

"The family physician! Oh no, ma'am!" said Mr. Mountague, smiling.

"Eh!" said mademoiselle, "but dat is being too modest. Many take de titre of physician, I'll engage, wid less pretensions. And," added she, looking graciously, "absolument, I will not have you call yourself de family apothicaire."

At this moment Lord George came in, and shook his family apothecary by the hand, with an air of familiarity which astounded mademoiselle. "Qu'est ce que c'est?" whispered she to Dashwood, who followed his lordship: "is not dis his apothicaire?" Dashwood, at this question, burst into a loud laugh. "Mr. Mountague," cried he, "have you been prescribing for mademoiselle? she asks if you are not an apothecary."

Immediately Lord George, who was fond of a joke, especially where there was a chance of throwing ridicule upon any body superior to him in abilities, joined most heartily in Dashwood's mirth; repeating the story, as "an excellent thing," to every one, as they came down to breakfast; especially to Lady Augusta, whom he congratulated, the moment she entered the room, upon her having danced the preceding evening with an apothecary. "Here he is!" said he, pointing to Mr. Mountague.

"Ma chère amie! mon coeur! tink of my mistaking your Mr. Mountague for such a sort of person! If you had only told me, sir, dat you were Miladi Augusta's partner last night, it would have saved me de necessity of making ten million apologies for my stupidity, dat could not find it out. Ma chère amie! Mon coeur! Miladi Augusta, will you make my excuse?"

"Ma chère amie! mon coeur!" repeated Mr. Mountague to himself: "is it possible that this woman can be an intimate friend of Lady Augusta?" What was his surprise, when he discovered that Mlle. Panache had been her ladyship's governess! He fell into a melancholy reverie for some moments. "So she has been educated by a vulgar, silly, conceited French governess!" said he to himself; "but that is her misfortune, not her fault. She is very young, and a man of sense might make her what he pleased." When Mr. Mountague recovered from his reverie, he heard the company, as they seated themselves at the breakfast-table, begin to talk over the last night's ball. "You did not tire yourself last night with dancing, my lord," said Dashwood.

"No; I hate dancing," replied Lord George: "I wish the ladies would take to dancing with one another; I think that would be an excellent scheme." An aunt of his lordship, who was present, took great offence at this suggestion of her nephew. She had been used to the deference paid in former times to the sex; and she said she could not bear to see women give up their proper places in society. "Really, George," added she, turning to her nephew, "I wish you would not talk in this manner. The young men now give themselves the strangest airs. Lady S—, I will expose him; do you know, last night, he was lolling at his full length upon a bench in the ball-room, while three young handsome ladies were standing opposite to him, tired to death."

"They could not be more tired than I was, I am sure, ma'am."

"Why, you had not been dancing, and they had."

"Had they, ma'am? that was not my fault. I did not ask 'em to dance, and I don't see it was my business to ask 'em to sit down. I did not know who they were, at any rate," concluded his lordship, sullenly.

"You knew they were women, and as such entitled to your respect."

Lord George gave a sneering smile, looked at Dashwood, and pulled up his boot.

"Another thing—you were in the house three weeks with Miss Earl last summer; you met her yesterday evening, and you thought proper not to take the least notice of her."

"Miss, Earl, ma'am; was she there?"

"Yes, close to you, and you never even bowed to her."

"I did not see her, ma'am."

"Mrs. Earl spoke to you."

"I didn't hear her, ma'am."

"I told you of it at the moment."

"I didn't understand you, ma'am."

"Besides, ma'am," interposed Dashwood, "as to Miss Earl, if she meant that my lord should bow to her, she should have curtsied first to him."

"Curtsied first to him!"

"Yes, that's the rule—that's the thing now. The ladies are always to speak first."

"I have nothing more to say, if that be the case. Lady Augusta, what say you to all this?"

"Oh, that it's shocking to be sure!" said Lady Augusta, "if one thinks of it; so the only way is not to think about it."

"An excellent bon-mot!" exclaimed Dashwood. "It's thinking that spoils conversation, and every thing else."

"But," added Lady Augusta, who observed that her bon-mot was not so much admired by all the company as by Dashwood, "I really only mean, that one must do as other people do."

"Assurément," said mademoiselle; "not dat I approve of the want of gallantry in our gentlemen, neider. But, I tink, Mademoiselle Earl is as stiff as de poker, and I don't approve of dat, neider—Je n'aime pas les prudes, moi."

"But, without prudery, may not there be dignity of manners?" said the old lady, gravely.

"Dignité!—Oh, I don't say noting against dignité, neider; not but I tink de English reserve is de trop. I tink a lady of a certain rank has always good principes enough, to be sure, and as to the rest qu'importe?— dat's my notions."

Mr. Mountague looked with anxiety at Lady Augusta, to see what she thought of her governess's notions; but all that he could judge from her countenance was that she did not think at all. "Well, she has time enough before her to learn to think," said he to himself. "I am glad she did not assent to mademoiselle's notions, at least. I hope she has learnt nothing from her but 'the true French pronunciation.'"

No sooner was breakfast finished than Lord George — gave his customary morning yawn, and walked as usual to the window. "Come," said Dashwood, in his free manner—"come, mademoiselle, you must come down with us to the water-side, and Lady Augusta, I hope."

"Ay," whispered Lord George to Dashwood, "and let's settle our wager about mademoiselle and my blackamore—don't think I'll let you off that."

"Off!—I'm ready to double the bet, my lord," said Dashwood aloud, and in the same moment turned to mademoiselle with some high-flown compliment about the beauty of her complexion, and the dangers of going without a veil on a hot sunny day.

"Well, Mr. Dashwood, when you've persuaded mademoiselle to take the veil, we'll set out, if you please," said Lady Augusta.

Mr. Mountague, who kept his attention continually upon Lady Augusta, was delighted to see that she waited for the elderly lady, who, at breakfast, had said so much in favour of dignity of manners. Mr. Mountague did not, at this moment, consider that this elderly lady was Lord George's aunt, and that the attention paid to her by Lady Augusta might possibly proceed from motives of policy, not from choice. Young men of open tempers and generous dispositions are easily deceived by coquettes, because they cannot stoop to invent the meanness of their artifices. As Mr. Mountague walked down to the river, Lady Augusta contrived to entertain him so completely, that Helen Temple never once came into his mind; though he had sense enough to perceive his danger, he had not sufficient courage to avoid it: it sometimes requires courage to fly from danger. From this agreeable tête-à-tête he was roused, however, by the voice of Mlle. Panache, who, in an affected agony, was struggling to get away from Dashwood, who held both her hands—"No! no!—Non! non! I will not—I will not, I tell you, I will not."

"Nay, nay," said Dashwood; "but I have sworn to get you into the boat."

"Ah! into de boat à la bonne heure; but not wid dat vilain black."

"Well, then, persuade Lord George to send back his man; and you'll acknowledge, my lord, in that case it's a drawn bet," said Dashwood.

"I! not I. I'll acknowledge nothing," replied his lordship; and he swore his black Tom should not be sent away: "he's a capital boatman, and I can't do without him."

"Den I won't stir," said mademoiselle, passionately, to Dashwood.

"Then I must carry you, must I?" cried Dashwood, laughing; and immediately, to Mr. Mountague's amazement, a romping scene ensued between this tutor and governess, which ended in Dashwood's carrying mademoiselle in his arms into the boat, amidst the secret derision of two footmen, and the undisguised laughter of black Tom, who were spectators of the scene.

Mr. Mountague trembled at the thoughts of receiving a wife from the hands of a Mlle. Panache; but, turning his eye upon Lady Augusta, he thought she blushed, and this blush at once saved her, in his opinion, and increased his indignation against her governess. Mademoiselle being now alarmed, and provoked by the laughter of the servants, the dry sarcastic manner of Lord George, the cool air of Mr. Mountague, and the downcast looks of her pupil, suddenly turned to Dashwood, and in a high angry tone assured him, "that she had never seen nobody have so much assurance;" and she demanded, furiously—"how he could ever tink to take such liberties wid her? Only tell me how you could dare to tink of it?"

"I confess I did not think as I ought to have done, mademoiselle," replied Dashwood, looking an apology to Lady Augusta, which, however, he took great care mademoiselle should not observe. "But your bet, my lord, if you please," added he, attempting to turn it off in a joke: "there was no scream—my bet's fairly won."

"I assure you, sir, dis won't do: it's no good joke, I promise you. Ma chère amie, mon coeur," cried mademoiselle to Lady Augusta—"viens—come, let us go—Don't touch that," pursued she, roughly, to black Tom, who was going to draw away the plank that led to the shore. "I will go home dis minute, and speak to Miladi S—. Viens! viens, ma chère amie!"—and she darted out of the boat, whilst Dashwood followed, in vain attempting to stop her. She prudently, however, took the longest way through the park, that she might have a full opportunity of listening to reason, as Dashwood called it; and before she reached home, she was perfectly convinced of the expediency of moderate measures. "Let the thing rest where it is," said Dashwood: "it's a joke, and there's an end of it; but if you take it in earnest, you know the story might not tell so well, even if you told it, and there would never be an end of it." All this, followed by a profusion of compliments, ratified a peace, which the moment he had made, he laughed at himself for having taken so much trouble to effect; whilst mademoiselle rested in the blessed persuasion that Dashwood was desperately in love with her; nay, so little knowledge had she of the human heart as to believe that the scene which had just passed was a proof of his passion.

"I wonder where's Miladi Augusta? I thought she was wid me all this time," said she.

"She's coming; don't you see her at the end of the grove with Mr. Mountague? We have walked fast,"

"Oh, she can't never walk so fast as me; I tink I am as young as she is."

Dashwood assented, at the same time pondering upon the consequences of the attachment which he saw rising in Mr. Mountague's mind for Lady Augusta. If a man of sense were to gain an influence over her, Dashwood feared that all his hopes would be destroyed, and he resolved to use all his power over mademoiselle to prejudice her, and by her means to prejudice her pupil against this gentleman. Mademoiselle's having begun by taking him for an apothicaire, was a circumstance much in favour of Dashwood's views, because she felt herself pledged to justify, or at least to persist, in her opinion, that he did not look like un homme comme il faut.

In the mean time Mr. Mountague was walking slowly towards them with Lady Augusta, who found it necessary to walk as slowly as possible, because of the heat. He had been reflecting very soberly upon her ladyship's late blush, which, according to his interpretation, said, as plainly as a blush could say, all that the most refined sense and delicacy could dictate. Yet such is, upon some occasions, the inconsistency of the human mind, that he by no means felt sure that the lady had blushed at all. Her colour was, perhaps, a shade higher than usual; but then it was hot weather, and she had been walking. The doubt, however, Mr. Mountague thought proper to suppress; and the reality of the blush, once thoroughly established in his imagination, formed the foundation of several ingenious theories of moral sentiment, and some truly logical deductions. A passionate admirer of grace and beauty, he could not help wishing that he might find Lady Augusta's temper and understanding equal to her personal accomplishments. When we are very anxious to discover perfections in any character, we generally succeed, or fancy that we succeed. Mr. Mountague quickly discovered many amiable and interesting qualities in this fair lady, and, though he perceived some defects, he excused them to himself with the most philosophic ingenuity.

"Affectation," the judicious Locke observes, "has always the laudable aim of pleasing:" upon this principle Mr. Mountague could not reasonably think of it with severity. "From the desire of pleasing," argued he, "proceeds not only all that is amiable, but much of what is most estimable in the female sex. This desire leads to affectation and coquetry, to folly and vice, only when it is extended to unworthy objects. The moment a woman's wish to please becomes discriminative, the moment she feels any attachment to a man superior to the vulgar herd, she not only ceases to be a coquette, but she exerts herself to excel in every thing that he approves, and, from her versatility of manners, she has the happy power of adapting herself to his taste, and of becoming all that his most sanguine wishes could desire." The proofs of this discriminative taste, and the first symptoms of this salutary attachment to a man superior to the vulgar herd, Mr. Mountague thought he discerned very plainly in Lady Augusta, nor did he ever forget that she was but eighteen. "She is so very young," said he to himself, "that it is but reasonable I should constantly consider what she may become, rather than what she is." To do him justice, we shall observe, that her ladyship at this time, with all the address of which so young a lady was capable, did every thing in her power to confirm Mr. Mountague in his favourable sentiments of her.

Waiting for some circumstance to decide his mind, he was at length determined by the generous enthusiasm, amiable simplicity, and candid good sense which Lady Augusta showed in speaking of a favourite friend of hers, of whom he could not approve. This friend, Lady Diana, was one of the rude ladies who had laughed with so much ill-nature at Helen's white and black shoes at the archery ball. She was a dashing, rich, extravagant, fashionable widow, affecting bold horsemanlike manners, too often "touching the brink of all we hate," without exciting any passions allied to love. Her look was almost an oath—her language was suitable to her looks—she swore and dressed to the height of the fashion—she could drive four horses in hand—was a desperate huntress—and so loud in the praises of her dogs and horses, that she intimidated even sportsmen and jockeys. She talked so much of her favourite horse Spanker, that she acquired amongst a particular set of gentlemen the appellation of my Lady Di Spanker. Lady Augusta perceived that the soft affectations remarkable in her own manners were in agreeable contrast in the company of this masculine dame; she therefore cultivated her acquaintance, and Lady S— could make no objection to a woman who was well received every where; she was rather flattered to see her daughter taken notice of by this dashing belle; consequently, Lady Di. Spanker, for by that name we also shall call her, frequently rode over from Cheltenham, which was some miles distant from S— Hall. One morning she called upon Lady Augusta, and insisted upon her coming out to try her favourite horse. All the gentlemen went down immediately to assist in putting her ladyship on horseback: this was quite unnecessary, for Lady Diana took that office upon herself. Lady Augusta was all timidity, and was played off to great advantage by the rough raillery of her friend. At length she conquered her fears so much as to seat herself upon the side-saddle; her riding mistress gathered up the reins for her, and fixed them properly in her timid hands; then armed her with her whip, exhorting her, "for God's sake, not to be such a coward!" Scarcely was the word coward pronounced, when Lady Augusta, by some unguarded motion of her whip, gave offence to her high-mettled steed, which instantly began to rear: there was no danger, for Mr. Mountague caught hold of the reins, and Lady Augusta was dismounted in perfect safety. "How now, Spanker!" exclaimed Lady Di., in a voice calculated to strike terror into the nerves of a horse—"how now, Spanker!" and mounting him with masculine boldness of gesture—"I'll teach you, sir, who's your mistress," continued she; "I'll make you pay for these tricks!" Spanker reared again, and Lady Di. gave him what she called "a complete dressing!" In vain Lady Augusta screamed; in vain the spectators entreated the angry amazon to spare the whip; she persisted in beating Spanker till she fairly mastered him. When he was perfectly subdued, she dismounted with the same carelessness with which she had mounted; and, giving the horse to her groom, pushed back her hat, and looked round for applause. Lord George, roused to a degree of admiration, which he had never before been heard to express for any thing female, swore that, in all his life, he had never seen any thing better done; and Lady Di. Spanker received his congratulations with a loud laugh, and a hearty shake of the hand. "Walk him about, Jack," added she, turning to the groom, who held her horse; "walk him about, for he's all in a lather; and when he's cool, bring him up here again. And then, my dear child," said she to Lady Augusta, "you shall give him a fair trial."

"I!—Oh! never, never!" cried Lady Augusta, shrinking back with a faint shriek: "this is a trial to which you must not put my friendship. I must insist upon leaving Spanker to your management; I would not venture upon him again for the universe."

"How can you talk so like a child—so like a woman?" cried her friend.

"I confess, I am a very woman," said Lady Augusta, with a sigh: "and I fear I shall never be otherwise."

"Fear!" repeated Mr. Mountague, to whom even the affectation of feminine softness and timidity appeared at this instant charming, from the contrast with the masculine intrepidity and disgusting coarseness of Lady Diana Spanker's manners. The tone in which he pronounced the single word fear was sufficient to betray his feelings towards both the ladies. Lady Di. gave him a look of sovereign contempt. "All I know and can tell you," cried she, "is, that fear should never get a-horseback." Lord George burst into one of his loud laughs. "But as to the rest, fear may be a confounded good thing in its proper place; but they say it's catching; so I must run away from you, child," said she to Lady Augusta. "Jack, bring up Spanker. I've twenty miles to ride before dinner. I've no time to lose," pulling out her watch: "faith, I've fooled away an hour here; Spanker must make it up for me. God bless you all! Good bye!" and she mounted her horse, and galloped off full speed.

"God bless ye! good bye to ye, Lady Di. Spanker," cried Dashwood, the moment she was out of hearing. "Heaven preserve us from amazons!" Lord George did not say, Amen. On the contrary, he declared she was a fine dashing woman, and seemed to have a great deal of blood about her. Mr. Mountague watched Lady Augusta's countenance in silence, and was much pleased to observe that she did not assent to his lordship's encomium. "She has good sense enough to perceive the faults of her new friend, and now her eyes are open she will no longer make a favourite companion, I hope, of this odious woman," thought he. "I am afraid, I am sadly afraid you are right," said Lady Augusta, going up to the elderly lady, whom we formerly mentioned, who had seen all that had passed from the open windows of the drawing-room. "I own I do see something of what you told me the other day you disliked so much in my friend, Lady Di.;" and Lady Augusta gave the candid sigh of expiring friendship as she uttered these words.

"Do you know," cried Dashwood, "that this spanking horsewoman has frightened us all out of our senses? I vow to Heaven, I never was so much terrified in my life as when I saw you, Lady Augusta, upon that vicious animal."

"To be sure," said Lady Augusta, "it was very silly of me to venture; I almost broke my neck, out of pure friendship."

"It is well it is no worse," said the elderly lady: "if a fall from a horse was the worst evil to be expected from a friendship with a woman of this sort, it would be nothing very terrible."

Lady Augusta, with an appearance of ingenuous candour, sighed again, and replied—"It is so difficult to see any imperfections in those one loves! Forgive me, if I spoke with too much warmth, madam, the other day, in vindication of my friend. I own I ought to have paid more deference to your judgment and knowledge of the world, so much superior to my own; but certainly I must confess, the impropriety of her amazonian manners, as Mr. Dashwood calls them, never struck my partial eyes till this morning. Nor could I, nor would I, believe half the world said of her; indeed, even now, I am persuaded she is, in the main, quite irreproachable; but I feel the truth of what you said to me, madam, that young women cannot be too careful in the choice of their female friends; that we are judged of by our companions; how unfairly one must be judged of sometimes!" concluded her ladyship, with a look of pensive reflection.

Mr. Mountague never thought her half so beautiful as at this instant. "How mind embellishes beauty!" thought he; "and what quality of the mind more amiable than candour!—All that was wanting to her character was reflection; and could one expect so much reflection as this from a girl of eighteen, who had been educated by a Mlle. Panache?" Our readers will observe that this gentleman now reasoned like a madman, but not like a fool; his deductions from the appearances before him were admirable; but these appearances were false. He had not observed that Lady Augusta's eyes were open to the defects of her amazonian friend, in the very moment that Lord George — was roused to admiration by this horseman belle. Mr. Mountague did not perceive that the candid reflections addressed to his lordship's aunt were the immediate consequence of female jealousy.

The next morning, at breakfast, Lord George was summoned three times before he made his appearance: at length he burst in, with a piece of news he had just heard from his groom—"That Lady Di. Spanker, in riding home full gallop the preceding day, had been thrown from her horse by an old woman. Faith, I couldn't believe the thing," added Lord George, with a loud laugh; "for she certainly sits a horse better than any woman in England; but my groom had the whole story from the grand-daughter of the old woman who was run over."

"Run over!" exclaimed Lady Augusta; "was the poor woman run over?—was she hurt?"

"Hurt! yes, she was hurt, I fancy," said Lord George. "I never heard of any body's being run over without being hurt. The girl has a petition that will come up to us just now, I suppose. I saw her in the back yard as I came in."

"Oh! let us see the poor child," said Lady Augusta: "do let us have her called to this window." The window opened down to the ground, and, as soon as the little girl appeared with the petition in her hand, Lady Augusta threw open the sash, and received it from her timid hand with a smile, which to Mr. Mountague seemed expressive of sweet and graceful benevolence. Lady Augusta read the petition with much feeling, and her lover thought her voice never before sounded so melodious. She wrote her name eagerly at the head of a subscription. The money she gave was rather more than the occasion required; but, thought Mr. Mountague,

"If the generous spirit flow
Beyond where prudence fears to go
Those errors are of nobler kind,
Than virtues of a narrow mind(2)."

(Footnote 2: Soame Jenyns.)

By a series of petty artifices Lady Augusta contrived to make herself appear most engaging and amiable to this artless young man: but the moment of success was to her the moment of danger. She was little aware, that when a man of sense began to think seriously of her as a wife, he would require very different qualities from those which please in public assemblies. Her ladyship fell into a mistake not uncommon in her sex; she thought that "Love blinds when once he wounds the swain(3)." Coquettes have sometimes penetration sufficient to see what will please their different admirers: but even those who have that versatility of manners, which can be all things to all men, forget that it is possible to support an assumed character only for a time; the moment the immediate motive for dissimulation diminishes, the power of habit acts, and the real disposition and manners appear.

(Footnote 3: Collius's Eclogues.)

When Lady Augusta thought herself sure of her captive, and consequently when the power of habit was beginning to act with all its wonted force, she was walking out with him in a shrubbery near the house, and mademoiselle, with Mr. Dashwood, who generally was the gallant partner of her walks, accompanied them. Mademoiselle stopped to gather some fine carnations; near the carnations was a rose-tree. Mr. Mountague, as three of those roses, one of them in full blow, one half blown, and another a pretty bud, caught his eye, recollected a passage in Berkeley's romance of Gaudentio di Lucca. "Did you ever happen to meet with Gaudentio di Lucca? do you recollect the story of Berilla, Lady Augusta?" said he.

"No; I have never heard of Berilla: what is the story?" said she.

"I wish I had the book," said Mr. Mountague; "I cannot do it justice, but I will borrow it for you from Miss Helen Temple. I lent it to her some time ago; I dare say she has finished reading it."

At these words, Lady Augusta's desire to have Gaudentio di Lucca suddenly increased; and she expressed vast curiosity to know the story of Berilla. "And pray what put you in mind of this book just now?" said she.

"These roses. In Berkeley's Utopia, which he calls Mezzorania—(every philosopher, you know, Mr. Dashwood, must have a Utopia, under whatever name he pleases to call it)—in Mezzorania, Lady Augusta, gentlemen did not, as amongst us, make declarations of love by artificial words, but by natural flowers(4). The lover in the beginning of his attachment declared it to his mistress by the offer of an opening bud; if she felt favourably inclined towards him, she accepted and wore the bud. When time had increased his affection—for in Mezzorania it is supposed that time increases affection for those that deserve it—the lover presented a half-blown flower; and, after this also was graciously accepted, he came, we may suppose not very long afterwards, with a full-blown flower, the emblem of mature affection. The ladies who accepted these full-blown flowers, and wore them, were looked upon amongst the simple Mezzoranians as engaged for life; nor did the gentlemen, when they offered their flowers, make one single protestation or vow of eternal love, yet they were believed, and deserved, it is said, to be believed."

(Footnote 4: Gaudentio di Lucca, p. 202.)

"Qu'est ce que c'est? Qu'est ce que c'est?" repeated mademoiselle several times to Dashwood, whilst Mr. Mountague was speaking: she did not understand English sufficiently to comprehend him, and Dashwood was obliged to make the thing intelligible to her in French. Whilst he was occupied with her, Mr. Mountague gathered three roses, a bud, a half-blown and a full-blown rose, and playfully presented them to Lady Augusta for her choice.—"I'm dying to see this Gaudentio di Lucca; you'll get the book for me to-morrow from Miss Helen Temple, will you?" said Lady Augusta, as she with a coquettish smile took the rose-bud, and put it into her bosom.

"Bon!" cried mademoiselle, stooping to pick up the full-blown rose, which Mr. Mountague threw away carelessly. "Bon! but it is great pity dis should be thrown away."

"It is not thrown away upon Mlle. Panache!" said Dashwood.

"Dat maybe," said mademoiselle; "but I observe, wid all your fine compliment, you let me stoop to pick it up for myself—á l'Anglaise!"

"A la Française, then," said Dashwood, laughing, "permit me to put it into your nosegay."

"Dat is more dan you deserve," replied mademoiselle.—"Eh! non, non. I can accommodate it, I tell you, to my own taste best." She settled and resettled the flower: but suddenly she stopped, uttered a piercing shriek, plucked the full-blown rose from her bosom, and threw it upon the ground with a theatrical look of horror. A black earwig now appeared creeping out of the rose; it was running away, but mademoiselle pursued, set her foot upon it, and crushed it to death. "Oh! I hope to Heaven, Mr. Mountague, there are none of these vile creatures in the bud you've given me!" exclaimed Lady Augusta. She looked at her bud as she spoke, and espied upon one of the leaves a small green caterpillar: with a look scarcely less theatrical than mademoiselle's, she tore off the leaf and flung it from her; then, from habitual imitation of her governess, she set her foot upon the harmless caterpillar, and crushed it in a moment.

In the same moment Lady Augusta's whole person seemed metamorphosed to the eyes of her lover. She ceased to be beautiful: he seemed to see her countenance distorted by malevolence; he saw in her gestures disgusting cruelty; and all the graces vanished.

When Lady Augusta was a girl of twelve years old, she saw Mlle. Panache crush a spider to death without emotion: the lesson on humanity was not lost upon her. From imitation, she learned her governess's foolish terror of insects; and from example, she was also taught that species of cruelty, by which at eighteen she disgusted a man of humanity who was in love with her. Mr. Mountague said not one word upon the occasion. They walked on. A few minutes after the caterpillar had been crushed, Lady Augusta exclaimed, "Why, mademoiselle, what have you done with Fanfan? I thought my dog was with us: for Heaven's sake, where is he?"

"He is run, he is run on," replied mademoiselle.

"Oh, he'll be lost! he'll run down the avenue, quite out upon the turnpike road.—Fanfan! Fanfan!"

"Don't alarm, don't distress yourself," cried Dashwood: "if your ladyship will permit me, I'll see for Fanfan instantly, and bring her back to you, if she is to be found in the universe."

"O Lord! don't trouble yourself; I only spoke to mademoiselle, who regularly loses Fanfan when she takes him out with her." Dashwood set out in search of the dog; and Lady Augusta, overcome with affectation, professed herself unable to walk one yard further, and sank down upon a seat under a tree, in a very graceful, languid attitude. Mr. Mountague stood silent beside her. Mademoiselle went on with a voluble defence of her conduct towards Fanfan, which lasted till Dashwood reappeared, hurrying towards them with the dog in his arms—"Ah, la voilà! chère Fanfan!" exclaimed mademoiselle.

"I am sure I really am excessively obliged to Mr. Dashwood, I must say," cried Lady Augusta, looking reproachfully at Mr. Mountague.

Dashwood now approached with panting, breathless eagerness, announcing a terrible misfortune, that Fanfan had got a thorn or something in his fore-foot. Lady Augusta received Fanfan upon her lap, with expressions of the most tender condolence; and Dashwood knelt down at her feet to sympathize in her sorrow, and to examine the dog's paw. Mademoiselle produced a needle to extract the thorn.

"I wish we had a magnifying-glass," said Dashwood, looking with strained solicitude at the wound.

"Oh, you insensible monster! positively you shan't touch Fanfan," cried Lady Augusta, guarding her lapdog from Mr. Mountague, who stooped now, for the first time, to see what was the matter. "Don't touch him, I say; I would not trust him to you for the universe; I know you hate lapdogs. You'll kill him—you'll kill him."

"I kill him! Oh no," said Mr. Mountague; "I would not even kill a caterpillar."

Lady Augusta coloured at these words; but she recovered herself when Dashwood laughed, and asked Mr. Mountague how long it was since he had turned brahmin; and how long since he had professed to like caterpillars and earwigs.

"Bon Dieu!—earwig!" interrupted mademoiselle: "is it possible that monsieur or any body dat has sense, can like dose earwig?"

"I do not remember," answered Mr. Mountague, calmly, "ever to have professed any liking for earwigs."

"Well, pity; you profess pity for them," said Mr. Dashwood, "and pity, you know, is 'akin to love.'—Pray, did your ladyship ever hear of the man who had a pet toad?"(5)

(Footnote 5: Vide Smellie's Natural History, vol. ii.)

"Oh, the odious wretch!" cried Lady Augusta, affectedly; "but how could the man bring himself to like a toad?"

"He began by pitying him, I suppose," said Dashwood. "For my part, I own I must consider that man to be in a most enviable situation whose heart is sufficiently at ease to sympathize with the insect creation."

"Or with the brute creation," said Mr. Mountague, smiling and looking at Fanfan, whose paw Dashwood was at this instant nursing with infinite tenderness.

"Oh, gentlemen, let us have no more of this, for Heaven's sake!" said Lady Augusta, interposing, with affected anxiety, as if she imagined a quarrel would ensue. "Poor dear Fanfan, you would not have any body quarrel about you, would you, Fanfan?" She rose as she spoke, and, delivering the dog to Dashwood to be carried home, she walked towards the house, with an air of marked displeasure towards Mr. Mountague.

Her ladyship's displeasure did not affect him as she expected. Her image—her gesture stamping upon the caterpillar, recurred to her lover's mind many times in the course of the evening; and in the silence of the night, and whenever the idea of her came into his mind, it was attended with this picture of active cruelty.

"Has your ladyship," said Mr. Mountague, addressing himself to Lady S—, "any commands for Mrs. Temple? I am going to ride over to see her this morning."

Lady S— said that she would trouble him with a card for Mrs. Temple; a card of invitation for the ensuing week. "And pray don't forget my kindest remembrances," cried Lady Augusta, "especially to Miss Helen Temple; and if she should have entirely finished the book we were talking of, I shall be glad to see it."

When Mr. Mountague arrived at Mrs. Temple's, he was shown into the usual sitting-room: the servant told him that none of the ladies were at home, but that they would soon return, he believed, from their walk, as they were gone only to a cottage at about half a mile's distance.

The room in which he had passed so many agreeable hours awakened in his mind a number of dormant associations—work, books, drawing, writing! he saw every thing had been going forward just as usual in his absence. All the domestic occupations, thought he, which make home delightful, are here: I see nothing of these at S— Hall. Upon the table, near a neat work-basket, which he knew to be Helen's, lay an open book; it was Gaudentio di Lucca. Mr. Mountague recollected the bud he had given to Lady Augusta, and he began to whistle, but not for want of thought. A music-book on the desk of the piano-forte caught his eye; it was open at a favourite lesson of his, which he remembered to have heard Helen play the last evening he was in her company. Helen was no great proficient in music; but she played agreeably enough to please her friends, and she was not ambitious of exhibiting her accomplishments. Lady Augusta, on the contrary, seemed never to consider her accomplishments as occupations, but as the means of attracting admiration. To interrupt the comparison, which Mr. Mountague was beginning to enter into between her ladyship and Helen, he thought the best thing he could do was to walk to meet Mrs. Temple; wisely considering, that putting the body in motion sometimes stops the current of the mind. He had at least observed, that his schoolfellow, Lord George —, seemed to find this a specific against thought; and for once he was willing to imitate his lordship's example, and to hurry about from place to place, without being in a hurry. He rang the bell, inquired in haste which way the ladies were gone, and walked after them, like a man who had the business of the nation upon his hands; yet he slackened his pace when he came near the cottage where he knew that he was to meet Mrs. Temple and her daughters. When he entered the cottage, the first object that he saw was Helen, sitting by the side of a decrepit old woman, who was resting her head upon a crutch, and who seemed to be in pain. This was the poor woman who had been ridden over by Lady Di. Spanker. A farmer who lived near Mrs. Temple, and who was coming homewards at the time the accident happened, had the humanity to carry the wretched woman to this cottage, which was occupied by one of Mrs. Temple's tenants. As soon as the news reached her, she sent for a surgeon, and went with her daughters to give that species of consolation which the rich and happy can so well bestow upon the poor and Miserable—the consolation not of gold, but of sympathy.

There was no affectation, no ostentation of sensibility, Mr. Mountague observed, in this cottage scene; the ease and simplicity of Helen's manner never appeared to him more amiable. He recollected Lady Augusta's picturesque attitude, when she was speaking to this old woman's grand-daughter; but there was something in what he now beheld that gave him more the idea of nature and reality: he heard, he saw, that much had actually been done to relieve distress, and done when there were no spectators to applaud or admire. Slight circumstances show whether the mind be intent upon self or not. An awkward servant girl brushed by Helen whilst she was speaking to the old woman, and with a great black kettle, which she was going to set upon the fire, blackened Helen's white dress, in a manner which no lady intent upon her personal appearance could have borne with patience. Mr. Mountague saw the black streaks before Helen perceived them, and when the maid was reproved for her carelessness, Helen's good-natured smile assured her "that there was no great harm done."

When they returned home, Mr. Mountague found that Helen conversed with him with all her own ingenuous freedom, but there was something more of softness and dignity, and less of sprightliness, than formerly in her manner. Even this happened to be agreeable to him, for it was in contrast with the constant appearance of effort and artificial brilliancy conspicuous in the manners of Lady Augusta. The constant round of cards and company, the noise and bustle at S— Hall, made it more like town than country life, and he had often observed that, in the intervals between dressing, and visiting, and gallantry, his fair mistress was frequently subject to ennui. He recollected that, in the many domestic hours he had spent at Mrs. Temple's, he had never beheld this French demon, who makes the votaries of dissipation and idleness his victims. What advantage has a man, in judging of female character, who can see a woman in the midst of her own family, "who can read her history" in the eyes of those who know her most intimately, who can see her conduct as a daughter and a sister, and in the most important relations of life can form a certain judgment from what she has been, of what she is likely to be? But how can a man judge what sort of wife he may probably expect in a lady, whom he meets with only at public places, or whom he never sees even at her own house, without all the advantages or disadvantages of stage decoration? A man who marries a showy, entertaining coquette, and expects that she will make him a charming companion for life, commits as absurd a blunder as that of the famous nobleman, who, delighted with the wit and humour of Punch at a puppet-show, bought Punch, and ordered him to be sent home for his private amusement.

Whether all or any of these reflections occurred to Mr. Mountague during his morning visit at Mrs. Temple's we cannot pretend to say; but his silence and absence seemed to show that his thoughts were busily engaged. Never did Helen appear to him so amiable as she did this morning, when the dignity, delicacy, and simplicity of her manners were contrasted in his imagination with the caprice and coquetry of his new mistress. He felt a secret idea that he was beloved, and a sober certainty that Helen had a heart capable of sincere and permanent affection, joined to a cultivated understanding and reasonable principles, which would wear through life, and ensure happiness, with power superior to the magic of passion.

It was with some difficulty that he asked Helen for Gaudentio di Lucca, and with yet greater difficulty that he took leave of her. As he was riding towards S— Hall, "revolving in his altered mind the various turns of fate below," he was suddenly roused from his meditations by the sight of a phaeton overturned in the middle of the road, another phaeton and four empty, and a group of people gathered near a bank by the road-side. Mr. Mountague rode up as fast as possible to the scene of action: the overturned phaeton was Lord George's, the other Lady Di. Spanker's; the group of people was composed of several servants, Lord George, Lady Di., and mademoiselle, all surrounding a fainting fair one, who was no other than Lady Augusta herself. Lord George was shaking his own arms, legs, and head, to make himself sure of their safety. Lady Di. eagerly told the whole story to Mr. Mountague, that Lord George had been running races with her, and by his confounded bad driving had overturned himself and Lady Augusta. "Poor thing, she's not hurt at all, luckily; but she's terrified to death, as usual, and she has been going from one fainting fit to another."

"Bon Dieu!" interrupted mademoiselle; "but what will Miladi S— say to us? I wish Miladi Augusta would come to her senses."

Lady Augusta opened her beautiful eyes, and, just come sufficiently to her senses to observe who was looking at her, she put aside mademoiselle's smelling-bottle, and, in a soft voice, begged to have her own salts. Mademoiselle felt in one of her ladyship's pockets for the salts in vain: Lady Di. plunged her hand into her other pocket, and pulled out, in the first place, a book, which she threw upon the bank, and then came out the salts. In due time the lady was happily restored to the full use of her senses, and was put into her mother's coach, which had been sent for to convey her home. The carriages drove away, and Mr. Mountague was just mounting his horse, when he saw the book which had been pulled out of Lady Augusta's pocket, and which, by mistake, was left where it had been thrown upon the grass. What was his astonishment, when upon opening it, he saw one of the very worst books in the French language; a book which never could have been found in the possession of any woman of delicacy—of decency. Her lover stood for some minutes in silent amazement, disgust, and, we may add, terror.

These feelings had by no means subsided in his mind, when, upon his entering the drawing-room at S— Hall, he was accosted by Mlle. Panache, who, with no small degree of alarm in her countenance, inquired whether he knew any thing of the book which had been left upon the road. No one was in the room but the governess and her pupil. Mr. Mountague produced the book, and Lady Augusta received it with a deep blush.

"Put a good face upon the matter at least," whispered her governess in French.

"I can assure you," said her ladyship, "I don't know what's in this book; I never opened it; I got it this morning at the circulating library at Cheltenham: I put it into my pocket in a hurry—pray what is it?"

"If you have not opened it," said Mr. Mountague, laying his hand upon the book; "I may hope that you never will—but this is the second volume."

"May be so," said Lady Augusta; "I suppose, in my hurry, I mistook—"

"She never had the first, I can promise you," cried mademoiselle.

"Never," said Lady Augusta. The assertions had not the power to convince; they were pronounced with much vehemence, but not with the simplicity of truth. Mr. Mountague was determined to have the point cleared up; and he immediately offered to ride back to Cheltenham, and return the second volume. At this proposal, Lady Augusta, who foresaw that her falsehood would be detected, turned pale; but mademoiselle, with a laugh of effrontery, which she thought was putting a good face upon the matter, exclaimed,

"Eh! listen to me—you may spare yourself de trouble of your ride," said she, "for the truth is, I have de first volume. Mon Dieu! I have not committed murder—do not look so shock—what signify what I read at my age?"

"But Lady Augusta, your pupil!" said Mr. Mountague.

"I tell you she has never read one word of it; and, after all, is she child now? When she was, Miladi S— was very particular, and I, of consequence and of course, in de choice of her books; but now, oder affaire, she is at liberty, and my maxim is—Tout est sain aux sains."

Mr. Mountague's indignation was now strongly raised against this odious governess, and he looked upon her pupil with an eye of compassion. "So early, so young, tainted by the pernicious maxims of a worthless woman!"

"Eh, donc, what signify your silence and your salts?" cried mademoiselle, turning to her.

"If I could be spared this scene at present," said Lady Augusta, faintly—"I really am not well. We had better talk over this business some other time, Mr. Mountague:" to this he acceded, and the lady gained more by her salts and silence than her governess did by her garrulous effrontery.

When she talked over the business with Mr. Mountague, she threw all the blame upon mademoiselle, and she appeared extremely shocked and alarmed at the idea that she had lessened herself by her folly, as she called it, in the esteem of a man of superior sense and taste. It was perhaps possible that, at this moment of her life, her character might have taken a new turn, that she might really have been awakened to higher views and nobler sentiments than any she had ever yet known; but the baleful influence of her constant attendant and conductress prevailed against her better self. Mademoiselle continually represented to her, that she did not know or exert the whole of her power over Mr. Mountague; and she excited her to caprice and coquetry. The fate of trifling characters is generally decided by trifles: we must beg leave to relate the important history of a turban.

Mlle. Panache, who piqued herself much upon her skill as a milliner, made up a certain turban for Lady Augusta, which Dashwood admired extremely, but which Mr. Mountague had the misfortune not to think perfectly beautiful. Vexed that he should dare to differ from her in taste, Lady Augusta could not rest without endeavouring to make him give up his opinion: he thought that it was not worth while to dispute about a trifle; and though he could not absolutely say that it was pretty, he condescended so far as to allow that it might perhaps be pretty, if it were put on differently.

"This is the way I always wear it—every body wears it so—and I shall not alter it," said Lady Augusta, who was quite out of temper.

Mr. Mountague looked grave: the want of temper was an evil which he dreaded beyond measure in a companion for life. Smiles and dimples usually adorned Lady Augusta's face; but these were artificial smiles: now passions, which one should scarcely imagine such a trifle could excite, darkened her brow, and entirely altered the air of her whole person, so as to make it absolutely disagreeable to her admirer. Lord George, who was standing by, and who felt delighted with such scenes, winked at Dashwood, and, with more energy than he usually expressed upon any subject, now pronounced that, in his humble opinion, the turban was quite the thing, and could not be better put on. Lady Augusta turned a triumphant, insulting eye upon Mr. Mountague: he was silent—his silence she took as a token of submission—in fact, it was an expression of contempt. The next day, at dinner, her ladyship appeared in the same turban, put on sedulously in the same manner. Lord George seated himself beside her; and as she observed that he paid her unusual attention, she fancied that at length his icy heart would thaw. Always more intent upon making cages(6), Lady Augusta bent her mind upon captivating a new admirer. Mr. Mountague she saw was displeased, but she now really felt and showed herself indifferent to his opinion. How variable, how wretched, is the life of a coquette! The next day Lord George's heart froze again as hard as ever, and Lady Augusta lightened upon the impassive ice in vain. She was mortified beyond measure, for her grand object was conquest. That she might triumph over poor Helen, she had taken pains to attract Mr. Mountague. Dashwood, though far beneath her ladyship in fortune and in station, she deemed worth winning, as a man of wit and gallantry. Lord George, to be sure, had little wit, and less gallantry; but he was Lord George, and that was saying enough. In short, Lady Augusta exacted tribute to her vanity without any discrimination, and she valued her treasures by number, and not by weight. A man of sense is mortified to see himself confounded with the stupid and the worthless.

(Footnote 6: Swift)

Mr. Mountague, after having loved like a madman, felt it not in the least incumbent upon him to love like a fool; he had imprudently declared himself an admirer of Lady Augusta, but he now resolved never to unite himself to her without some more reasonable prospect of happiness. Every day some petty cause of disagreement arose between them, whilst mademoiselle, by her silly and impertinent interference, made matters worse. Mademoiselle had early expressed her strong abhorrence of prudes; her pupil seemed to have caught the same abhorrence; she saw that Mr. Mountague was alarmed by her spirit of coquetry, yet still it continued in full force. For instance, she would continually go out with Lord George in his phaeton, though she declared, every time he handed her in, "that she was certain he would break her neck." She would receive verses from Dashwood, and keep them embalmed in her pocket-book, though she allowed that she thought them "sad stuff."

However, in these verses something more was meant than met the ear. He began with addressing a poem to her ladyship, called The Turban, which her silly mother extolled with eagerness, and seemed to think by no means inferior to the Rape of the Lock. Lady Augusta wrote a few lines in answer to the Turban—reply produced reply—nonsense, nonsense—till Dashwood now and then forgot his poetical character. Lady Augusta forgave it; he, of course, forgot himself again into a lover in prose. For some time the sonnets were shown to Lady S—, but at length some were received, which it was thought as well not to show to any body. In short, between fancy, flattery, poetry, passion, jest, and earnest, Lady Augusta was drawn on till she hardly knew where she was; but Dashwood knew perfectly well where he was, and resolved to keep his ground resolutely.

When encouraged by the lady's coquetry, he first formed his plans; he imagined that a promise of a wedding-present would easily secure her governess: but this was a slight mistake; avarice happened not to be the ruling, or, at least at this time, the reigning passion of mademoiselle's mind; and quickly perceiving his error, he paid assiduous court to her vanity. She firmly believed that she had captivated him, and was totally blind to his real designs. The grand difficulty with Dashwood was, not to persuade her of his passion, but to prevent her from believing him too soon; and he thought it expedient to delay completing his conquest of the governess till he had gained an equally powerful influence over her pupil. One evening, Dashwood, passing through a sheltered walk, heard Lady Augusta and Mr. Mountague talking very loudly and eagerly: they passed through the grove so quickly that he could catch only the words "phaeton—imprudence."

"Pshaw! jealousy—nonsense."

"Reasonable woman for a wife."

"Pooh, no such thing."

"My unalterable resolution," were the concluding words of Mr. Mountague, in a calm but decided voice; and, "As you please, sir! I've no notion of giving up my will in every thing," the concluding words of Lady Augusta pronounced in a pettish tone, as she broke from him; yet pausing for a moment, Dashwood, to his great surprise and concern, heard her in a softer tone add a but, which showed she was not quite willing to break from Mr. Mountague for ever. Dashwood was alarmed beyond measure; but the lady did not long continue in this frame of mind, for, upon going into her dressing-room to rest herself, she found her governess at the glass.

"Bon Dieu!" exclaimed mademoiselle, turning round: "Miladi told me you was gone out—mais qu'est ce que c'est? vous voilà pâle—you are as white—blanc comme mon linge," cried she, with emphasis, at the same time touching a handkerchief, which was so far from white, that her pupil could not help bursting out into a laugh at the unfortunate illustration. "Pauvre petite! tenez," continued mademoiselle, running up to her with salts, apprehensive that she was going into fits.

"I am not ill, thank you," said Lady Augusta, taking the smelling bottle.

"But don't tell me dat," said mademoiselle: "I saw you walking out of de window wid dat man, and I know dis is some new démêlé wid him. Come, point de secret, mon enfant. Has not he being giving you one good lecture?"

"Lecture!" said Lady Augusta, rising with becoming spirit: "no, mademoiselle, I am not to be lectured by any body."

"No, to be sure; dat is what I say, and, surtout, not by a lover. Quel homme! why I would not have him to pay his court to me for all de world. Why, pauvre petite, he has made you look ten years older ever since he began to fall in love wid you. Dis what you call a lover in England? Bon, why, I know noting of de matter, if he be one bit in love wid you, mon enfant."

"Oh, as to that, he certainly is in love with me: whatever other faults he has, I must do him that justice."

"Justice! Oh, let him have justice, de tout mon caeur; but I say, if he be a man in love, he is de oddest man in love I ever happen to see; he eat, drink, sleep, talk, laugh, se possede tout comme un autre. Bon Dieu! I would not give noting at all myself for such a sort of a lover. Mon enfant, dis is not de way I would wish to see you loved; dis is not de way no man ought for to dare for to love you."

"And how ought I to be loved?" asked Lady Augusta, impatiently.

"La belle question! Eh! don't every body, de stupidest person in de world, know how dey ought to be love? Mais passionnément, éperdument—dere is a—a je ne sais quoi dat infailliblement distinguish de true lover from de false."

"Then," said Lady Augusta, "you really don't think that Mr. Mountague loves me?"

"Tink!" replied mademoiselle, "I don't tink about it; but have not I said enough? Open your eyes; make your own comparaisons."

Before Lady Augusta had made her comparisons, a knock at the door from her maid came to let her know that Lord George was waiting.

"Ah! milord George! I won't keep you den: va t'en."

"But now, do you know, it was only because I just said that I was going out with Lord George that Mr. Mountague made all this rout."

"Den let him make his rout; qu'importe? Miladi votre chère mère make no objections. Quelle impertinence! If he was milord duc he could not give himself no more airs. Va, man enfant—Dis a lover! Quel homme, quel tyran! and den, of course, when he grows to be a husband, he will be worserer and worserer, and badderer and badderer, when he grows to be your husband."

"Oh," cried Lady Augusta, snatching up her gloves hastily, "my husband he shall never be, I am determined. So now I'll give him his coup de grace."

"Bon!" said mademoiselle, following her pupil, "and I must not miss to be by, for I shall love to see dat man mortify."

"You are going then?" said Mr. Mountague, gravely, as she passed.

"Going, going, going, gone!" cried Lady Augusta, who, tripping carelessly by, gave her hand to the sulky lord; then springing into the phaeton, said as usual—"I know, my lord, you'll break my neck;" at the same time casting a look at Mr. Mountague, which seemed to say—"I hope you'll break your heart, at least."

When she returned from her airing, the first glance at Mr. Mountague's countenance convinced her that her power was at an end. She was not the only person who observed this. Dashwood, under his air of thoughtless gaiety, watched all that passed with the utmost vigilance, and he knew how to avail himself of every circumstance that could be turned to his own advantage. He well knew that a lady's ear is never so happily prepared for the voice of flattery as after having been forced to hear that of sincerity. Dashwood contrived to meet Lady Augusta, just after she had been mortified by her late admirer's total recovery of his liberty, and, seizing well his moment, pressed his suit with gallant ardour. As he exhibited all those signs of passion which her governess would have deemed unequivocal, the young lady thought herself justified in not absolutely driving him to despair.

Where was Lady S— all this time! Where?—at the card-table, playing very judiciously at whist. With an indolent security, which will be thought incredible by those who have not seen similar instances of folly in great families, she let every thing pass before her eyes without seeing it. Confident that her daughter, after having gone through the usual routine, would meet with some suitable establishment, that the settlements would then be the father's business, the choice of the jewels hers, she left her dear Augusta, in the meantime, to conduct herself; or, what was ten times worse, to be conducted by Mlle. Panache. Thus to the habitual indolence, or temporary convenience of parents, are the peace and reputation of a family secretly sacrificed. And we may observe, that those who take the least precaution to prevent imprudence in their children are most enraged and implacable when the evil becomes irremediable.

In losing Mr. Mountague's heart, Lady Augusta's vanity felt a double pang, from the apprehension that Helen would probably recover her captive. Acting merely from the impulse of the moment, her ladyship was perfectly a child in her conduct; she seldom knew her own mind two hours together, and really did not foresee the consequences of any one of her actions. Half a dozen incompatible wishes filled her heart, or, rather, her imagination. The most immediate object of vanity had always the greatest power over her; and upon this habit of mind Dashwood calculated with security.

In the pride of conquest, her ladyship had rejoiced at her mother's inviting Mrs. Temple and her daughters to an entertainment at S— Hall, where she flattered herself that Mr. Mountague would appear as her declared admirer. The day, alas! came; but things had taken a new turn, and Lady Augusta was as impatient that the visit should be finished, as she had been eager to have the invitation sent. Lady S— was not precisely informed of all that was going on in her own house, as we have observed; and she was, therefore, a little surprised at the look of vexation with which her daughter heard that she had pressed Mrs. Temple to stay all night. "My dear," said Lady S—, "you know you can sleep in mademoiselle's room for this one night, and Miss Helen Temple will have yours. One should be civil to people, especially when one sees them but seldom." Lady Augusta was much out of humour with her mother's ill-timed civility; but there was no remedy. In the hurry of moving her things at night, Lady Augusta left in her dressing table drawer a letter of Dashwood's—a letter which she would not have had seen by Miss Helen Temple for any consideration. Our readers may imagine what her ladyship's consternation must have been, when, the next morning, Helen put the letter into her hand, saying, "There's a paper you left in your dressing-table, Lady Augusta." The ingenuous countenance of Helen, as she spoke, might have convinced any one but Lady Augusta that she was incapable of having opened this paper; but her ladyship judged otherwise: she had no doubt that every syllable of the letter had been seen, and that her secret would quickly be divulged. The company had not yet assembled at breakfast. She retired precipitately to her own room, to consider what could possibly be done in this emergency. She at length resolved to apply to Mr. Mountague for assistance; for she had seen enough of him to feel assured that he was a man of honour, and that she might safely trust him. When she heard him go down stairs to breakfast, she followed, and contrived to give him a note, which he read with no small degree of surprise.

"How to apologize for myself I know not, nor have I one moment's time to deliberate. Believe me, I feel my sensibility and delicacy severely wounded; but an ill-fated, uncontrollable passion must plead my excuse. I candidly own that my conduct must appear to you in a strange light; but spare me, I beseech you, all reproaches, and pardon my weakness, for on your generosity and honour must I rely, in this moment of distress.

"A letter of mine—a fatal letter from Dashwood—has fallen into the hands of Miss Helen Temple. All that I hold most dear is at her mercy. I am fully persuaded that, were she to promise to keep my secret, nothing on earth would tempt her to betray me; but I know she has so much the habit of speaking of every thing to her mother, that I am in torture till this promise is obtained. Your influence I must depend upon. Speak to her, I conjure you, the moment breakfast is over; and assure yourself of my unalterable gratitude.

"AUGUSTA —."

The moment breakfast was over, Mr. Mountague followed Helen into the library; a portfolio, full of prints, lay open on the table, and as he turned them over, he stopped at a print of Alexander putting his seal to the lips of Hephaestion, whom he detected reading a letter over his shoulder. Helen, as he looked at the print, said she admired the delicacy of Alexander's reproof to his friend; but observed, that it was scarcely probable the seal should bind Hephsestion's lips.

"How so?" said Mr. Mountague, eagerly.

"Because," said Helen, "if honour could not restrain his curiosity, it would hardly secure his secrecy."

"Charming girl!" exclaimed Mr. Mountague, with enthusiasm. Helen, struck with surprise, and a variety of emotions, coloured deeply. "I beg your pardon," said Mr. Mountague, changing his tone, "for being so abrupt. You found a letter of Lady Augusta's last night. She is in great, I am sure needless, anxiety about it."

"Needless, indeed; I did not think it necessary to assure Lady Augusta, when I returned her letter, that I had not read it. I gave it her because I thought she would not like to have an open letter left where it might fall into the hands of servants. As she has mentioned this subject to you, I hope, sir, you will persuade her of the truth; you seem to be fully convinced of it yourself."

"I am, indeed, fully convinced of your integrity, of the generosity, the simplicity of your mind. May I ask whether you formed any conjecture, whether you know whom that letter was from?"

Helen, with an ingenuous look, replied—"Yes, sir, I did form a conjecture—I thought it was from you."

"From me!" exclaimed Mr. Mountague. "I must undeceive you there: the letter was not mine. I am eager," continued he, smiling, "to undeceive you. I wish I might flatter myself this explanation could ever be half as interesting to you as it is to me. That letter was not mine, and I can never, in future, be on any other terms with Lady Augusta than those of a common acquaintance."

Here they were interrupted by the sudden entrance of mademoiselle, followed by Dashwood, to whom she was talking with great earnestness. Mr. Mountague, when he had collected his thoughts sufficiently to think of Lady Augusta, wrote the following answer to her letter:—

"Your ladyship may be perfectly at ease with respect to your note. Miss Helen Temple has not read it, nor has she, I am convinced, the slightest suspicion of its contents or its author. I beg leave to assure your ladyship, that I am sensible of the honour of your confidence, and that you shall never have any reason to repent of having trusted in my discretion. Yet permit me, even at the hazard of appearing impertinent, at the still greater hazard of incurring your displeasure, to express my most earnest hope that nothing will tempt you to form a connexion, which I am persuaded would prove fatal to the happiness of your future life. I am, with much respect, Your ladyship's obedient servant, F. MOUNTAGUE."

Lady Augusta read this answer to her note with the greatest eagerness: the first time she ran her eye over it, joy, to find her secret yet undiscovered, suspended every other feeling; but, upon a second perusal, her ladyship felt extremely displeased by the cold civility of the style, and somewhat alarmed at the concluding paragraph. With no esteem, and little affection for Dashwood, she had suffered herself to imagine that her passion for him was uncontrollable.

What degree of felicity she was likely to enjoy with a man destitute equally of fortune and principle, she had never attempted to calculate; but there was something awful in the words—"I earnestly hope that nothing will tempt you to form a connexion which would prove fatal to your future happiness." Whilst she was pondering upon these words, Dashwood met her in the park, where she was walking alone. "Why so grave?" exclaimed he, with anxiety.

"I am only thinking—that—I am afraid—I think this is a silly business: I wish, Mr. Dashwood, you wouldn't think any more of it, and give me back my letters."

Dashwood vehemently swore that her letters were dearer to him than life, and that the "last pang should tear them from his heart."

"But, if we go on with all this," resumed Lady Augusta, "it will at least break my mother's heart, and mademoiselle's into the bargain; besides, I don't half believe you; I really—"

"I really, what?" cried he, pouring forth protestations of passion, which put Mr. Mountague's letter entirely out of her head.

A number of small motives sometimes decide the mind in the most important actions of our lives; and faults are often attributed to passion which arise from folly. The pleasure of duping her governess, the fear of witnessing Helen's triumph over her lover's recovered affections, and the idea of the bustle and éclat of an elopement, all mixed together, went under the general denomination of love!—Cupid is often blamed for deeds in which he has no share.

"But," resumed Lady Augusta, after making the last pause of expiring prudence, "what shall we do about mademoiselle?"

"Poor mademoiselle!" cried Dashwood, leaning back against a tree to support himself, whilst he laughed violently—"what do you think she is about at this instant?—packing up her clothes in a band-box."

"Packing up her clothes in a band-box!"

"Yes; she verily believes that I am dying with impatience to carry her off to Scotland, and at four o'clock to-morrow morning she trips down stairs out of the garden-door, of which she keeps the key, flies across the park, scales the gate, gains the village, and takes refuge with her good friend, Miss Lacy, the milliner, where she is to wait for me. Now, in the mean time, the moment the coast is clear, I fly to you, my real angel."

"Oh, no, upon my word," said Lady Augusta, so faintly, that Dashwood went on exactly in the same tone.

"I fly to you, my angel, and we shall be half way on our trip to Scotland before mademoiselle's patience is half exhausted, and before Miladi S— is quite awake."

Lady Augusta could not forbear smiling at this idea; and thus, by an unlucky stroke of humour, was the grand event of her life decided.

Marmontel's well-known story, called Heureusement, is certainly not a moral tale: to counteract its effects, he should have written Malheureusement, if he could.

Nothing happened to disconcert the measures of Lady Augusta and Dashwood.

The next morning Lady S— came down, according to her usual custom, late to breakfast. Mrs. Temple, Helen, Emma, Lord George, Mr. Mountague, &c., were assembled. "Has not mademoiselle made breakfast for us yet?" said Lady S—. She sat down, and expected every moment to see Mlle. Panache and her daughter make their appearance; but she waited in vain. Neither mademoiselle, Lady Augusta, nor Dashwood, were any where to be found. Every body round the breakfast-table looked at each other in silence, waiting the event. "They are out walking, I suppose," said Lady S—, which supposition contented her for the first five minutes; but then she exclaimed, "It's very strange they don't come back!"

"Very strange—I mean rather strange," said Lord George, helping himself, as he spoke, to his usual quantity of butter, and then drumming upon the table; whilst Mr. Mountague, all the time, looked down, and preserved a profound silence.

At length the door opened, and Mlle. Panache, in a riding habit, made her appearance. "Bon jour, miladi! Bon jour!" said she, looking round at the silent party, with a half terrified, half astonished countenance. "Je vous demande mille pardons—Qu'est ce que c'est? I have only been to take a walk dis morning into de village to de milliner's. She has disappointed me of my tings, dat kept me waiting; but I am come back in time for breakfast, I hope?"

"But where is my daughter?" cried Lady S—, roused at last from her natural indolence—"where is Lady Augusta?"

"Bon Dieu! Miladi, I don't know. Bon Dieu! in her bed, I suppose. Bon Dieu!" exclaimed she a third time, and turned as pale as ashes. "But where den is Mr. Dashwood?" At this instant a note, directed to mademoiselle, was brought into the room: the servant said that Lady Augusta's maid had just found it upon her lady's toilette—mademoiselle tore open the note.

"Excuse me to my mother—you can best plead my excuse.

"You will not see me again till I am

'Augusta Dashwood.'"

"Ah scélérat! Ah scélérat! Il m'a trahi!" screamed mademoiselle: she threw down the note, and sunk upon the sofa in real hysterics; whilst Lady S—, seeing in one and the same moment her own folly and her daughter's ruin, fixed her eyes upon the words "Augusta Dashwood," and fainted. Mr. Mountague led Lord George out of the room with him, whilst Mrs. Temple, Helen, and her sister, ran to the assistance of the unhappy mother and the detected governess.

As soon as mademoiselle had recovered tolerable composure, she recollected that she had betrayed too violent emotion on this occasion. "Il m'a trahi," were words, however, that she could not recall; it was in vain she attempted to fabricate some apology for herself. No apology could avail: and whilst Lady S—, in silent anguish, wept for her own and her daughter's folly, the governess, in loud and gross terms, abused Dashwood, and reproached her pupil with having shown duplicity, ingratitude, and a bad heart.

"A bad education!" exclaimed Lady S—, with a voice of mingled anger and sorrow. "Leave the room, mademoiselle; leave my house. How could I choose such a governess for my daughter! Yet, indeed," added her ladyship, turning to Mrs. Temple, "she was well recommended to me, and how could I foresee all this?"

To such an appeal, at such a time, there was no reply to be made: it is cruel to point out errors to those who feel that they are irreparable; but it is benevolent to point them out to others, who have yet their choice to make.

THE KNAPSACK (1)

(Footnote 1: In the Travels of M. Beanjolin into Sweden, he mentions having, in the year 1790, met carriages laden with the knapsacks of Swedish soldiers, who had fallen in battle in Finland. These carriages were escorted by peasants, who were relieved at every stage, and thus the property of the deceased was conveyed from one extremity of the kingdom to the other, and faithfully restored to their relations. The Swedish peasants are so remarkably honest, that scarcely any thing is ever lost in these convoys of numerous and ill-secured packages.)

DRAMATIS PERSONAE
COUNT HELMAAR, a Swedish Nobleman.
CHRISTIERN, a Swedish Soldier.
ALEFTSON, Count Helmaar's Fool.
THOMAS, a Footman.
ELEONORA, a Swedish Lady, beloved by Count Helmaar.
CHRISTINA, Sister to Helmaar.
ULRICA, an old Housekeeper.
CATHERINE, Wife to Christiern.
KATE and ULRIC, the Son and Daughter of Catherine—they are six and seven years old.
Serjeant, and a Troop of Soldiers, a Train of Dancers, a Page, Peasants, &c.

ACT I

SCENE—A cottage in Sweden.—CATHERINE, a young and handsome woman, is sitting at her spinning wheel.—A little Boy and Girl, of six and seven years of age, are seated on the ground eating their dinner.

CATHERINE sings, while she is spinning.
Haste from the wars, oh, haste to me,
The wife that fondly waits for thee;
Long are the years, and long each day,
While my loved soldier's far away.
Haste from the wars, &c.

Lone ev'ry field, and lone the bow'r; Pleasant to me nor sun nor show'r: The snows are gone, the flow'rs are gay—Why is my life of life away? Haste from the wars, &c.

Little Girl. When will father come home?

Little Boy. When will he come, mother? when? To-day? to-morrow?

Cath. No, not to-day, nor to-morrow, but soon, I hope, very soon; for they say the wars are over.

Little Girl. I am glad of that, and when father comes home, I'll give him some of my flowers.

Little Boy (who is still eating). And I'll give him some of my bread and cheese, which he'll like better than flowers, if he is as hungry as I am, and that to be sure he will be, after coming such a long, long journey.

Little Girl. Long, long journey! how long?—how far is father off, mother?—where is he?

Little Boy. I know, he is in—in—in—in—in Finland? how far off, mother?

Cath. A great many miles, my dear; I don't know how many.

Little Boy. Is it not two miles to the great house, mother, where we go to sell our faggots?

Cath. Yes, about two miles—and now you had best set out towards the great house, and ask Mrs. Ulrica, the housekeeper, to pay you the little bill she owes you for faggots—there's good children; and when you have been paid for your faggots, you can call at the baker's, in the village, and bring home some bread for to-morrow (patting the little boy's head)—you that love bread and cheese so much must work hard to get it.

Little Boy. Yes, so I will work hard, then I shall have enough for myself and father too, when he comes. Come along—come (to his sister)—and, as we come home through the forest, I'll show you where we can get plenty of sticks for to-morrow, and we'll help one another.

Little Girl sings.

That's the best way, At work and at play, To help one another—I heard mother say—To help one another—I heard mother say—

(The children go off, singing these words.)

Cath. (alone.) Dear, good children, how happy their father will be to see them, when he comes back!—(She begins to eat the remains of the dinner, which the children have left.) The little rogue was so hungry, he has not left me much; but he would have left me all, if he had thought that I wanted it: he shall have a good large bowl of milk for supper. It was but last night he skimmed the cream off his milk for me, because he thought I liked it. Heigho!—God knows how long they may have milk to skim—as long as I can work they shall never want; but I'm not so strong as I used to be; but then I shall get strong, and all will be well, when my husband comes back (a drum beats at a distance). Hark! a drum!—some news from abroad, perhaps—nearer and nearer (she sinks upon a chair)—why cannot I run to see—to ask (the drum beats louder and louder)—fool that I am! they will be gone! they will be all gone! (she starts up.)

(Exit hastily.)

SCENE changes to a high road, leading to a village.—A party of ragged, tired soldiers, marching slowly. Serjeant ranges them.

Serj. Keep on, my brave fellows, keep on, we have not a great way further to go:—keep on, my brave fellows, keep on, through yonder village. (The drum beats.)

(Soldiers exeunt.)

Serj. (alone.) Poor fellows, my heart bleeds to see them! the sad remains, these, of as fine a regiment as ever handled a musket. Ah! I've seen them march quite another guess sort of way, when they marched, and I amongst them, to face the enemy—heads up—step firm—thus it was—quick time—march!—(he marches proudly)—My poor fellows, how they lag now (looking after them)—ay, ay, there they go, slower and slower; they don't like going through the village; nor I neither; for, at every village we pass through, out come the women and children, running after us, and crying, "Where's my father?—What's become of my husband?"—Stout fellow as I am, and a Serjeant too, that ought to know better, and set the others an example, I can't stand these questions.

Enter CATHERINE, breathless.

Cath. I—I—I've overtaken him at last. Sir—Mr. Serjeant, one word! What news from Finland?

Serj. The best—the war's over. Peace is proclaimed.

Cath. (clasping her hands joyfully.) Peace! happy sound!—Peace! The war's over!—Peace!—And the regiment of Helmaar—(The Serjeant appears impatient to get away)—Only one word, good serjeant: when will the regiment of Helmaar be back?

Serj. All that remain of it will be home next week.

Cath. Next week?—But, all that remain, did you say?—Then many have been killed?

Serj. Many, many—too many. Some honest peasants are bringing home the knapsacks of those who have fallen in battle. 'Tis fair that what little they had should come home to their families. Now, I pray you, let me pass on.

Cath. One word more: tell me, do you know, in the regiment of Helmaar, one Christiern Aleftson?

Serj, (with eagerness.) Christiern Aleftson! as brave a fellow, and as good as ever lived, if it be the same that I knew.

Cath. As brave a fellow, and as good as ever lived! Oh, that's he! he is my husband—where is he? where is he?

Serj, (aside.) She wrings my heart!—(Aloud)—He was—

Cath. Was!

Serj. He is, I hope, safe.

Cath. You hope!—don't look away—I must see your face: tell me all you know.

Serj. I know nothing for certain. When the peasants come with the knapsacks, you will hear all from them. Pray you, let me follow my men; they are already at a great distance.

(Exit Serj. followed by Catherine.)

Cath. I will not detain you an instant—only one word more—

(Exit.)

SCENE.—An apartment in Count Helmaar's Castle.—A train of dancers.—After they have danced for some time,

Enter a Page.

Page. Ladies! I have waited, according to your commands, till Count Helmaar appeared in the ante-chamber—he is there now, along with the ladies Christina and Eleonora.

1st Dancer. Now is our time—Count Helmaar shall hear our song to welcome him home.

2nd Dancer. None was ever more welcome.

3rd Dancer. But stay till I have breath to sing.

SONG.
I.
Welcome, Helmaar, welcome home;
In crowds your happy neighbours come,
To hail with joy the cheerful morn,
That sees their Helmaar's safe return.

II.
No hollow heart, no borrow'd face.
Shall ever Helmaar's hall disgrace:
Slaves alone on tyrants wait;

Friends surround the good and great.

Welcome Helmaar, &c.

Enter ELEONORA, CHRISTINA, and COUNT HELMAAR.

Helmaar. Thanks, my friends, for this kind welcome.

1st Dancer (looking at a black fillet on Helmaar's head). He has been wounded.

Christina. Yes—severely wounded.

Helmaar. And had it not been for the fidelity of the soldier who carried me from the field of battle, I should never have seen you more, my friends, nor you, my charming Eleonora. (A noise of one singing behind the scenes.)—What disturbance is that without?

Christina. Tis only Aleftson, the fool:—in your absence, brother, he has been the cause of great diversion in the castle:—I love to play upon him, it keeps him in tune;—you can't think how much good it does him.

Helmaar. And how much good it does you, sister:—from your childhood you had always a lively wit, and loved to exercise it; but do you waste it upon fools?

Christina. I'm sometimes inclined to think this Aleftson is more knave than fool.

Eleon. By your leave, Lady Christina, he is no knave, or I am much mistaken. To my knowledge, he has carried his whole salary, and all the little presents he has received from us, to his brother's wife and children. I have seen him chuck his money, thus, at those poor children, when they have been at their plays, and then run away, lest their mother should make them give it back.

Enter ALEFTSON, the fool, in a fool's coat, fool's cap and bells, singing.

I.
There's the courtier, who watches the nod of the great;
Who thinks much of his pension, and nought of the state:
When for ribands and titles his honour he sells—
What is he, my friends, but a fool without bells?

II.
There's the gamester, who stakes on the turn of a die
His house and his acres, the devil knows why:
His acres he loses, his forests he sells—
What is he, my friends, but a fool without bells?

III.
There's the student so crabbed and wonderful wise,
With his plus and his minus, his x's and y's:
Pale at midnight he pores o'er his magical spells—

What is he, my friends, but a fool without bells?

IV.
The lover, who's ogling, and rhyming, and sighing,
Who's musing, and pining, and whining, and dying:
When a thousand of lies ev'ry minute he tells—
What is he, my friends, but a fool without bells?

V.
There's the lady so fine, with her airs and her graces,
With a face like an angel's—if angels have faces:
She marries, and Hymen the vision dispels—
What's her husband, my friends, but a fool without bells?

Christina, Eleonora, Helmaar, &c.—Bravo! bravissimo!—excellent fool!—Encore.

(The fool folds his arms, and begins to cry bitterly.)

Christina. What now, Aleftson? I never saw you sad before—What's the matter?—Speak.

(Fool sobs, but gives no answer.)

Helm. Why do you weep so bitterly?

Aleft. Because I am a fool.

Helm. Many should weep, if that were cause sufficient.

Eleon. But, Aleftson, you have all your life, till now, been a merry fool.

Fool. Because always, till now, I was a fool, but now I am grown wise: and 'tis difficult, to all but you, lady, to be merry and wise.

Christina. A pretty compliment; 'tis a pity it was paid by a fool.

Fool. Who else should pay compliments, lady, or who else believe them?

Christina. Nay, I thought it was the privilege of a fool to speak the truth without offence.

Fool. Fool as you take me to be, I'm not fool enough yet to speak truth to a lady, and think to do it without offence.

Eleon. Why, you have said a hundred severe things to me within this week, and have I ever been angry with you?

Fool. Never; for, out of the whole hundred, not one was true. But have a care, lady—fool as I am, you'd be glad to stop a fool's mouth with your white hand this instant, rather than let him tell the truth of you.

Christina (laughing, and all the other ladies, except Eleonora, exclaim)—Speak on, good fool; speak on—

Helm. I am much mistaken, or the lady Eleonora fears not to hear the truth from either wise men or fools—Speak on.

Fool. One day, not long ago, when there came news that our count there was killed in Finland—I, being a fool, was lying laughing, and thinking of nothing at all, on the floor, in the west drawing-room, looking at the count's picture—In comes the Lady Eleonora, all in tears.

Eleon. (stopping his mouth.) Oh! tell any thing but that, good fool.

Helmaar (kneels and kisses her hand). Speak on, excellent fool.

Christina and ladies. Speak on, excellent fool—In came the Lady Eleonora, all in tears.

Fool. In comes the Lady Eleonora, all in tears—(pauses and looks round). Why now, what makes you all so curious about these tears?—Tears are but salt water, let them come from what eyes they will—my tears are as good as hers—in came John Aleftson, all in tears, just now, and nobody kneels to me—nobody kisses my hands—nobody cares half a straw for my tears—(folds his arms and looks melancholy). I am not one of those—I know the cause of my tears too well.

Helm. Perhaps they were caused by my unexpected return—hey?

Fool (scornfully). No—I am not such a fool as that comes to. Don't I know that, when you are at home, the poor may hold up their heads, and no journeyman-gentleman of an agent dares then to go about plaguing those who live in cottages? No, no,—I am not such a fool as to cry because Count Helmaar is come back; but the truth is, I cried because I am tired and ashamed of wearing this thing—(throwing down his fool's cap upon the floor, changes his tone entirely)—I!—who am brother to the man who saved Count Helmaar's life—I to wear a fool's cap and bells—Oh shame! shame!

(The ladies look at one another with signs of astonishment.)

Christina (aside). A lucid interval—poor fool!—I will torment him no more—he has feeling—'twere better he had none.

Eleon. Hush!—hear him!

Aleft. (throwing himself at the counts feet). Noble count, I have submitted to be thought a fool; I have worn this fool's cap in your absence, that I might indulge my humour, and enjoy the liberty of speaking my mind freely to the people of all conditions. Now that you are returned, I have no need of such a disguise—I may now speak the truth without fear, and without a cap and bells.—I resign my salary, and give back the ensign of my office—(presents the fool's cap).

(Exit.)

Christina. He might well say, that none but fools should pay compliments—this is the best compliment that has been paid you, brother.

Eleon. And observe, he has resigned his salary.

Helm. From this moment let it be doubled:—he made an excellent use of money when he was a fool—may he make half as good a use of it now he is a wise man.

Christina. Amen—and now I hope we are to have some more dancing.

(Exeunt.)

SCENE—By moonlight—a forest—a castle illuminated at a distance.—A group of peasants seated on the ground, each with a knapsack beside him.—One peasant lies stretched on the ground.

1st Peasant. Why, what I say is, that the wheel of the cart being broken, and the horse dead lame, and Charles there in that plight—(points to the sleeping peasant)—it is a folly to think of getting on further this evening.

2nd Peasant. And what I say is, it's folly to sleep here, seeing I know the country, and am certain sure we have not above one mile at furthest to go, before we get to the end of our journey.

1st Peasant (pointing to the sleeper). He can't walk a mile—he's done for—dog tired—

3rd Peasant. Are you certain sure we have only one mile further to go?

2nd Peasant. Certain sure—

All, except the sleeper and the 1st Peasant. Oh, let us go on, then, and we can carry the knapsacks on our backs for this one mile.

1st Peasant. You must carry him, then, knapsack and all.

All together. So we will.

2nd Peasant. But first, do you see, let's waken him; for a sleeping man's twice as heavy as one that's awake—Hollo, friend! waken! waken!—(he shakes the sleeper, who snores loudly)—Good Lord, he snores loud enough to waken all the birds in the wood.

(All the peasants shout in the sleeper's ear, and he starts up, shaking himself.)

Charles. Am I awake?—(stretching.)

2nd Peasant. No, not yet, man—Why, don't you know where you are? Ay; here's the moon—and these be trees; and—I be a man, and what do you call this? (holding up a knapsack.)

Charles. A knapsack, I say, to be sure:—I'm as broad awake as the best of you.

2nd Peasant. Come on, then; we've a great way further to go before you sleep again.

Charles. A great way further! further to-night!—No, no.

2nd Peasant. Yes, yes; we settled it all while you were fast asleep—You are to be carried, you and your knapsack.

(They prepare to carry him.)

Charles (starting up, and struggling with them). I've legs to walk—I won't be carried!—I, a Swede, and be carried!—No! No!—

All together. Yes! Yes!

Charles. No! No!—(he struggles for his knapsack, which comes untied in the struggle, and all the things fall out.)—There, this comes of playing the fool.

(They help him to pick up the things, and exclaim,)

All. There's no harm done—(throwing the knapsack over his shoulder).

Charles. I'm the first to march, after all.

Peasants. Ay, in your sleep!

(Exeunt, laughing.)

Enter CATHERINE'S two little Children.

Little Girl. I am sure I heard some voices this way—suppose it was the fairies!

Little Boy. It was only the rustling of the leaves. There are no such things as fairies; but if there were any such, we have no need to fear them.

Little Boy sings.

I.
Nor elves, nor fays, nor magic charm,
Have pow'r, or will, to work us harm;
For those who dare the truth to tell,
Fays, elves, and fairies, wish them well.

II.
For us they spread their dainty fare,
For us they scent the midnight air;
For us their glow-worm lamps they light,
For us their music cheers the night.

Little Girl sings.

I.

Ye fays and fairies, hasten here,
Robed in glittering gossamere;
With tapers bright, and music sweet,
And frolic dance, and twinkling feet.

II.

And, little Mable, let us view
Your acorn goblets fill'd with dew;
Nor warn us hence till we have seen
The nut-shell chariot of your queen:

III.

In which on nights of yore she sat,
Driven by her gray-coated gnat;
With spider spokes and cobweb traces,
And horses fit for fairy races.

IV.

And bid us join your revel ring,
And see you dance, and hear you sing:
Your fairy dainties let us taste,
And speed us home with fairy haste.

Little Boy. If there were really fairies, and if they would give me my wish, I know what I should ask.

Little Girl. And so do I—I would ask them to send father home before I could count ten.

Little Boy. And I would ask to hear his general say to him, in the face of the whole army, "This is a brave man!" And father should hold up his head as I do now, and march thus by the side of his general.

(As the little Boy marches, he stumbles.)

Little Girl. Oh! take care!—come, let us march home:—but stay, I have not found my faggot.

Little Boy. Never mind your faggot; it was not here you left it.

Little Girl. Yes, it was somewhere here, I'm sure, and I must find it, to carry it home to mother, to make a blaze for her before she goes to bed.

Little Boy. But she will wonder what keeps us up so late.

Little Girl. But we shall tell her what kept us. Look under those trees, will you, whilst I look here, for my faggot.—When we get home, I shall say, "Mother, do you know there is great news?—there's a great many, many candles in the windows of the great house, and dancing and music in the great house, because the master's come home, and the housekeeper had not time to pay us, and we waited and waited with our faggots; at last the butler—"

Little Boy. Heyday!—What have we here?—a purse, a purse, a heavy purse.

Little Girl. Whose can it be? let us carry it home to mother.

Little Boy. No, no; it can't be mother's: mother has no purse full of money. It must belong to somebody at the great house.

Little Girl. Ay, very likely to dame Ulrica, the housekeeper, for she has more purses and money than any body else in the world.

Little Boy. Come, let us run back with it to her,—mother would tell us to do so, I'm sure, if she was here.

Little Girl. But I'm afraid the housekeeper won't see us to-night.

Little Boy. Oh, yes; but I'll beg, and pray, and push, till I get into her room.

Little Girl. Yes; but don't push me, or I shall knock my head against the trees. Give me your hand, brother.—Oh, my faggot! I shall never find you.

(Exeunt.)

SCENE—Catherine's Cottage.

CATHERINE, spinning, sings.
I.
Turn swift, my wheel, my busy wheel,
And leave my heart no time to feel;
Companion of my widow'd hour,
My only friend, my only dow'r.

II.
Thy lengthening thread I love to see,
Thy whirring sound is dear to me:
Oh, swiftly turn by night and day,
And toil for him that's far away.

Catherine. Hark! here come the children. No, 'twas only the wind. What can keep these children so late?—but it is a fine moonlight night—they'll have brave appetites for their supper when they come back—but I wonder they don't come home.—Heigho! since their father has been gone, I am grown a coward—(a knock at the door heard)—Come in!—Why does every knock at the door startle me in this way?

Enter CHARLES, with a knapsack on his back

Charles. Mistress! mayhap you did not expect to see a stranger at this time o' night, as I guess by the looks of ye—but I'm only a poor fellow, that has been a-foot a great many hours.

Cath. Then, pray ye, rest yourself, and such fare as we have you're welcome to.

(She sets milk, &c., on a table. Charles throws himself into a chair, and flings his knapsack behind him.)

Charles. 'Tis a choice thing to rest one's self:—I say, mistress, you must know, I, and some more of us peasants, have come a many, many leagues since break of day.

Cath. Indeed, you may well be tired—and where do you come from?—Did you meet, on your road, any soldiers coming back from Finland?

Charles (eats and speaks). Not the soldiers themselves, I can't say as I did; but we are them that are bringing home the knapsacks of the poor fellows that have lost their lives in the wars in Finland.

Cath. (during this speech of Charles, leans on the back of a chair. Aside) Now I shall know my fate.

Charles (eating and speaking). My comrades are gone on to the village beyond with their knapsacks, to get them owned by the families of them to whom they belonged, as it stands to reason and right. Pray, mistress, as you know the folks here-abouts, could you tell me whose knapsack this is, here, behind me? (looking up at Catherine.)—Oons, but how pale she looks! (aside). Here, sit ye down, do. (Aside) Why, I would not have said a word if I had thought on it—to be sure she has a lover now, that has been killed in the wars. (Aloud) Take a sup of the cold milk, mistress.

Catherine (goes fearfully towards the knapsack). 'Tis his! 'tis my husband's!

(She sinks down on a chair, and hides her face with her hands.)

Charles. Poor soul! poor soul!—(he pauses.) But now it is not clear to me that you may not be mistaken, mistress:—these knapsacks be all so much alike, I'm sure I could not, for the soul of me, tell one from t'other—it is by what's in the inside only one can tell for certain. (Charles opens the knapsack, pulls out a waistcoat, carries it towards Catherine, and holds it before her face.)—Look ye here, now; don't give way to sorrow while there's hope left—Mayhap, mistress—look at this now, can't ye, mistress?

(Catherine timidly moves her hands from before her face, sees the waistcoat, gives a faint scream, and falls back in a swoon. The peasant runs to support her.—At this instant the back door of the cottage opens, and ALEFTSON enters.)

Aleft. Catherine!

Charles. Poor soul!—there, raise her head—give her air—she fell into this swoon at the sight of yonder knapsack—her husband's—he's dead. Poor creature!—'twas my luck to bring the bad news—what shall we do for her?—I'm no better than a fool, when I see a body this way.

Aleft. (sprinkling water on her face.) She'll be as well as ever she was, you'll see, presently—leave her to me!

Charles. There! she gave a sigh—she's coming to her senses.

(Catherine raises herself.)

Cath. What has been the matter?—(She starts at the sight of Aleftson.)—My husband!—no—'tis Aleftson—what makes you look so like him?—you don't look like yourself.

Aleft. (aside to the peasant.) Take that waistcoat out of the way.

Cath. (looking round, sees the knapsack.) What's there?—Oh, I recollect it all now.—(To Aleftson) Look there! look there! your brother! your brother's dead! Poor fool, you have no feeling.

Aleft. I wish I had none.

Cath. Oh, my husband!—shall I never, never see you more—never more hear your voice—never more see my children in their father's arms?

Aleft. (takes up the waistcoat, on which her eyes are fixed.) But we are not sure this is Christiern's.

Charles (snatching it from him). Don't show it to her again, man!—you'll drive her mad.

Aleft. (aside.) Let me alone; I know what I'm about. (Aloud) 'Tis certainly like a waistcoat I once saw him wear; but perhaps—

Cath. It is his—it is his—too well I know it—my own work—I gave it to him the very day he went away to the wars—he told me he would wear it again the day of his coming home—but he'll never come home again.

Aleft. How can you be sure of that?

Cath. How!—why, am not I sure, too sure?—hey!—what do you mean?—he smiles!—have you heard any thing?—do you know any thing?—but he can know nothing—he can tell me nothing—he has no sense. (She turns to the peasant.) Where did you get this knapsack?—did you see—

Aleft. He saw nothing—he knows nothing—he can tell you nothing:—listen to me, Catherine—see, I have thrown aside the dress of a fool—you know I had my senses once—I have them now as clear as ever I had in my life—ay, you may well be surprised—but I will surprise you more—Count Helmaar's come home.

Cath. Count Helmaar!—impossible!

Charles. Count Helmaar!—he was killed in the last battle, in Finland.

Aleft. I tell ye, he was not killed in any battle—he is safe at home—I have just seen him.

Cath. Seen him!—but why do I listen to him, poor fool! he knows not what he says—and yet, if the count be really alive—

Charles. Is the count really alive? I'd give my best cow to see him.

Aleft. Come with me, then, and in one quarter of an hour you shall see him.

Cath. (clasping her hands.) Then there is hope for me—Tell me, is there any news?

Aleft. There is.

Cath. Of my husband?

Aleft. Yes—ask me no more—you must hear the rest from Count Helmaar himself—he has sent for you.

Cath. (springs forward.) This instant let me go, let me hear—(she stops short at the sight of the waistcoat, which lies in her passage).—But what shall I hear?—there can be no good news for me—this speaks too plainly.

(Aleftson pulls her arm between his, and leads her away.)

Charles. Nay, master, take me, as you promised, along with you—I won't be left behind—I'm wide awake now—I must have a sight of Count Helmaar in his own castle—why, they'll make much of me in every cottage on my road home, when I can swear to 'em I've seen Count Helmaar alive, in his own castle, face to face—God bless him, he's the poor man's friend.

(Exeunt.)

SCENE—The housekeeper's room in Count HELMAAR'S Castle.

ULRICA and CHRISTIERN.

CHRISTIERN is drawing on his boots.—Mrs. ULRICA is sitting at a tea-table making coffee.

Mrs. Ulrica. Well, well; I'll say no more: if you can't stay to-night, you can't—but I had laid it all out in my head so cleverly, that you should stay, and take a good night's rest here, in the castle; then, in the morning, you'll find yourself as fresh as a lark.

Christiern. Oh! I am not at all tired.

Mrs. Ulrica. Not tired! don't tell me that, now, for I know that you are tired, and can't help being tired, say what you will—Drink this dish of coffee, at any rate—(he drinks coffee).

Christiern. But the thoughts of seeing my Catherine and my little ones—

Mrs. Ulrica. Very true, very true; but in one word, I want to see the happy meeting, for such things are a treat to me, and don't come every day, you know; and now, in the morning, I could go along with you to the cottage, but you must be sensible I could not be spared out this night, on no account or possibility.

Enter Footman.

Footman. Ma'am, the cook is hunting high and low for the brandy-cherries.

Mrs. Ulrica. Lord bless me! are not they there before those eyes of yours?—But I can't blame nobody for being out of their wits a little with joy such a night as this.

(Exit Footman.)

Christiern. Never man was better beloved in the regiment than Count Helmaar.

Mrs. Ulrica. Ay! ay! so he is every where, and so he deserves to be. Is your coffee good? sweeten to your taste, and don't spare sugar, nor don't spare any thing that this house affords; for, to be sure, you deserve it all—nothing can be too good for him that saved my master's life. So now that we are comfortable and quiet over our dish of coffee, pray be so very good as to tell me the whole story of my master's escape, and of the horse being killed under him, and of your carrying him off on your shoulders; for I've only heard it by bits and scraps, as one may say; I've seen only the bill of fare, ha! ha! ha!—so now pray set out all the good things for me, in due order, garnished and all; and, before you begin, taste these cakes—they are my own making.

Christiern (aside). 'Tis the one-and-twentieth time I've told the story to-day; but no matter. (Aloud) Why, then, madam, the long and the short of the story is—

Mrs. Ulrica. Oh, pray, let it be the long, not the short of the story, if you please: a story can never be too long for my taste, when it concerns my master—'tis, as one may say, fine spun sugar, the longer the finer, and the more I relish it—but I interrupt you, and you eat none of my cake—pray go on—(A call behind the scenes of Mrs. Ulrica! Mrs. Ulrica!)—Coming!—coming!—patience.

Christiern. Why, then, madam, we were, as it might be, here—just please to look; I've drawn the field of battle for you here, with coffee, on the table—and you shall be the enemy.

Mrs. Ulrica. I!—no—I'll not be the enemy—my master's enemy!

Christiern. Well, I'll be the enemy.

Mrs. Ulrica. You!—Oh no, you sha'n't be the enemy.

Christiern. Well, then, let the cake be the enemy.

Mrs. Ulrica. The cake—my cake!—no, indeed.

Christiern. Well, let the candle be the enemy.

Mrs. Ulrica. Well, let the candle be the enemy; and where was my master, and where are you—I don't understand—what is all this great slop?

Christiern. Why, ma'am, the field of battle; and let the coffee-pot be my master: here comes the enemy—

Enter Footman.

Footman. Mrs. Ulrica, more refreshments wanting for the dancers above.

Mrs. Ulrica. More refreshments!—more!—bless my heart, 'tis an unpossibility they can have swallowed down all I laid out, not an hour ago, in the confectionary room.

Footman. Confectionary room! Oh, I never thought of looking there.

Mrs. Ulrica. Look ye there, now!—why, where did you think of looking, then?—in the stable, or the cockloft, hey?—(Exit Footman.)—But I can't scold on such a night as this: their poor heads are all turned with joy; and my own's scarce in a more properer condition—Well, I beg your pardon—pray go on—the coffee-pot is my master, and the candle's the enemy.

Christiern. So, ma'am, here comes the enemy full drive, upon Count Helmaar.

(A call without of Mrs. Ulrica! Mrs. Ulrica! Mrs. Ulrica!)

Mrs. Ulrica. Mrs. Ulrica! Mrs. Ulrica!—can't you do without Mrs. Ulrica one instant but you must call, call—(Mrs. Ulrica! Mrs. Ulrica!)—Mercy on us, what do you want? I must go for one instant.

Christiern. And I must bid ye a good night.

Mrs. Ulrica. Nay, nay, nay,—(eagerly)—you won't go—I'll be back.

Enter Footman.

Footman Ma'am! Mrs. Ulrica! the key of the blue press.

Mrs. Ulrica. The key of the blue press—I had it in my hand just now—I gave it—I—(looks amongst a bunch of keys, and then all round the room)—I know nothing at all about it, I tell you—I must drink my tea, and I will—(Exit Footman). 'Tis a sin to scold on such a night as this, if one could help it—Well, Mr. Christiern, so the coffee-pot's my master.

Christiern. And the sugar-basin—why here's a key in the sugar-basin.

Mrs. Ulrica. Lord bless me! 'tis the very key, the key of the blue press—why dear me—(feels in her pocket)—and here are the sugar tongs in my pocket, I protest—where was my poor head? Hers, Thomas! Thomas! here's the key; take it, and don't say a word for your life, if you can help it; you need not come in, I say—(she holds the door—the footman pushes in).

Footman. But, ma'am, I have something particular to say.

Mrs. Ulrica. Why, you've always something particular to say—is it any thing about my master?

Footman. No, but about your purse, ma'am.

Mrs. Ulrica. What of my purse?

Footman. Here's your little godson, ma'am, is here, who has found it.

Mrs. Ulrica (aside). Hold your foolish tongue, can't you?—don't mention my little godson, for your life.

(The little boy creeps in under the footman's arm; his sister Kate follows him. Mrs. Ulrica lifts up her hands and eyes, with signs of impatience.)

Mrs. Ulrica (aside). Now I had settled in my head that their father should not see them till to-morrow morning.

Little Girl. Who is that strange man?

Little Boy. He has made me forget all I had to say.

Christiern (aside). What charming children!

Mrs. Ulrica (asid). He does not know them to be his—they don't know him to be their father. (Aloud) Well, children, what brings you here at this time of night?

Little Boy. What I was going to say was—(the little boy looks at the stranger between every two or three words, and Christiern looks at him)—what I was going to say was—

Little Girl. Ha! ha! ha!—he forgets that we found this purse in the forest as we were going home.

Little Boy. And we thought that it might be yours.

Mrs. Ulrica. Why should you think it was mine?

Little Boy. Because nobody else could have so much money in one purse; so we brought it to you—here it is.

Mrs. Ulrica. 'Tis none of my purse. (Aside) Oh! he'll certainly find out that they are his children—(she stands between the children and Christiern). 'Tis none of my purse; but you are good, honest little dears, and I'll be hanged if I won't carry you both up to my master himself, this very minute, and tell the story of your honesty before all the company.

(She pushes the children towards the door. Ulric looks back.)

Little Boy. He has a soldier's coat on—let me ask him if he is a soldier.

Mrs. Ulrica. No—what's that to you?

Little Girl. Let me ask him if he knows any thing about father.

Mrs. Ulrica (puts her hand before the little girl's mouth). Hold your little foolish tongue, I say—what's that to you?

(Exeunt, Mrs. Ulrica pushing forward the children.)

Enter, at the opposite door, THOMAS, the footman.

Footman. Sir, would you please to come into our servants'-hall, only for one instant: there's one wants to speak a word to you.

Christiern. Oh, I cannot stay another moment: I must go home: who is it?

Footman. 'Tis a poor man who has brought in two carts full of my master's baggage; and my master begs you'll be so very good as to see that the things are all right, as you know 'em, and no one else here does.

Christiern (with impatience). How provoking!—a full hour's work:—I sha'n't get home this night, I see that:—I wish the man and the baggage were in the Gulf of Finland. (Exeunt.)

SCENE—The apartment where the COUNT, ELEONORA, CHRISTINA, &c., were dancing.

Enter Mrs. ULRICA, eading the two children.

Christina. Ha! Mrs. Ulrica, and her little godson.

Mrs. Ulrica. My lady, I beg pardon for presuming to interrupt; but I was so proud of my little godson and his sister, though not my goddaughter, that I couldn't but bring them up, through the very midst of the company, to my master, to praise them according to their deserts; for nobody can praise those that deserve it so well as my master—to my fancy.

Eleonora (aside). Nor to mine.

Mrs. Ulrica. Here's a purse, sir, which this little boy and girl of mine found in the woods as they were going home; and, like honest children, as they are, they came back with it directly to me, thinking that it was mine.

Helmaar. Shake hands, my honest little fellow—this is just what I should have expected from a godson of Mrs. Ulrica, and a son of—

Mrs. Ulrica (aside to the Count). Oh, Lord bless you, sir, don't tell him—My lady—(to Christina)—would you take the children out of hearing?

Eleon. (to the children). Come with us, my dears.

(Exeunt ladies and children.)

Mrs. Ulrica. Don't, sir, pray, tell the children any thing about their father: they don't know that their father's here, though they've just seen him; and I've been striving all I can to keep the secret, and to keep the father here all night, that I may have the pleasure of seeing the meeting of father and mother and children at their own cottage to-morrow. I would not miss the sight of their meeting for fifty pounds; and yet I shall not see it after all—for Christiern will go, all I can say or do. Lord bless me! I forgot to bolt him in when I came up with the children—the bird's flown, for certain—(going in a great hurry).

Helmaar. Good Mrs. Ulrica, you need not be alarmed; your prisoner is very safe, I can assure you, though you forgot to bolt him in: I have given him an employment that will detain him a full hour, for I design to have the pleasure of restoring my deliverer myself to his family.

Mrs. Ulrica. Oh! that will be delightful!—Then you'll keep him here all night!—but that will vex him terribly; and of all the days and nights of the year, one wouldn't have any body vexed this day or night, more especially the man, who, as I may say, is the cause of all our illuminations, and rejoicings, and dancings—no, no, happen what will, we must not have him vexed.

Helmaar. He shall not be vexed, I promise you; and, if it be necessary to keep your heart from breaking, my good Mrs. Ulrica, I'll tell you a secret, which I had intended, I own, to have kept from you one half hour longer.

Mrs. Ulrica. A secret! dear sir, half an hour's a great while, to keep a secret from one when it's about one's friends: pray, if it be proper—but you are the best judge—I should be very glad to hear just a little hint of the matter, to prepare me.

Helmaar. Then prepare in a few minutes to see the happy meeting between Christiern and his family: I have sent to his cottage for his wife, to desire that she would come hither immediately.

Mrs. Ulrica. Oh! a thousand thanks to you, sir; but I'm afraid the messenger will let the cat out of the bag.

Helmaar. The man I have sent can keep a secret—Which way did the Lady Eleonora go?—Are those peasants in the hall? (Exit Count.)

Mrs. Ulrica (following). She went towards the west drawing-room, I think, sir.—Yes, sir, the peasants are at supper in the hall. (Aside) Bless me! I wonder what messenger he sent, for I don't know many—men I mean—fit to be trusted with a secret. (Exit.)

SCENE—An apartment in Count HELMAAR'S Castle.—ELEONORA.—CHRISTINA.—Little KATE and ULRIC asleep on the floor.

Eleon. Poor creatures! they were quite tired by sitting up so late: is their mother come yet?

Christina. Not yet; but she will soon be here, for my brother told Aleftson to make all possible haste. Do you know where my brother is?—he is not among the dancers. I expected to have found him sighing at the Lady Eleonora's feet.

Eleon. He is much better employed than in sighing at any body's feet; he is gone down into the great hall, to see and reward some poor peasants who have brought home the knapsacks of those unfortunate soldiers who fell in the last battle:—your good Mrs. Ulrica found out that these peasants were in the village near us—she sent for them, got a plentiful supper ready, and the count is now speaking to them.

Christina. And can you forgive my ungallant brother for thinking of vulgar boors, when he ought to be intent on nothing but your bright eyes?—then all I can say is, you are both of you just fit for one another: every fool, indeed, saw that long ago.

(A cry behind the scenes of "Long line Count Helmaar! Long live the good count! long live the poor man's friend!")

Christina (joins the cry). Long live Count Helmaar!—join me, Eleonora—long live the good count! long live the poor man's friend!

(The little children waken, start up, and stretch themselves.)

Eleon. There, you have wakened these poor children.

Ulric. What's the matter? I dreamed father was shaking hands with me.

Enter Mrs. ULRICA.

Little Kate. Mrs. Ulrica! where am I? I thought I was in my little bed at home—I was dreaming about a purse, I believe.

Mrs. Ulrica. Was it about this purse you were dreaming?—(shows the purse which the children found in the wood)—Come, take it into your little hands, and waken and rouse yourselves, for you must come and give this purse back to the rightful owner; I've found him out for you—(Aside to Christina and Eleonora). And now, ladies, if you please to go up into the gallery, you'll see something worth looking at.

(Exeunt.)

SCENE—A hall in Count HELMAAR'S Castle.—Peasants rising from supper in the back scene.

1st Peasant. Here's a health to the poor man's friend; and may every poor man, every poor honest man—and there are none other in Sweden—find as good a friend as Count Helmaar.

Enter CHARLES, eagerly.

Charles. Count Helmaar! is he here?

Omnes. Heyday! Charles, the sleeper, broad awake! or is he walking in his sleep?

Charles. Where's Count Helmaar, I say?—I'd walk in my sleep, or any way, to get a sight of him.

1st Peasant. Hush! stand back!—here's some of the quality coming, who are not thinking of you.

(The peasants all retire to the back scene. Count HELMAAR, CHRISTINA, and ELEONORA, appear, looking from a gallery. Enter ALEFTSON and CATHERINE at one door, Mrs. ULRICA at the opposite door, with CHRISTIERN, followed by the two children.)

Cath. (springs forward.) Christiern! my husband! alive!—is it a dream?

Christiern (embracing her). Your own Christiern, dearest Catherine.

(The children clap their hands, and run to their father.)

Ulric. Why, I thought he was my father; only he did not shake hands with me.

Kate. And Mrs. Ulrica hid me hold my tongue.

Christiern. My Ulric! my little Kate!

Mrs. Ulrica. Ay, my little Kate, you may speak now as much as you will.—(Their father kisses them eagerly.)—Ay, kiss them, kiss them; they are as good children as ever were born—and as honest: Kate, show him the purse, and ask him if it be his.

Kate. Is it yours, father?—(holds up the purse).

Christiern. 'Tis mine; 'twas in my knapsack; but how it came here, Heaven knows.

Ulric. We found it in the wood, father, as we were going home, just at the foot of a tree.

Charles (comes forward). Why, mayhap, now I recollect, I might have dropped it there—more shame for me, or rather more shame for them—(looking back at his companions)—that were playing the fool with me, and tumbled out all the things on the ground. Master, I hope there's no harm done: we poor peasant fellows have brought home all the other knapsacks safe and sound to the relations of them that died; and yours came by mistake, it seems.

Christiern. It's a very lucky mistake; for I wouldn't have lost a waistcoat which there is in that knapsack for all the waistcoats in Sweden. My Catherine, 'twas that which you gave me the day before I went abroad—do you remember it?

Charles. Ay, that she does; it had like to have been the death of her—for she thought you must be dead for certain when he saw it brought home without you—but I knew he was not ead, mistress—did not I tell you, mistress, not to give way to sorrow while there was hope left?

Cath. O joy! joy!—too much joy!

Aleft. Now are you sorry you came with me when I bade you?—but I'm a fool!—I'm a fool!

Ulric. But where's the cap and coat you used to wear?

Kate. You are quite another man, uncle.

Aleft. The same man, niece, only in another coat.

Mrs. Ulrica (laughing). How they stare!—Well, Christiern, you are not angry with my master and me for keeping you now?—but angry or not, I don't care, for I wouldn't have missed seeing this meeting for any thing in the whole world.

Enter Count HELMAAR, ELEONOKA, and CHRISTINA.

Christina. Nor I.

Eleon. Nor I.

Helmaar. Nor I.

The Peasants. Nor any of us

Helmaar (to little Ulric). My honest little boy, is that the purse which you found in the wood?

Ulric. Yes, and it's my own father's.

Helmaar. And how much money is there in it?

(The child opens the purse, and spreads the money on the floor.)

Ulric (to Mrs. Ulrica). Count you, for I can't count so much.

Mrs. Ulrica (counts). Eight ducats, five rixdollars, and let me see how many—sixteen carolines(2):— 'twould have been pity, Catherine, to have lost all this treasure, which Christiern has saved for you.

(Footnote 2: A rixdollar is 4s. 6d. sterling; two rixdollars are equal in value to a ducat; a caroline is 1s. 2d.)

Helmaar. Catherine, I beg that all the money in this purse may be given to these honest peasants. (To Kate) Here, take it to them, my little modest girl. As for you and your children, Catherine, you may depend upon it that I will not neglect to make you easy in the world: your own good conduct, and the excellent manner in which you have brought up these children, would incline me to serve you, even if your husband had not saved my life.

Cath. Christiern, my dear husband, and did you save Count Helmaar's life?

Mrs. Ulrica. Ay, that he did.

Cath. (embracing him.) I am the happiest wife, and—(turning to kiss her children)—the happiest mother upon earth.

Charles (staring up in Count Helmaar's face). God bless him! I've seen him face to face at last; and now I wish in my heart I could see his wife.

Christina. And so do I most sincerely: my dear brother, who has been all his life labouring for the happiness of others, should now surely think of making himself happy.

Eleonora (giving her hand to Helmaar). No, leave that to me, for I shall think of nothing else all my life.

Maria Edgeworth was born at Black Bourton, Oxfordshire on January 1st 1768, the second child of Richard Lovell Edgeworth and Anna Maria Edgeworth (née Elers).

Her early years were with her mother's family in England. Sadly, her mother died when Maria was only five. When her father married his second wife, Honora Sneyd, in 1773, the family went to live at his estate, Edgeworthstown, in County Longford, Ireland.

Maria was later sent to Mrs. Lattafière's school in Derby after Honora fell ill in 1775. There she studied dancing, French and other subjects. After Honora died in 1780 Maria's father married Honora's sister, Elizabeth, causing much social disapproved.

Maria transferred to Mrs. Devis's school in Upper Wimpole Street, London. Her father began to focus more attention on Maria in 1781 when she nearly lost her sight to an eye infection.

She returned home to Ireland at 14, and took charge of her younger siblings. She herself was home-tutored by her father in Irish economics and politics, science, literature and law. Despite her youth literature was in her blood.

She became her father's assistant in managing the Edgeworthstown estate, which had become run-down during the family's absence. Maria would now live and write there for the rest of her life.

With her father she began a lifelong academic collaboration. She meticulously detailed daily Irish life; a valuable lodestone of references for later use in her novels. Maria mixed with the Anglo-Irish gentry, and her aunt, Margaret Ruxton of Blackcastle, supplied her with the novels of Anne Radcliffe and William Godwin and encouraged her ambition to write.

Edgeworth's first published work in 1795 was 'Letters for Literary Ladies'. That same year 'An Essay on the Noble Science of Self-Justification', written for a female audience, states that the fair sex is endowed with an art of self-justification and women should use their gifts to continually challenge the force and power of men, especially their husbands, with wit and intelligence.

In 1796 her first children's book, 'The Parent's Assistant', which included the much loved short story 'The Purple Jar' was published.

In 1798 her father married for the fourth and last time, this time to Frances Beaufort. Frances was a year younger than Maria and they quickly became close.

'Practical Education' (1798) is a progressive work on education that combines the ideas of Locke and Rousseau with scientific inquiry. Edgeworth believed that "learning should be a positive experience and that the discipline of education is more important during the formative years than the acquisition of knowledge." The ultimate goal of Edgeworth's system was to create an independent thinker who understands the consequences of his or her actions.

Her first novel, 'Castle Rackrent' (1800) was published anonymously without her father's knowledge. It was an immediate success and firmly established Maria's appeal to the public.

'Belinda' (1801), was her first full-length novel. It dealt with love, courtship, and marriage, and she examined these as conflicts within her "own personality and environment; conflicts between reason and feeling, restraint and individual freedom, and society and free spirit." Startlingly, 'Belinda' also included a depiction of interracial marriage between an African servant and an English farm-girl. Later editions of the novel, in line with unforgiving times, removed these sections.

Frances also pushed the family to travel more first London (1800), the Midlands (1802) and later the continent; first to Brussels and then to France. They met all the notables, with Maria even receiving a proposal of marriage from a Swedish courtier.

'Tales of Fashionable Life' (1809 and 1812) is a 2-series collection of short stories that often had its focus on the life of women. The second series was so successful that she was now the most commercially successful novelist of her age and ranked alongside her contemporaries Jane Austen and Sir Walter Scott.

On a visit to London in 1813, she met many notables including Lord Byron. She entered into a long correspondence with Sir Walter Scott after the publication of 'Waverley' in 1814, in which he acknowledged her influence, and they formed a lasting friendship. She visited him in Scotland at Abbotsford House in 1823 and the following year he visited Edgeworthstown.

After debating the issue with the economist David Ricardo, Maria came to believe that better management and the further use of science in agriculture would raise food production and help to lower prices. They were both in favour of Catholic Emancipation, enfranchisement for Catholics without property restrictions, agricultural reform and increased educational opportunities for women.

She worked particularly hard to improve the living standards of the poor in Edgeworthstown and to provide schools for the local children whatever their denomination.

After her father's death in 1817 she edited his memoirs, and extended them with her biographical addenda. Her father had married 4 times and sired 22 children. At the height of her creative endeavours, Maria had written, "Seriously it was to please my Father I first exerted myself to write, to please him I continued."

Maria worked for the relief of the famine-stricken Irish peasants during the Irish Potato Famine. She wrote 'Orlandino' and gave the proceeds to the Relieve Fund. However, during the famine her 'business head' insisted that only those tenants who had paid their full rent would receive any relief. She also punished any tenants who voted against her Tory preferences.

'Helen' (1834) is Maria Edgeworth's final novel, the only one she wrote after her father's death. Here the focus was on characters and situation and not moral lessons.

William Rowan Hamilton was elected president of the Royal Irish Academy and Maria's advice was constantly sought especially regarding literature in Ireland. She suggested that women should be allowed to participate in Academy events. Hamilton made Maria an honorary member in 1837.

After a visit to see her relations Maria was struck with severe chest pains and died suddenly of a heart attack in Edgeworthstown on 22nd May 1849. She was 81.

Maria Edgeworth is buried in the family tomb at St. John's Church, Edgeworthstown, Longford, Ireland.

Maria Edgeworth – A Concise Bibliography

Letters for Literary Ladies (1795) Second Edition (1798)
An Essay on the Noble Science of Self-Justification (1795)
The Parent's Assistant (1796)
Practical Education (1798) (2 Vols; collaborated with her father and step-mother)
Castle Rackrent (1800) Novel
Early Lessons (1801)
Moral Tales (1801)
Belinda (1801) Novel
The Mental Thermometer (1801)
Essay on Irish Bulls (1802)
Popular Tales (1804)
The Modern Griselda (1804)
Moral Tales for Young People (1805) (6 Vols)
Leonora (1806)
Essays in Professional Education (1809)
Tales of Fashionable Life (1809)
Ennui (1809) Novel
The Absentee (1812) Novel
Patronage (1814) Novel
Harrington (1817) Novel
Ormond (1817) Novel
Comic Dramas (1817)
Memoirs of Richard Lovell Edgeworth (1820) Editor
Rosamond: A Sequel to Early Lessons (1821)
Frank: A Sequel to Frank in Early Lessons (1822)
Tomorrow (1823) Novel
Helen (1834) novel
Orlandino (1848) Temperance novel

www.ingramcontent.com/pod-product-compliance
Lightning Source LLC
Chambersburg PA
CBHW020417260626
47156CB00007B/2436